The Great War Diary
of
A. T. Champion

Major, 11th Bn. South Lancashire Regiment

Lt-Col., 2nd Bn. West Yorkshire Regiment

1914-1919

Edited by David Risley

St. Helens Townships Family History Society

First published in the United Kingdom in 2015 by

St. Helens Townships Family History Society

ISBN 978-0-9929745-1-0

Printed and bound by Bell & Bain Ltd, Glasgow

The Great War Diary
of
A.T. Champion

A. T. Champion at Grantham in 1915

Contents

Acknowledgements

The editor gratefully acknowledges the assistance of The Lancashire Infantry Museum, Fulwood Barracks, Preston, in providing research material and granting permission to use copyright material.

In particular, the ever helpful Museum Curator, Jane Davies; the Chairman of the Friends Management Committee, David Rogan, for his support in this venture; and Major (retd) Douglas Farrington who originally brought the diary to my attention.

Thanks go also to those who helped with transcription; Bryan Ball, Chris Bluck, Carol Farrar, Peter Harvey, Susan Risley. And finally, the Heritage Lottery Fund without which publication of the transcribed diary would not have been possible.

David Risley
1 November 2015

Glossary

2Lt	Second Lieutenant
A/	Acting
AA	Anti-Aircraft
ADMS	Assistant Director Medical Services
Adj	Adjutant
AOC	Army Ordnance Corps
AQMG	Assistant Quartermaster-General
ASC	Army Service Corps
A&SH	Argyll & Sutherland Highlanders
BHQ	Battalion Headquarters
BMGO	Battalion Machine Gun Officer
Capt	Captain
CCS	Casualty Clearing Station
CO	Commanding Officer
CO2	Second in Command
Col	Colonel
Cpl	Corporal
CQMS	Company Quartermaster Sergeant
CRA	Commanding Royal Artillery
CRE	Commanding Royal Engineers
CRT	Canadian Railway Troops
CSM	Company Sergeant Major
CT	Communications Trench
DAA	Director Army Accounts
DADMS	Deputy Assistant Director Medical Services
DAQ	Deputy Assistant Quartermaster
DCM	Distinguished Conduct Medal
DH.Q.	Divisional Headquarters
DLI	Durham Light Infantry
DMO	Director Military Operations
DSO	Distinguished Service Order
F.Co	Field Company
FGCM	Field General Court Martial
GOC	General Officer Commanding
GS	General Service
HAC	Honourable Artillery Company
HAG	Heavy Artillery Group
HE	High Explosive shells
KLR	King's Liverpool Regiment
KORLR	King's Own Royal Lancaster Regiment

KSLI	King's Shropshire Light Infantry
L/Cpl	Lance Corporal
LF(us)	Lancashire Fusiliers
Lt-Col	Lieutenant-Colonel
Maj	Major
ManR	Manchester Regiment
MC	Military Cross
MID	Mentioned in Despatches
MO	Medical Officer
OO	Orderly Officer
OP	Observation Post
OTC	Officer Training Corps
PT	Physical Training
QM	Quartermaster
RAMC	Royal Army Medical Corps
RAVC	Royal Army Veterinary Corps
RE	Royal Engineers
RFC	Royal Flying Corps
RGA	Royal Garrison Artillery
RHA	Royal Horse Artillery
RIF	Royal Irish Fusiliers
RNAS	Royal Naval Air Service
ROD	Railway Operating Division
RSF	Royal Scots Fusiliers
RSM	Regimental Sergeant Major
RSR	Royal Sussex Regiment
RTO	Railway Transport Officer
Sgt	Sergeant
SL(R)	South Lancashire (Regiment)
SWB	South Wales Borderers
TF	Territorial Force
TM	Town Major
TMB	Trench Mortar Battery

Introduction

Alan Treweeke Champion was one of three brothers who were commissioned as officers of the 11th Battalion South Lancashire Regiment, St. Helens Pals (later St. Helens Pioneers), shortly after its formation in September 1914. They appear to have gone to St. Helens to join their uncle, Major Frederick Osborne Evans, who was one of the battalion's first officers. Alan's older brother, Charles Coverley Champion, eventually became the battalion's commanding officer, whilst his younger brother, Eric Osborne Champion, was killed near Menin in 1917. A.T.C. commanded 'A' Company of the Pals from early 1915 until late 1917 when he began short attachments to a number of units before his transfer to 2nd Battalion West Yorkshire Regiment in 1918, where he became its commanding officer.

He was born 21 May 1890, to Francis and Amelia Champion. The family lived in Greenwich until the death of Francis when they moved to Silverdale near Carnforth. Alan was in Ebor House at Rugby School and before he left in 1909 he played for the Scool XI, being described as "A medium-paced right-hand bowler who swerves from the leg. Has bowled steadily throughout the season. Can bat well but is too impatient. A fine field in the slips." He then went into manufacturing in Wolverhampton, working as an electrical engineer; leaving there in 1914 to join the St. Helens Pals. In 1915 he married Katherine Malcolm, with whom he was to have three sons and three daughters. After the war he returned to Wolverhampton and rejoined the Efandem company (later part of Ever Ready). In 1923, he and J. Eaton patented "an improvement in motor driven systems" which was used in air raid sirens during the Second World War. 1936 saw the first reunion of the St. Helens Pals and he was a stalwart for the next few years, even proposing a tour of the battlefields in 1939, that of course had to be abandoned. In May 1940 he formed 'B' Company of the Wolverhampton Battalion, Local Defence Volunteers, and later served as Lt-Col. of the new 26th Battalion of the Home Guard. He died in 1944 after collapsing at the South Staffordshire Golf Club, where he had recently been elected to a second year as club captain.

The diary comprises two large, thick volumes and gives the appearance of having been written after the war; presumably compiled from pocket diaries and notebooks. This view is strengthened by the diary containing daily entries for 1914 and early 1915 in the middle of entries for 1917. This may explain why the diary begins with generalised entries for 1914 and early 1915. It is assumed that the latter were written from memory before the daily entries were found. Some rearrangement has taken place to put the entries into their chronological sequence. The diary also contains original copies of Operation Orders, telegrams and drawings of billet areas. Some punctuation has been introduced to aid clarity.

Introduction

Unfortunately the diary often isn't easy to read and has faded in places, resulting in gaps in the narrative. Where these gaps occur the missing words or letters have been replaced by '.....'. Similarly, where words are uncertain they have been 'shaded'. Hopefully this doesn't detract too much from what is a fascinating insight into one man's war. If any reader has corrections or suggestions as to e.g. place names, officers' names or helpful footnotes they should contact the editor via enquiries@lancashireinfantrymuseum.org.uk.

Oriel Lodge,
Ford Houses,
Wolverhampton.

Joined XIth S.Lancs.Reg. & gazetted 2nd Lieut.	October 5th 1914
Gazetted 1st Lieut.	Oct. 16th 1914
Gazetted Captain	Jan. 22nd 1915
Left England for France	Nov. 5th 1915
Left France for six months exchange	Oct. 19th 1917
Attached 52nd Welch Batt.	Nov. 26th 1917
Left 52nd Welch Reg.	April 25th 1918
Left England for France	May 7th 1918
Reported XIth S.Lancs.Reg.	May 9th 1918
Gazetted Major	May11th 1918
Left for Base	May 14th 1918
Reported 2nd E.Lancs.Reg.	June 19th 1918
Transferred to 2nd R.Berks Reg.	July 18th 1918
Appointed Second-in-Command 2nd W. York.R.	Sept. 16th 1918
Took over 2nd West Yorkshires	Sept. 23rd 1918
Armistice	Nov. 11th 1918
Landed in England	April 19th 1919
Demobilised	June 14th 1919

1914

5 Oct 1914
St Helens

Battalion formed about Sept 5 1914. I joined on Oct 5 1914 - I saw Colonel Thomas Sept 29 1914, motoring up from Wolverhampton via Nantwich & Warrington with A. E. Clarence Smith[1]. Had lunch at Barracks - only officers in the Regiment then were C.O. Colonel Thomas[2], Adj. Lt Potter T., Capt Earl & Capt Bonnyman & attached was Lt Goodwin also the temp M.O. was Mr Edwards. We returned back via Chester to get uniform at Smiths & finally joined in civilian clothes Monday Oct 5 1914. Was gazetted 2nd Lieut Oct 25 & then Lieut Oct 16 & finally dated 2nd Lieut to Oct 5.

The men lived in old glass works of Messrs Pilkington & had no uniform for some months other than grey.

The officers first lived at the Fleece Hotel. I had 4 days in mufti before my uniform came. Various officers joined & left. Those that came were

Dixon C. J. 12-10-14	Hurst H. H. W. 12-10-14
Brooke H. J.	Bacon S. C. F. 12-10-14
Hitchen J. H. 12-10-14	Fry D. C.
Hitchen W. G. 19-10-14	Evans F. O.
Burn R. W. 13-10-14	Champion E. O. 5/12/14
Sagar J. H.	Ward Barrington V. M. 14/10/14
Radcliffe	Pethick J. E. S. 15-10-14
Rowley H. B.	Douglas
Walker A. D 10/1/15	Thompson W. R. 29-9-14
Parr B. 19-10-14	Langford J. W. 23-12-14
Gardner A. 29-1-15	Edwards H. W.
Boshell W.	

Then various ones left. Capt Earle who was then Maj & joined a Bantam Reg of the Line to be their C.O. & with him Bacon, Fry & Hurst left to join the same regiment. H. A. C. Goodwin not wanting to go across the water left & went to a musketry School & afterwards became a musketry instructor to some Brigade. I had as my servant Pt Green all the time & he acted as my chauffeur & was quite good.

---

[1] A.E.C. Smith also joined the battalion.
[2] Lt-Col. Robert W.H. Thomas, late 5th Battalion South Lancashire Regiment (T.F.)

We trained mostly at Sherdley Park[3] in close order & open order training. Rifles were very short - only 25 per company at first. We also did a good bit of Route marching - to Liverpool & other places - at Liverpool Sefton Park I met Radcliffe's people. We also had a good many lectures - I gave only one & that on discipline. We also taught them semaphore - scouting & .....ination range. Mother gave us flags. Colonel Pawle joined us later when Colonel Thomas gave up - but he became very ill & had pneumonia & appendicitis at Windle Hall[4]. The officers had shifted from The Fleece to The Raven owing to the uncleanliness of the former - Mrs A. Pilkington of Windle Hall had taken some of us in then & Colonel Pawle[5] was ill up there. There at Windle Hall were - Bonnyman, myself & ....., Karl[6], Uncle Fred[7], Eric[8] & Radcliffe. Sir J. Harrington KCMG KCVO CB then took over just before we moved from there to Bangor. The Sergt Major was RSM Taylor & then RSM Eaves.

Eaves was first full C.S.M. of 'A' Co. I had my Singer at the Barracks & found it very useful - especially for running home & Lancaster on weekends & to Liverpool in the evening. It took about 2 hours to go to Lancaster & about 30 minutes to Liverpool. One famous occasion when we went to the latter place was when Dunn & I met Bonnyman, Pawle & Potter at the Adelphi[9] & went to the Olympia after. I took Pawle back in car. He slept all the way. He had a nasty fall down the steps leading up to the WC in the theatre. Potter was not altogether. Burn tried to get Bonnyman back but missed him temporarily on the platform. Luckily he turned up after. One day taking Douglas over he was sitting on the step & got his face covered in mud. I also visited the museum in Paradise Street. We saw Monsieur Brancain there with Kaye[10] & Mother. Also the Pantomime many times (Shuffle!!) I also ran on to Chester once or twice & met the Craddocks - Bonnyman & I stayed the night there once. I also kept two monkeys & 3 Bantams in the duty room as pets but we had to

---

[3] The home of Captain Michael Hughes, late 2nd Life Guards.
[4] The St. Helens home of the glass-making Pilkington family.
[5] Lt-Col. Alfred G. Pawle, V.D., late 10th Battalion London Regiment (T.F.)
[6] Charles Coverley Champion. A.T.C.'s older brother, also referred to as C.C. or Karl.
[7] Major Frederick Osborne Evans; uncle, by marriage, of the Champion brothers, also referred to as F.O.E..
[8] 2/Lt. Eric Osborne Champion, A.T.C.'s younger brother, also referred to as E.O.
[9] When opened in 1914, regarded as the most luxurious hotel outside London.
[10] A.T.C.'s fiancée Catherine Malcolm, also referred to as K.

send them back as they made too much mess. They were very funny though. Bonnyman had a rough haired fox terrier called Charles Bragg.

Towards the end in January they formed a fifth company & I was put O.C. of it (Jan 22nd). My subalterns were A D Walker, Rowley & Manning. At that time company commanders were Earle & then Potter of 'D' company, Evans of 'C', Ward of 'B' & Bonnyman of 'A'. When Potter took 'D' Co C.C. took Adj. We were inspected fairly often Lord Derby[11] for one. We had a private interview with Lord Derby just the company commanders at Windle Hall ..... about Bonnyman getting the Battalion. We went to Bangor about Feb 22 1915. Great scenes on platform & going down to station as we went off.

We used to go to the Baths fairly often, one time I was there a man in 'E' Co nearly drowned himself. I had Spencer as my C.S.M. & Patterson as my CQMS A man committed suicide while in 'E' Co & I had to attend the inquest. Madness was found in the family. Rowley created a bad scene in the parade for the dependents as he came in splendidly drunk. Luckily Bonnyman saw it. The Battalion went in 2 trains about 10 & 12 o'clock & got to Bangor about 3 & 5.
Lt-Col Harrington[12] took over on Feb 8th 1915
Used to play bridge at Dr Massens with Col Pawle & Bonnyman.

---

[11] The battalion had been raised by Lord Derby at St. Helens in September 1914.
[12] Lt-Col. Sir John L. Harrington, K.C.M.G., K.C.V.O., C.B.(Maj. ret. Indian Army)

4-10-14	Motored to St Helens from Lancaster. Had dinner with Karl, Bonnyman & Potter. Mr & Mrs Earl came in after.
5-10-14	Barracks at 8.30. ACS then stayed in & saw Colonel Thomas. Uncle Fred arrived about 12.0. Aft[13] route march with Karl, 'A' & 'B' Cos 5-6 miles. Evening saw boxing at Engineers Hall[14]. Changed to Clarence's room.
6-10-14	Parade 8.30. Parade ground with Karl. Evening Uncle Fred & I went to Brevis, Clerk to the magistrates, Colonel there.
7-10-14	Route march with Bonnyman & Karl about 7 miles. Aft on Parade ground. O.C. for day. Thompson & Burn arrived.
8-10-14	Parade 8.30. Route march with Bonnyman. Evening to N.C.O.s mess.
9-10-14	Parade but rained. Orderly room all aft. Smith, Uncle, Boshell & self bridge. Hart O.O.
10-10-14	6.0. a.m. day. Sub parade at 9.0. S.M. drilled us. Kit inspection at 10.0. Wal..... not on his sword, belt etc. Watched match St Helens v Widnes. Dinner with Boshell. Slept at Barracks, violent disturbance. Bonnyman away.
11-10-14	Church Parade 10.30. Lunch at Huyton with Goodwin. Evening at Ravenshoe[15] Bob Burlyn Smith & Uncle Fred. Edwards carried news of Antwerp falling. Bonnyman away.
12-10-14	Parade in morning. Subaltern Drill. Bacon & Hurst came. Evening Pethick[16], Uncle, Karl & I bridge. Bonnyman away.
13-10-14	Drill in morning on parade. Sub drill in aft. Completely lost voice. Potter, Uncle, Edwards & self bridge. Bonnyman away.

---

[13] A.T.C. frequently uses this to mean 'In the afternoon'.
[14] Drill Hall of 1st and 2nd Field Coys, West Lancashire Division, Royal Engineers (T.F.)
[15] The home of George and Edith Bramwell. Edith was A.T.C.'s aunt.
[16] Captain John E.S. Pethick, 'A' Coy. 11th Bn. South Lancs., son of a Dr. Pethick of Woolton, Liverpool.

14-10-14	Parade ground. Capt Sub parade. Bridge, Kent, Fletcher & Smith. Parade at 10 p.m. Marched out about 3 miles & night ops. Back at 1 a.m.
15-10-14	Parade at 10.0. In orderly room with Bonnyman. Aft Sub parade & orderly room. Alarm went but did not attend. Bridge, K, Edwards & Burn.
16-10-14	Route march - 12½ miles. Aft pay 'B' Co & orderly room work. Bridge , K. Burn & Smith.
17-10-14	Barracks till 11.0. Kit inspection. To Ravenshoe, mother & K there. Aft lunch Karl & Uncle came & all went over barracks. Aft dinner billiards. Clarence turned up.
18-10-14	Church parade at 10.0. Mother, Kaye, June & Miss Wigley turned up. Lunch at Hotel & round to Ravenshoe after & billiards.
19-10-14	Route march in morning. To theatre The Lady Sla......, frightful rot.
20-10-14	O.O. for day. Down at 9.0. Advance guard march in aft. Parade ground in morning. To cards & billiards in evening at Dr T.....ffs. Turned out guard at 12.30 a.m.
21-10-14	O.O. for day. Route march in morning. Board for Sergt mess. Sub drills in aft. Sub lecture by Goodwin.
22-10-14	Orderly room all day. Mess night. David Gamble[17] to mess. Bridge, Karl, Earl, Edwards & Bonnyman.
23-10-14	Morning half company squad drill, aft pay. To Wolv[18] with Karl to get Singer. Kaye rang up. To TEC. Saw Gregory. After dinner 'A' Co off went to smoking concert given by No 1 Platoon at Wheatsheaf.
24-10-14	Kit inspection. Ord room till 11.30. Caught 2.45 to Liverpool with Ward, Karl, Uncle, Bonnyman & Burn, had a Turk[19], dinner at Adelphi. 3 caught 9.30, we caught 11.40. Goodwin & ..... there.

---

[17] Sir David Gamble, Mayor of St. Helens.
[18] Wolverhampton.
[19] Turkish bath.

25-10-14   Church Parade. Uncle & I to Ravenshoe for lunch. Karl, Smith & ward round after. Stayed tea & supper. Frank Jones in.

26-10-14   Co route march, stayed in O Room. Bonnyman away. Aft took 'A' & 'B' on parade ground. All decided to go to Raven.

27-10-14   Wet day. Short while on parade ground & then route march. Aft Goodwin lectured NCOs. Platoon drill.

28-10-14   Route march in morning. Stayed Ord room in aft. To Ravenshoe for .... Bonnyman turned up & all went to Pals concert.

29-10-14   Route march in morning. Drill in aft. Concert in evening.

30-10-14   Morning Parade ground. Route march in aft. Left by 5.30 got to Wolv with Karl by 9. Dai away, Hilda at home, Macdonald there.

31 10 14   Left Oakhill 9.45. Left Wolv at 10.30 arrived Lancaster 4.15. Karl to Oaklea[20].

1-11-14   At Lancaster. Karl called for me at 9.0., ... at 9.15 St Helens 11.30. V.G. run.

2-11-14   Route march 9.0 till 12.45 at H..... Back at 2.30. Fetched Bonnyman from .....

3-11-14   Drill morning. Fletcher came to me in aft. Bonnyman saw Colonel & arranged for me to get second star.

4-11-14   M....ates rang in morning. Took Bonnyman to range. Col had officer meeting & inspection. 6 of us to theatre & saw "Mind Your Business" V.G.

5-11-14   Barracks all day. Rained. Comp drill in aft. Platoon drill in morning. Jones & Ralph came to mess. Rowdy evening & initia.....s

6-11-14   Barracks all day. Paid men in aft. 6.50 tug of war. Back for breakfast. After breakfast saw about putting up boards for sleeping wards & another tug of war at 11.30. O.O. for day.

---

[20] The Champion family home at Silverdale, near Carnforth.

7-11-14   To town to fetch Colonel & Bonnyman. Tug of war at 12.0. 'A' beat staff 2 & 1. Caught 1.5 with Uncle, Karl & Edwards. Kaye, Mother, Mrs MacFarlane met us at Liverpool. All to tea at Royal & saw Scarlet Pimpernel. Back by 5.30 Kaye & Mr sM went on home. Mother to Ravenshoe, we all back to Raven. After mess bridge with Ward.

8-11-14   Sammy's Birth. Church parade in morning. Took Uncle, Karl to Ravenshoe for lunch & rest of day there. Mother there.

9-11-14   Batt parade morning & Inspection by C.O. aft. Co drills & going through finance report & defaulters sheets. Lectures in evening.

10-11-14   All day in Barracks moving ..... Kit put straight, afternoon changing our beds. After mess played nap. Emden[21] reported sunk.

11-11-14   Rained hard morning & aft. Morning Batt drill put off. At 4 Bonnyman, Burn, Goodwin & I went to Liverpool for hair cut. Dinner at Adelphi & then Mrs Goodwin came & all went to Gipsy Lee. Should have gone to Jones to dinner but cried off.

12-11-14   General Inspection by Sir General Mackinnon[22] all morning. Afternoon Col H, Bonnyman & I went to Chester. Got back just in time for mess & napped till 2.0.

13-11-14   At Barracks all day. Rained most of day. Paid men in morning & drill. Early to bed. Bridge with Uncle, Karl & Burn.

14-11-14   In Orderly room all morning. Lunch at 12.30 with Karl & Clench. Motored to Warrington. Karl & I played two rounds giving Uncle OS ½ stroke beat them 3&1. Tea at Golf Club & then dinner at Sunnyside & back about 11.0 got back about 12.0.

15-11-14   Lord Roberts[23] died. Church parade. Pouring with rain just before but stopped for us & was not raining when we returned. Went straight on to Warrington & had lunch. Wrote all aft & played bridge all evening. Returned at 11.0 & got back about 12.0. Snow in morning on lawn etc.

---

[21] German light cruiser, the "Scourge of the Indian Ocean", sunk by HMAS *Sydney*.
[22] Sir William H. Mackinnon (1852-1929), G.O.C. Western Command.
[23] Field Marshall Frederick S. Roberts, late Commander-in-Chief of the British Army.

16-11-14   Stayed in in morning & took Bonnyman down to town. Went route march with Bab[24] in afternoon, awfully silly & did not talk. New Colonel came. In evening played billiards at Hotel with Karl etc. Won pool both times.

17-11-14   Stayed in in the morning & company drill in afternoon. Afternoon took Bonnyman to Hospital & then round to Ravenshoe. Mother, Evelyn & Bob there.

18-11-14   Route march in morning. Waited to take Bonnyman home. Sent 5 & 6 shooting in aft. Also took Gym in morning. Took Ward & Burn to Goodwins to dinner at 8.15. V. jolly evening.

19-11-14   Route march in morning. Sent 7 & 8 shooting in afternoon. Things for .... night rather interesting. Uncle ..... to men. Weather changed to warm again.

20-11-14   Stayed in all morning with cold. O.O. for day. Helped pay the men in aft. Ward Ord Capt for week. Brought him up & down in evening. Slept at Barracks.

21-11-14   Kit insp in morning. Men to baths. Bonnyman in fearful temper. Put kit right with 2 NCOs & Eaves. After lunch at Barracks. Karl & I set off for Lancaster. Huge fog. Set off at 2.15 & landed at Lancaster at 4.15. Karl went on to Silverdale.

22-11-14   All to Kirk but Mrs M who went to Barracks. Stayed in all day with women. Karl called at 8.30 for me & set out at 9.0. Arrived 11.30. Car went badly very cold.

23-11-14   Started at 9.0. for Pecks Hill[25]. Got there at 11.0. Had an attack on a farm house then lunch. Marched back & arrived at 4.30. Bridge with Colonel, Kuny[26] & Potter till 11.30.

24-11-14   March off to big field & open order in morning. Stayed in with Bonnyman all aft. Set out with Burn at 5.15 to change, call at

---

[24] Possibly Lt. John H. Fletcher, who is referred to as 'Baboon' in a photo caption.

[25] Pexhill, at Cronton, rising to only 200 ft (61 m) above sea level; covered with heather and gorse. On the top are the Widnes Corporation reservoirs, formed in 1868.

[26] Captain Simon A. Kuny, RAMC, the battalion Medical Officer.

Huyton & go on to Adelphi & Potash & Perlmutter[27]. V. good. Called in at Huyton on way back. Nasty dirty day.

25-11-14   Musketry all day. Went & came by train. In evening Bonnyman & I went to dine at Burn's. Played bridge & returned 12.45.

26-11-14   March out to Pecks Hill & manoeuvres. In evening out to concert. Aunty Edie there, took her home. Car handed over to mother.

27-11-14   Shooting in morning. Capt Potter told me to go with him to Town[28] & caught 4.36. Got to Town 9.15. Burn met us & went to Lupin & then supper at Princes Street. Mrs Brown & Mrs Phyllis Smith, Kathleen Jackson & Colgrave. After supper went to 400 Club & then to 4 Mount Street. Got back at 4.0.

28-11-14   Breakfast in town at 10.30. Went round to MacGregors & then lunch with Roy, Mr & Mrs Brown at Princes. Aft at 4 Mount St. & dinner then met 2 subalterns friends of Roy's & then Alhambra. Back at 4 Mount Street & home at 1.15.

29-11-14   Got up at 10.0. Met Potter with Douglas, Rutherford & Davidson in smokeroom. Last two went off at 12.0. We went round to Troc and had lunch & then went on to Burns. Douglas left at 3.45. Tubby at Burns. We four had tea & played Bridge. I & Pat v Mr B & Potter & Mr Burns. We won by 4 in 6 rubbers. Then went round to Princes for dinner & met Phyllis Smith. Saw Ro....y off at 12.10 & then back to bed.

30 11 14   Got up at 9.30. Breakfast & caught 10.0 train back with Potter. Saw Huntingdon at Widnes & got back at 2.30. Lunch on train. Earle not gone, stayed in all the time.

1-12-14   Elected on mess committee. Got cert drilling at Sherdley. Did mess accounts all aft. Wet & bad day. Karl at Chester.

2-12-14   All day shooting. Got flu in evening, to bed early. Cold & wet day.

3-12-14   In bed all day.

---

[27] An ethnic Jewish comedy by Montague Glass and Charles Klein for a 1913 Broadway play.
[28] London.

4-12-14   Bed till 12.0. Rest of day in sitting room.

5-12-14   Went up to Barracks & fished about for Eric. He turned up via Liverpool. Took him to town & watched football match. Went round with Colonel & Bury to Dr Masons. Colonel Thomas there stayed till 12.15.

6-12-14   ..... B...th. Went to morning church Parade with Ward. Aft writing & playing Bridge & evening too. Ward, Bing, Burn & I. Bed at 12.0. St. James fete day.

7-12-14   Stayed behind when rest went to attack towards Crank[29] & stayed in all day & practiced firing with Bury v Pro..... Mother, Eric & I met at 5.59. All went to Ravenshoe & had dinner. Col Thomas turned up afterwards.

8-12-14   Took Company out to Parade ground in morning, back early as it rained & formed up in shed & drill & flag ..... Started at 6.0 for Chester & had dinner & stayed night at Chester.

9-12-14   Got up at 6.30 in Chester & after breakfast went to Smith. Met aunty May & then to Arthur Dodds. Spent aft with Mrs Craddick & returned at 5.30 Dense fog & took from 6.30 to 9.0. to get from Warrington.

10-12-14   General Inspection by Lord Derby in morning & aft, shooting. Mess night & nap. Mother wired whether to come down on Sat & wired yes.

11-12-14   Route march in morning. Aft drills, Burn Bury & myself went to Liverpool & dined. Met young Heap.

12-12-14   March about all morning. Mother & Kaye arrived 10.50. Took Bonnyman round in afternoon round Rugby & Soccer matches & to Goodwins who was ill in bed with cold in the kidneys. Aft we went to Lancaster. Kaye & mother then Karl & I & Eric came later.

13-12-14   At Ravenshoe all day. Kaye & mother then Karl, Eric & Smith all turned up. Billiards etc. Bed at 10.30.

---

[29] A village about a mile or so north of St. Helens.

14-12-14   Took shooting in morning & flag signalling in afternoon. Karl, Ward & I to Theatre to Mill Girls Secret, awful rot. Many other officers there.

15-12-14   Drilling in Barn all day & signalling too. Went to Liverpool in morning with Bury, Burn & Radcliffe, motored in & out. Rather a wet night.

16-12-14   Signalling competition in morning. Collier won. Aft in ..... off Arthur Dodds & Craddock & played 'B' Co Rugger. I played & we won 13-4. O. Officer for day.

17-12-14   Started at 9.0. Ord Off. Had ..... field day at Bullings Barn. 'A' 'B' & 'D' Co v 'C' Co, no definite result given. Very tired & stiff. Bridge with Colonel, Bonnyman & Evans.

18-12-14   Got money & things in morning. Bonny. & I motored to Chester. Lunch at Craddocks. I had Bath Bun & then tea & got back at 5.45. Poured with rain. Early to bed.

19-12-14   Barracks all morning. Aft to football match. Poured with rain. Burn & I returned & went to Liverpool. Tea at Adelphi. Saw J M Heap, Di..... Col P..... & Bonnyman & on to Olympia aft brought W..... home.

20-12-14   Up at 10.0 & round to see Bonnyman. After lunch to Huyton, Ward & I lost to Karl & W..... They gave us a half 2 & 1. After golf bridge all evening. Bed at 10.15.

21-12-14   Drilled all day. Took Radcliffe to Liverpool & had dinner with Burn, came back in the ..... Bad day. Bury on leave.

22-12-14   Marched to Liverpool. Lunched at Radcliffe's. Back different way with Burn. Bob took advance guard. V. cold.

23-12-14   Shooting in morning. Lunch at Barracks. Motored up via Upholland to Lancaster. Got there for tea. Bury came back.

24-12-14   Down town & bought all sorts of stuff.

25-12-14   Present Inspection at 9.30. Golf in afternoon. Mr & Mrs M in ..... Dinner at night. Dr & Mrs M....., Mr & Mrs Catterall & Dr Henderson & Mr Duncan.

26-12-14   Golf in aft. ..... down town. Mr Malcolm .... Went to .....
concert at ..... Hall. V good.

27-12-14   To church in morning. Rest of day indoors. Wet.

28-12-14   Down town in morning. Aft Irene Saul came. Evening concert at
Barracks. Left at 10.35. Got to St Helens at 12.30. Sat up with
Burn & Bonnyman till 3.0.

29-12-14   Nothing all day. Cold & raining. Bridge in evening. Colonel, Bury
& Douglas.

30-12-14   O.O. Bury had inspection everything went wrong. Stayed in all
day. Slept at Barracks & did some mess accounts.

31-12-14   Burn left for holidays. Wrote out small books[30] all aft. To theatre
in evening & played bridge after. Saw New Year in with Karl,
Douglas & Bury.

---

[30] The small book (Army Form B-50) was an essential part of a soldier's kit before the
war. Its stated purpose was to provide the soldier with a record of his service in the
Army, and provide him with certain information, which he will find useful during his
service. It served as his personnel file and acted as a handbook.

1915

Jan 1   Tug of War v 'D' Co in morning lost. Half day off. Aft did accounts. To Ravenshoe for dinner. Pouring wet day. Bridge at barracks till 3 a.m. with both Bury & Douglas.

2   Bath parade in morning. Bury & T.P. made a mess all on my coat. Aft on mess accounts. Tea with Pethick at Raven & then to Liverpool. Met Brown, scrappy dinner & to Panto, Old King Cole at the Court v.g. Got 11.40 back ¾ h late.

3   Took Church Parade. To Ravenshoe for dinner & supper. Bob & Joselyn there. Mess accounts all aft.

4   Goodwin returned. Barracks all aft. Route march in morning. Liverpool in aft with Douglas, Brooke, Pethick. Met Frank Jones. Returned 11.40.

5   In barracks all day. Inspection by Brigadier. Burn returned. Only Uncle, Colonel & self in at night. Kaye not too well.

6   Barracks all day. Burn & Potter & I to Liverpool in evening & to Hippodrome. Mrs Potter & Dixon there. Back by 11.40. Karl turned up.

7   Started at 7.0 to march to Warrington. Rained very shortly & we turned back. Got back at 12.30. In aft took summary of evidence & defaulter sheets. In evening went with Colonel & Bonnyman to Dr Martin's. Stayed till 3.0

8   Got up in slacks & ran Bury & Burn over to Liverpool. Lunch with at Adelphi. Stayed in all aft & had tea with them. Came back at _ Went with B _ & Karl to Mersey Market.

9   At barracks all morning. Went with Karl to Manchester. Got 1st Lieut dated back until Oct 17. Ward & Pethick joined us. Saw Betty & motored back in 57 min. Betty quite good.

10   Got up at 10.0. Col, Bury & Burn & I went to Pilkington's for lunch, tea & supper. Asked us to go & stay. Rained all day.

11   Had Colonel's Kit inspection in morning. Aft spent in Barracks. Evening up at Pilkington's Windle Hall. Rained all day.

12   Spent in Barracks. Company inoculated. Route march in morning.

13   Caught 10.0 train to Lancaster from Barracks. Lunch at ..... Concert at Hippodrome. Kaye singing. Maj. Holmes inoculated me at 5.0. Back at 9.0. Mother to lunch, saw her off by 5.37.

14   Spent day in bed.

15   Bed until 11.0. Major Holmes to see me but did not come. Left at 2.0 for Manchester. Arrived 4.30. Tea & then Mr Malcolm turned up. Saw Brook of WPB there. Went to B.....y a bit groggy. Bed at 11 o'clock. Wet day.

16   Breakfast at 9.30. Walked round with Kaye. Lunch 12.45. Saw M. Brancain. Saw Karl Bury & Eric. Left by 5.45 train. Back at 7.30. Belsize[31] turned up. Karl gazetted.

17   Stayed in all day. Started car after port trouble.

18   Stayed in all morning. To Palladium with Rosalind & Holmes while Kaye had music lesson. Caught 3.30 to St Helens, to Barracks & YMCA. Green took car to Wigan. Slept at Pilkington's. Colonel got pneumonia.

19   Spent whole day running between Barracks & YMCA. Colonel v bad.

20   Spent all day between YMCA & Barracks. Colonel still bad. Two sisters came. Karl to Ravenshoe.

21   Took Bury & P to Widnes in aft. Spent all day messing about. Uncle much better.

22   Took Major Waugh to Manchester to our Brigadier. Spent day in Manchester ordered leggings etc. Returned at 6.0. Dinner at Mrs Pilkington.

23   Paid Company. 12.0 recruiting until 6.0. Evening at Ravenshoe.

---

[31] A car, manufactured by Belsize Motors of Manchester.

24	Took Bury & Karl to Barracks at 10.0. Waited till 12.30 & then took K to Ravenshoe. Mother there. Left at 7.30. At 11.30 Bury woke me up & I had to go & fetch Karl up to decipher telegram. Got to bed at 3.0.
25	Capt Nixon arrived & lectured us for 1 hr in morning & aft. Did nothing otherwise all day.
26	In all day & worked out things for 'E' Co[32].
27	In all day about 'E' Co. Took Nixon to Pilkington Works & station. All went out to dinner but Mother. Karl & I.
28	Spent day arranging for orderly room with Rowley. Saw last of Colonel's sister.
29	Took over 'E' Co. Spent all day arranging for quarters with Rowley.
30	Took orderly room & spent day moving men around. Karl & I motored to Lancaster. Tea there & then on to Silverdale. Kaye to dance at Holmes.
31	Went over to Lancaster to fetch Kaye. Left Silverdale at 7.30 to St Helens arrived 10.15 dropping Kaye en route.
Feb 1	In barracks all day.
2	In barracks all day. Rained. Capt Nixon returned.
3	In all day. Lecture from Capt Nixon. Potter & Ward dined at Windle.
4	In all day. Bat parade for Dr at 3.0. Lord Derby came in morning & spoke to company. Route march. Mr & Mrs Pilkington to dinner.
5	Barracks all day. Came back early to go to Panto. Mr & Mrs P. Bury, Burn, Radcliffe & self all to Panto. Dined at Adelphi. Talked to Bury about going after Karl & Eric left for later.
6	Paid men. Saw Ward. Took Douglas & Woods to Liverpool. Had photo taken. Back at 6.0. & saw Colonel Day at Windle trying to persuade Bury to stay. Burn went to tea.

---

[32] In early January local newspapers had run an advert for a fifth company.

7   To Barracks & got letters. Took Rolly[33] up to Rainford Hall[34] & brought Douglas to Windle. Took Bury to hospital after tea. Potter came to Windle too. Saw Smith at Hospital.

8   Square drill. Ball to Liverpool. Aft half to Bath half to parade. Colonel Harrington came at 2.30. Evening at Windle.

9   In all day. Batt Parade to hand over to New Colonel. In all afternoon. Burn returned at night.

10   In all day. Men did section drills & route march in aft. Was going to Chester with Bury but had a row & did not go. Karl & Eric returned. Left car at Ormskirk.

11   All company inoculated in morning & paid. Left after lunch & got to Lancaster at 5.0. Innoculated at 8.0 Kaye to a rehearsal.

12   In bed all day.

13   In bed all day. Dr to see me in evening.

14   In bed till midday. Maj Holmes came & in said I was not to leave till Sunday. Went over with Kaye & saw mother, Uncle & Aunty Hills.

15   In bed for breakfast. After lunch to Maj Holmes. Left at 4.30 got in at 6.20. Col.   Sister in.

16   On Parade all day.

17   On parade all day. General Inspection in morning - all well by General Dixon.

18   Parade all day. Went in big car to Manchester. Pilkington for dinner. Good fun. Talked to Burn till 1 o'clock.

19   Barracks all morning & aft. Mother to Ravenshoe & we had dinner there.

20   In Barracks all morning. To Manchester in afternoon to order gaiters. Dinner at Ravenshoe.

[33] Capt. Harold B. Rowley.
[34] The home of Col. W. N. Pilkingon DSO, 5th Bn. South Lancashire Regiment (T.F.)

21	To Barracks & to church. Spent aft packing up. Tea at Ravenshoe Dinner at Liverpool with Pilkington.

| 22 | Left St Helens at 9.15. Got to Barracks at 6.15. Got to Bangor at 12.30. Company in two halves. Aft billeting & all evening. Kaye to Hilda's. |

Bangor
22/2/15
to
4/5/15

We arrived there in the afternoon - Potter & some men had gone on to Billet. We took about 2 hours to billet the Battalion & even there they were not ..... anything like finally. 'E' Co were down by the shore. 'A' Co up on the top in higher Bangor. 'B' Co near station - 'C' Co all down the main street & 'D' Co over at   near the pier & towards the College. The officers were in the Castle & the British Hotels. Rowley was ill for a week or so when we first arrived. There was a distinct unpleasantness between the C.O. & Bonnyman until he left & then between the C.O. & F.O.E. until he left. Bonnyman took over some of the Fusiliers of the Public School Regiment & F.O.E. did nothing till he became second in command to a similar regiment. When Bonnyman left I got 'A' Co, Ward had 'B'. C.C.C. got 'C' Co. Potter still had 'D' & Evans took 'E'. At the same time Brooke took the Adjutancy. Later Ward left to take over as RTO ..... in France.

Several officers arrived.

Woolcock H J	5-4-15
Hopwood A E	1-4-15
Diplock A B	21-4-15
Bretherton W	3-5-15
Craig F	24-4-15
Featherby C R	27-3-15
Miller R W R	8-4-15
Garton R W	

We trained in Penrhyn Park. Lord Penrhyn's Park. Lord Penrhyn was commander of Craig when he was in the Life Guards. Also did some marches & company & battalion training. Our horses & tools arrived then but not full amount of transport, mules or tools. I met Mr Hodgson & Dr Jones & Roberts of Carnarvon - Douglas Mount over the Castle when we were there once for dinner. Spent Easter at Conway with Mr & Mrs Malcolm, Tommy & Mrs Pearce. Kaye at Ash Hill with mumps. Played footer once vs 'B' Co & we won. 'B' & 'D' companies had a hunt for German officers who had escaped but did not find them - they had a very hard day indeed in the mountains in mist & rain. We went over to Bull Bay twice - Dai & Hilda -

Mother, & Kaye came up & stayed at the George & Hilda & Dai brought their car. I had mine & took Mr & Mrs Manning on run over to Bettys Coed & Llanberis & back to Karl's. Mine broke the propeller shaft & was sent to Coventry by train with Karl's to be got from there when we went there. My servant Green got appendicitis while here & I had to have Pte Durkin instead. Also Pte Hindley previously Goodwin's chauffeur took over the driving of my car. We left Bangor in 2 trains & the fifth company went back in a 3rd to St Helens. Clarence Smith took charge & Edwards went with him. Major Evans was also transferred with them & he was put in command at the depot[35]. Our Brigadier was Brig MacKenzie & his Staff Capt was Capt Montgomery.

---

[35] The old watchworks in Prescot; previously used as a barracks for Liverpool Pals.

IVY BUSH ROYAL HOTEL,
CARMARTHEN,
'PHONE 38.

LION HOTEL,
MACHYNLLETH,
'PHONE '48,

MARION EDWARDS,
PROPRIETRESS.

'PHONE 39

Belle Vue Royal Hotel,
Aberystwyth.

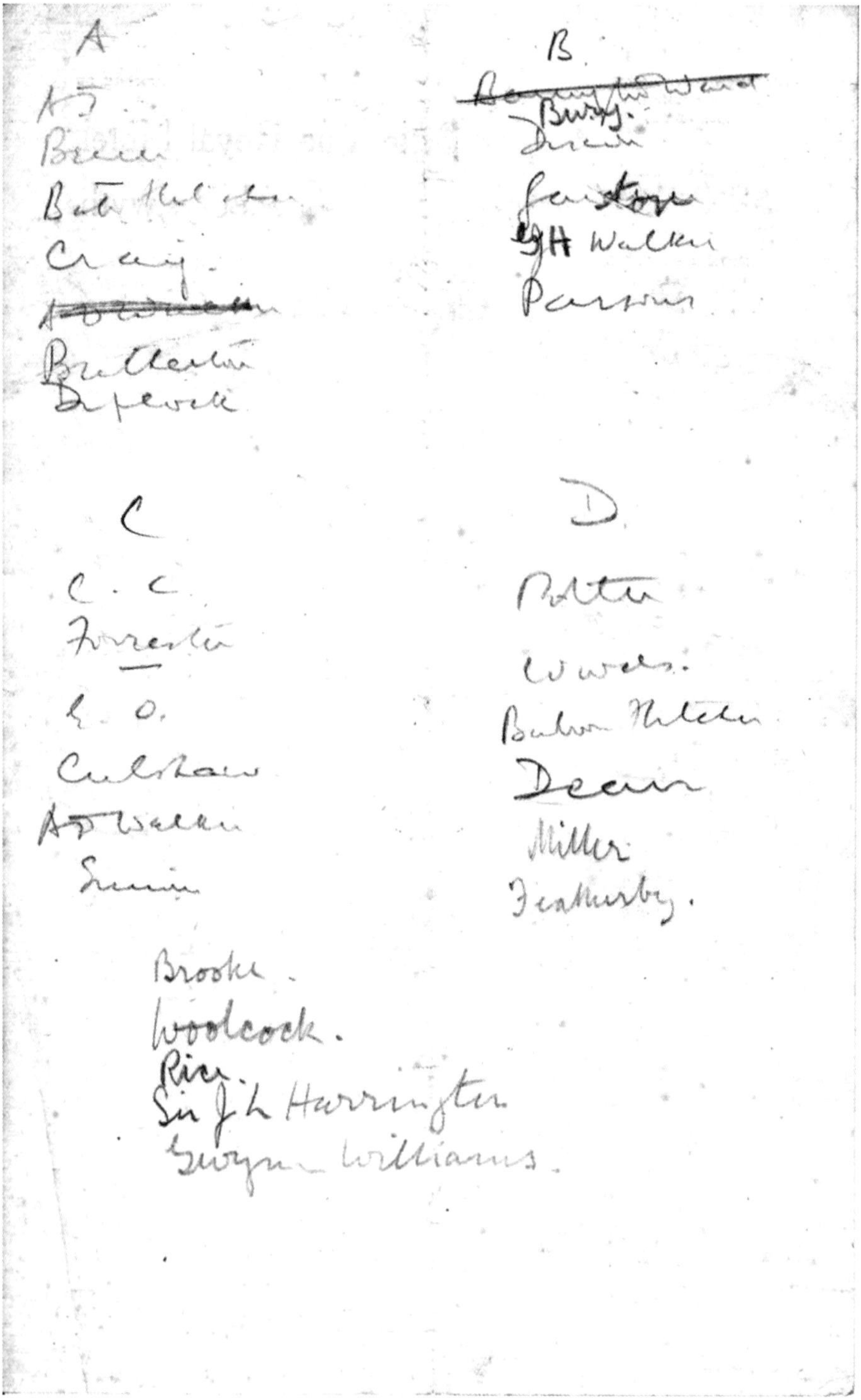

A

A T.
[illegible]
[illegible]
Craig.
~~[illegible]~~
[illegible]
[illegible]

B.

~~[illegible]~~
Burry.
[illegible]
[illegible]
G H Walker
Parsons

C

C. C
Forrester
E. O.
Culshaw
~~A D~~ Walker
[illegible]

D

Potter
Woods.
[illegible]
Dean
Miller
Featherby.

Brooke.
Woolcock.
Rice.
Sir J L Harrington
Gwynne Williams.

23	Up to 9.0 parade. Drill at Penrhyn Park[36]. Route march in afternoon. Stayed in to get orderly room settled. Snowed in morning.
24	Penrhyn Park in morning & afternoon. Up to 9.0 Parade. Fine all day.
25	Penrhyn Park morning & aft. Up for 9.0 parade.
26	Penrhyn Park all day. Karl & Eric innoculated & went to Mother in Menai Terrace.
27	Paid in morning also Billets. At work all day. Gazetted to Capt & dated back to Jan 29. Went up at 5.0 & saw Rowley & also went to mother. Karl, Eric & Uncle Fred up there early.
28	Got up at 9.0 To orderly room & the A Billets. Lunch with mother. Karl & Eric & I went to meeting of Lloyd George[37]. Tea & supper at Mount View Terrace with Uncle, Mother, Karl & Eric.
March 1	Drill all day. Busy in evening over sports. Blue clothes came.
2	Drill all day. Wore blue clothes for first time. Rained in evening.
3	Were on route march but rained so hard billet inspection & drill.
4	Batt. Route march in morning. Aft paid men & they were all inoculated.
5	In orderly room.
6	Paid Billets. Caught 3.30 with Karl to Liverpool, Bonnyman & Langford by same train got through to Liverpool. Dinner at Euchamp. To Ormskirk got Karl's car. Spent night at Pilkington's.
7	Left Windle Hall at 11.0. Called at Barracks. Lunch at Chester 12.45 to 2.45. Got to Bangor for 6.15. Good day but rotten road.
8	Comp work all day. Karl bad with Flu. Dean got mumps.
9	Usual Company training. Karl little better. Bonny[38] returned late at night.

---

[36] The estate of the Pennant family, now owned by the National Trust.
[37] Chancellor of the Exchequer at the time.

10   Batt route march. Rugger v Normal College[39] won 8-5 in aft. Hilda got mumps. Mess night. Karl much better.

11   Comp training. Maj. Evans & self out to dinner at Mr Holmes. Met Dr. Jones at Carnarvon. Karl to Menai View Terrace. Mother arrived.

12   Tried entrenching. Brigadier came round. C.O. to Town.

13   Physical drill & pay. Uncle & I beat Karl & Eric one up. To tea & supper with Mother.

14   Took company to church. Lunch with Mother. Mother not too well. Took Mr & Mrs Manning on run in Karl's car though Bethesda, Capel Curig, Betws, Llanberis Fan Carnaen & back. Billiards with Holmes & Dr Jones & Uncle Fred.

15   Penrhyn Park all day. Officers meeting in evening. ..... by C.O.

16   Penrhyn Park all day. Went up at 11.0 p.m.to fetch Mrs Radcliffe from Station with Bonnyman.

17   Park all day. Batt route march put off till Friday.

18   Billets all day. Snowed hard. Up in evening to Holmes & with Forester to Beaumaris.

19   All day in Park. Lunch then tea. C.O. returned. Bonny out.

20   In aft went fishing with Bonny, Edwards & Smith. Caught nothing. Tea at George[40]. Back to George after with Bury, Clench & Edwards.

21   Spent day with Clench, Holmes & Douglas at Bull Bay[41]. To George after dinner. Started at 9.30 back at 7.30.

22   Penrhyn Park all day. Started Brigade lectures.

23   Park all day.

---

[38] Major Francis J. Bonnyman.
[39] An independent teacher training college, now part of the University of Bangor.
[40] The George Hotel, Bangor; now Grade II listed.
[41] A village and bay on the northern coast of Anglesey.

24	Park all day. Night ops.

25	Park all day.

26   Route March towards Bethesda & Capel Curig. 'B' Co did ambushes. Rode Horse. Kaye started mumps. Met Mr & Mrs Pilkington.

27   Park all morning. Comp officers met at 2.0 by golf links & played with Mr & Mrs Pilkington. Dinner with them at George. Mother came down.

28   Took Church Parade. Lunch at George. To Bull Ring Mrs O'.....tery, Mrs P. & ..... Had snow storm. Nasty. Dinner at George.

29   Took over 'A' Co from Evans & he took over 'E'. Spent day taking over.

30   Penrhyn Park all morning. Mrs Malcolm rang up from Conway.

31   Park all day. Fine day. Very busy. Kaye much better.

April 1   Park all day. Brigadier round.

2   Took Church Parade. Lunch at Conway with Mr & Mrs & Tony Malcolm & Parker. Round with Mr Malcolm halved. My car smashed. Karl lent me his. Returned after dinner.

3   Worked all day in Park. Dinner with mother.

4   Saw C.O. all evening. Lunch with Malcolm at Conway. Two rounds of golf won 1 up & 4 & 6. Returned after dinner. Talked to Burn.

5   Brooke to town. I took on adjutancy. Brigade Concentration in Park. Mother to tea. Burn went off to Town on sick leave. Bonneyman went sick. Dined at George.

6   Act Adj. Wet all day. To dinner at Manning's with Uncle Fred.

7   Act Adj.

8   Act Adj.

9	Act Adj. Douglas & I went at night to Carnarvon. Saw ..... driver at Dr Jones. Met Dr Lloyd Roberts. Returned at 12.30.
10	'D' & 'B' Co sent out to locate German officers. Brooke returned. C.O. away all day. Golf in afternoon. Eric & Karl beat Uncle & I. Hilda, Dai & Kaye at Church Stretton. Dinner at George.
11	To Kirk. Rest of day at George. Hilda, Kaye & Dai still at Church Stretton.
12	Wet day. Morning shooting, afternoon Park.
13	Trench digging & shooting.
14	Attack with Potter over A & B areas. Aft practising it.
15	Park all afternoon. Morning with Potter, outposts on Carnarvon road.
16	Route March in rain to Bethes[42]. Hilda, Kaye & Dai turned up from Aberdovey. Mother at George. Dined there.
17	Park. Trench digging. Aft took Kaye a run in Dai's car. Evening at George.
18	Did not go to Church. Morning a walk with Kaye. Mother Karl & Dai to Anglesea monument in aft. Dai took Karl, Eric Kaye & self to Bull Bay. Tea there.
19	Line of Outposts towards Bethesda. Karl attacked. Saw Kaye Dai & Hilda on their way home. Photoed in aft & dug Trenches at night.
20	Dug trenches & shot all day. Wet. C.O. at Carnarvon. Kaye to Lancaster.
21	Batt outposts. Brigadier came along. Bed early.
22	Outposts with 'D' Co. Wet so early back & did knots & lashups in Penrhyn Hall. Aft entrenching. To Lloyd Roberts & Dr Jones with Douglas at night.
23	Park in morning. Lecture at night.

---

[42] Bethesda.

24   Medical Board at Hospital at 11.0. Aft with Kaye & Mother at George. Staff Raids put off.

25   Morning with C.O. arranging transfers. Aft & evening with Kaye. Burn to dinner.

26   Morning in Park. General Dixon round to see us working. Aft Park & nights ops.

27   Trench digging & musketry all day. To dinner with Douglas at Holsons.

28   Batt Parade. 'A' 'B' & 'D' Co attack. 'B' out all day. Very hot & tiring.

29   All day in Park.

30   All day in Park.

May 1   Wet all day. Aft at golf club with Karl & Eric. Could not get a game.

2   Took Church Parade. Aft lunch golf with Karl & Eric. Tea & supper at Holsons. Billiards with Holson. Saw Lloyd Roberts at lunch.

3   Aft Batt Sports. Douglas & Major Liam at Holston's until 2.30 a.m. Played bridge with Brig Jarvis.

4   Left Bangor at 7.0 for Grantham. Batt Parade at 6.15. Slept all the way. Arrived 1.30. Rest of day settling down.

Grantham   The Battalion lived in hutments for the first time. We arrived at about 1.0 met by Div & taken to lines which are just outside Belton Park, near Londonthorpe village. The 24th Man[43] were next to us & the 17th Liverpools had their officers lines practically in ours. I first of all lived in Barracks & then after returning from 1 weeks leave & being married lived at The Angel & then we got a house at 16 Harrowby Road just opposite the cemetery. I got a weeks leave from July 20th. I left at about 3.0 & motored via Nottingham Derby Leek Knutsford Warrington Wigan Preston & arrived Lancaster at about 10.45. I got home to Silverdale at 12.0. Hilda & Dai, Karl & mother, Mabel & aunt Edie came to the wedding. Karl with boils acting as best man. We Karl & I ran over in the Singer & left it at Atkinson &

---

[43] Manchester Regiment

motored up with mother to the church. At the reception & dinner were ..... the Malcolm's. The Rev & Mrs Bardsley, Mr Duncan, Mr & Mrs Heath, Kevin Irwin, Rev Griffiths & Mrs & Rev Hain. We left just after lunch & motored up to Lowood - had a ripping week there & motored back to Lancaster for lunch on Wed Aug 4th. Then down to Hilda's & arrived there at 7.0. Next day we ran on after lunch via Melton Mowbray, Oakham to Grantham & I resumed work on Friday. We had very good run indeed & only failed once on Red Bank, the west side of Grasmere. Davis & Hilda & Rosalind came to Harrowby Road the first free weekend & the others with Jock for a week. Mother stayed a bit at Woodhall Spa - when Karl had a few ..... with boils & we ran over there quite a lot. We also ran out Hilda's on weekend - through a fearful storm - the rain bounced down on the bonnet & as we went through a puddle came over the screen rail - luckily we were saved by the ..... rug.

The men trained a bit in R.E. work in revetting & in trench work & we built some communication trenches revetted in various ways for the Division. We got our Khaki & about 400 new S.L. Rifles. We also shot on the Range parts 1 & 2 - also we had a separate exam for the officers which I had to take just before I went on leave. We had a bit of Route marching - Brigade work & also a bit of Battalion Schemes. Kaye had a friend Mrs .....build who lived at Belton Rectory & we went ..... there. We also went up to town for weekends ..... before I was married & used to stay at 4 Mount Street - Roy Burns house - we always did Princes - Alhambra & then Murray's or the 400. I also went up one ..... & stayed at the Euston & met Kaye & Mrs Malcolm & we went off also to Th..... also stayed at H..... - it was very good indeed.

Various officers came & some left

Came

Maj Gwynn Williams	2nd Lt Dean A G 4-6-15
2nd Lt Williams S.A. 30/6/15	2nd Lt Culshaw J G 10-6-15
Lt Craythorne S.A. 1/7/15	2nd Lt Humphreys E H 14-6-15
2nd Lt Symon CHN 14-5-15	2nd Lt Struthers 14-6-15
2nd Lt Davison W 31-5-15	2nd Lt Parsons J 6-9-15
2nd Lt Bradley A 2-6-15	Lt Rice A H 6-5-15
2nd Lt Ryder A H 4-6-15	Capt Berry F 14-6-15
2nd Lt Nash L.A.H. 14-6-15	Capt Peck C E 6-7-15
2nd Lt Watson S.K. 14-6-15	Smith G E 6-7-15

Kaye & I had a ripping little house there & were thoroughly happy. I left the car in a garage belonging to Mr Lee only about 50yds down the road. We did some night ..... & went over to Belvoir ..... then over an area over the castle which belongs to the Duke of Rutland. Another time I took Woolcock & the Vet to a great monster of a mule there. We used also to motor over to Nottingham & go to theatre. Potter got ill from ague & was laid up for a few weeks. I had many ..... on Jane[44] being 3 times thrown through her coming down twice on the road - to the side..... & in the rut overgrown with grass & also jump the ditch at the bottom of the football field - also trying to ride a mule. Bradley also was thrown off Broncho. We used to have officers out to dinner & ended up with the theatre & saw Gipsy Lee & M..... ..... Quite good. The C.O. lived in Hound Lodge Belton. One run Kaye & I did was Nottingham, Thetford, Lincoln & home. At a Pa.....wah by Brigadier, Potter talked of seeing men ..... on a wall like lotuses & also about a coal sack (cul-de-sac). This happened at Bangor. C.O.2 took over mess until mess meeting. Very funny when Potter took it on. Became 91st Brigade in 30th Div under General Fry & Brig. Gen. Rumforth, Maj Grant being Brig Major - later on became Pioneer Batt & 30 Div T..... C.S.M. Coates[45] & Sergt Collier[46] both left for Inns of Court O.T.C. & got commissions. Sergt Prescott became C.S.M.

May 5	All day fatigues. Huge thunderstorm at night.
6	Fatigues. Spent evening putting up C.O.'s telephone.
7	Fatigues.
8	Motored over with Burn to Uppingham[47]. Returned for mess.
9	Up to Town with Burn. Lunch at Princes & dinner also. Went to Romford to see Burn family & Billy Lawson.
10	Min..... gang & fatigues.
11	Musketry & cleaning.
12	Wet all day. Bayonet in Pk Drill later.

---

[44] One of the officers' horses.
[45] Capt. Manchester Regt.
[46] 2nd Lt. Manchester Regt.
[47] Uppingham public school, Rutland. Capt. Roddam Burn was an ex-pupil.

13   Wet no parades.

14   Route March to Ancaster & Belton Park[48] with 'B' Co. Musketry.

15   With Burn to Town. Aft at Princes, Alhambra & then to Murrays. Met A. Challenor.

16   To lunch & bridge all afternoon. Met Mr Newman. Caught 11.0 to Grantham.

17   Outposts. Bayonet .....

18   In all day. Musketry.

19   March to Aiwars & back. Half. With C.C. & C.O. to Northampton & saw "Oh I Say". Back at 7.20.

20   Inspection by Col. Higginson in Ancaster Park of the attack. Aft foot inspection.

21   General inspection by General Fry G.O.C. Div. Very pleased.

22   With Eric & Burn to Town. Tea with Ronald Townsend at Constitutional & dinner at Princes & the Empire & back.

23   Took Church Parade.

24   Took Karl & Eric to Skegness & a round of golf & back via Lincoln for dinner. Lot of trouble with jet & tyres.

25   Musketry.

26   Route March to Belvoir & back - round castle.

27   'C' & 'D' to Park to practice attack.

28   'C' & 'A' to Willoughby[49] & practiced attack under C.O.2.

29   General Inspection all morning. Caught 11.40 to Town. Lunch at Princes with Burn. Empire Rack. Roy stayed in Town.

---

[48] The family home of the 3rd Lord Brownlow. 30th Division came together there.
[49] West Willoughby Hall, at Ancaster.

30	Returned by 1.15 train. Got up at 4. Went to 4 Mount St lunch & dinner at Princes & back.
31	Batt in attack on P
June 1	Light March under C.O.2.
2	Inspection by G.O.C. inc Batt V.G. Officers V.B. All stayed. Men given half duty, not over till 5.0.
3	Whole holiday for Kings Batt. To Town & met Kaye. Lunch with Mr & Mrs M & Kaye at Troc. Matthew Gui..... dinner at Euston.
4	March to Huncaster. Brigadier, Company Commanders ..... lecture.
5	Kit foot & Hut inspection. 12.13 to Town. Spent aft with Kaye. Dinner at Savoy. To The Monarch. Stayed at Home & back to Euston.
6	Wrelkin Park. Lunch at Princes. Tea at Tou.....nds. Dinner at Euston.
7	Musketry lecture & fatigues.
8	ditto
9	ditto. To Town. Kaye, I & Burn. Dinner at Savoy & to Alhambra.
10	Musketry & fatigues.
11	ditto
12	Musketry, Hut & Boot Inspection. With Karl & Eric to Woodhall Spa[50] golf & saw Mother.
13	Woodhall Spa. Golf all day.
14	Route March & attack at Willoughby Hall under C.O.
15	Musketry.

---

[50] Woodhall Spa, Lincolnshire. Home of the 'Dambusters' in WW2.

16	General Inspection by General Dinham Halt. To Woodhall Spa with K & Eric.
17	Brigade March & foot inspection.
18	Musketry.
19	To Woodhall Spa. Round of golf self K & E. Edith there.
20	Took Church Parade & then to Woodhall. Picked up Edith & on to Skegness. Golf with Jack Karl & Sue. Got back after dinner.
21	With 'B' & 'D' Co on Park.
22	Route March under Capt Bury to Ingoldsby. 'A' Co advance ft & flank guards.
23	Musketry & Half Holiday. Officers lectured by C.O. K & I to Woodhall.
24	Musketry, no parade in aft. Night ops till 7.0 a.m.
25	Trench digging, Musketry. By myself to Woodhall & saw Kitty & Mother. Slight rain.

The Battalion left about 9.0 in 3 detachments - Kaye met us in the town.

Salisbury
Larkhill
/9/15
5/11/15

The Battalion arrived about 3.0 p.m. & was met by Dixon & A. D. Walker who had been sent on to prepare hutments etc. We are in Camp No 25 in Larkhill about 2000 due N. of Stonehenge. Dixon got rooms at Old Sarum, London Road, Shrewton, about 4 miles away. Kaye did not come down till a few days later. I met her at Amesbury & took her to Shrewton & after that I lived altogether there. Sometimes I rode over on Jane & sometimes motored. But Hindley bringing the car from Grantham ran into a gate & it took some time mending & then towards the end I broke the propeller shaft or rather back axle. We managed 2 or 3 runs. One to Cheddar Gorge & then back to Warminster. We had lunch at the Swan Inn at Wells & tea at Warminster with Lt & Mrs Fair wife of an RAMC Lieut. We went up to town for weekend & stayed at Westminster Palace. Ronald & Hope dined with us at the Savoy & then went to Hippodrome & then supper at Savoy & so home. We went & had tea with Miss Hill, Ronald's aunt & so back to Salisbury. Karl went over to see Dr Arnley somewhere near Bath - he also took us a beautiful run through the New Forest & we had tea at Lindhurst - ..... to have plenty of ..... out to dinner but not as much as at Grantham. The men did much more R.E. work & built bridges & barbed wire entanglements & that sort of thing. We also did a lot of tunnelling for the R.E. I watched one divisional attack from trenches & was not impressed, they came out & had to go back again. Sir Arthur Paget[51] was down to watch it. We also did one in which we ..... took - had to run from Stonehenge Line to past the Artillery School carrying Barbed Wire entanglements! We also finished our musketry, did Field Firing practice & also our Revolver practice, the latter in pouring rain. A very funny incident happened when 'B' Co fired at 500 yds & a man was behind the 300 yds elevated firing point, he lay flat & refused to move! Just before leaving Berry went off to arrange about the coming of the Division. The C.O. lived at Durrington Manor, a huge red brick house. At the last minute my servant Durkin left to go Munition Making. I got ill on the Thursday Nov 3 just before leaving & had to go to bed while we were mobilizing. Potter had 'D' Co out all day standing to - what he called "Primly Mobling" he meant a Preliminary Mobilisation. I took on Pte Bennett instead of Durkin. At the last minute all the equipment & Boots were changed for new ones. I got leave for ..... 4 days on   /10/15. Kaye & I caught the 6.0

---

[51] General Sir Arthur Paget (1851-1928), Commander-in-Chief, Ireland, prior to the war.

o'clock at Salisbury & we got up to town & met Ronald & had dinner with him at a Restaurant. We then caught the 11.50 from London & got sleepers for Glasgow. Hope had a friend staying with her so could not come to dinner. We had a very good journey up but instead of getting in at 8.20 we did not get into Glasgow till 11.0. Had breakfast & then went for a motor run after lunch. Left Glasgow at 10.0 next morning for Manchester, spent that night there going out to tea with the Holmes & then had night with mother. That meant we had Wednesday night at Francis again & left by 8.30 to Wolverhampton. Met T B Adams at Stafford & spent day with Hilda. Caught 11.30 to there & spent afternoon .....ing with Ronald & caught 7.0 to Salisbury & landed in about 7.30. We had a day with the 20th Manchesters who came over on a pouring wet day - had sports which we won easily, all Rugger & soccer games - very funny officer T..... was on horse back & then ended up with a concert given by them that was very good. Col Petin was on good form. C.S.M. Prescott began to show weakness on the mobilising parades & CQMS Scott was very good. Mrs Fenn was Mary Shuttleworth.

5-11-15   The Battalion left Salisbury at 2 a.m. & went by two trains to Salisbury where they remained all day & embarked at 5.0 by the Mona Queen[52]. They were allowed into the town & most of the officers had breakfast & haircut at the Hotel. I left at 1.15 p.m. with the Divisional signallers including Lieut Hindle whom I had got to know. I got up about 7.30 & Kaye & I motored to Salisbury where we picked up mother & Aunty Hatty & we saw old Kaye off to Town & then Home. Mother, Aunty Hatty & I motored back to Larkhill & went to the Camp to the room they had left. We found Scott & a farmer there but the others gone, there had been a mishap to 'D' Co cooker & it was still there. I motored to Amesbury station wearing my pack for the first time. I got to Salisbury about 3.30 & entrained on the Mona Queen. The C.O. was with the transport on another. We had one Destroyer as escort & got out about 6.0. We had a beautiful crossing & I had a lunch all to myself & slept nearly all the way. We did not disembark at Havre till about 7.0 a.m. the next morning.

6-11-15   Disembarked about 7.0 a.m. & marched up to rest camp under canvas till we entrained again about 11.0 leaving the camp about 9.30. The officers arrived in a rest camp mess & were doing quite well. The men got a bit of sleep. Some officers went out into the town & got a

---

[52] S.S. *Mona's Queen*, a paddleboat of the Isle of Man Steam Packet Company that carried half a million troops to France during the war.

bath & food at one of the Hotels, personally I did not. The C.O. joined us later having not seen us since we left Southampton.

7-11-15   After travelling all night on the train in a most uncomfortable carriage 2nd class, in which there were 5 officers of 'A' Co, we landed at Pont Remy about 11 & all then had lunch. After much confusion we got on the march & marched to Bussus Bussuel which we reached about 4.30 after having tea on the way. It was a very exhausting & hot march after the last very hard & tiring days in wet & train & many men fell out. We experienced great difficulty in ..... with our parades. The billeting at Bussus was not arranged well at all. We had a very bad ..... who ..... us first & when we got there it took us about 2 hours to get billeted. The arrangements were approximately as the map shows.

Bussus   We marched then via Franciere & Ailly Le Haut Clocher where DHQ
8-11-15   were. H.Q. & 'A' Co had mess together, things were rather strained
to   owing to behaviour of C.O. & M.O., who would ask the C.O. for a
17-11-15   driver ..... in French language. About the 11th a new interpreter came.
            M. Marcel Maille..... Politzer - commonly known as Polly - he had been out during the whole of the war & very favourably impressed us. He was attached to H.Q. mess. The messing was in C.O.2 & Buchanan's hands & worked out 5 francs a head. The Major came to mess & ..... a way along old road & ..... long stayed. On the 13/11/15 & 14/11/15 I rode over to St Riquier & saw the 16th Manchesters ..... Capt Griff-Taylor & also H..... & the M.O. It snowed hard & froze hard during the last part of our stay there. Potter & I lost our

way coming back from St Riquier. We had a lot of Batt training under C.O.2 & the chill was very ..... as he left us saying by the right when in ..... column & then into his left ..... & on the left f..... ..... which put as all out! 'A' Co then made its reputation for latrines owing to the straw ..... we ..... up for the C.O. Bury left the Batt to become claims officer to the Division & we saw no more of him except very occasionally. We heard some of the men of the ..... stood .... to train ..... billets ..... very badly. On Tuesday 16-11-15 Brooke had to go to DH.Q. & was not heard of again that day also no signs of his horse Tawny.

17-11-15   Marched from Bussus to Bethencourt via ..... & St Ouen ..... having to ..... sur B..... Cross Roads by 11.0. Very hard marching on roads area covered in snow & in places ice, very hard on transport which took distinctly longer to get in than we did & went a long way too far ..... this way by not turning off right. We had a very good Billet. Burn had to sleep on the floor of my billet. We got in about 3.0 & left at 9.0 the next morning. Still no news of Bosch.

Flesselles   Batt marched to Flesselles via Vignacourt. Burn was sent on to billet
18-11-15   ahead & we got there about 1.0. DH.Q. was there. Brooke turned
   to   up in a very dirty state having been sent there two days before to
25-11-15   billet DH.Q. & troops, he had sent a message to C.O. which had
            never got to him. He made a fearful hash of things on a whole & the billeting for Officers & 'B', 'C' & 'D' Companys was very unsatisfactory. 'A' Co was very well off & did not have to shift at all. The Rev Lloyd Matthews there joined our mess & was a .... making things very lively & playing bridge with Fletcher v Diplock & myself every night. We did a bit of Batt training under C.O. & C.O.2 & also some bombing. Also all the Batt went through gas test in room under Capt Hartley only that by the time 'A' Co had got to room the gas was nearly all used up & I could go in without helmet on. Did a bit of Company training & also made a few straw huts under Bradley for C.O. & Division.

26-11-15   'A' & 'B' Companies left Flesselles under C.O.2 for Mailly Maillet. We marched the first day to Rainneville near Rubempré via Villers Bocage. Burn & G H Walker went on ahead to Billet. 'A' Co were very comfortable in a very big farm yard in barns all round. The officers were in an empty shooting box & then was the time G.W. began to make himself objectionable. He first of all messed with 'B' Co & quite ignored 'A'. He ..... help the H.Q. mess ..... & he ordered 'A' Co waiters to get some more wood for our fire & he issued reams & reams of orders & told Burn to do all the Billetting formalities with

Mayor etc. showing he did not know anything about them himself. Craig in charge of Transport.

27-11-15   We left early as we had a long march before us, the weather was very cold & frosty. 'A' Co was late in starting & S.M. Prescott began to show signs again of incompetence. We were to do the rest of the march that day. We went via Henincourt - Toutencourt - Harponville - Varennes - Forceville to Mailly. The same day B & D & H.Q. left Flesselles for Berneuil. The men stuck the march very well & we did not have our lunch till we got to the other side of Forceville. The transport had to take the wagons up to Mailly & then return & billet in Forceville. Again Burn & Walker & Galsworthy[53] were sent out to billet. We got the men in very well & officers had all got billets. 'A' Co were given an empty house for its mess which we found quite impossible. 'B' Co had quite a good mess in a Café. We had no H.Q. or Q.M.S. or C.H.Q. & on the whole except for getting men in the billeting was not done well at all. Burn met us with standing orders at Maille - great excitement on C.O.2's part for showing them me before him. He never showed me them after all.

28-11-15   Visited Trenches in morning with C.O.2 & Dixon & Capt Martel R.E. I did not recognize him at first but both knew we had known each other but could not think when or where, till we realised about the middle of the morning that it had been at Stratheden House[54] about 17 years before. We went to the Sucrerie - all down Roman Road - Taupin - Cheero - Delamay - Monk trench, where we were to dig trenches parallel & in front to ..... the German dug outs, but Monk trench was in such bad condition they could not use it & from Monk Trench to Firing line & back by Le Cateau - Observation Wood[55] - Excema & Waterloo Bridge - we got back late for lunch & had afternoon to ourselves. Three reliefs had to go down to trenches that night. Starting at 4.0 p.m.- 7.0 p.m.- 10 p.m. Dixon took first - myself second & Burn the third. We arranged reliefs alright & had guides but the C.O.2 thought they had dug all which the R.E.s had marked out & so put Parsons on to mark out more but he missed a communicate with Monk trench & luckily I found the real trench marked out by R.E.s.

---

[53] Pte. 20000 Robert W. Galsworthy, 'A' Coy.
[54] The Knightsbridge home of Mitchell Henry M.P., demolished about 1900.
[55] There were two; one just north of the village of Hem on the Somme itself; the other at the northern end of the battlefield between La Signy Farm and Touvent Farm.

28-11-15   When parading for party some man let off his rifle which luckily hit no one. The ground was fearfully hard owing to frost & we only dug down about 2 feet - much too much notice was taken at first to Star pistols & odd rifle bullets but the men soon got used to them. To let Burn's party in we got into the trench 'B' had dug & let him get into the trench we had been digging. We then got back. The men were pretty nervous but on the whole things went very well. In getting there we nearly missed a platoon. But it turned up later. Met D Bart Marchal in Maille. Entwistle Pt. lost his rifle.

29-11-15   We did nothing all day but took to Billets. Q.M. Stores were changed from 'B' Co lines to 'A' Co & we changed our mess from the empty House to same place as Q.M. Stores. That day it rained all day & it was too bad to work at all. First party went down to work but it was so much stuck & the trenches so bad we sent them ..... back in D..... & they turned us back & we turned the third party back.

30-11-15   Still raining. 'A' Co got turned out of mess to make it a drying room & Q.M. Stores & went to 'A' Co old house. C.O.2 lost his temper with Burn. & myself. 'A' Co joined 'B' Co in mess. C.O.2 went & billeted & messed by himself at corner near the men's billets. & there we all stayed till the end of the visit. 'A' Co found a C.H.Q. opposite Bat. H.Q. That night we had 2 shifts to carry material down - Burn & the first one came back with C.O.2 to Sucrerie to change trench boots. We had to wait ¾ hour for the boots & then it took us 3 hours to get to Charing X Dump & from there to Monk Trench - full up with water. C.O.2 only sent us down as sort of spite as he said it was no use at all. Craig & Bretherton came with him. That day Craig & Diplock changed places in transport. Board on Entwistle lost rifle. No orders appeared. Pres & Committee (members) by C.O.2.

1-12-15   Still raining. Did nothing all day. Had kit inspection & cleaning up billets. Changed my servant Bennett[56] for Rogerson[57]. Dinner with Martel at R.E.

2-12-15   Both Companies went into trenches. 'A' Co with 1st Batt R.I.F. 'B' Co with R.I.R. 'A' Co had to be at Auchonvillers at 3.0. Met by an R.I.F. guide who took us down 3rd Avenue to the Tenderloin[58]. Then

---

[56] Pte. 20055 Henry Bennett.

[57] Either Pte. 20194 James Rogerson or Pte. 20196 John Rogerson, who were brothers.

[58] Tenderloin trench was situated on the high ground overlooking the track that leads up the 'White City' area.

I met Maj. Moon C.O. R.I.F. who was dressed in Mackintosh & Sowester & a huge stick with pack. They were just changing H.Q. He was very decent & we had a guide to take each platoon to the Company.

No 1 Plat to A.Co.   No 3 Plat to C.Co.   Burn had No 2
No 2 Plat to B.Co.   No 4 Plat to D.Co.

I went to B.H.Q. 'C' Co had right bit of line from about point 62 - 64 incl. 'A' from pt 65-68 inclusive. 'B' from 69 round Redan[59] to 72 incl.

O.C. 'A' Co. was Capt Parr
O.C. 'B' Co. was Capt Synolt (Spider)
O.C. 'C' Co. was Capt O'Donovan
O.C. 'D' Co. was 2nd Lieut Russell
Adj. Capt Lerching
M.G. Officer
Scout officer Lt Williams

Nothing could have been nicer than the way the R.I.F. took us in - all officers were taken into the messes & made to feel at Home instantly - the men looked after our men - gave them Braziers & rum & rations which owing to the bad condition of the trenches the ..... was afterwards unable to be used - had not come at first. I sent CQMS Slater & C.S.M. Prescott up with Burn. Diplock was still in charge of the Transport. The rations did not turn up till about 11.30 & as CQMS & C.S.M. being up in the Redan - Sergt Dennett. took them & contacted both his own platoon Sergt & CQMS as a matter of fact - CQMS should have been left in Billet. I had a stretcher in H.Q. to sleep on & it was quite comfortable only the roof leaked horribly. I had a very good night's .....

3-12-15   Had a very good breakfast indeed & after telephoning for CQMS & C.S.M. I set out on the rounds. I set out to 'A' & 'C' Companies & visited with them & then got back for lunch (V G) & then went round to Redan - did not see Burn but some of the men. Burn was not too happy the Redan being in a frightfully dirty & wet state & the dug outs being in very bad condition. Everyone seemed cheery & shouting for rations. We made one very great mistake in having fresh instead of tinned meat rations. I attended conference of C.

---

[59] Redan Ridge, on the road to Beaumont Hamel.

Commanders at 12.0. It was very interesting to listen to what had been noticed one way & another as regards the Bosch. Several men were stuck in the mud & had to return by transport including my servant Rogerson. Diplock came down with Rations.

4-12-15   Did rounds of platoon as day before & found all quiet & settling down. The platoons instead of being part of the double sentry of the day before now joined up & found a platoon of the Company & acted as such. Maj. Moon raised question of syphoning the Redan into crater & 'A' Co trench into Watling Street. I reported the idea quite feasible. C.O.2 & S.M. Prescott came along midday. I did not see the former but C.S.M. remained - his story was that he & CQMS Slater had lost their way after getting my message & started for the Tenderloin - he ..... and Slater asked for the 10th line instead of Tenderloin. They went also along Talland & Roman[60] road & came to a clearing station where they had been given rum & then gone on to H.Q. of a Batt there where the C.O. said our .... had gone out of the trenches and back to Maillet after giving them stuff to drink. Slater had stuck in the mud & given up all hope & told Prescott to leave him to die. Prescott had ..... just .... by getting onto a parapet to pull Slater out. Slater had turned up nearly down to ..... & his .... bad state & Prescott was rather ..... C.O.2 brought him down the next day. He stayed with Dennett after that & Slater stayed back at Maillet. Rations came up for the next day & the weather changed a bit.

5-12-15   Visited platoons as previous day - only Redan in the morning. All quiet again. That night a Bosch working party was scuppered by R.I.F. machine gun.

6-12-15   Spent all morning preparing to come out of Trenches. Went up to 'A' & 'C' Companies. We ought to have left at 3.0 but did not leave till 3.30. Platoons left as they arrived at the Trenches & we reorganised at Auchonvillers. Crathorne[61] was mining officer at Auchonvillers & we met him there as we came away. Men are fearfully dirty & tired but in good spirits & managed to raise a song as they came back into billets at Maillet. We occupied the same areas as before going up to the trenches - they had had fires & hot food got for them by party sent up early in the morning - also a lot of clean straw. We had only one case of genuine Trench feet & that was Sergt Small. Dixon came

[60] The old Roman road from Bapaume to Albert.
[61] 2nd Lt. Alfred Crathorne, Royal Engineers.

out the same day. Apparently the R.I.R.'s had not treated 'B' Co as well as we had been treated. Like us they had had no casualties but a Sergt of the R.I.R.'s had taken 2 men out for inspection on the parapet & through our wire on patrol. He missed his way & found himself right up against the Bosch wire, had lost his head & b....d back. Our men got back as best they could but left a hat (11S Lancs) on the Bosch barbed wire. 'B' Co had a near shave coming out of the trenches as the story goes they were having a sort of inspection in the open by Waterloo bridge when they were spotted & shelled pretty badly one shell very nearly hitting Garton & another Dixon - hitting the side of the trench - luckily the ground was so soft it only splashed them with mud. A bit of shell went through Sergt Sharratt's pack & broke his mess tin. All through the shelling although everyone else had gone to earth pretty quickly 2 men had hold of one rifle on the parapet & got quite heated arguing whose rifle it was 'That's my ----- rifle'

7-12-15   Spent all day cleaning themselves & cleaning up billets etc. rained hard all day.

8-12-15   Started on day work repairing & cleaning up communication trenches uniting Roman Road & Tarquin trench. Special men were told off for repairing billets under W. Parsons.

9-12-15   Still on repairing Roman Road etc - also put Fletcher & No 4 Plat on 4th Avenue. Also ch..... Special parties still under Parsons. Crathorne called in & saw us all at tea.

10-12-15   Still on clearing up trenches & special work. Orders came through that C.S.M. Boden 'B' Co & myself are to go to the 3rd Army School of Instruction at Flixecourt. C.O.2 told me to arrange for car with Brigade office. As we were moving the next day orders came out for the move & in them were "Horses & mules to report to transport officer by 8.0 am"

Notes on fortnight at Maille.

Some officers were acting the spy & reporting what went on to C.O. We thought it was Dixon or W.G. Walker. We - Burn & I, wrote a note to Brooke[62] as follows

2-12-15 Dear Brooke. Just a line to let you know we are alive & kicking in the mud. We have been in the trenches & it is delightfully wet there. Just as you would love it! But it is very quiet. Swimming is impossible - perfectly rotten & altogether a ? but still rather amusing. Everyone is well & send you various messages. I'd like Rice to be here it would suit him admirably. A spent bullet nearly took my nose off last night & destroyed my .... but I enjoyed myself all the same. A T says he is the ..... Service he was not, in fact "in ..... sans ....." (Burn notes that then) I ..... the last sentence & if you like you can tell J.L.H. that I have never wished for gentlemanly behaviour more - certain the ways are better off!! ATC (Then Burn again) Send me a line if you have a moment. C..... Remember us to all yours A.B.

Somehow C.O. got to know all of it & he had Burn up about it (& not saluting him) & told him he had heard from higher authorities about the note - now as a matter of fact we never sent it at all & Brooke never heard anything about it of course. C.O.2 all the time we were there made Company Commanders arrange everything. Wished very good mess & officers ..... then & in all ..... then - the men got 2 ..... at Maille & one at Auchonvillers where there was also a good canteen & also the field ..... M..... told us a good story of a German called Hans Mueller who almost always turned on M.G. etc when he came along. Hans ..... always gave us warning by shouting "I am Hans Mueller, I am Hans Mueller" & slowly getting up & waving us down. When 'C' & 'D' were in the trenches C.C. was quite good & had no nerve in fact the C.O. was very annoyed with him because he hopped up on the parapet in daylight to escape having to go through some mud in the trench. Potter on the other hand was very bad & lost his nerve entirely. Brooke was about the best of that Company I was told. Total Casualties of 2 Companies 7. 'C' Company 2 1 Dead. 'D' Company 5 all died. Many stories were told of Potter & others. He & his men did the .....dgeon stroke all down some road one night to get to his work at Vallard & not a sound was allowed. Potter kept on saying "Hush! Hush!" They were met by a G.S. wagon making the devil of a noise & the driver shouting for all he was worth. Another

---

[62] Capt. Harry K. Brooke, 11/SLR.

time when some bullets came over his men in the middle of the night he made them all lie down & he went along the trench & tried to attract the Bosche's fire by exhibiting his cap on his stick over the trench (midnight), this was in ..... - the nearest point being 1150 yards. He also used to have what he called "predominations" (premonitions) if his men were going to be wounded but as soon as he told his subaltern that the next evening he did not have them a man was killed. He also talked about Salonoco (Salonika) & Uskbug (Us.....) The C.O., R.S.M., Polly & Padre were being were being conducted once over the front line when they lost the guide & nearly wandered into the Bosches. Luckily they found out in time & returned - wiser for their experience. Crathorne told us how he had shown a French officer round Auchonvillers - he had all the necessary passes & the same afternoon very accurate German shooting on Auchonvillers & all the important houses etc.

11-12-15   Companies left at 9.0 leaving C.S.M. Boden & myself behind. Bretherton took advance guard which met the C.O. with the rest of the Batt but C.O.2 & main body missed them (possibly on purpose & certainly they ..... not ..... acting C.O.2 fault!) Polly & Miller turned up before for Billeting Party but as I had all cut & dried they did not loiter. Polly got fearfully excited but I did not show him anything - I heard he had been a failure before. Battalion was in in about 10-15 minutes. Had tea with 'D' Co. Brooke had given up the adjutancy & become C.O.2 to 'D' Co. R.S.M. Payne had taken on the adjutancy. Had dinner with C.O. Polly & Matthews. They went & I had a long talk with C.O. about C.O.2 He told me C.O.2 had reported badly on Burn & told him Burn was a ..... funk[63] but I contradicted it & he was awfully pleased as he had always had great faith in Burn. I had a long talk & I think I put a spoke in the C.O.2 wheel - the fifth wheel of the cart! I slept that night on C.C.'s bed as my luggage had to go to transport at Forceville that night as I had to be at 7 a.m. next morning at Hedanville to meet the bus.

12-12-15   I got up at 6.0. C.C. lent me his horse & I went over to Hedanville. Woolcock sent my luggage & a groom to get C.C.'s horse. C.S.M. Boden & Henshall walked over. Bus started at 7.0 a.m. for officers & baggage & one for N.C.Os & servants. My valise would only just go in. We went to Flixecourt & I met Synott 1st R.I.F. on bus, via Warloy - Vadencourt - Contay - Herrisart - Rubempré - Villers Bocage - Flesselles - Vignacourt - Flixecourt - getting there about

---

[63] A person in a state of nervousness.

11.30. We went into the White Chateau & there given a paper with billet in ..... B..... Rue de Remy de Ceylan. A very good billet with electric light & a fire place & very good eiderdown & bed. Also a paper to say I was in No 1 Syndicate with Maj Stansfield & in No 2 was Capt Bartlett Mess president in the big Chateau (belonging to M. Saint of Saint Freres)

Staff of School
Commandant Lt Col Kentish DSO 1st R.I.F.
Adj. Capt Armstrong 16 I.C.
Chief Instructor Maj Hill RF DAQMG 7th Div
Syndicate Commanders
No 1 Maj Standfield DSO 2nd Yorks
No 2 Maj Brownlow R.R.
No 3 Maj Harris Gordon H.
No 4 Capt Yates I.C.
No 5 Capt Bartlett Buffs
No 6 Capt Kelly MC R.E. I.A
No 7 Capt Ramsden 2nd Yorks
No 8 Capt Hudson Seaforths
Attached
Capt G.....-White R.E.
Capt Briers RAMC
Capt Davidson Warwick
Capt Fletcher Warwicks
Capt Hesketh Pritchard
Capt   Yorks QM
M. Bazithen Interpreter

Col Kentish was late of 1st R.I.F. with whom 'A' Co were in trenches. A very good leader but no organiser - good lecturer & a very energetic man. Good footballer & an advocate of football in England - favourite ..... which became a byword - demand ..... a bad show. Maj Stansfield & Capt Ramsden came to 30th Div. Capt Bartlett was at Rugby in A.S.O. Capt Kelly knew R.S. Rai....en ..... of Indian R.E. Capt Hudson lived at Bedford & knew Edith Hawton. Capt ..... White was a cousin of the ..... White in Staffs. Capt Hesketh Pritchard was the cricketer & expert on sniping being a big game shooting.

No 1 Syndicate officers
Capt Jordan   High Point   8th Devons
Capt Eckhart W.H.   Evy (Evolution)   14th Warwicks

Capt Cassels	George Roly	17 HLI[64]
Capt Fowler	General French	Gloucester
Capt McDougall		Seaforths
Capt Cutter		Warwicks
Capt Ellis C.A.B.		Leicesters
Capt Synot	Spider	R.I.F.
Capt Williams	Tick	3 Monmouths
Capt Renshall		18 Manchesters
Capt Elstob	Murphy	16 Manchesters
Capt Madden	Murphy 2	17 Manchesters
Capt Peterson	Dolly	Gordons
Capt Vernon	Humpty	
Capt Leith A.L.W.	.....ter	4th Gloucesters
Capt Bundy		Warwicks
Capt Matthews H.S.		14th Warwicks
Capt Hart W.T.	Golliwog	11th Warwicks
Capt Langdale	Scourge	R.R.
Capt Boyle	Broncho Bill	
Capt Mulvanney		Gordons
Capt Cross A.R.		3rd Gordons
Capt Millard A.J.	Mother Goose	11th Warwicks
Capt Fletcher	B..... Ypres	1st Cambridgeshires
Capt ATC		11 S Lancs
Lt Chadwick	Ivy 2	Warwicks

Other Messes
Capt Reilly W.P.B. Rugby
Capt Parker S..... Off No 2 Syndicate
Capt Hartford V..... Expert S..... at ..... Garden

Jordans	O.C. Company - his batt went over first at Mons. His Batt at Ailly sur Somme.
Cassells	knew Ronald T..... the rest of the Glasgow people where he came from.
Fowler	came from Argentina
McDougall	was billeted at Bedford before he came out.
Miller	his Batt had the 24th Man in the trenches with it for instruction - they know none of the equipment & stuff away in Dumps & things.

---

[64] Highland Light Infantry

Synott	O.C. B Co R.I.F. was in charge of Burn when we were in the trenches. Had been through Ypres ..... St Julien & Loos.
Elstob	in same Company as Mal.... - brother of the Haileybury[65] master. He was a master himself before war. Knew P.S. F.....
Pitman	nephew of Cherry Pitman who married Hilda Dorkin - of course he knew all the Dorkins.
Vernon	His brother lived at High Wycombe & had Sylvia Dorkin out to tea when she was there.
North	Had Military Cross for getting in wounded men we're told.
Harts	Batt came to our Div ..... to his order not-a..... he stayed on his own.
Boyle	was a Capt in the Life Guards before war & also ran a ranch out in America.

No 1 Syndicate dined at big Chateau with C.O., Adj., etc. Stansfield - Kelly - Bartlett - Ramsden - Hudson & a few French men dined at No 1 mess.

In my billet was Maddens Purcell & ..... - Elstob was supposed to be there but he got another as there were only 4 rooms. Spider on one side & Jordan on the other. Mr Saint had big canvas ..... there & also 22 other mules of ..... on ..... about France - one at St Ouen. He had built 3 others for his children. 2 of them weren't finished.

They gave us a Syllabus of Works it was intended to try & do as follows:-

1. Ladies lip	a. Its meaning.
	b. How to acquire the gift of.
2. Discipline	a. General behaviour & conduct of the Off.
	b. Personal appearance - Physical fitness - punctuality - Saluting.
3. Morale	Its meaning & importance - Responsibility of Officers & N.C.Os engendering it - Patriotism - Esprit de Corps - Esprit de Brigade - Esprit de Division - Esprit d'A..... - Psychology of the War.
4. Discipline & Command	Necessity of system of command so as to ensure continuity - Bearing of Officers & N.C.O.s towards their men.
5. Organisation	Batt - Brigade - Div. Chain of Responsibility

---

[65] Public school in Hertfordshire where C.C. Champion had been the science master.

6. Care of Arms	Rifle, Bayonets, Ammunition - Equipment Smoke Helmets - Clothing - Iron rations.
7. Sanitation	(a) In Trenches, Billets, Bivouacs, Line of March
	(b) Care of feet: Standing orders on subject
	(c) First aid, use f Field Dressing
	(d) Evacuation of the wounded, general principles of.
8. Billet Life	How to care for & get the best out of the men in billets. N.B. This is a special subject with a very special importance which was not realised at the commencement of the last Winter Campaign.
9. Duties of Platoon & Section Commanders	(a) System of Billeting
	(b) In the line of march (Discipline)
	(c) In the Trenches
	(d) In the attack
10. Protection	Adv. Guard. Rear & flank. Outposts.
11. Principles of Attack Normal.	(a) Organisation ..... to.
	(b) Distribution of troops .....
	(c) Formation with regard to ground
	(d) Formation with regard to .....
	(e) Close communication with troops in Flanks
12. Fire Discipline	(a) Combination of ..... with movement
	(b) Fire control
	(c) Description of Target
	(d) Judging Distance
	(e) Use of Range-finders
13. Defence Normal	(a) Principle lines of Discipline
	(b) Taking up a ..... line
	(c) Sighting of Trenches by day & night
	(d) Telling off & Distribution of Wa..... Points
14. Trench Warfare (attack)	(a) Organisation for an attack from trenches (Supply of Ammo, for an attack from trenches supply of ammo, grenades, rations, H.Q.)
15. Defence	(a) Construction of trenches
	(b) Construction of parapets
	(c) Construction of traverses
	(d) Revetting, Sandbags, fascias wire hurdles & other impediments.
	(e) Construction of splinter Proof
	(f) Loopholes, sighting & construction of, types of limitations
	(g) Sniping posts
	(h) Listening Posts

(k) M. Gun emplacements

(l) Sapping principles of

(m) Entrenching tools use of

(n) Entanglements

(o) Use of telescopes & periscopes

(p) Sniping ..... & methods to be employed in

16. Trench   (a) Al..... necessity for
    Orders   (b) Organisation of work
              (c) Allotment of horses for watch work ..... etc

17. Machine   1. How to fire Maxim Lewis Gun
    Guns   2. Principles of employment in attack & defence

18. Grenades (a) Description of
              (b) Handling of
              (c) Limitations of
              (d) Uses in attack & defence
              (e) Training of formations
              (f) Organisation of grenadiers in attack & defence
              (g) Carrying of
              (h) Supply of

19. Patrol   (a) Importance of
    Work   (b) How to organise

20. Map   (a) Sample scales & meaning of
    Reading   (b) How to read a map / explain how it should be
              looked upon as a ..... & not a puzzle
              (c) Compass. Variation of, taking of angles,
              conversion of magnetic into true bearing
              (d) Setting a map by compass & other methods.

21. Co-operation Importance of & method of.
    Of other ..... Co-operation of Staff & Reg Officers.

22. Messages (a) Official letters writing of
    & Reports (b) Memoranda
              (c) Minutes
              (d) Field messages method of writing
              (e) Verbal messages limitations of
              (f) Reports - how to be written
              (g) Reconnaissance simple form of
              (h) Trench Reports

23. Arrest   (a) Rules of
              (b) Telling off & disposal of prisoners
              (c) Crime & punishment on active service
              (d) Field G.C.M.
              (e) Army (Suspension of S.....) Act 1915

24. Intelligence (a) Service of security

	(b) Information
	(c) Prisoners of war
	(d) their treatment & disposal
25. G.R.O.	Extracts from S.....y, Dress, Discipline, Correspondence
26. Gas	Use of Protection methods of dealing with organisation of attack.
27. System of Supply	(a) Ammunition (b) Supplies
28. Drill	(a) Importance of as a means to an end (b) Squad with arms (c) Platoon (d) Company
29. Riding	(a) ..... on (b) Saddling & Bridling a horse (c) Stable management
30. Physical Training	(a) Bayonet Fighting (b) Swedish Drill (c) Foot Call
31. Revolver	(a) Method of using (b) Short course in use of

TO. ABBEVILLE.

→ H

A

TO
LON'?

G

B

TO ST OUEN.

Rail. ←Longpré

ST ouen →

TOWN.

FLIXECOURT

J. Elliott Billet -

TO AMIENS.

A. Chateau No.2 MESS

B H.Q Chateau.

C. My Billet -

D. Tadani Billet -

E. Spiden Billet.

G. Newtti's Billet -

F. Tich.
Elliott
Mottenson   } Billet -
Langdale

H. Parade ground

I. Pitman
McDougall } Billet -
Forlin

13-12-15 9. a.m.   Dispersal of Syndicate Commanders - we had all our
                        past history gone into & also were told the general idea
                        of the course.
          10.30 a.m.   Officers - Inspection of by Commandant; followed by
                        Commandant's address. General idea etc of course.
          2. p.m.   Drill parade for all Syndicates.
          5. p.m.   Lecture by Commandant on "Leadership"

14-12-15 8.45   D.S.C. Repeat of day before
          10.15 a.m.   Squad drill
          11.45 a.m.   Lecture on Fire Control by Maj. Hill.
          2 - 3 p.m.   Grenades Lecture. Mills No 5 Mark 1
          3.15 p.m.   Communication Drill - order of command
          6 p.m.   Lecture by Commandant on Leadership

15-12-15	8.45	Squad Drill
	10.15 a.m.	D.S.C.
	11.45 a.m.	Entrenched order Drill
	2 - 3 p.m.	Grenades - lecture
	3.15 p.m.	Communication Drill
	6 p.m.	Lecture on Gas - Capt. Hartly 3rd Army
	8.15	Concert by Cambridgeshires. Very good indeed.

Burn & Diplock came over on horse back. Had tea at café.

16-12-15	8.45	D.S.C.
	10.15	Marching Drill
	11.45	Entrenched order Drill - signals - Fire position - how to ..... up & .....
	2 - 3 p.m.	Grenades Lecture - hand grenades
	3.15 p.m.	Communication Drill
	6 p.m.	Lecture by Commandant " Esprit de Corps"

17-12-15	8.45	Rain. D.S.C.
	10.15	Gas L..... Drill
	11.45	Gas Test on helmets. Capt Hartley sent gas over trenches in which was a platoon of Cambridgeshires & then demonstrated efficiency of V..... sprayer. Also they advanced through a cloud of gas & smoke.
	2.0 p.m.	Grenades Lecture
	3.0 p.m.	Entrenched order Drill. Fire position & Fire Orders
	6.0. p.m.	Lecture by Commandant - Esprit de Corps
		Entertainment by Major & Capt Wood son of Sir Evelyn Wood - very funny & a ..... animal - he had been on stays which ..... any before - demonstrated against the inadequacy of pay before war - the contestant was quite good.

18-12-15	8.45 a.m.	Ceremonial Drill very interesting.
	10.15	Grenades Throwing
		Inspected by French officers. Had to double back to punch thing having arrived earlier than Commandant asked. Very hard work.
		In afternoon we went by Bus to Amiens - Jordan & I went in together - had bath in public baths then they had ..... we had baths & then the maid brought in hot towels & ..... you up & you were supposed to recline on a sofa. Had Shampoo & a dinner at 7.0 at Le Café des

Huites on the R..... Corps road sans ..... Funny place - went through a dirty shop & then a clean kitchen where an ..... officiated & then up stairs where one ..... ran up & down. Upstairs there were about 24 dining including Maj. Hill-....., Capt Bartlett, Ramsden, Davidson & M. Braz..... Had a very good dinner of Lobster (cray fish) Sole, Crab-stick, R..... omelette, fruit & chablis Heavy ..... cigars. Caught 9.15 bus back. S.....d the worse for drink & then was sick all over Jordan myself on the bus.

19-12-15		Went to church parade opposite the big chateau. Officers saluted during singing of National Anthem. Spent the rest of the day writing letters etc.
20-12-15	9. a.m.	Drill as a company - Formation applicable to Fire. Parade ground.
	10.30	Formation applicable to Fire in Field
	11.30	Fire Control
		Major Hill took us on this - we went in columns of platoons in lines in fours & they went through a wood & then came back & a company of Cambridgeshires attacked a wood ..... were retreated & cavalry & machine guns appeared & also a battery. Ridiculously funny.
	3. p.m.	Platoon Drill
	4. p.m.	Grenade throwing. Threw Mills. Burn came over to see us at lunch time but could not stay.
	6. p.m.	Lecture Maj. Stansfield on Battle of Loos & preliminary preparations from point of view of Infantry. The lecture was very good but it showed us how fearfully difficult everything is. ..... & cheers 8th Devons but 19 officers out of 19.
21-12-15	9. a.m.	Demonstration Drill attack by a company of the 1st Cambridgeshire Regiment. As a matter of fact we attacked ..... & had no C.R. with us at all. It was fearfully heavy going & we had to run miles also it was raining hard. We had about 200 yds charge over ploughed field & then another 300 yds after to make good the other side. We had busses to take us back to Flixecourt from Ville-de-Marclet.
	2. p.m.	Platoon Drill
	3. p.m.	D.S.C.

	6. p.m.	Lecture Capt Gr..... R.E. Battle of Loos & .... preparations from point of view of R.E.s. Very good & gave us some idea of the ..... work to be done by the R.E.s before the attack. All their work is practically before.
22-12-15	9. a.m.	Officers ..... in any reconnaissance before an attack as a Drill ..... Assault & reorganise - as matter of fact it rained so hard it had to be put off.
	2. p.m.	D.S.C.
	3. p.m.	Platoon Drills - marching in lines.
	6. p.m.	Lecture by Lt. Col Tach... DA. Attack on the battle from the point of view of the R Artillery. He was in command of the L & T Batteries there & 'L' Battery was the one which took up a position between original first-lines. Very good.
23-12-15	9. a.m.	Attack by the attached Battalion. Student officers in command. As a matter of fact the combined ..... did it all & we just looked on & criticised.
	2. p.m.	Company Drill
	3. p.m.	bayonet
	6. p.m.	Lecture by General Vaughan - Role of Cavalry in the present war & probability of their use in the future. He never got onto the second part of the lecture but his first part was usefully good & showed how useful the cavalry were ..... on in the war. General Vaughan had Lt. Jos Wardell in attendance on him. He turned over his maps etc for him.
24-12-15	9. a.m.	Attack scheme to be worked out on ground. No 1 & 2 went together towards Vanchells & did attack on La Follie Aubeyn. Vernon, Boyle, Elliott & I worked together our scheme was as Maj Stansfield.
	2. p.m.	Bayonet
	3. p.m.	Company Drill
	6. p.m.	Lecture by Commandant "Esprit de Corps"

25-12-15   Christmas day. Breakfast at 8.0 & caught 9.15 to Amiens - got there about 12.0 with Jordan & Mother Goose. Tried to get rooms at Rest. Go..... where the dinner was to be but failed. Finally settled in Hotel du Rhin, could not get them anywhere else. Had lunch there with those two. Had a bath in aft & then had tea with Spider, Tick &

Elliott. After tea went to Cathedral with Elliott & listened to service going on. Had dinner at Rest. Gudul. C.O. turned up late but in very good form. Had ripping good meal. Fowler & Mrs Dougal misheard ..... through excess of licquer with ..... the servant. I got to bed about 1.15.

26-12-15   Got up about 11.15 had no breakfast as I could not draw anyone's attention. Had lunch at R..... with Chadwick. Had tea with Vernon & Boyle - caught the 6.15 back to Flixecourt. Got back in time for mess.

27-12-15   9. a.m.   Lecture - Capt Kelly - laying out trenches, tasks, tools, followed by practical demonstration on the work dealt with in the lecture & building of a sandbag revetments.

2. p.m.   Company Drill.

3. p.m.   D.S.C.

6. p.m.   Lecture by Capt J.G.Q. Mantell R.E. Trenches of the 4th Division. Lecture was not much good as he talked to the ..... & was far too disjointed & the subject too varied.

28-12-15   'A' Company came to St Ouen from Beu...iel

8.45 a.m.   Use of entrenching Tool, sandbag Revetments. Had to dig in ourselves to lying position & then to kneeling position. I got deeper than any other officer. Had no time to do more - very hard & wet work.

2. p.m.   Gas & Smoke Demonstration by Capt Hartley Chemical Advisor 3rd Army.

1. Test of t...h Helmet by wearing them in room containing chlorine - we were in for about 10 minutes - Tick was affected & was ill after.

2. Demonstration of formation of gas cloud by allowing gas to escape rapidly in the open.

3. Demonstration of gas mixed with smoke cloud. Seemed very efficient to hide advancing troops.

4. Formation of a frontal smoke screen by means of smoke candles placed at 20 yards intervals. The smoke is i..vail.ing & men will advance through it to show concealment given.

5. Demonstration of F...ite Grenades will burst in the open & in a trench to show:-

(1) Radius over which burning material is scattered.

(2) Nature of smoke

(3) Efficiency & character of smoke screen produced.

(4) Distance to which the screen is effective

(5) Incendiary effect of grenades burst in a trench

6. Similar demonstration with the R.E. Phosphorous Grenade.

7. Demonstration of the production of a flank screen with Red Phosphorous Grenades in order to protect the flank of an Infantry advance from aimed fire. The screen will be made by throwing the grenades by hand & by West Bomb Thrower. A good stunt.

8. Bursting of I.S.K. Bombs to show lachrymatory effect & protection afforded by goggles with & without the Tabs Helmet. Had great effect on eyes.

The whole thing was a very good stunt & we saw the exact thing - very interesting.

	5.30 p.m.	Laying out trenches by night. We went out at 6.0. & had to just dig 6" down after being extended & put into position.
29-12-15	8.45 a.m.	Clearing & revetting a damaged trench. As a matter of fact we did not clear anything but revetted with Rabbit netting - a very dirty job as I had to hold posts to be beaten in by Boyle. Bolton was full of mud.
	2. p.m.	D.S.C.
	3. p.m.	Company Drill. Capt Heath the S.M. Guardsman at Chelsea School of Instruction came & jiggered us about. It was fearfully funny the way some men absolutely lost themselves. We were not very much improved there being far too much of the "as you were" business about it - we did not pay any attention to the first 4 or so words of command.
	6. p.m.	Lecture by Commandant - Discipline. General Allenby 3rd Army G.O.C. came down in afternoon.
30-12-15	8.45 a.m.	Laying out wire entanglement.
	2. p.m.	Ceremonial Drill.
	3. p.m.	D.S.C.
	6. p.m.	Lecture by Commandant - Esprit de Corps.

Kent came over & I took him up to tea at chateau.

31-12-15	8.45	Lecture on Construction of Sniping point, Dug outs & M.G. emplacements. Then we went & dug ourselves in with entrenching tools - hard work in chalk. I got down

further than anyone else in No 1 - Boyle ran one close, there was very little to choose between us - he was bigger & I was deeper.

2.0 p.m.	D.S.C.
3. p.m.	Ceremonial Drill
6. p.m.	Commandant - Esprit de Corps

That night we sat up playing bridge - Hardan, Madden, Hunt & myself. We saw the new year in singing Auld Lang Syne. Any..... but all the syndicate there but it was quite a good show & many of them had certainly had as much as was good for them. Murphy was quite funny.

1916

1-1-16	8.45	Ceremonial Drill under Commandant.
	10.30 a.m.	We turned up very late nearer 11.30.

We did an output scheme towards Amiens & got back at 2.0. Jane was brought over to me by young Ellison, Thompson being under arrest for drunkenness. I rode to St Ouen about 2 to 3 miles & I rode on & had tea & mess with Burn & Co at St Ouen. A concert at 6.0. was given by Rev L Matthews so we went to that. It was awfully good & we thoroughly enjoyed it. They sang Auld Lang Syne after & joined hands. Col. Wheatley C.O. 3rd Div. A.C. was crossing hands with Matthews - a private & a drunk Sergt!! I rode back on a byke & the wind blew me over into the side of the road & the thick mud & I had the greatest difficulty in getting up. Mud about 6" thick. Had to walk practically the whole way back. Wind too strong. Met Craig on the way there & he was in an awful state being sodden with whiskey. His horse was having a very bad time indeed. He did not stay to mess. In morning scheme Boyle Vernon Elliott & I worked together on scheme agreed with Maj. Stansfield.

2-1-16

Did not go to church parade - & so as it was in front of the big chateau I missed breakfast. Rode back on byke to St Ouen & saw Burn. In the afternoon Brooke, Dixon, Garton & Walker came along & stopped tea. Parsons was there temporarily attached to 'A' Co. I had lunch .... there & then went rode back on Jane & Elliott walked over & took Jane back.

3-1-16	9 a.m.	Defence of village. We ventured into Surcamp & put that in state of defence. Vernon Boyle & I worked together. We had a difficult "keep" etc, but after ..... way they still thought we had got the best one.
	2 p.m.	Lecture on machine gun with sample gun by Cambs. Officer.
	3 p.m.	D.S.C.
	5.30 p.m.	Lecture by Commandant on March.
	9 p.m.	Lecture by M. Bazellon - Napoleon as a leader (voluntry) - this was extraordinarily good as a lecture but

we got rather tired of his monotone french-english. There was a very good attendance of NCOs as well.

4-1-16	9 a.m.	Scheme defence of a town - the Follie Auberge. Grovewhite gave an ideal scheme - Elliott & I worked together - we are not very much like the original but quite a good scheme - we misunderstood the time given to be 4 hours instead of 24.
	2 p.m.	Machine gun. Lecture on gun & faults as before.
	3 p.m.	D.S.C.
	6 p.m.	Lecture by Lt Col Holbeck 20th London Regt. Loos Defensive Flank. This did not take place & we had only Major Brimelow on Interior Economy - not up to much. C.C.C. came over to tea.

5-1-16	9 a.m.	Lecture by Yates Grenade Attack. Quite good but did not know much about the subject - got it all from pamphlet etc.
	10.15 a.m.	Bombing up Trench.
	11.15 a.m.	D.S.C. Lecture by C.O. on Patrols.
	2 p.m.	Machine gun. Lecture as before.
	3 p.m.	D.S.C.
	6 p.m.	Lecture by Colonel Saunders on Intelligence. C.O. Int Dept 3rd Army. A very interesting lecture but rather too much read & so monotonous.

The C.O. doubled us back from lecture to the chateau & had lunch with us - personally I was very down! Orderly officer of the day.

6-1-16	9 a.m.	Visit to Flying Squadron. We set out by bus & went to Bertangles via Belloy, La Chausee, St Sauveur, just missed Vaux. The Aerodrome was close to the railway but we went up to Bertangles to try & find someone to show us round - they had not prepared anyone - we arrived about 12.30. We got hold of an observer & he showed us a Sopwith & told us all about it & then went on to a Bristol Byplane - then they started taking us up. A friend of Pitman's was there. The Squadron had only been out a fortnight & all very enthusiastic. I got a flight in & thoroughly enjoyed the stunt - was up for about 15 minutes. Only about 12 out of us got up - they hadn't enough time. We then got back in time for lecture at

		night without any tea having had only 1 sandwich going there, but I thoroughly enjoyed the show.
	6 p.m.	Lecture by Capt Yates & Kelly - Work of the Indian Army with the Wertun Exp. Fua. As a matter of fact they tossed for it & Kelly lost so he gave the lecture - a very good one & it showed us how well the Indians had stood the campaign & that their illness was really less than the whites - also they did stirling good work.
7-1-16	9 a.m.	Lecture by Commandant followed by Demonstration on Relief of Trenches - the lecture was good - on the book "Trench Order" he wrote. But the demonstration very weak - we did it first without any order or previous reconnaissance & it was a fearful pain. We doubled back to lunch.
	2 p.m.	Machine gun. Firing Vickers Light Gun in a quarry - Raining & a fearful echo off quarry - I did not stay long for that reason.
	3 p.m.	D.S.C.
	5.30 p.m.	Lecture by Maj. McClean 8th Squad. R.F.C. Aircraft in War. A very interesting lecture. McClean is Hope's brother. I had gone over to Abulady with him in the car - from Glasgow once with Ronald & Co. Spoke to him.
	8.30	Lecture on Experiences when Flying by Capt Cross & Lt Child. Very interesting & a real good stunt. They were very unfortunate for what they had done. Child came to mess at the mess & I sat next to him - we had speeches etc & a rare time at night the French officers departing.
	9 p.m.	Address by Maj. General Bols[66] Chief of the Staff 3rd Army. The most imperious address I have ever heard - a small very firm looking fellow with very commanding eyes - you could have heard a pin drop any minute of the address which was for 20 minutes. He told us the situation in the west was extraordinary ..... & we had 150,000 troops to the Bosches 35,000 in the 3rd Army area. We all cheered him hard. Hope to hear him again.
8-1-16	9 a.m.	Explanation of, followed by Attack from the trenches. We had demonstration by Ca...ls on the attack a.....al e.g.

[66] Lt-General Sir Louis Jean Bols, KCB, KCMG, DSO (1867-1930), born in Cape Town and educated at Lancing College in England.

from trenches. Was not a good show as we could not get near enough to see what went on in the trenches. Also we were kept standing about before until we were frozen & our ..... feet!! Three generals came & also a lot of red Hats. The show was humorous in parts as they blew up a mine & bombed each other with bombs made out of tins which exploded like ..... After lunch Elstob & I walked towards Amiens & were picked up by a motor lorry just before Belloy & taken as far as Picquigny. We then saw the ambulance man but he had nothing to give us & told us his Colonel had to go in by train they are so strict owing to people abusing the privilege. We walked on to Builly & then a French T.....y picked us up in a Studebaker & ran us in to the outskirts of Amiens where we took a train & got in at 4.0. & then people tried to catch goods trains & other trains at Hangert & all sorts of other means but did not get in till at least an hour later. We then had a bath - both in the same bathroom & then tea & found Parker then - did a bit of shopping & then haircut & finally just got to the Rest. Godbert[67] in time for the final ..... syndicate dinner. A very good dinner & good fun in the way of dancing etc after - we caught the 12.15 to Hangert - 2 English ladies from the staff at Doulen on the train. Got to Hangert at 1.15 & walked back to Flixecourt[68] via Bourdon - got in at 2.0 a.m.

9-1-16   During the ..... I had quite a lot of bridge & played at various times with Hudson - Fowler - McDougall - Hart & Madden. I got up about 8.30 & had breakfast at 9.0. Had to see the Commandant at 10.0 as he did not know me. Was kept waiting till 12.15. Then he saw me & showed me my fatuous report & after a horrid lunch he addressed us all at 12.30. We gave him three cheers & also the instructors of the school. Jordan made a pretty little speech for the occasion. We left by bus at 1.30 each Division having a bus. Our busman did not know where the 30th Div H.Q. was - but we knew they were somewhere near Bray so we set out there via Vignacourt - Flesselles Rainneville - St Gratien - very steep hill up into St Gratien - Querrieu - Corbie - & then Bray. Following officers on the bus -
Capt Elstob 16 Man

---

[67] Café Godbert in Amiens was an exclusive restaurant much frequented by officers.
[68] The site of 3rd Army Training School.

Capt Madden 17 Man
Capt Renshaw 18 Man
1 Off from 2nd Wilts & 1 from 2nd W. Ridings
Also the N.C.O.s & servants. On landing at Bray I saw Brig Maj of 13 & also 14 Brig who were handing over to 30th Div. Also Town Major[69] office but no one in it & was directed to Billets of South Lancs at Froissy about 1½ miles from Bray due South. Then I saw the C.O. & he made us dine with him. I was very thankful. I slept in Polly's room on a stretcher!

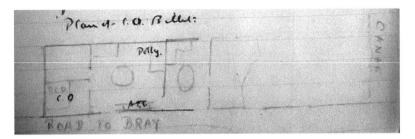

10-1-16   Wandered about all day & saw various people. Lectured for 45 minutes to officers & N.C.O.s of 'B' & 'C' Companys, on what I had learned at the course. Got up very late in the morning & walked all round billets.

11-1-16   Wandered about all day but also wrote up a bit of diary. Still living with the C.O. Karl came to dinner. Rained most of the day. Straffing being pretty heavy all day & night. Letter from Hilda - parcel from mother. Got up very late. Drew from Canteen.

12-1-16   Did nothing all morning. Rode in during afternoon at 3 on M.O. old man - used to be the C.O.'s, to Suzanne via Cappy, to 'D' Company. Had tea there. Officers had properly got the wind up - all a bag of nerves. Potter was rushing about in a very excited condition - he rushed me out & showed me some pot holes in the distance where they had been shelling in the afternoon. I lectured to their Officers & N.C.O.s on the course again & then came back to Bray over the top - a fearfully bad road - all mud. Got back in time for mess with the C.O. Buchanan went off to Amiens.

---

[69] Staff officer (not necessarily a major) responsible for billeting arrangements in a town or village behind the lines.

13-1-16   Got up earlier & spent the morning wandering about the lines. Bradley in bed not very fit, with malaria. Gave the M.O. a lecture on first aid!! Wrote a bit more in diary after lunch. Karl had a bit of an experience in which his men were working on the top of a hill - the Bosches started shelling a battery behind it & the first shell fell within 5 yards of Pavlova[70] & luckily was a dud; the men were rather wondering how to take it so C.C. looked at his watch & said only 10 minutes more so we'll just finish. They watched the shooting till it was over - no damage done. Capt Stern 17 Liverpools came to mess, also Bradley & Forester - Stern got the Town Commandant at Bray. Buchanan returned from Amiens with some stores he had got for us, which he left at Rail Head.

14-1-16   Got up at 7.0 to see Valin etc ready at 8.0 for cart to leave for Puchevillers. Went & saw all ready but it did not leave by wagon till 8.45. Servant etc all went with it. had a wander round in morning as usual & saw everyone & then lunch with C.O. & Polly. Left Froissy at 2.45 on Dixon's horse the old Adj. bay Tommy. Just before I left the stuff Buchanan bought at Amiens came in & I brought along with us a Port-Salut[71] Cheese afterwards known as "Jack". I met Brown & his party as I left Bray & then came via Bray - Morlancourt - Ville - Buire - Lavieville - Hennencourt - Warloy - Vadencourt - Toutencourt - Puchevillers. Arrived at 5.30. Wagon arrived at 4.0. Found Billets very comfortable & with great possibilities.

15-1-16   Worked hard all day arranging for improvements in billets etc. Getting canteen running. 2nd Lieut Lichfield of 9th Devons came to lunch. He was acting as their billeting officer. The 2 companies & H.Q. turned up about 4.30 in afternoon. 2nd Lieut Noone the S.O. of 7th Corps came in at dinner time & talked seemed a very decent sort of fellow. Promised to take 2 officers in to Amiens on Tuesday. Went to bed early.

16-1-16   Nothing much doing all day but Railway work. 16th R.I.R.s came to village - only one company - but went right through & after found billets in Raincheval. Visit from Sanitary inspector of 3rd Army. Started canteen going. Good day from start.

17-1-16   Went round work morning & afternoon. Burn told story of Col Wheatley - C.O. 30th D.A.C. who lived on Bull Beef & tea & cheese

---

[70] A horse often ridden by Carl Champion.
[71] A semi-soft cheese from the Loire, developed by Trappist monks in the 19th century.

at St Ouen - hearing the buzzer of the string factory "stood to" thinking it was an alarm. He turned all his men out. Saw Lt Bickley R.E. on the railway & as he was coming to Puchervillers to billet asked him to join our mess which he readily accepted. Drew from cashier. Lectured to Officers & N.C.O.s at 3.0 as it rained hard & we did no work. A general lecture on the course at Flixecourt.

18-1-16 Worked hard all day. Galsworthy went off for tea to Corbie. Bickley R.E. joined the mess. He was on the rail work we were working on. Moore was to take 2 officers to Amiens & come on to mess but was unable to come. Fletcher & Craig were going. He came into mess but could not stop & apologised most profusely. Gave the Off & N.C.O. a lecture on organisation & working practices.

19-1-16 Road Jane all morning. Did usual Railway work. In afternoon Moore took me over in his car - a Sunbeam 4 seater - to his place at Maricourt & I walked on with him to see Maj. McClean at the aerodrome there of No 8 Squadron R.F.C. Found he had left for England & taken over the Scottish Wing. Went to tea with Child in the H.Q. mess there & walked down & had another with Moon who had come down first before tea. Found Barney Hunter up there to tea - he belongs to the 6th Squad R.F.C. Moon motored me back just in time to give lecture to the Off & N.C.O.s Defence of a House. C.O. replied to 2 notes I sent him on business in a very jocular way.

20-1-16 Men put on a new job about 1½ miles away from old cutting in afternoon. Rode up then we had to put lunch back till 12.15 & have tea late to try & get the thing through as it was keeping the track back if it lasted till next day. Moore came to mess had quite a good one he is a very good sort & has done some Naval work at the beginning of the war on a despatch boat. Capt Tasker of No 1 Sect D.A.C. (Welsh Div) turned up as mess finished to find out about billets. We gave him something to eat as he had had nothing & also took a violent dislike to him. Lecture on Consolidation of mine crater & Flying.

21-1-16 Work all day. Just finished job in time to prevent the track being delayed. Started at 8.0 parade. Craig took them out to finish off the cutting. Rode out to see them - they finished there & started on cutting again. No 3 & 4 had bath in morning at 9.0. No 1 & 2 in afternoon. Had accident on the line - buffer locking owing to excess of speed on the straight. 2 men killed & 14 injured - blocked the line for the next two days. Saw moon at midday. Got order for Craig & Robertshaw to report as soon as possible at H.Q. at Bray. Neither wanted to go. Craig was very sick & so were us all that he had to go. Lecture on Patrols.

22-1-16   Work all day - had two sections out for digging themselves in. Craig, Robertshaw & Hankinson[72], Craig's servant went off by the Wagon at 10.0. We worked all afternoon. Sent Galsworthy for noon bus to Corbie. Rode Jane all the morning. Boots came from Wolverhampton by post - they were a bit small but hope they will work alright. Also a letter from Kaye by the post - Galsworthy came at night & brought a second kindly here as well which is better.

23-1-16   No parade in morning till 12.0 when an inspection for opaque goggles for lachrymatory shells[73] took place. Had breakfast at 9.45 & then went on ride on Jane wearing my new boots which were rather tight but Burn lending me thin socks made a lot of difference. We rode along the line back toward Canders to the scene of the smash - fearfully sloppy on the top of the hill. The smash was just before I got to the Beauquesne road. 3 wagons were smashed to bits & in various postures. Rode back by Beauquesne & got back at 12.0. Met the Sanitary Inspector of 3rd Army in Beauquesne. Spent afternoon making out Balance Sheet for Canteen - showed a profit of about 67 Francs. Evening writing letters. Spent afternoon writing letters. Heavy draught horse - the better of our two blacks died in evening of cholic - we got the Sergt of the Welsh D.A.C. up but it was no good & she had ..... down & got a ..... Remained in all morning.

24-1-16   Spent morning drilling two sections No 8 & 9. Fletcher took 1½ platoons to a new place at Raincheval & dug them all day. A rotten day as it was a wintry sort of rain all day. Spent aft looking round. Had various visits in evening - one from V.O. at Toutencourt - to see the dead mare - he went back & promised to come next day - then the A.D.V.S. 32 Div came along also but he went back to relieve a cow ..... down the village - he had tea - was a Maj - very young with DSO - had been out with the Heavy Cavalry early on in the war. Payed company. Train got to within about 1 mile of Puchevillers. Got a big post in - from C.O. etc - he sent me a wagon to take stuff back the next day to Bray - 700 Francs worth. Boots getting more comfortable. Got invitation to S.M. do the next day.

---

[72] Probably Pte. 20217 Thomas Hankinson, k.i.a. 8.6.17.
[73] Shells containing tear gas, compelling men to wear masks for long periods.

25-1-16   Had 2 Sections No 11 & 12 for drilling - the V.O. from Toutencourt came & cut up horse which was buried in afternoon. Rode out to furthest point at Raincheval in aft. V.O. brought in death from inflammation of C...ls. L/Cpl went back to H.Q. with wagon about 12.0. Went to Sergts Mess dinner at 5.45. Had an impromptu concert after - funny sketches on ...ing & Orderly Rooms by Pilkington & Crompton & Sergt Jackson - also songs by Sgt Dennett - Cpl Culley & Cpl Smart & Cpl Jones. All officers including Beckley attended. Got back about 9.30 & had supper. Railway nearly got to Puchevillers. Wrote mother & Kaye & C.O. Jane reshod aft.

26-1-16   Had Sect 13 & 14 for drill. Jane turned out in morning lame - took her back & they took off her shoe which had been put on the day before. She had been shod both aft. legs with mules shoes as we had not got any more - Thompson said that she was lame as a nail had pinched her - the farrier said it was owing to the mule shoes having only one clip instead of two as she was used to. Sergt Jones knowing nothing about it said it was due to her having no heel on the shoes made her twist her fetlock. Could not use her all day. Thompson put on bran mash poultice. Still on railway work up at Raincheval. Two Royal Scot officers a Captain & a subaltern came in after tea to talk about billets. Expected C.O. all day as he said he was coming over one day this week. Did not turn up.

27-1-16   Jane still lame she stayed in all day. Men still on railway work. Expected C.O. all day but he did not turn up. Had Sect 15 & 16 for drill all the morning. No lecture - had a talk to S.M. Prescott & told him he was not satisfying me. But only warned him. Galsworthy went Doulen. Burn asked 2 Scotch fellows in to mess the next night. Had a post in. Letters from Kaye, Mother & others & also a parcel from Mother. One new H.D. horse turned up to replace one died. Train blocking Amiens road.

28-1-16   Sects 1 & 2 for drill the rest up to cutting at Raincheval - nothing doing all afternoon. I gave a lecture at 6.0 on Div. Troops - two officers turned up. Burn said he had gone to sleep & had not woken up in time - impertinence. I made a mental resolution to give him something to go to sleep for. The others said they thought it was for N.C.O.s only - teach them to read orders. Capt Liddell & Lt Paulin of the Royal Scotts came to dinner. We had a good dinner but beastly tough chickens - they stayed till 12.0 & we played ving-et-un. Was to have had a bath but too late in going to bed. I found that Capt Liddell knew Pitman who was at the course at Flixecourt & Vera

Pitman his sister who used to stay with the Dorkins whom I met. Paulin knew Pat F..... in Edinburgh & was a very great friend of his. Train blocking Toutencourt road. Galsworthy got mess bill.

29-1-16   Made Burn go up with working party to Raincheval - Diplock had to inspect harness of transport in aft. Had Sect 2 & 3 for drill in morning. Rode out to working party in aft. Jane went ..... lame out there & when she returned was sweating all over & very lame. Sent for V.O[74]. When I got there I found they had finished the job & were coming back having wanted some time. Burn very annoyed & trying to annoy me - he will find it won't pay. Train had got past Puchevillers & across Toutencourt Road. The letter cart from H.Q. ..... met ours as usual at Senlis & ours after waiting 4 hours came back. Had a bath after dinner.

30-1-16   No work all day as had Kit Inspection & Bath. One section worked on lane by cutting to make ramp but no new work . Jane was very lame & the Vet came to see her in morning. He said it was a sprain in the Hock or higher. A S.M. of Arm. Column said thrush & a farrier sergeant said ricket hock. We rubbed her & she seemed to ..... a lot. Spent most of the morning in trying to make up canteen accounts, could not make it agree so turned them in to Slater who could not make any more of it. Spent afternoon in mess. All ..... by Bob's were at café with Gorman. Bretherton & Diplock went to dinner at Royal Scots. Played Bridge at night. All Company got Bath & Kit Inspection. Great rumours about what is happening at Sausanne & Bray. No news about letters etc miscarrying the day before.

31-1-16   Jane a bit better. Thompson had done a lot of rubbing. Put onto railway cutting & following up train on lines. The train came off twice in afternoon. In evening we paid & then letters arrived. Birks said the Bosches had shelled Suzanne & round there from Thursday till Sunday continuously & that was the reason that the cart had been unable to come on the Saturday. They had one killed, Mason the policeman & one wounded, Rigby. Woolcock's horse had been killed & several mules damaged. Suzanne had been quite wiped out & nothing had been heard of 'D' Co. the headquarters had been changed into Bray from Froissy. I got a parcel from Mother & 2 letters from Kaye to which I replied! The two Royal Scots came in after mess & played cards - they had had orders that Liddell was to move to Morlancourt & they could not find it. We had a nasty shock

---

[74] Vetinary Officer.

because Slater came back with the tale that the A.S.C. man had had orders not to supply us with any more rations after today, which looked as though we were moving but as we heard nothing we did nothing. Bretherton went to .... & sprained his ankle so had to lie up.

1-2-16   Still on cutting & various little jobs. Jane getting better. Paulhen Royal Scot fellow borrowed byke as he had to go to Toutencourt. Some Batt of Argyle & Sutherland went through with pipes etc. Received the following order at lunch time.

Coy 11 S.Lancs at Puchenvillers should proceed today to La Vicogne & billet there for the night. Tomorrow they should proceed to Querrieu & will be billeted under arrangement of the 10th Corps. Billetting officer to report there. On the 3rd they will proceed from Querieux to H.Q. of 30th Div at Etinehem to come under orders of that Division. Acknowledge. Addressed O.C. Coy 11th S.Lancs at Puchevillers repeated 10th Corps & 30th Division. From 13th Corps. P. Hudson Lt Col A.Q.M.G. 13th Corps.

I wired back. Shall need 2 G.S. wagons before I can move. Could make Querrieu tomorrow if transport is forthcoming. Cannot move today in any case. Awaited the reply all afternoon & made what arrangements I could but could not make many.
Pte Bullock asked me which powers were in the "Triple Enten" meaning the "Triple Entente"! Gave a lecture after tea on Div. Staff duties. Liddell & Paulin came to dinner - after all Liddell had not to go as they were only sending half the original detachment & were sending a subaltern instead of Liddell. At about 8.0 two A.S.C. wagons turned up from the 7th Army Sub. Aux H.T. Sect & also orders to move to Etinehem via Querrieu the next day. We had a good finish off to the evening & a sing song by Liddell at the piano - which had a few strings gone & they left about 12.0. Burn talked in my room till about 1.0.

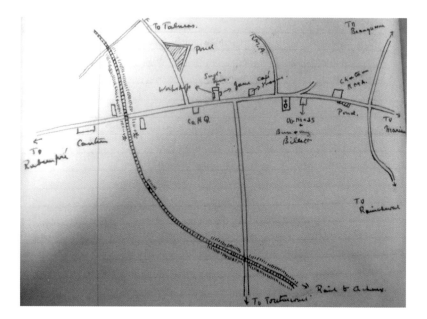

2-2-16   Parade ordered for 10.0. Had breakfast at 8.0. C.S.M. Prescott made a great hash over packing blanket. Saw Liddell & Paulin & the latter & Beckley saw us off. Liddell had to go over to Beauquesne to see the C.O. or something. Burn went on ahead to Billet the Company at Querrieu on a pushbike. Slater & a G.S. Wagon went to Marieux to draw rations for the following day. He then went on to Querrieu. Jane was still a bit lame so I let Thompson lead her all the way. Diplock was in charge of the transport & got it out up to time. We started punctually at 10.0. We took tender farewells from the School Mistress & the Scots officers took over our billets there. The others also bade farewell to the fair Yvonne. We marched via Rubempré - Beaucourt - Bellancourt - Pont Noyelle. At Rubempré two mules (pack) got behind a long way so Jones went back to look after them. We saw no more of him till we got to Pont Noyelle - he went via Pierregot - Molliens - St Gratien & to Querrieu where he billeted the mules on the old billet they had before - but had to take them out. He got there before us. We did not go that way although it was shorter owing to the steep hill into St Gratien. I knew it from the bus ride from Flixecourt to Bray. After the halt at Rubempré I sent Sergt Fleming on with an advance guard of No 1 Section which went the wrong way & we passed it & it caught us up at the last halt just after Bethencourt. Thompson & Jane did the same. She was very lame at first but seemed to be going quite well towards the end. The road was quite bad from half way between Rubempré & Beaucourt till

Bethencourt but the transport managed it very well under Diplock. It was a beautiful day to start off with but clouded over towards the end & got rather cold. We had lunch just before we got into Beaucourt. I had it behind a haystack - of course Booth was not quite ready & we had to wait 20 minutes. Burn had quite forgotten to have any sandwiches made for the officers. I told Hignett as I got up to make some of tongue & he told me at breakfast there was no tongue so I told him to make them of ham - at 9.30 I got a message that the ham had gone queer so I told him to make them of jam & made him run back & make some for me. Burn met us in Pont Noyelle & showed us our billet which was just in Pont Noyelle by the river - the other side being Querrieu. The Div Baths was in the Billet - all men & officers were in the same farm yard where the men's quarters were made with wood partitions & floors. I had a billet across the road & a bed which an old woman gave up for me - it was in Querrieu. The men stood the march very well indeed considering they had done no marching for so long & also they had done so much digging. We drew 2 days rations there - having Slater for the next day as well. So we were two days in hand. When leaving Puchevillers I gave orders for all Off rations to be on the blanket wagon. I found they were not so woke up the S.M. about it & had them altered.

3-2-16   We started off at 9.30. Jane was very rotten about the belly so I had to have her in the R.E. Signalling stable & arrange with them to take her over. I left Thompson there too with saddle etc. Burn left on the cycle at 9.0 to report to the 30th Div at Etinehem & Slater left about then with Galsworthy to leave a few empty barrels at the brewery at Corbie. We all were ready at 9.15. Went round billets & found a lot of old tins & mess - made 3 men from each platoon fall out & clean up. S.M. made great fuss about blaming N.C.O.s. We started at 9.30 exactly. In spite of all orders my valise was put on another wagon, not on the blanket one. We had done rather well on the journey having an extra G.S. Wagon & also 2 extra days rations in hand. Up the steep hill towards Corbie out of Pont Noyelle my valise slipped off the wagon owing to bad packing & we had to have Jones & a man & the wagon to put it straight. They caught us up at the halt on top off the hill. It was a ripping day again though rather a strong & very cold wind blowing. Burn & I had arranged for him to put a stick with a destination on at the corner of the road leading off to Etinehem from the Bray-Corbie road. As our orders were to report at Etinehem & I knew the Batt was at Bray. We had our lunch at an old Brick Manufacture place - to get out of the wind. The S.M. was very bad at keeping order & the fellows sloped off a lot & ..... went into a café near by. I also noticed that the men were feeling the march very badly & were very straggly & the S.M. had no idea of pulling them together & ..... shouted at them from the head of the column. Just before the old Div dump at the Bois de Tailles - but which was changed today to Morlancourt we met Polly on a horse going to Corbie to change some money for the C.O. He was very cheery & I was very pleased to see him. Burn met us just after the dump & told us we had to go to Etinehem as one company was to be attached to Div. H.Q. pro tem for Road making & we were that company till D came from Suzanne when we would go there. We got in about 3.30 & met Lloyd Matthews as we went in. We found the men's billets not bad but not too good but officers were very bad indeed in fact the worst we had yet had. Thin ..... & beds made of wood & canvas & wire netting on top very hard & uncomfortable. We managed a Mess room & cook house in the house in which Burn & I slept but which was quite empty & no furniture in. We also got a Sergts Mess & orderly room combined. I went off straight at 4.30 to H.Q. by byke via Bray, having heard that they had moved to dug outs. Saw Steen as Town Commandant. He directed me to the dug outs N.E. of Bray about 1 mile to 1½ miles. I went out on the cycle & just past the R.E. Dump met Garten & a party of men - as I left Bray they dropped a few shells into Bray. I left the road & h..... ..... along a track a short way. I met C.C. & E.O.[75] with another small party then just as I got to the dug outs. I met the C.O.2 & Williams 'C' Co & spoke to them. C.O.2 said he was living in Bray as he had a comfortable billet & did not like being uncomfortable in a dug out. Later the C.O. told me he said that he thought the dug outs would be shelled badly & that was why the C.O. inferred he wanted to stay in Bray. I then saw Payne & then went in to the C.O. He seemed quite comfortable in his dug out. The C.O. was in splendid form & told me Williams was actually leaving. He told me about his interview with the General & the letters which followed. He also said Potter was improving & Dixon was pretty hopeless. Also while he had been at Bray he messed the 'C' Co & while they were at tea a shell dropped just outside & broke all the windows etc & cut Woods hand - no other damage was done. I showed him Burn's & my letter to Brooke from Meuille & he was very amused. He told me they worked the horses on & off & I was to stay at Etinehem for a day or two & then relieve 'D' Co at Suzanne. I had tea with him & left about 6.0 making my way back straight across country pushing the cycle & hitting the Corbie Bray road & then riding from then. I got back in time for dinner & then straight to bed.

---

[75] Eric Champion.

C.S.M. woke me at 11.0 as rations had arrived & he had to hand on the Rum to me. Burn then snored so loud I stayed awake for 2-3 hours. On arrival Fletcher inspected the blankets & found all sorts of foreign matter.

4-2-16   Got up about 9-0 had kit etc inspection. Told the C.S.M. that he would have to give up his crown[76] he took it very well - I told him he was a square peg in a round hole & that seemed to satisfy him - I also told him I would recommend him to the C.O. as having tried & done his best. The men did nothing for the rest of the day - it was a nasty wet & very windy day. Burn went over to see the C.O. & just returned for a few minutes to get an indent for boots & then returned to mess there. Three old spies -2 men & 1 woman were taken from no 3 Billet in afternoon apparently for heliographing[77]. I was in Diplock's & Bretherton's billet when 2 shells dropped quite warmably close. We waited up till 9.30 for the post but it did not turn up. They also shelled Bray in the afternoon & one shell woke up Parsons & Garton sleeping in the brewery. I went to bed & was woken up at 12.30 by Burn returning with Bradly considerably drunk. He got to bed & Bradly returned We tried Pye at the mess for cook & it seemed satisfactory to start off with.

5-2-16   Bradley came in about 9.0 & got every man onto Roads. Burn & I had a walk round & then Polly turned up about 11.30 & had a drink at the mess. A beautiful day & a lot of aeroplanes about. One very sporting one of the Bosches which was very heavily shelled & fired at by M.G. but to no purpose. Lunch as usual very late. Got orders to relieve 'D' Co at Suzanne on Monday. Burn went over to Headquarters in afternoon. Got about 4 letters from Kaye - also boots from mother & cakes from Hilda - wrote Kaye a long letter & sent her £40.

6-2-16   Burn took church parade - Diplock & Fletcher went to Suzanne to see Potter. Bretherton went to Heilly to stores. I walked over to H.Q. & talked to him while he got up - saw most of the officers. C.O. was talking about canteen - mess - leave & odds & sods. Woolcock got it in the neck. C.C., Williams & myself walked back to lunch & had aft talking & then tea - just after this the C.O. called in on his way to the General to enquire about leave. We stayed till he came back. Diplock & Fletcher came back in the meantime & came back with great

---

[76] Badge of rank, a crown worn on the sleeve.
[77] Signalling using flashes of sunlight reflected by a mirror.

stories of 'D' Co making things very uncomfortable for themselves & ...ing going up above board. Stories of the men being fearfully crammed & dirty - it seemed a very bad look out for the first night but possibilities of making the place quite comfortable. Bretherton returned about 6.0 & then the C.O. came in & said leave was quite out of the question at present but ought to come along very soon. Then there went off & we tried to settle the business about going in to Suzanne. We had orders to leave at 5.0 & go by half platoon at ..... 100 yards apart.

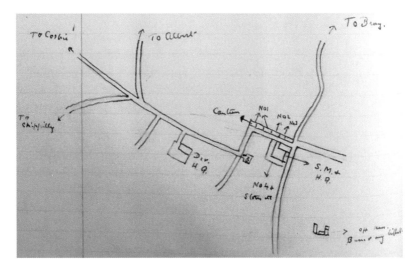

7-2-16   Men working as usual on roads as the day before in the morning. I got everything arranged for moving at 5.0. At 2.45 I went round with Bury to Div H.Q. & then met Hindle who was motoring over to Bray & the car was taking a Brig. Signaller over to Susanne so as the two had such a difference of opinion ..... I sent over to 'D' Co. The same day I determined to go over early & see Potter. I went over in the car & got off to Potter about 2.45 getting there at 3.15. Had tea with Potter & his crowd in a beastly dug out in horrible mess! I walked round & saw the work. Potter & his crowd fearfully keen to get out of it - we went down to B.H.Q. & saw Montgomery the Brig. Maj. The company turned up about 6.30 - the transport was all directed off a different way so my scheme of 1 party then 1 wagon so that our party unloaded each wagon. The whole thing fell through but we got all through & 'D' Co loaded up very quickly & got all away by about 8.30. We all got in comfortably into the cellar - Burn sleeping up above it. I got a bed into the cellar & was quite comfortable.

8-2-16   Got up for breakfast at 9.0. Craig had rejoined us & Buchanan was messing with us. We set to clean up all the farm & place & got onto the trench & the dug outs. had 50 Manchesters working for us in the afternoon. Major Mellor R.H.A. came to tea & in the middle we were badly strafed[78] by the Bosches. Two duds & 2 H.E. 5.9 fell in the midden heap in the middle of the billet yard. Plenty of shells on the road outside. Only one casualty & Fletcher seemed ..... the fellow. Ogden - not at all badly - cut in bicep. It started at 5.10 & left off at 5.45. We remained in cellar. Went down & saw Brig. After it all but nothing doing. Not half as much damage done as I expected. Dinner as usual & then bed. Sergt Harper 'D' Co stayed over to show us the strings - he was fearfully surprised at the Sergts mess

9-2-16   Got up for breakfast at 9.0. Burn & I went down to see where trench cuts the road & got it badly. We had to run through the horse standings & then across the swamps for 200 yds & then up the hill. We got back for orderly room at 11.30 - very hot & tired having had it thoroughly taken out of us by the run. Had a quieter afternoon. It snowed in the morning & was fearfully cold. About 12.30 at night they started a real strafe & went on for 1¼ hours. Very bad one - some damage done to chateau etc. Nothing very near us. We started building a dug out near the cooker for the officers servants - cooks & Sergts mess servants.

10-2-16   Got up for 9. Breakfast all on dug outs & trench. Went round with Montgomery & he showed me works to be done. In aft the C.O. turned up for tea - we had had a very quiet day of it - he was in very great form & so was Payne who came too. They did not stay long it was too hot for them!! Letter from Kaye & also Mr Townsend. Nothing doing that night at all. We sat & talked a lot at night.

11-2-16   Very quiet early morning only about 4 or 5 shells over. Rained hard all day & we only worked on dug outs all day. Nothing doing still improving all the time. Saw Town Major at night who was very bad mannered over the dug out accommodation. A Major in the 16th Manchesters had made a fuss over something to do with billets.

12-2-16   Got up about 9.0 & walked over after breakfast to H.Q. on the top of the hill. Frightfully muddy & hard work. When I got there intending

---

[78] Strafe - (1) To machine gun, especially from the air. (2) General bombardment. From German Strafen, to punish. Gott Strafe England (God punish England) was a popular song and greeting in Germany during the war years.

to see the C.O. about going on Monday but he was out. I saw the C.O.2 who had cut his face falling from his horse. He landed with his face on his field glasses. Also Williams, Culshaw, Rick Walker, the M.O. & C.C.C. who was in bed with nettle rash & a b.....p but he seemed to be improving & was quite cheerful. I talked to him a bit & then I rode back. Woolcock had sent me his horse - I met him on the way & he promised me to find one. He sent his own which was a huge camel & very old & lazy. We met Burns on the Bray-Corliss Road digging the trench from Bray to Sussane & then came home for lunch. Burn & Craig went on in the afternoon to try & see the C.O. & I went on the work. The 16th Manchesters were coming into the dug outs & Elstob was down there & he came into tea & he was very pleased with what we had done. No straffing up to 6.0 o'clock at least. Nothing doing that evening. Had a ripping bath. Burns & Craig returned late having got the C.O. to say we were not returning on Monday but probably we should be returning on the Wednesday. They were both fairly tight & had had a good time. Craig caught a magpie on the way. The C.O. was in great form but was very angry at being told by Weber G.S.O.1. that he should not have mentioned the Div. was supposed to be going to be relieved on the 16th. He had determined to go over to see him. I got various letters - mother & others. Two Zeppelins are supposed to have flown over about 2.30 a.m. They returned from B.H.Q. Craig & Burn in a motor ambulance & were impressed by the .... of the road.

13-2-16   Things began to wake up in the morning as guns seemed to be firing on all sides. Being Sunday I had short hours 8-11.45 & 2-4 as Holy Communion was at 12.0 & service at 6.30. Men working on everything as usual all morning. Elstob & Worthington O.C. 'A' Co. 16 Man -were asked to tea at 2.30 then the Bosche started straffing the town- about 3.0. 2 officers were seen riding over, they seemed to be from the H.Q. direction but when they saw us being shelled they apparently turned round & went back. The shelling went on for about 1 hour then ceased for a bit. We found the cooker shed had been hit & also the Sergts mess which was stove right in. It also killed a hen. The shelling started again after a few minutes & went on till about 5.30. It then went on from about 5.45 to about 7.30 & then we got up for dinner as the things had been on the fire all the time. We had dinner & then came down & had vingt-et-un & a ..... Corpl Emery & about 20 Manchesters are working down on dug outs by the Chateau & a shell hit the trees above & wounded 7 of the Manchesters but did not touch Emery or Private Lane - we had no casualties luckily. There were about 14-20 casualties in the

Manchesters. The night was quiet except for a letter through that the French had captured Bois de Vache & Bois de Segnal & the trenches between & also 100 Bosch prisoners. Thompson & Jones came to Bray. Parr, Gardner & Symon turned up at H.Q. & Struthers to follow. No reason why they all turned up given. C.O. very annoyed. 350 shells in according to "comic cuts"[79].

14-2-16   Very windy & bad day - normal round of works in the morning & then went up to the mess. Had asked Woolcock for a horse & he sent over Tommy & Thompson at 11.30. The C.O.2 & G.H. Walker turned up just before I left. G.H.W. had had a brother come out with a draft to the 20th Liv & had come out to see him but he was at Bray so G.H.W. stayed to mess. The C.O.2 left & I caught him up later just past Cappy corner. I went round the lower road. Tommy did not appreciate the guns. Got to H.Q. & saw the C.O. about staying & he said he wasn't coming back at any rate for 10 days to a fortnight - he was going very shortly on 7 days leave. Stayed to lunch there. Buchanan turned up too. Impression of the mess very bad. Very uncomfortable - no chairs or table cloth - only roast beef & stewed figs & nothing else. The C.O. had whiskey & soda port & shandy - so I had a fairly good lunch but the others -! I had a good argument with the Adj & then accompanied Brooke & Polly to extricate a motor Met C.C. & E.O. on the way. I saw the motor but neither was any good. We returned over the top & it rained & hailed hard on the way back. I got back about 3.30 went & saw the Brig.Major & then Worthington & Eliott came to dinner. No straffing at all during the day. Beastly wet & cold windy day. Letter through at 12.0 that Bosches were going to make an attack on 15th. All to sleep with boots & puttees on.

15-2-16   Nothing doing in the morning - fearfully windy day - blew all sorts of things about & down. C.C.C. & E.O.C. came in to lunch - also Slack a 2nd Lieut. in the 16th Manchester. C.O. had C.C.C. living on a job in 'U' defences. I had to take it on so Burn & Craig went to see it in aft. Gardner turned up just about lunch time - he brought all sorts of stories from Depot - everyone seemed either ill or signing on for home defences only. Skunks. No straffing during the day. Managed to put gard...alin in the cellar. Letter from Kaye -rather sick of Ashhill. Had not had a letter from me for over a week. Craig hurt his leg in the morning coming back from putting 3 men to work in a

---

[79] Slang for Corps Intelligence Summary.

sap[80] at Vaux. Things were very quiet all the evening. We played vingt. et un till midnight! As Gardner's kit was to come on the Rations Wagon it did not turn up till then. Craig went out & put up screen in East Street again.

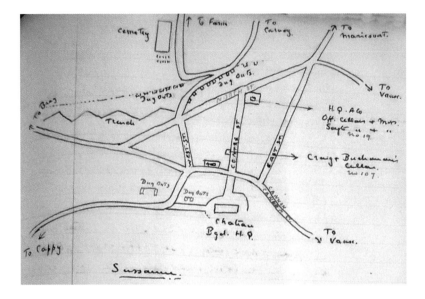

16-2-16   Frightfully windy & raining. Burn & Bretherton went out to 'U' defences. Burn returned about 2.0. soaking wet & very exhausted. Went round in morning & found Craig's screen blown down. Took Gardner round the work. Manchesters left off work at 11.30. Rained hard all day so did very little. Saw Brigade Major at night. Very quiet all day. Very windy. Craig went down to Vaux to see rails for dug outs. C.O. went on leave at 1.30 a.m.

17-2-16   Ordinary work as usual - another frightfully windy day but no rain. Walker + 35 of 'B' Co. turned up at 10.0 They came to work on Z2 defences. C.O.2 & Dickens turned up at 11.0 to go round with Walker- had lunch after us at about 3.0. He tried to put the work on me but I would not take it. Was going up to 'U' defences in afternoon but did not go. Burn went. Had no working parties working for us. Shelling went on about 6.30 but only very slight. C.O.2 said W.O. would not let him have the battalion. Also we are to go back ..... very shortly. Went down to Brigade Major at night. Splendid story of

---

[80] A trench dug forwards towards the enemy lines.

Potter told when someone mentioned Bairnsfather[81] book of pictures. Potter said he "did not know Bairnsfather was an artist". All played vingt-et-un at night. Burn with Pipsqueak up to the Trenches.

18-2-16   Went up to 'U' defences immediately after breakfast - pouring wet day. Went up with Burn; had on trench boots - no tunic - cardigan leather jerkin - mackintosh cape - & sowester. Soon found trench boots making my feet very sore & that I had too much on. We went up across country & got into the Billon Avenue close to wood to left of Maricourt & close to P..... Avenue. Very heavy going in trenches & feet frightfully sore - we went round all the 'U' defences & saw each of the cuttings - I took off my jerkin & sent Sergt Hunwick back with it. Craig & Diplock were up there. The trenches were very upright & deep & some had good footing & some very bad. After going round every one Diplock joined us & we made our way back. Only very few Wizbangs[82] went over & practically no shelling at all. We got back at about 12.45 to find Garton & Parsons there - the former went straight back to his work & the latter stayed on for lunch. I had a jolly good wash & shampoo & found my heels were only slightly blistered & then lunch. I went out after lunch & showed Parsons where I thought it best for the Bray trench to go & then returned. Bedford officers from Chipilly came in to tea. I saw their Colonel in the afternoon & sympathised with him & his lack of men! After dinner had a short game of vingt-et-un & then a bath & bed. Wrote Edith, Mrs Pilkington & Mrs Townsend. Bedford officer was named Read.

19-2-16   Had order in the morning from last night's wagon to send Fletcher to Chipilly - wrote Adj. about it. Also Heutuker's lectures arrived - letters from Hilda & Kaye. Went round in morning only skimpily as feet still very sore. C.O.2 & Adj turned up about 12.0. Great argument about Fletcher going to Chipilly. Ultimately Diplock had to go. He went off about 3.0. Nothing much doing all day. 2nd Lt Blower RFA 30th Div came to dinner & stayed till about 11 o'clock talking. Rather a boring individual. Got letter from Kaye.

---

[81] Captain (Charles) Bruce Bairnsfather; humorist whose best-known character, Old Bill, featured in his weekly "Fragments from France" cartoons published in "The Bystander".

[82] 77mm field gun shells. These travelled faster than sound and troops would hear the whizzing sound of one travelling through the air only just before they heard the bang of the gun. They gave virtually no warning of incoming fire.

20-2-16   Being Sunday we only worked from 9-11.30 & 2-4. There being
           services at 12.0 & 6.0. We had no one over to any meals & had a
           fairly quiet day. 50 Bedfords working for us in the morning but no
           one over in the afternoon. By the evening post came a note from
           C.O.2 to the effect that leave for officers was starting & that Karl &
           Potter were going on the 24th & I & himself were going on the 28th.
           Mother sent a "simnel"[83] cake & some more sulphur candles[84] turned
           up. Vingt-et-un in the evening.

21-2-16   Ordinary work. Had 70 16th Man working for us in afternoon. C.O.2,
           Dixon & Adj came over just before lunch & went up to see Walker's
           work. Adj. remarked how nice it was to have someone nice to talk to
           & also I told him of Diplock not being wanted by C.R.E. & he said
           that is what C.R.E. told C.O.2. Cully started on French Saps. Sergt
           Watkins slightly wounded by Whiz bang. Bosch had a gas attack on 2
           villages 9 miles South of Somme - both failed - in early morning. Saw
           Brig. Major. A few shells dropped in Susanne in very early morning.
           A lot of airplanes dud shells also dropped. Also started reservoir dug
           out. C.O.2 said leave was for 8 clear days in England. He & I are
           going together & then Dixon & Forrester & then Burn & Brooke.
           This meant O.C. companys & O.C.2 of companys were all away at
           one time.

22-2-16   Nothing doing - all work went on alright during morning &
           afternoon. Guns fairly lively. Snowed hard about lunch time & was
           very cold - all afternoon it was inclined to snow. Tried sulphuring
           blankets for lice - tried Sergts first. Just after tea Capt M B Buchanan
           Adj of 2nd R.S. Fus. Came in about a letter I had written to him that
           his men did not turn out of the Dug outs early enough. He
           recognised me as being an O.R.[85] He had been at Rugby in
           Stallard's[86]. I did not recognise him. He would not stay to mess. He
           knew Bretherton & Walker.

---

[83] A light fruit cake with two layers of almond paste or marzipan, toasted and normally
   eaten during the Easter period.
[84] A fumigator and disinfectant used in greenhouses.
[85] Old Rugbeian.
[86] Mr George Stallard M.A., assistant master at Rugby School.

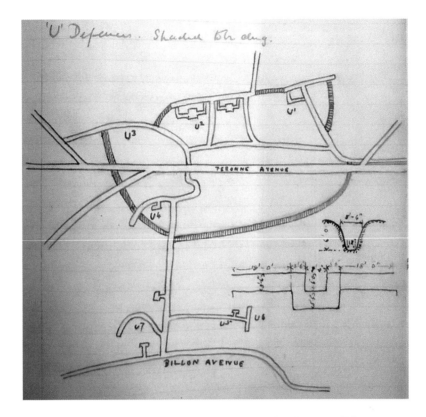

23-2-16   Nothing doing all morning. Hard frost at night. C.O.2 & Dixon came
up to see Walker's work. It started to snow about 11 o'clock &
snowed hard all afternoon. Had no working parties all afternoon.
C.O.2 told me leave started for me on Sunday at last. I left Maricourt
on Sunday. I got till the 6/3/16 that is till Monday - I leave Monday
4.0 p.m. from Waterloo. Played cards till about 7 o'clock & then
waited writing in bed till ration came in. Cat slept in my room for first
time & no mice came near. Pipsqueak was still sleeping in every night.
C.O. not turning up till tomorrow night. Started reading awful book
called "3 Weeks" by Elinor Glyn[87]. Potter & C.O. went on leave.

24-2-16   Very cold again - not much snow during the night. Went down & saw
Brig. Maj. at 10.0. Went down French Sap, horrible performance.
Thompson turned up with a horse for me but as C.O. was not
returning till tonight I did not want it till tomorrow. Diplock came to
lunch but as he was very rude when meeting me & did not even

---

[87] A British author who wrote romantic fiction which caused an uproar in the early 1900s
because of its straightforward dealings involving sex, extra-marital affairs and betrayal.

salute I gave him the cold shoulder. Got a few shells on Maricourt Road - one or two gas over besides. About mess time a wire came through from Brig. to say all leave was stopped. We played cards up till 11.30 waiting for the rations wagon & I lost about 60 francs. Great excitement - nasty cold & snowy night. Pip slept out. C.O. did not return. W.G. Walker wired for urgently to see D.A.Q. about German prisoners. R.W. Garton turned up at 5 o'clock to take his place

25-2-16   Snowing hard in morning - Dixon came in about 10.0 to see Garton who had taken Walker's place & slept in Diplock's bed. Rumour had it he was to go to a German internment camp for prisoners & go in as a prisoner to see what he could pick up from them as he knew German so well. Dixon left about 11.30. I got an invitation to G.O.C. lunch - Got there about 1.30. At lunch there were G.O.C Brig Genl. Stevenson - Major Montgomery 90 Inf. Brig. Maj. Maj. Seymour 89th Brig. Maj. Lt Col. Stanley 149th Brig. RFA County Palatine Artillery. A Lt.Col. Territorial Artillery of 57 Div. Capt Arthur Taylor the Staff Capt. A Signal & Manchester Subalterns besides. Rather dry but a very good lunch. Steak & Kidney pie - apple & jam tart - cheese etc - s...ing good. Whisky & Soda & Masala. Came away about 2.30. Nothing doing much in afternoon. Horrible snow & cold all day. Went to bed early, ration wagon did not turn up till about 3.0 a.m. C.O. returned about 2.30 p.m.

26-2-16   Went round dug outs in morning. Burn went up to Maricourt. At 11.15 I rode over to H.Q. Thompson coming for me. I got over there about 12.30 & had lunch with C.O. After I had a talk with him & he said he would send Diplock back, send up supplies for the canteen & anything else practically I required was very nice indeed but seemed absolutely fagged out with his weeks so called leave. He had been at it all the time as hard as he could go. Had been up to St Helens & seen C.O. of Depot, Daly & Thomas, Mrs Pilkington & also Bonnyman in the distance. He had spent the whole time working - had given the reports of the St Helens bumph ..... in t.... His servant had returned a day earlier than usual by mistake on the date of his pass. He told me a lot about things at St Helens. All dark as pitch, no lights in churches etc after 7 o'clock. The clock on the church & also Beecham's Tower were not allowed to strike. Everyone seemed to have the wind up properly. He had seen several of the munitions workers etc including Kirkham who was still waiting for his job & Durkin who was at Prescot wire works. He had a lot more stories also - How Serg. Keith had robbed the working girls of money by saying he was getting up a waggonette party affair. He was apparently a R.P.M. on trains. I had a talk to Eric as he was slack at O.Off duties & had missed some guard mounting & Orderly Room although the Batt. Orders had said the duties of O.O. could be seen up in orderly room. His excuse was that the Subalterns never saw Batt. Orders in 'C' company. Left there about 3.30 & rode back - it had thawed hard & then began to rain & snow. I got in about 4.0 & they said a few shrapnel had come over. Burn brought back a report on 'U' defences & it was not good - apparently the officers had inspected it & a traverse had gone wrong - so I spoke to them all severely at 6.0. Cap. Worthington & Elstob of 16th Manchesters came in to dinner & we had quite a good dinner for them.

Hors d'euvre   - Salmon & Sardines
Soup   - Brown
Joint   - Duck & Roast Beef
Sweets   - Jam roll & Pears & Peaches
Savoury   - Welsh Rarebit
Port & Liquers

But the Bosche started intermittent shelling & we had to return to the cellar about 3 times & ultimately took up an ..... there & finished the meal there - they left about 10.15. Shelling still going on. Wrote to Kaye in afternoon.

27-2-16   Started off at 9.15 to 'U' defences - quite a nice day. Got up there to find round 'U' the work was shockingly bad but the rest of the work was not so bad. I pointed out to Fletcher what he was to do. About 5 Whiz bangs over us at the time. Got back for orderly room at 12.30 with very sore head. After dinner as arranged I went round to see 2nd R.S.F. & saw Maj. Lambeter about the Battle Dugouts - we walked out to them & I had some idea what to do. Got back about 3.30 & had tea & then went to see Brig. Maj. who said the Corps wanted us to have dug outs for Brig. H.Q. & also our Batt. at North Street in a week's time. Got back & was just going to start dinner & the Bosche started dropping them over & we had to take dinner downstairs, Bretherton & 10 men went out to work a night job on 'U' defences to start in the way over from U^{ii} to U^{i}. Corpl Davies was taken bad again & Diplock took him down on a stretcher to the dressing station. Craig & Buchanan had to wait for a long time & turned up about 8 o'clock. About 30 men went to spend the aft. at Bray the rest worked 9-11.30, 2-4 & inspections at 5 o'clock. Quite a heavy strafe at night. We had cards in cellar & also dinner.

28-2-16   Expected the C.O. & Adj. to lunch so had the place thoroughly cleaned up & mess room put straight. Went round & found all going on satisfactorily C.O. did not turn up. We had a good lunch ready for him of soup minced chicken etc. Went over rounds after dinner. Went to see Brig. Transport Off. & Chaplain's dug out - a cellar very weak so said I would help them to straighten it. Saw Knockton & Rogerson after tea - they were working in Vaux Sap. They said the Bosch Prussian guard had attacked seeing they were a working party but had been sent back. We had had quite a few casualties - they had not been to sleep for 24 hours as the casualties had been so numerous coming in & they slept near the entrance to the dug out. They also said a Manchester Corp. had been captured & all his equipment etc. taken off, but they had left him a bomb hidden under his shirt - he had been put in the charge of only one guard - had knocked him down & thrown the bomb on him & cleared off back quite safe. We had a few shells over at 5.45 p.m. Felt rather rotten & head aching all day. Wrote to Kaye. Struthers turned up at Batt. H.Q. Garton went over at midday - apparently the C.O. had had a parade & cussed 'B' &' D' Co. left & right & said 'C' Company was the best company etc - he did not mention 'A'

29-2-16   After breakfast took plans down to 2nd R.S.F. of Battle Dug outs, these were passed & then I put Sergt. O'Brian on - after that Craig & I started off to Vaux to see the men on the sap. Bosch started straffing & we heard them going over - one H.E. landing in center street killed Pte Howard[88], Gartons's servant & wounded Mills[89], Bretherton's servant in the arm so that they thought his arm would have to come off. L/Cpl Owen helped a man down who was very hurt & did very well. Also Sergt Jones helped about 9 men, the guard who were badly caught. Craig & I got down there & saw Knockton & Rogerson very cheery souls they had about 1 months work before them about 80 yards. They said a dead Bosch had been brought in that morning off the marshes he had ..... Khaki suit on & an overcoat like French in shape & very good underclothing. Also a Bosch bayonet had been found with a saw edge on the back. We got back about 12.0 just as the Strafe had stopped. Burn went over to Batt. H.Q. & saw the C.O. who was in very good form & told him Struthers was not coming & also that we were to stay over here for some time more. He stayed for lunch which was awful. I saw Brig. Maj. in afternoon about starting dug outs in Quarry & had to start

---

[88] In fact, Pte. 20486 Robert Howard died of wounds on 1.3.16.
[89] Pte. John W. Mills died of wounds on 10.3.16.

there with 16 continual working parties in 10 days. Had plans of that made. Burn came back for tea. Night was quiet up till 7 o'clock at least. Ponto & Pipsqueak still missing. When in Brig. Office they were talking of Bosch pushing over marshes & barrages of shrapnel etc over marshes from us. No letter by post in this day before & that night. Nothing doing for the rest of the night.

1-3-16   Went rounds in morning - Buchanan came with me - we started on Brig. H.Q. dug outs in the quarry. Everything going on alright. In afternoon went with Craig round the horse standings of Manchesters - found that the 16th needed very little doing to them. The C.O. was seeing the General & came back then to tea. A fine day but nothing much doing. Then B.M.G.O. Lt Gibbon came in before lunch to talk to Buchanan - wild rumours of the Bosch going to attack & massing troops behind Cappy

2-3-16   Went round in the morning & down the French sap. Everything going alright. Also in the afternoon. Bosch dropped a few shells over in afternoon but no damage done to my ..... Elstob asked me to dinner at 7 o'clock. Gardner found to be slacking & not going round the outer jobs - did not go to Battle dug outs or to Manchester horse lines. Went to see Maj. Lambeter Act. C.O. 2nd R.S.F. about Battle dug outs & said if material was forth coming they ought to be finished in a week or so. The British attacked N. of Ypres & took back all the objectives required. I went round at 7.0 to 'A' Co 16 Man mess for dinner - Worthington very kindly came round to see me to show me to show me the way. Elstob was in very good form & we had a very good dinner. Herrings. Soup. Steak & kidney pie - Custard - Welsh rabbit - champagne & coffee (not black). There were three other officers there. We had a four at bridge after, I played against Elstob. I left about 10.15 & got back & went to bed-about 1.30 a.m. I was woken up by an orderly who said a dug out had fallen in on some of the Manchesters. Bob was first up & then I got down & then Burn - we found Gregg & Johnson down there too. There were 3 men injured & supposed to be 3 men buried - after about 1 hours work we found all out - 2 dead & 2 men badly squashed & a third cut about the head. Having got all them out we got the rest out & put them in the reservoir dug out & the barn behind our billet - we gave them stew & hot tea & Gregg & Johnson came in for a drink. We got to bed about 4.15 a.m. Elstob was going off for the next day at Amiens & had to get up at 5.15 a.m.

3-3-16   Got up at usual time & went straight down after breakfast & saw the
General - he did not seem very much astounded but had not heard
anything about it. I then went round & went after to see Colonel
Peters who had come down in the night with Adj. He was out but I
saw Gregg & then Adj. both were very nice - then went round again.
Col. Panet C.R.E. came round while I was away & said we had made
excellent progress but our timbering was too light & a few technical
hints - side p.....s etc. I ordered the props & cross pieces to be
doubled in number & then the Brig. Maj. called for me & told me
what Panet had said. We went round to see the new B.H.Q. dug outs
& then one of the town ones & then I went round more & after that
found Emery's men waiting for him as he had been to bath. Burn
went round & spent the afternoon at a board of enquiry on the
accident at which was Capt Gregg & Worthington & a subaltern.
Thompson turned up with two light draft horses in place of the M.S's
two mules. At 5.0 C.O.2 & Dixon came in just before lunch & were
going up to see 'U' defences. A pipsqueak of an R.E. officer called
Day came round to see about the Battle Dug outs as he said he had
the job in hand - so we left it at that to see the Brig. Maj. to know
who exactly had it in hand. Buchanan & Garton went on to B.H.Q.
& brought back wonderful rumours of Struthers who thought
because our working party got bothered by Whiz bangs they ought to
make a bayonet charge. Also because a few shells dropped in Bray the
Bosch had made an attack & retreated on Fuanne - he meant
Suzanne. No post to speak of turned up except papers. Huge
rumours going about (I) That the Turks had given up altogether. (II)
The French were taking over our bit of the line. (III) The Div. was to
be relieved by the 7th Div. on the 10th of March.

4-3-16   Beastly snowy & frightfully windy day. Went round in the morning
nothing much doing all over doubling their props & covering timbers
Burn went to a board on the death of the three men. Stayed in all
afternoon - after tea went down & returned Army List to Staff Capt
which I had borrowed in afternoon. I saw Brig. Maj. about a note
from 14th Brig. R.F.A. to Div & sent on by A.A. & Q.M.S. that we
are seriously encroaching on the road from Suzanne to the cemetery -
I assured him we had not taken an inch more room than Potter had
so that he said all was well. The night was quieter much lighter but
very cold. Had stove erected in my room (cellar). Letters from Kaye
& Mother. Ripping ..... from C.O. about accident to Manchesters in
dugout.

5-3-16   Very fine morning indeed - lots of aeroplanes about. Being Sunday we only worked the usual Sunday hours 9-11.30 - 2.0-4.0. I had a good slack & did not do much - just going round in the morning & stayed in all afternoon. Stove going strong in cellar. Burn & I worked Mess Bills out for month & they came to only 2 frs a day. Hospital cases are mounting very rapidly we had 27 in - due to Bronchial Catarrh & Flu. A few dud aeroplane Bosch ..... came into the town in morning but no big shells up to 4.0. At 4.30 they started putting heavy stuff over but no casualties in our lot. Later 2 Manchesters were hit - about 30. Had cards after dinner - very poor post nothing for me. Wrote Kaye & Mother. Turned to rain in afternoon & evening.

6-3-16   Nothing doing much in morning - quite a nice fine day. Went round in morning. C.C. came over just as we were starting lunch & had lunch with us. Bosch sent one or two over at the finish & we had to retire to the cellar where we spent the afternoon talking. Dixon just called in on his way up to & from Garton's job. C.C. went off at 3.45 he would not stay to tea as he had to see some men at 4.30. He told us ..... about leave & a few rumours but nothing much. Nothing doing in evening. I got a letter from Woolcock stating Buchanan had written to the C.O. re the two horses coming up here - he had apparently got no objection & the first intimation I had was the letter from Woolcock - so I wrote Buchanan to the effect that I did not want to see him in 'A' Co Mess till he had given a satisfactory explanation of the incident - I got a letter from Kaye & one from Mother.

7-3-16   Buchanan came up to breakfast & I saw him about his letter to the C.O. about the horses etc. he gave no excuse except that he had no command over them up here. I told him I did not want him in the mess if that was the case. Burn went over to get money & to see the C.O. about Buchanan etc. The Brigade Maj. came up & talked about the new work & how many we could have in the dug outs. Apparently he had got orders about us all going in Support trench in Z2 No 14-17. Just after he left I got orders from B. H.Q. to say all the company were to go in support trenches. Burn then returned just after lunch & told me that the C.O. has said Buchanan ..... not mess with us & the horses were to stay. I was also to switch all my men onto support trenches. The Brig. Maj. also then asked us for a report on Dug outs which I wrote out & went down & saw him & he said he only wanted a report exactly on North Street dug outs. I saw Panet as I went in. I then wrote out another report showing work under construction & amount to do & time to do it. I sent that in & then waited results. I heard a funny story about Potter talking about Lord Asquith[90] & Mr Runciman[91] & then trying to say a bird in the hand etc started "a stitch in time what is it?" Just before tea Buchanan came back & threw a letter on the table & said that was his authority for staying in the mess. I told him it wasn't whereupon he cleared out. I wrote him telling him his authority was when I had seen the other officers & asked them would they let him in. After seeing them I wrote & told him he could return whereupon he wrote & said he thanked 'A' Co officers for their consideration & he would not return until he got further instructions from the C.O. I stopped the work at 4.0 & spoke to the men telling them I was damned proud of them for this last month's work & told them other companies did not relish coming up here & would they prefer to go back or to stay here another fortnight - they said stick it out another fortnight. I felt damned proud of them & told them after I would reduce the hours & take the consequences! Wrote to Kaye. Burn reported C.O. seemed rather livery & not very well.

8-3-16   Worked all morning on usual work - I arranged all men & reliefs etc for new Trench work. Support Trenches 14-17 & then the C.O. arrived at 1.30. I saw Worthington in morning for a few minutes. Bosch shelled us & Burn & I made our way to Brig.Maj. but he was out & I saw G.O.C who said keep on Vaux & also night shift on Whitehall which is the G.O.C's dug outs in Quarry. C.O. & Adj. to lunch - gave them a good lunch. He was very luched. After he called for Buchanan who got a jolly good telling off & was very undiplomatic about it. We had an afternoon off. I was still trying to arrange the reliefs. Buchanan came back to mess with a very bad grace indeed. I sent 20 men off to the trenches under Craig at 6.30. Garton went off too. Asked Greig of 16th Man. 'D' Co to mess at night - he accepted. C.O. was in very good form & very jolly - he seemed much better. He left about 3.0 saw Elstob for a minute or two but not very long. Small (Serg) refused to revert to L/Sergt unpaid to give Jones & Holmes their standing rank. Arranged to go up with Garton to trenches tomorrow. Got a letter from Kaye in morning post.

---

[90] Prime Minister of the Coalition Government.
[91] Prominent Liberal between the 1900s and 1930s; President of the Board of Trade 1914 to 1916.

9-3-16   In morning I went up with Garton to see support trenches no 14-17. We went via Maricourt Road & Communication Trench Yew, Batt. Head Qrs into C5 & then along Fargay Wood Avenue & so to 14. We walked up the trench as far as 16 where they had cleared to & no further: it was fearfully hard going - in one or two places being above the knee & being very heavy thick mud which clogged on so much it felt like lifting one up. We met Dixon on the way back & came out across the road. Dixon told us the C.O.2 was down with Bright's ..... & had gone to hospital. We walked back to H.Q. & Di..... went straight in. After lunch I went a turn round & then got back & Gregg wanted me to give evidence on a board of enquiry about the collapse of No 24 dug out. My evidence was that I considered the dug out safe for partial occupation but advised the Town Maj. not to overcrowd them. I then got back & had a note from G.O.C. he wanted to see me. I went down & he was very annoyed & asked me had I received any orders from Panet. I said only the one about all the company on 14-17 support trenches - he fumed & said I ought to have had orders that aft. I also saw Montgomery who said the C.R.E. had said the R.E's were going to take over all dug outs & that all the work we had done would have to be taken down & reconstructed. He ordered me to put on about 20-30 men. I came back & arranged that. Craig & Garton took a party up to support trenches again to clear them. I then got a wire to say Buchanan was going to the 91st Brigade & Craig was to take over the M.G. Section. No letters in the post. Col. Peters asked me to go & "advise" about strengthening their house. I told him tomorrow. Gregg asked me to dine with them but I refused & said I was going out.

10-3-16   Fletcher & I went down to see Peter's plan. We found them at breakfast. I had a look at their cellar & advised propping it & putting rubble on top floor. Then I rode over about 10.30 to see the C.O. He was occupied so I went in & saw Brooks, Q.M. Dixon - Walker, Potter & Woods. Saw the C.O. riding off so rode back with him - told him about G.O.C. the night before - he said Panet had told him he would have to indent on 201st Field Co. R.E. to get materials & have his indents countersigned G.O.C that company - he had got 2 motor lorries from the Corps & got his stuff direct! We met C.C.C. just by the road & the C.O. turned back he was going to see Lord Derby who was at Etinehem. The C.O. said when I asked him for a second star for Diplock that he was arranging it that in about a months time there would be there would be a lot of second stars a few majorities about the place. I then left him & rode back saw Bradley on the way on the road & had an argument with him. Got back at about 1 o'clock. Found that Craig had to go to Etinehem for a board (medical) He went off about 1 o'clock. Burn told me he loathed Garton. A bit of news. Petrie told me that via Haig's sister who married Merriman's brother who was a Major in 19 or 20th Man & so to 16th Man - leave was to start on the 11th!! Gardner asked me if he might apply for the reserve machine gun officer so I asked the C.O. who said yes. After mess a junior R.E. Subaltern came round to take over N. Street dug outs so I told him I had no orders & I could not hand them over in the dark. Had a bath & then bed. Craig returned about 7 o'clock they had kept him actually on the ward till 6.0 & there had been heaps there. The C.O. had had something to do with it.

11-3-16   Sent Diplock over to H.Q. to see the C.O. He & Buchanan went over. I went round & saw everyone. Diplock got back just in time for lunch. Dixon came in about 10.30-11.30 & told us that the rumours that we are to be attached to the 7th Div at Fricourt to live in tents & also we are going near Albert. Diplock & Buchanan came back & said the C.O. was fearfully sick with Panet & also the same rumours as Dixon. Bradley came in just after & had lunch & he & Buchanan left about 2.30 the latter for good to be attached to 91st Brig M.G.O. Craig took over our M.G.S. Just at tea I got a wire to hand over Dug outs to R.E.'s 2nd Lt Murphy came round & Fletcher showed him round. He obviously knew nothing about mining by such remarks as - putting infantry on the face - split logs were no good! I went down with Craig to see Brigadier at 7.0. He was furious but said he had very good things to say for the Pioneers & no-one knew but himself how much the Pioneers had done for him. I was to tell the men. The first wire was that we had to put 20 men to work for the R.E.'s & later on a whole platoon & an officer just as I was going to bed. We heard heavy straffing going on about 6.0-8.0 & rumours the Bosch was attacking Fanny Hill. Craig came down to the Brigade office & we met Worthington there - we scuttled back as soon as possible. Bretherton brought us back a very good night cap.

12-3-16   I rode over in the morning to see the C.O. It was a ripping morning. I got over there about 11.30 no one was up. I talked a long time to the C.O. & told him exactly what statements the silly subaltern had made who was taking over the dug outs. He told me he & Panet were having a row about it all. He also said Potter was going also Brooke & Dixon was to ..... C.C. was to be second in command. I stayed to lunch & saw nearly all the officers - rotten lunch. Rode back to tea. Culshaw & Parsons came to dinner & got very uproarious & really quite tight. I sent them back on the buggy with Thompson & he dropped them where the road to the Grovetown dug outs branches off. Young Murphy came up 2 or 3 times to see me but got absolutely no change. Brooke looked very bad & Forrester had a bad throat. I took Culshaw & Parsons round the dug outs & their opinion was our timbering was too strong & the tunnelling could almost be done without timber. Letter to Kaye.

13-3-16   Burn & I went up to the 'U' defences to put it right. Beautiful day - plenty of aeroplanes over all the time & also guns registering etc. I decided what was to be done to put the bad bits right & then got back about 1 o'clock. The afternoon I spent doing orderly room work & then in the evening I spoke to the men about giving them a false impression about working on dug outs when they stayed for the extra week. Usual inspections & then Burn took a party of about 12 men up to the 'U' defences to put them right. Got orders that we were to leave here on 15th evening. Parcel from mother & Hilda. Wrote to Kaye.

14-3-16   Sent men up to 'U' defences & to 14-17 Trenches as usual. About 10.0 orders came for 3 G S wagons to be here at 2.0 p.m. 15-3-16 & we were to leave at 4.0 p.m. Potter & Dixon came over at 11.0. Potter had been to see C.O. the day before & had been told he was windy & would have to go - he said he would fight it & so had come over to see Stevenson & get a recommendation. He went down & I with him to Brig. H.Q. Stevenson was engaged with a French General. They were looking at the Bosch things captured at the D.....ch Pat F..... point. Potter got an interview & told & told me that Stevenson had backed him up & so he & Dixon went off happy before lunch & Burn. Burn lost Thompson somewhere & sent the buggy back as he had to stay & see the C.O. who wasn't returning till 4.0 Thompson returned later. We were slightly shelled about 4.30 -7.0. Thompson & Diplock went to see a ..... cap & a shell came over so they both got into the same shell hole & then ran for it. They sent shells over 4 every ¼ hour. Burn turned up & said we could not have more transport on 15th but could have 2 wagons tonight. They turned up & we got them loaded & sent off with all tools & a lot of mess stuff. Bosch shelled heavily at about 11 p.m. Burn said Potter had 5-1 on beating the C.O. at best - the C.O said 50! Jones & Fleming were very nearly hit by a 5.9 on top of the dug outs but luckily they were only covered in mud. Fleming was a bit silly that night but they gave him hot drink & put him to bed & he was quite alright the next day - Jones was alright.

15-3-16 Had no work on except 6 men & Bretherton going up to the 'U' defences to finish revetting the bad places & cutting trench so no mistake could be made. Rest on clearing up & we got all the tools & stores (including 17 off. boxes) down to the end billet in West Street so that transport could come up unseen & could be loaded up under cover. We had orders to move at 4.0. & Transport to be arriving at 2.0 p.m. Transport was late owing to Div. muddling up things. I heard after from Adj. that order for Batt. had been to move two companies & H.Q. company to Ville & two companies to Meaulte - that then they had to put 5 motor lorries to move with. After that they got a wire from the A.S.C. saying as you are only moving 2 companies from Grovetown they would only supply two wagons. This was the first intimation that the other order did not hold good. The C.O. then wired for definite orders & had orders to send 2 companies to Meaulte - 2 to stay in huts at Grovetown opposite the old dug outs - H.Q. company to go to Ville & the transport to go to Dernancourt. So they had to get tents for two companies & hence the transport was very late for us. It turned up about 2.30 & we loaded it as it came & returned - we were given 3 G.S wagons & one R.E. limber. I gave Craig the R.E. limber, Garton 1 G.S. & myself 2. As a matter of fact Garton did not take quite one so we put a lot of our things on it - as we could not get all ours on 2 G.S. wagons. The Bosch started shelling at about 3.30 & as Dippy[92] & Serg Jones were doing something on top of the last G.S. wagon a shell dropped on the billet & knocked the roof off & also Dippy & Sergt Jones were closing something on top of one last G.S. wagon a shell dropped in the billet & knocked the top off & also Dippy & Jones off the G.S. wagon. I inspected each lot as it was ready for moving off & sent them back to clean their buttons they were so dirty. I got off two parties before the shelling so sent the rest by the Bray Trench & through the new lines so they all got off safely that way. We took all sorts of things with us - sandbags - expanded metal - barrows & also about 19 hens. We handed our mess over to some Manchesters & then dug outs too - I heard later from Suter[93] that they were turned out of our mess for someone else who was coming in later. Suter had orders to take the relieving M.G. section the Brig. Co up to Eclusier by day at 2.0 p.m. this was from B.M.G.O. Lt Gibbon - I persuaded Scot... to show it to Stevenson the Brig. who laughed at it & told him to relieve at night. The original scheme was absolute madness as it was in full view of the Bosch quarries & ..... & no trench or anything

---

[92] Lt. Alfred Diplock, 11/SLR.
[93] Lt. E. J. Suter, Manchester Regt.

to go up by. He had great trouble as the M.G. Co had only just come out from Grantham & had practically no training & had only come to Suzanne the night before. They did not appreciate the shelling at all. As soon as I had seen Fleming & the last party leave I rode over by the short way to Bray. When I got up to the top I found there were starting Barbed wire all along the top of the hill but luckily by riding along a bit to the left I found where it was only posts & new wire put up so got through & got in about ¼ hour before the first party - I was on the C.O.2's horse. I passed Garton & his first party just off the road on the way to Grovetown I saw the C.O. & had a chat with him about going on to Meaulte etc. & he said he would give us not only that he doesn't send 'B' & 'D' Co to go there & so was keeping 'B' & 'C' at Grovetown & we had to move up. Then the company arrived & I & Burn put them into tents. I got the C.O.2's dug out. We had an uproarious dinner & although still having this confounded flu I had much too much to drink - Kümmel[94] about a glass full - got horribly bleary & having a scrum with Woods got hit in the stomach so retired to the dug out & was as sick as a dog. Went off to sleep & had a jolly good night. Eric was in very priceless form.

16-3-16   It was a great effort to get up as I still had flu & felt rotten from last night's debauch. I did not get up till about 9.30 a.m. & had breakfast in bed. The company was inspected for cleanliness about 11 o'clock & were not bad but not as good as I would have liked. I saw Woolcock about Jane & we agreed that she should be cast as she seemed no better after 7 weeks. We were at first supposed to be leaving at 3.0 with 'D' Co. to go to Meaulte but Woods who had been to Meaulte about our billets returned & said it was not safe to go there in daylight. So we postponed it till dusk about 6.30 p.m. H.Q. & our transport went off at 3 o'clock. We had a most awful lunch imaginable - cold beef & that's all no potatoes or sweet cheese & bread & butter. I hadn't any it was far too raw but got a tongue from 'A' Co. mess box. We then had all to shift out & go to the tents. I had chocolate & cake with Brooke & then tea & cake with C.C.C. Potter moved at about 5.30 when it seemed to me scarcely dark enough. We moved about 6.15 p.m. Both of us went off by platoon with about 3-400 yards interval. Burn going with the first platoon - Bob brought up the rear. We moved across country & I brought up the rear on C.O.2's horse at last. I saw them all off & then rode up to the front & over took Burn just when he got to the roads. I rode on expecting

---

[94] A sweet, colourless liqueur flavoured with caraway seed, cumin and fennel; first distilled in Holland by Lucas Bols during the 16th century.

anytime to overtake 'D' Co. but got right into Meaulte without seeing them & started looking round my billet. 'D' Co came up very shortly & Potter explained his first platoon had gone wrong!! We got in very soon after & had a very small snack & ..... & then bed. We all slept in 'D' Co. café a huge place with a balcony where we slept. We had 2 motor lorries to carry our transport - we made a journey in the morning & then both made one in the afternoon besides our G.S. wagons & R.E. Limber. Dixon sent a Sergt over to Suzanne to get the sheep & calf & also my cat. We found Pip Squeak at H.Q. & brought him along with us to Meaulte - he slept in café in Burn's bed. I had never seen anything like the absolute state of depression at the H.Q. when we came there they seemed to be like so many lumps of chewed string. I got orders to see O.C. 95 R.E. Co. at 9.30 next morning

17-3-16   I had a fairly good night but was woken up hourly often by men swearing & by the pump going down stairs & servants making a noise downstairs too. Still had this flu & rather an effort getting up at 8.15. I had breakfast at our H.Q. place but as no latrines were up I hurried & went straight on to Maj. Dobson. He was very nice & we walked round his work. He told me he did not know we were coming till late the previous night - he showed me everything he could & a lot about the lines & we put up 3 or 4 notice boards to prevent men walking across exposed places etc. & then wandered up to see King's Avenue on which we were to work. He turned out to be a man who had been there when the Batt was being formed & had attested a few - he was sick & only allowed to join in Sept 15. He knew the Pilkington's - Gamble - Thomas - Cozens Hardy[95] etc & had been 4 years Adj. to the St Helens R.E.'s. So I got on very well with him. We wandered up King's Avenue to the Taurborn etc & then back. I had lunch with him & slacked all afternoon & evening feeling pretty rotten. The Bosch strafed Becordel while we were on the way up & they put in about 12 at 12 o'clock into Meaulte & about 30-50 after dinner luckily they were all at the far end by the church. Got a letter from Kaye & wrote her one.

18-3-16   Went up with all the company & all the officers bar Bretherton who was sick with flu & still in bed to King's Avenue at 8.30. A beautiful day. We started work at this end & put on a b..... & pulled up the trench boards. After seeing them started I came back with Diplock & met Maj. Dobson on the way & Lt Crowther. I turned back with

---

[95] A Director of the glass company, Pilkington Bros.

them & Dippy went on home. Maj. Dobson seemed quite satisfied with the work we were doing & chatted to some of the men but none of them knew him at all. I left him there & wandered back myself - had hardly been back ¼ hour when the C.O. & Adj. turned up - he was furious with 'D' Co. as he found a dirty man of theirs He seemed quite satisfied with my men. He strafed Miller for being dirty. The Adj. made a peculiar remark about the hole under the barn which the farmer used for throwing carrots, turnips etc being a splendid cellar. Diplock remarked that he would prefer to be out in the open field rather than in that death trap! They rode off back to the transport. Burn, Fletcher & Gardner went up to the trenches. Diplock, Bretherton & I had lunch together & after that wandered up to the alarm post in case of bombardment. Returned & all had tea together & then I went along took orderly room & then went on & saw Dobson who wanted us to work further up nearer the Tambour & have a night & day shift. Burn paid the company - after dinner we played vingt et un & then bed - there was no shelling of Meaulte up till then.

19-3-16   Being Sunday I did not get up till about 10.0. Burn & Fletcher & Diplock went up with Croxton to the trenches to see the new work. At 11.0 I rode over to Ville to lunch with the C.O. Wilson & witnesses were taken over by Slater but C.O. could not hold orderly room so he had to come back. Craig, Payne & Rice were there to lunch. They have a ripping place. The C.O. informed me I was to go on leave on 23rd. I left there about 3 o'clock with Craig & we came back via Danencourt so that he could pick up his horse - he came over to tea - at lunch time the Bosch dropped a few shrapnel over & killed about 5 men - one landed at the entrance to an off. mess & made a bit of a mess, slightly wounded 2 men & Booth the cook went to hospital with shell shock. They had apparently dropped shrapnel in 2 or 3 places up the street & ours was the furthest point they got to. Craig only stayed to tea & then went back. When the shell dropped Woods was in at our mess & they say they have never seen anyone run right out into the field so quickly - everything was quiet after - the mess servants seemed rather scared! Potter asked Burn what I had said when I came in & saw the damage. Two men were killed ..... down - in each case they had their legs blown right off - in the one by our gate instantly killed - the others died later. We played vingt et un after dinner & had quite a good. Bab & Bretherton both being out & very ..... it got the wind up fairly easily Burn said.

20-3-16   Waited about after breakfast for C.O. who was supposed to arrive
about 11 o'clock. Got every place cleared up & the offices were
whitewashed & canvas put up. About 10.30 I got a note from the
adjutant saying the C.O. was in bed with flu & would not be over - so
I sent over to see if he would be holding orderly room & sent at case
& witnesses over. Having no reply Bab, Diplock & I went on a walk
towards Ville & then to Dernancourt & saw Woolcock there & then
back. Got back for lunch. After lunch Potter & I rode over to Ville &
saw the adjutant. The C.O. was in bed & unable to see anyone. Came
back via Dernancourt & saw Woolcock again. Got orders & warrant
for leave & they said I should have to hear from Corbie so I went
round with Burn & saw Carr the Staff Capt. he knew nothing about it
but explained that the 30th Div was at Corbie & so could go from
there - our being on detachment was different. Gardner made a devil
of a hash of things on the trenches in the day having boards & things
up & sandbags all over the place. Nothing doing all evening. Then
Bab went up at night & was nearly killed by a trench mortar or some
infernal machine of the Bosch. Luckily he came to no harm.

21-3-16   Rode over after breakfast to Mericourt to see about leave train & &
found I could board it there & then rode back to Ville going both
ways via Treux. Saw Adj. & quartermaster & then rode on to
Grovetown via Morlancourt & then across country. Got there &
found Dixon, Brooke & Forrester. C.C. was out so stayed lunch -
C.C. came in later on - after lunch I rode over to Dernancourt & saw
Woolcock about getting my coat & things over to Mericourt by mess
cart - got back in time for the tea - heard about Gardner's bad work
on trench. Going through Mericourt on my way from Grovetown to
Dernancourt & I saw Merriman (Maj) in 22nd Man & & we had a
short chat. Packed up things in evening.

22-3-16   Got up at 7.0 & had breakfast & left Meaulte with Diplock at 8.0 a.m.
Called at Ville on the way & saw C.O.; he was in bed & looked very
rotten - saw adj. about my letters but were none. Forrester had
walked over from Grovetown to H.Q. one day before & slept the
night there & was walking on to Mericourt to catch the train. The
train left Mericourt at 9.35. When Diplock got there we found the
mess cart alright & the groom to take back my horse. Forrester
turned up just in time to catch the train. Arrived at Amiens about
10.15 & left about 11.40. We got coffee & rolls for breakfast there &
also a luncheon bag consisting of bottle of beer, bread - ham & veal,
jam etc in a blue bag. We met Hindle there. I went in to next carriage
& played bridge with Hindle & Wyatt (S.S.O.) & Cranston the salvage

officer in charge of the salvage company. In our carriage was a signals officer of another Corps & an A.S.C. officer with M.C from the same Corps. In Hindle's carriage was Capt Kaufmann another A.S.C. officer of the 30th division. We arrived at Havre at 8.30 & got straight on the boat - the Connaught B.I.S.P.[96] Very bad commissariat - but I got a cabin & went straight to bed & slept on the wire mattress with a lifebelt as my pillow. We left about 12.30. I won about 5 francs at Bridge playing with Salvage v the other two. We had tea at Montresol - Buchy.

23-3-16   Arrived at Southampton about 8.0. I got up about 6.0 & walked the deck. I got no breakfast but ate some biscuits I had brought with me. By getting over the bridge I was the first off the boat & got the first train which left about 8.10. We arrived at Waterloo about 10.30. I went by Taxi straight off to Euston - wired up to Lancaster to find out what Kaye was doing as I had arrived a day earlier than expected. Then phoned up Ronald & found his address 36 Holland St. then went round to 4 Mount St & changed money at Cook's on the way - found that the Burns still at P..... so went round there, walked. Found Pat & stayed there drinking cocktails till 1.15. A girl I could not catch the name & Stella turned up & I rang up Mr Burn & told him I'd call in & see him at tea - then I took a taxi to Holland St - it took me to Holland Rd & we were ¾ of an hour late when we did find Holland St. there being no 36 at Holland Rd. Hope was in but Ronald had gone back so I had lunch & then went round & saw Ronald - he came along with her to Euston, having rung up to find a wire had arrived & a phone message to call one straight up to Lancaster. We had tea at Euston & I caught the 5.25 to Lancaster. On the train there was a Captain in the 8th S.L.R. & we talked a bit. I got up there about 10.30 - Kaye & Mrs Malcolm met us. Tommy was in bed with a slight attack of flu. We had the upstairs bedroom.

24-3-16   Had breakfast about 9.0 a.m. got straight into ..... We walked down there in the morning & met mother & Miss Waugh & Miss Hart Jackson - they could not stay as they were playing golf in the afternoon at Silverdale. Mr & Mrs Malcolm went to Manchester to see Gilbert & Sullivan D'Oyli Carte in something & so I took Mrs Malcolm to catch the 3.38 in afternoon in the Belsize & met Kaye at the County Hotel at some dress exhibition - also Mrs Helen W..... & Gladys there & when returning Greta in the town - Thomas got up in

---

[96] British & Irish Steam Packet Company. R.M.S. Connaught was torpedoed and sunk by U-48 on 3 March 1917.

afternoon & we had a quiet evening together. Trial by Jury was one thing Mr & Mrs Malcolm's saw.

25-3-16   K & I caught the 8.50 to Manchester - had a very comfortable journey & got in about 11.30. Went straight to Midland Hotel - Mr & Mrs Malcolm came in later I had arranged to be tried on by Smith's at 12 but he could not find one & I did not get tried on till 12.30 in the middle of lunch. Jolly good lunch & then we went to the Royal & saw Patience - it was awfully good - we got back for tea & caught the 5.45. We got in for dinner & Haggis.

26-3-16   We did nothing in the morning & no one went to church -a rather dark & very cloudy day. Mr Malcolm & I played golf in the afternoon. We got caddies & it was very jolly up there - very few out. I did approx 84 & Mr Malcolm 91. I gave him six strokes & beat him 4 & 3 & we halved the bye - I did a three at the 18th. Got back & changed & went to the Holmes for tea with Kaye & Tommy by car. Mr & Mrs Holmes, W..... & Greta, Gladys & Edgerton & Tom Holmes were there - on the way back we called in & saw ..... & Mrs Irwin - Lt.Col. Sylvester RAMC was there - nothing all evening. too tired. Karl went to Flixecourt for the months course.

27-3-16   Kaye & I went by car to town in the morning & did some shopping. I caught the 1. 7 to Glasgow - changing at Carlisle & getting tea on the train - two men in there talked about Whitehaven & Lancaster munitions works. Mr Townsend met me at 6.15 at Glasgow. Mr Townsend seemed very much better & very cheerful - he had been out & down to the club for the first time that day. He told me of the government wiring for the Glasgow Shipowners to advise them of the disposal of the shipload of Barley in 6 ships in the Black Sea! Also their failure over the Whiskey & both being bought. Bed about 11.0.

28-3-16   Breakfast at 8.15. Caught 10.10 to Lancaster. Mrs Townsend saw me off - I got lunch at Carlisle at Hotel - there was an S.L.[97] subaltern having lunch in the room. Kaye met me at 3.38 & Ta.....y in the car. We played Khun Khan[98] in the evening.

29-3-16   Kaye & I went over to Silverdale by car about 11.0. We went via Carnforth, Yealands & Story Hill & up Station Hill - called in at the Bartons in Carnforth & found Mary Humphries better, she had been

[97] South Lancashire.
[98] Nemo's Kuhn Khan, a 1912 card game by Chas. Goodhall & Sons.

ill & had killed the possibilities of having a child through an..... We did not do much all afternoon but talk & mooch around. I had Karl's car out for a run & found it was getting far too much petrol so that the ..... was all wrong - we did a puzzle at night. Mother seemed very fit & the house & garden was as usual pretty well. Mother ..... us Radcliffe (Capt) had been killed.

30-3-16   Burn left on leave. We left Silverdale at about 10.0 & got back to the Graves for lunch - we packed up for Wolverhampton & found Ta.....y had arranged to go to Bournemouth with Mrs & W..... Holmes by the same train. We caught the 2.13. Mrs Malcolm saw us off - Mr Malcolm & Miss Stenton came in to lunch. Mrs Malcolm gave me 100 Abdullas[99]. We travelled by ourselves to Preston & from there to Crewe with the others. At Crewe we found owing to telegraph wires being down that our train was not running we wired Dai - the wire arrived while we were having dinner at 8.0 & caught the 5.13. Got tea at Crewe. No one met us so we drove up in a cab. Hilda was just recovering from a severe cold. Dai seemed very fit. Uniform came - waist far too high so returned it.

31-3-16   Breakfast at 10 .0. Late for 9.0. Got Singer out & found it running very well but rattled & was very dirty - also tyre flat. Went up to the town with Kaye & & got her a brooch. After lunch went to the Efandem[100] - found Stra..... out but saw Gregory - the office very much improved. Went up & fetched Mrs MacClaren at 6.30 & she & Jack came to dinner & & we played flying petunia after-dinner. Got ..... cold - headache & sore throat. Kaye & I went out before lunch & saw Grand-mère & Mrs Wright. The company shifted from Meaulte to Grovetown & also 'D' Co. The C.O. being in Paris ill Potter was acting C.O. of the Battalion.

1-4-16   Breakfast at 9.15 - Khaki on - got packed up had persuaded Kaye not to come to town with me. Dai returned at 10.15. Kaye took a lot of photos. We all went to the station - found that the 10.45 was running for the first time this week owing to wires being down. Got off punctually - by myself in the dining car to Birmingham & very few in all the time. We absolutely crawled till we got to Watford all the wires being down & got in at 3.30 instead of 1.20. So had to go straight to Waterloo - found boat train going at 4.30 instead of 4.0. Met Wyatt

---

[99] Cigarettes by Abdulla & Co of New Bond St., London.

[100] A company formed in Birmingham in 1903 to manufacture batteries. In 1911 it moved to Wolverhampton and in the 1920s it was purchased by Ever Ready.

there who was now a Major & his father & Hindle & we all had tea together - after tea found Cranston, Salvage & Knapman who was also a Major now. We all got in the same carriage together & played bridge all the way while Knapman typed a letter. Hindle & & I were 1600 up on the others at Southampton. We crossed on the Mona Queen. There were only about 200 crossing owing to leave being stopped. Had dinner at about 7.0 & then strolled on deck with Maj. Knapman till the boat anchored off Netley Hospital[101] & then I went to bed - a glorious night & as calm as a mill pond.

2-4-16   Got up about 6 a.m. & had breakfast - quite a good breakfast & then had a sort of scruffy wash but no shave - we got off the boat about 9.0. Going into Havre we picked up the Viking with troops on. Got into a carriage with Hindle, Wyatt & Cranston Salvage. Played bridge all the way. We periodically had a ride in the observation box on the top of the next carriage. Forrester got in higher up & was made O.C. train. We got out at the place we had tea going & had omelettes & coffee for lunch - very good. We played all day & were only about 360 up in the end - Hindle & I. At Amiens we got there about 5.30 - we split up & they went off as they were motoring to their respective destinations - I got into Forrester's carriage - only Major was in besides he got out at Corbie - we got to Mericourt about 6.30. Found only Thompson with the C.O.2's horse & a grey - although Forrester had said on the train he would ride when he saw the grey he said he would prefer to walk so Thompson took his coat & pack & he walked. Thompson told me the C.O. was ill in Paris C.C.C. was at Flixecourt - Craig at a course at St Gratien & Miller at Corbie. I rode off through Treux - Ville - Morlancourt - then the d-d horse would not trot only gallop & was an awful nuisance - I ran into barbed wire just before we got to the camp & after getting off found my way through & got in about 8 o'clock - I saw Potter & as Burn was on leave & only Fletcher, Diplock & Bretherton there - I had to share a tent with Fletcher - beastly squash - & I went straight to bed. Jolly cold night.

3-4-16   Had breakfast about 10 o'clock Diplock was taking the company off to Suffolk Avenue for work. Stayed in camp all day. As we were changing the camp to the next valley. Went over there & arranged about getting it ready for us. Did nothing all day. Wrote to Kaye & Pat & Ronald. Found Co. gramophone had arrived

---

[101] A military hospital near Southampton; at the time the largest in the world.

4-4-16   Rode up with Diplock to see the trenches Bob was working up there. Very good & dug trenches but a bit dangerous. Got back about 1:15 p.m. lunch. In afternoon got a letter from Kaye & Craig turned up in time for lunch. Wrote to Kaye, Hilda & mother. The Sergeants had a match against the Bedfords & were beaten 0-2. Went over & watched it for a bit - but being so cold left early - it was a very cold dark & windy day rained at night. We played vingt-et-un all evening.

5-4-16   Had breakfast about 10.30 - did nothing all morning - had Batt parade at 2.30. Potter read out a letter from a General congratulating 'B' & 'C' Co on their night work. After that we changed camps & got into the next valley. Huge excitement - much grumbling but it did not take long - 'A' Co being out at work took longer but we were all in by 6.0 except the officers we got in about 8.0. Went off to bed early. Fletcher & I each had a tent of our own & Diplock & Bretherton had our .....

6-4-16   Breakfast at 9.0. Rode up to the trenches in Pau.....ua Got back about 12 o'clock. Spent aft till tea working out leave. After tea or as tea was coming in Maj. Dobson came to see me & we talked about trenches. After tea went to see Football match v Bedfords- their C.O., C.O.2 & 2 or 3 other officers were playing - we lost 3-0. Wrote Kaye. Bed about 10 o'clock. Nothing doing all day.

7-4-16   Got up fairly late & did nothing all day but work out leave & write letters. Got a letter from Kaye & wrote one after two parcels from Wolverhampton - cakes. C.O. came to tea. Cold & windy day. Diplock & I played Fletcher & Bretherton at Bridge in evening. Craig went to 'C' Co to mess. Had inspection in evening of everything.

8-4-16   M.O. Kuny went on leave. I rode up to the trenches & saw Bretherton there. Had a look round & on the way back went round & saw Woolcock about Thompson & my horse both doing well. I rode Pandora up there & back. Wrote all afternoon. At 4.30 there was a boxing contest between us & the Sussex & Bedfords. We won 5 & lost 3. I missed two owing tea being late. Eric & Walker came to tea. Capt Turnbull, Chaplain to Bedfords, came in just after & stayed tea at 'D' Co. Did nothing after mess.

9-4-16   Had a bath when I got up & had no breakfast. Church Parade Voluntary at 9.30. Lunch at usual time C.C. arrived in afternoon- did not look up to much - arrived in a car. Went with Potter to a concert given by the 3 Batt. W Sussex & Bedfords. Quite good in parts - we heard the Band 3 times they were jolly good.

L/C Hutton Sussex Comic Troubadour (Mediocre)
Pte Goodwin Bedford Fiddle de dee (Good)
Cpl Sullivan Sussex Hand's of our father (Mediocre)
Pte Witney Bedford Comic tableux Viewrama (Quite good.)
L/C Pensford Sussex " I've only come down for the day" (mediocre)
Pte Johnson SLR Story sentimental (Bad)
Lt Phillips Bedford My ain folk (Not bad at all)
Lt Whiting Sussex Comic (Quite good)
Sgt. Small SLR Virginian (really good)

We had to come away after that for dinner - Potter had Maj. Pattinson R.E. to mess - the C.O. was in our hut when I arrived - had a nasty headache & felt rotten so I went to bed early read. Wrote to Kaye & Hilda & got letter from Kaye.

10-4-16 Went up to the trenches in morning & saw Diplock up there - on the way back met Maj. Dobson down there - spent afternoon writing - leave tickets came through for Bob & Woods. Maj. Dobson called in just before tea again to tell us about the steps up from the trenches. Got letters from Mrs Townsend, Ronald & Pat. C.O. came round & talked to us about 6.0 & then Burn turned up having got to Mericourt early & so missed the mess cart. I had sent for him & Brooke & included a whisky & soda for each - Brooke did not come back having got 3 months extension for nephritis[102] (Kidneys). We greeted him with "we're glad to see you back dear lady"! on the gramophone. After dinner I went up to the trenches the horses meeting me at the bottom of Sussex Road. Saw Bretherton up there & stayed about 2 hours & then returned. Burn talked in my tent after I got into bed about 11 o'clock he went off.

11-4-16 Pouring wet day. Burn & I were going to ride up in the morning to the trenches but owing to the rain I sent the horses back - & put it off till after lunch but we left it too late & did not go up at all. Holmes was in charge of the party & seemed to carry on quite all right. No letters at all . Had a long talk to the C.O. in the afternoon with Burn.

---

[102] Inflammation of the kidneys.

12-4-16   Eric's birthday so had him round to mess. Potter went to Amiens with Douglas & that crowd. Another pouring wet day. But I rode up in it & saw Burn at the trenches - they were pretty muddy. While I was up there Maj. Dobson called & saw Diplock & Bretherton in bed & told them he wanted us to start Reserve trench from 70 St. end - the Borderers would do 68. I got back pretty wet & we played vingt et un after lunch. G.H. Walker came in & Simon stayed to tea. They have to go on night party so could not stay much. I had another long chat with C.O. He was rather infuriated with Maj. Patterson R.E. who tried to get the whole Batt. to work for him. Luckily the C.O. stopped it or I should have had to walk out there to Minden Post. Eric was only guest at mess & he brought his gramophone Burn having smashed ours. We had music & drink till about 12 - then Rice came in - Craig got up specially for the occasion as there was Haggis for mess. Rice was Four sheets in the wind & told us the same yarn about 5 times. Leave was all stopped & also we had orders we were moving to Vaux en Amienois on the 18th & the C.O. was to make all the arrangements!! At least 2 days march & no places stated to Billet. Potter turned up about 12 quite alright. I got to bed about 1.0

13-4-16   Did not go to the trenches - a nasty wet day all day bar the afternoon. Examined No 4 Plat. in afternoon - had C.O.'s orderly room at 12.30 & my own at 6.0. Had a long talk with the C.O. & had dinner usual time. I changed over from my tent to a dug out by the G.O.C's dug out. Ronald & Hope had a girl baby - heard late from Mrs Townsend.

14-4-16   Went up in morning to trenches. Chestnut out for the first time & a bit fresh. Found Bretherton up there & made a tour. On way back the groom's grey got away & it was near the R.E. Dump at Bray before I got it. Did nothing all afternoon - walked over & saw Eric but he was in bed & not up to much. Played Khun Khan after dinner & then bed. Dobson came in first before tea & I went & saw the C.O. after with Burn. New tunic turned up & sent old one for repair.

15-4-16   Woke up at 3 a.m. was feeling horribly sick & deposited my inside on the side of the bed at 4 a.m. Feeling horribly bad I stayed in bed all morning & only got up for lunch. Lay down all afternoon & went & lay down after tea & just got up for dinner & went to bed directly after dinner - got no letters. Horribly cold day.

16-4-16   Dobson saw me in bed just after breakfast which I had in bed - rode up at 10.30 to the trenches saw Diplock up there - beautiful day & very hot. When I got back I found Edwards in the mess. Bretherton cleared off at 10.0 to Corbie on a course with Sgt. Holmes. Platoon Commanders & Sergts course. Burn, Edwards & I went in & talked to the C.O. for a bit & then went over & saw C & B Co. officers. He stayed tea - he belonged to the 62 M.G. Co. at Ville at the time he had been up at Armentieres & in France about 2 months. Having stayed tea he went about 6.0. I went with him & Burn & saw the C.O. Craig & I - we rode through Morlancourt to Ville where he was billeted - I met Capt. Davidson 2nd Warwicks in Morlancourt & had a talk with him & then rode on. Got back for dinner. Went to bed early & read till about 12 o'clock. Miller returned from course at Corbie on which Bretherton was going & said it was very good & he had met C.C. in Amiens who said his course was very rotten. Got letters from Kaye & Kents & ginger bread from Mother.

17-4-16   No work. Horribly wet day. Arranging for leaving next day. G.O.C. came to tea & dinner. Got letter from Kaye - wrote Kaye, Mother & Hilda. Bob was wired to leave England that day. He said a huge crowd left at Waterloo & lot of boats at Southampton

18-4-16   Got up at 5.45. Pouring with rain. Had breakfast at 7.0 & all packed up ready to move at 8.30 but owing to the heavy rain & ground we did not move till abt 10.30. The C.O. rode in a motor lorry. We passed through Mericourt by the Bray Corbie road leaving the camp with 100 yards between each platoon & we joined up the other side of the Boise de Taille. Potter took over the Batt & I acted as C.O.2! We went through Mericourt & Heilly where we found C & D Co's blanket wagon broken down. C.O.C. was charged of the transport party for their purposes. The rations had gone all awry in the morning & we had caught up the Bedford's canteen of sausages & got 2 for each man, the other companies had only bread & butter. The result was my men stuck it very much better & at the end of the day out of about 35 none of 'A' Co fell out. We got to Lahoussoye about 4.30 & had some tea about then. I got a very measily bed but was so tired got to sleep about 10.0 o'clock. Forrester bagged my billet but I turned him out. The C.O. was pretty rotten - we had a mess in a kitchen nearby & did quite well. The M.O. & RSM returned from leave. Fletcher & Woods could not find a seat in the train at Havre & had to spend the night in the rest camp.

19-4-16   Got up at 6.30. Breakfast at 7.30. Hailed at 8.30. Potter again in charge & I C.O.2! Another pouring wet day worse than yesterday. The men again stuck it wonderfully - we marched through Querrieu-Allenville when as we left Potter missed the way - Poulainville & so to Vaux-en-Amienois. Querrieu was H.Q. of 4th Army. Three men out of abt 30 men 'A' Co. who fell out so we did pretty well. The weather cleared a bit after Poulainville, otherwise it rained incessantly the whole time. When we arrived we found our billets - all officers eat & sleep in the chateau & men in 2 billets Sergts in one - we found a mess of our own & the others all found beds - so we got fairly comfortable - had ham & eggs in a cafe & then dinner in our mess. Burn got toothache & a swollen face on one side of his face. Bob & Ward got the 7.30 H.O.I. train slept in it till 11.0. when it left Havre went to Grovetown via Mericourt & Bray & found we had left - slept at the Sucrerie the night. The C.O. was not very fit.

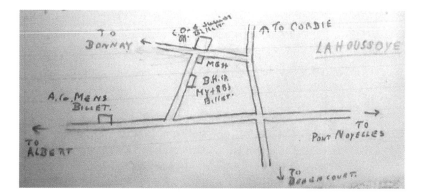

20-4-16   Got up at 10.0 & breakfast about 10.30, did nothing all day. Kit inspection at 3.0 for the men. I spent the afternoon sorting the mess boxes & then went in to see the C.O. he looked very bad & was very fed up. Bob turned up about tea time - he & Woods had got a lift by the Bedfords into Amiens & then got out from there. We had orders that the men would have to live on iron rations for 2 days so I made my arrangements for supplying them with lunch & porridge & other things for the two days. Eric came to mess at night & I also arranged for him to sleep in the little room adjoining mine - the dressing room - we had Khun Khan & then all toddled off to bed about 11 o'clock & I read till about 12 o'clock. Had a post in & got a letter from Kaye & one from mother.

21-4-16   Got up for breakfast at 9.0. Church parade under Potter at 10.15. Burn & I went for 'A' Co. Lenton Smith took it - & we held it behind the chateau. C.O. told us after that Fry G.O.C. Div was going to inspect the Battalion tomorrow so we had to spend the afternoon cleaning up. It rained hard all the afternoon & evening. I had an inspection of all equipment in pieces at 3.30 & several after that at

5.0, 6.0 & 7 o'clock. Could not have any drill or manual as it was raining so hard - had dinner early & then bed as I had to get up early tomorrow.

22-4-16   Got up at 6.30 for inspection of men - inspected them at 7.0 & then had breakfast & another inspection at 8.0 & then company fell in at 8.30 & I had one or two presents & fines. We marched up to the parade ground independently & drew up as a matter of fact we were with the Band & all companies in ..... march formation so it might have been the Batt. At 9.40 General Fry & Capt Jack Fry his son turned up & inspected us & then he spoke a few words & we marched off. Burn acted as Adj. We had Middlehurst faint but no-one else fell out. Got back about 10.30. Did nothing for the rest of the morning. Burn, Craig, Diplock & I were going out a ride after lunch but it started to rain. It rained hard all the afternoon & evening so we did not go. Williams came to dinner - C.O. to lunch.

23-4-16   Did not get up for church parade. Burn took the company. Diplock went to Amiens with Parsons & Bob. Was still ill in bed. Got up about 10.30 & had no breakfast. Eric stayed in bed all the morning. After lunch Burn Craig & I went out to Longpre passing Williams & Forrester to see some Div. equestrian sports we saw about 3 events - ½ mile - wrestling - tent pegging with Potter won & that was all & then got back to tea - went up to chateau & found that C.C. had returned & was closetted with the C.O. so went & talked to them & then returned to mess. Craig was out in W...ss he went to the Trench Mortar people. I went to bed early at 9.30.

24-4-16   Parade at 9.0. Gave the company 3 hours drill - close order - all ..... drill & physical drill. In afternoon Burn, Diplock & I went for a ride through Fricourt to Flesselles & had some coffee with our old Billet woman & got back for tea. Had a trench mortar demonstration at 7 o'clock CO & CC went to. Parsons came to dinner & we had Khun Khan after. Letter from Kaye & wrote her.

25-4-16   Burn, Eric & I rode into Amiens. I went to see the C.O. before going in & he gave me a telegram to send off. I had the grey, Burn a new arrival & Eric had Woollies. The mess cart was ordered for the afternoon. We got in about 12 o'clock & saw about the wire & then went & had a bath after we had lunch at the Restaurant des Huitres of oysters - sole - entrecotes - pineapple & 1906 Rochrer Cordiale ..... & coffee. Then we went & bought up grocers shops, the market etc & deposited it all in the mess cart. We then met Williams who had come in with Forester for the second day running - we sent off some chocolates to our Billet at Puchevillers, had tea at the other chocolate shop. Had good fun there - saw Forrester as we went in - rather tight. Went back to Hotel de la Pain where we had left the horses. Had a drink of Vittel water (Hotel water!). Eric & Williams clicked & we had to search the town for him, found him & left about 7.10. Got in at 7.55. Had dinner - we stayed & went up & talked with C.C.C. to C.O. till 11 o'clock. We got a pineapple - cauliflower - asparagus & some plaice for the C.O. Diplock in charge of company - he paid them.

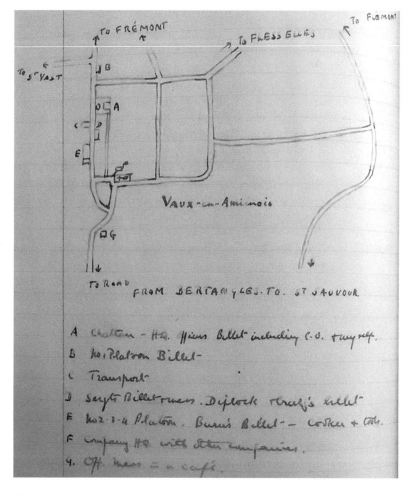

26-4-16   Had C.O.'s inspection at 9.30 after that we had a couple of hours drill. In afternoon we took down beds & put up wire over in place of wire & sand bags full of straw. Burn & I had dinner together alone. After Williams came in & chatted & we went to bed fairly early.

27-4-16   In morning we finished the beds & then had ceremonial drill for a bit - C.C. came up for it also RSM Boden & we had the band out. It was very good considering it was the first time we had tried it. After lunch Burn & I went over to Puchevillers & saw Yvonne. We went via Montonvillers - Villers Bocage - Rubempre & so to Puchevillers we stayed there about 1½ hours & then returned getting back about 7.30. Diplock went off in the morning to Corbie to see an exhibition of Flammenwerfer & smoke bombs etc - he Craig & Williams got back just in time for dinner & all came in. C.C. also came to dinner & we all had to feed off one small chicken. I rode Pavlova & Burn Neville. We got to bed about 10.30.

28-4-16   Had company drill etc in the morning at the usual place. Craig to Amiens with Eric. Bob did nothing. Diplock turned up late as I let him stay in bed owing to hard day yesterday. No letters. Burn & I rode to St Vaast & then on to La Chaussee & Tirancourt & back in aft. I was on a new horse no. 366 & Burn was on Neville. In evening there was a football match v. the village. Burn played, I talked to C.O. with C.C. Wrote Kaye & mother & sent a parcel of clothing to Kaye. No one to dinner. Eric came in afterwards & we went to bed early. Walker & Garton went on leave, also Slater, Routley & Barton.

29-4-16   Parade & kit inspection in the morning & finishing billets. Spent most of the morning talking to Rice. In afternoon C.C., Burns & I went for a ride - I was on 366 & Burn on a chestnut light draft - we went nearly to Montonvillers & then round by Bertangles to Vaux. Diplock went to Amiens. Had a short talk to C.O. & then came back & packed all the boxes we could. Got a letter from Kaye midday. Wrote Kaye but did not post it. Early to bed. An aeroplane caught alight in the air & crashed to the ground & the pilot Capt Mitchell[103] was killed. Lots of the Batt saw him.

30-4-16   Got up for breakfast 9.30. C.O. talked to us at 10 o'clock on amount of luggage & that the C. In C. Sir Douglas Haig was to inspect us on the march. Took church parade at 10.30 & after lunch went for a ride round with Burn & Craig. Diplock stayed the night in Amiens also Williams & Parsons & put us in a very awkward position. Rained a bit in the afternoon - We went passed where the aeroplane had fallen

---

[103] Flt. Cmdr. E. H. Mitchell, 24th Squadron RFC.

then round by Bertangles & just got in before the heavy rain - I was on no 366 & Burn on Neville.

1-5-16   Got leave to go to Amiens with C.C. & Burn. Just before starting a wire came from corps that two companies were to proceed to Chipilly tomorrow by motor bus so waited to see which companies. B & C were to go. They were to start at 7.30. I had a case of McManus[104] for drink for orderly room & so left Diplock to take it. Company were showed Lewis guns by the M.G. Section. C.C. & Burn on Neville & I as C.O.2. Set out about 10.30 to Amiens. Quite a fine day - got there about 11.45 & having ordered lunch at the restaurant ..... we had a bath. Forrester was there too. We had lunch after on Sole, Crayfish, chicken, pineapple, Sauterne, Grand Marnier & coronas. Finished about 3.30. Met Williams outside who had come in to tell Forrester about the move. Met Forrester in the tea shop & found the girl there could talk & understand English much better than I had thought - Burn & she talked hard - rather doubtfully. Started to rain slightly we bought up a few things including sticks. Left about 6.30. Burn & I had our horses in the Hotel de la Paix - C.C. in the Hotel Pomme de ..... behind the Hotel de Ville - Williams was up at the Universe. As we left a Taube was over the town dropping bombs - apparently trying to hit the station - Williams' runner came out so Burn & I rode on while C.C. & Williams stayed to put it right - got in to dinner . While there near the station we met Payne who was on his way back from leave. He turned up at the mess about 8 o'clock. I saw him again at H.Q.

2-5-16   Got up about 9.30. The other two companies 'B' & 'C' went off by lorry at 7.30. About 10 o'clock it started to rain hard. We stayed in & prepared for moving at 8.30 a.m. the next day to Corbie but at dinner time orders came in that all orders for tomorrow were cancelled - finally I found out that orders had come through there was to be no marching between 8 & 4. Bed early.

3-5-16   Lounged about all day till 3.30. Seeing everything finished off & tidy - breakfast at 10 o'clock. At 3.30 paraded & marched to Batt. parade. We got 3 lorries in the Batt extra transport & 'A' Co. got all of them. C.C. with Potter on parade marched us all out of the town & the C.O. took over when we got up to the top of the hill. It was very hot to start off with & men fell out fairly freely - we marched through Poulainville & then had tea & then got to Allonville - we made tea for

---

[104] Whisky.

the officers of 'A' Co - C.O. would not have any. From Allonville to Querrieu - Pont Noyelles & then Corbie - we got in at 10.10 p.m. about - men in tents but Bob who had joined us got the officers all billets. Williams kept my transport so I had to wait 50 min. & then H.Q. was the other end of the town so we had to report there & then got supper of an omelette & got to bed at about 12.30. Mounted officers were allowed to go without packs.

4-5-16 Messed about all morning, breakfast at 10.30 bought some Perrier & then after a very good lunch paraded at 3.20 & marched to the hill out of Corbie. 'A' Co. was behind - we had tea en route & after making up by the Bois des Tailles we arrived in about 8.0. I had to sleep in a dug out with Burn. The R.E.'s would not give us any beds which we had left so I went along & persuaded them, & we got to bed at about 11.30 after talking to the C.O. for a long time. I had orders to report to O.C. 202 F.Co.R.E. at 9.0 the next morning.

5-5-16 Got up & rode over with Diplock to see O.C. 202 F.Co.R.E. but he knew nothing about us so returned & reported - messed about & inspected till 4.30 when Diplock got orders from the Adj. to go to report to R.E. 200 F.Co. We waited & I had tea with him - Payne came up & although I asked him three times what he was telling Diplock to do he ignored us & was very rude so I got up after tea & went to the C.O. Met Payne & saw him so took him in & told the C.O. Payne tried to shift it & put it I was annoyed at Diplock being told to go without me being told a word about it. C.O. could not make it out so I referred it to C.C. Rode up with Diplock to Bray & saw 200 F.Co. R.E. but Maj. Keown was out & no one else knew about the work he wanted my two platoons to do. After dinner the C.O. talked to me about the row with Payne & C.C. had said I had spoken to Payne in a way to annoy him so the C.O. put it down to me - I think he also spoke to Payne. Anyhow it cleared the air a bit & Payne & I knew on what footing we stood. Burn went over in the afternoon to Chipily as both Forrester & Dixon were in hospital as O.S. Det. Got orders at 11.0 for 2 plat.[105] to report to Lt Bradley at station at 8.30 a.m.

6-5-16 Got up about 9.30. At 10.30 Rode out with Diplock who was going over to see the Billets at Suzanne - I met Bradley at the top of the hill & we went round the men's work - they were working at quarry Bray-Suzanne road, quarry Bray-Cappy road & Froissy Wood. At station &

[105] Platoons

Div. Dump. Got back at 1.0. Spent the afternoon trying to arrange about the two platoons going to Suzanne - having no orders at all. About 4 o'clock 'B' & 'C' Co. turned up - 'C' Co. to go on to Suzanne. Burn in charge for a few days. Much heat against Payne & his blithering want of orders - no one knew anything at all. Forrester went off to hospital in the morning & took Culshaw's servant without asking Culshaw at all. At 6.15 'C' Co & 2 platoons of 'A' & transport moved off to Suzanne. Diplock & I rode on at 6.50 to see Maj. Keown at H.Q. 200 F.Co.R.E. he was out so we rode over the top to Suzanne. The company turned up about 8.15 - I saw them in - they were billeted 'C' Co. in East Street & a bit in Canon St & No. 3 & 4 Plat in Canon Street. I came back with Gates in the dark over the top & called in & saw Keown again having his dinner & he explained what Diplock & the two platoons were to do - he wanted them to work in Napier's Keep at 9.0 the next morning - so I wired Diplock to report at 9.0 to Lieut. Richmond at Maricourt - which he did a bit late. I did not get any dinner when I got back but went pretty straight to bed.

7-5-16   Rode up with C.C to a ravine of the Valley of Death[106] to the left at 11 o'clock. We were going to take the short cut over the top to Suzanne but they were shelling it so we skirted down to the Right & got onto the Cappy-Suzanne Road. Got up there at 12 o'clock & found Rees (Capt. R.E.) Burn & Culshaw - I left them & went on & found Diplock in Maricourt - also I met Keown so he took us down to the trenches & showed us the trench he wanted to dig tomorrow night. He previously told us we could dig it by day when we got there we found it about 500 yds from the Bosch & on the facing slope. So we decided to dig it by night. I left him about 2.15 & got to my ..... about 2.45 got back about 3.15. Had some biscuits & Perrier & then tea. Bretherton turned up about 5 o'clock. Played bridge after dinner with C.C. against Woods & Miller. Lost a rubber but was up in points.

8-5-16   Did not get up till late. G.O.C. & W.G. Hitchen went on leave. Bretherton went to Heilly with the mess cart & got us some things for the men. Miller went to Corbie & got some officers mess boxes back. I did nothing all morning it was very cold & windy. In aft. I

---

[106] This valley was originally known to the troops as Happy Valley, and was taken during the advance of 14th of July, 1916 Although the Germans could not directly observe the road and the valley, this was the only route that could be used, and they pounded it with shells. After a while it became known, therefore, as Death Valley.

took Bretherton round No. 1 & 2 Platoons work. We walked to Froissy & saw 3 sections at work on station two & at Froissy one - the other two were on Suzanne-Maricourt road & Cappy-Suzanne road. Got letter from Kaye & a parcel from Mother also tunic back from Smiths. Wrote Kaye & Mother. In evening played bridge with Miller v. Woods & ~~Hopwood~~ Featherby. All square.

9-5-16 Got up late - at 11.30 I rode over to Suzanne with Thompson as orderly - saw working parties at Bray Station & Cappy-Suzanne road. Got there about 12.30 & found Burn just getting up. Stayed to lunch & at lunch there was Burn, Diplock, Culshaw, Gardener & Struthers, & Walker A.D. Had quite a good lunch & on the way back met Maj. Keown R.E. who wanted to find our headquarters so rode back with him & as Diplock saying what work we had done he seemed very satisfied - rode back over the top & it began to pour with rain - got back for tea - after tea I had a good talk with the C.O. & then held orderly room. Potter had a guest at night from the Sussex Capt De Jong their Adj. Capt De Jong. Also G.H. Walker & Garton turned up - they messed with us. We had 'D' Co. ..... going all night. No spring hardly in the beastly thing. Wrote K - Mother - Pat & Hilda. Bed about 11 o'clock. The Sussex man told us the Bedfords used Perrier Bottles full of lacrymatory gas during their attack.

10-5-16 Rode up at 12 with C.C. to Suzanne & had lunch with Burn & Diplock etc - but just before lunch - Keown took Diplock off to show him a new trench they were to dig - Keown was there when we arrived - so Diplock went without his lunch. C.C. had to meet Pavey at Mericourt at 2 o'clock. Burn rode back with me - I went round by Froissy & the Bray centre hill & so back - got back for tea. Bretherton went up to Suzanne to help Diplock. After tea Craig & I went on short ride behind the hill & back via the P.... Horn Camp. Bosch dropped a shell into Suzanne & cleared off the Sergts mess. Letter from Kaye - also glasses back from Harrods. Met Wathington while in Suzanne also met Wyatt motoring on the way up there & said a few words to him. Craig & I met Polly on the way out. Went to bed very early & read.

11-5-16 Heavy strafe 2.0 a.m.- 2.30 a.m. being asleep I did not hear anything of it. Got up at about 7.0 a.m. rode round the road parties in the morning met Baker on way to Cappy Corner & went on with him. Burn came over about 6.0 to see the C.O. I did nothing all afternoon. Got letter from Kaye - wrote Hilda. Suzanne was shelled the night before according to Burn but no damage done. Wrote Kaye. After dinner C.C. & I played Woods & Miller & won about 20 Fr. off them!! C.C. told me I had to meet the R.E. at 10.30 at Div. dump.

12-5-16   Got up early & Bob & I rode down & called in at 10.30 to see Panet at Div. dump. Not there so I rode on towards Suzanne. Panet in his car over took me just after leaving Bray & told me about the new roads to survey 1.a - Peronne area up to cross roads from road Billon-Carnoy & then the road meeting that one from 'U' defences.
I went on & got hold of Diplock & we saw the work 'A' Co No. 3 & 4 plat. had been doing in the trenches & then took a reconnaissance of the Peronne Rd & the other two - got back to 'B' Co. mess at about 1.45 - had lunch then with Walker G.H. & Garton & P..... & 3 R.E. officers - Day & Keily & some O.C. Co. who seemed rather an outsider & all would talk shop all the time. Left there about 2.30 & walked on to Suzanne had some tea there & heard that 'C' Co was still up digging out the sap Y3 that had fallen in on the top of some 18 Man. Bretherton, Culshaw & Struthers were there - got back about 4.0 - meeting Polly on the way. While on our walk round we met another Walker, the eldest of the three who is signalling officer to the 20th Liverpools - also Hepburn O.R. W...W who is a signalling subaltern. Went in still with Potter in the evening. After dinner played bridge with Potter v Woods & Miller & ended all square.

13-5-16   Woke up to a beastly wet day - very tired so decided to do nothing all day - spent the morning washing & the afternoon playing bridge with Featherby v Woods & Dean, ended all square. Got a letter from Kaye - long - wrote Kaye in evening. C.C. went up to Suzanne & saw Trigger Wood[107] we were to go to - secured very good sort of spot. The Bosch had 3 attacks on Y3 - just east of Maricourt last night - Culshaw was up there still trying to dig the 11 - 18th Man. fellows out & was in the middle of it. We had no casualties but the 18th had 50 - 60 & about 4 captured - we captured one Bosch. Culshaw came to dinner & expounded to us about the strafe - not mentioning that old Struthers was there too. After dinner Potter & I played bridge v Dean & Woods & drew. Bed about 11.30. Letter from Kaye & wrote Kaye & mother & aunty Edie.

14-5-16   Rode up to Suzanne seeing all the work parties en route. Not quite so mucky as yesterday but still pretty muddy. Saw Diplock & Burn up there. Got back to lunch owing to a board on the blankets returned.

---

[107] On the road between Bray sur Somme and Maricourt is Bronfay Farm. Trigger Wood was near the farm. It is now referred to as Bois de Longuis.

Woods & Featherby were on it & they both turned up late - it took us from 3.0 - 5.30 to examine them all & we finally burnt 6 of them - Burn came in at tea. Apparently I heard from Payne the C.O. had got a wire from Col. Fraser 18th Man. - saying that he & the officers & men of the 18th were very thankful for the work he & his men had done & thought they did exceedingly well. Burn & I had a talk after & he told me G.O.C. had the wind up - also that 'C' Co. had run away that night a few back & that the story was true & they had been frightened by 3 Liverpool officers with revolvers out who had been hunting for spies & had held them up. Also he told me that 'C' Co was pretty rotten at bottom. Bury came over & saw the C.O. for a short while - sent some records up to 'C' Co. & also some needles. Wrote Kaye. Got photo of ..... cups from Kaye. Played bridge with C.C against Potter & Woods. Lost. Sgt. Dermott returned from leave.

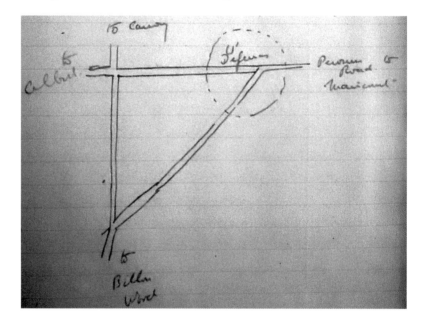

15-5-16   Beastly wet day so did nothing all day. C.O. left about 1 o'clock on leave. Payne appreciably more scrappy! Bob got hold of Bradley's ..... horse. Had bath at 6.15 p.m. Got Punch[108] but no letters. Wrote Kaye & Hilda. Wire came after dinner while C.C. & I were playing bridge v. Potter & Woods to say Potter was to take on the Battalion while C.O. was away. Potter had seen Sackville West at 8.0. Baby born at 8 a.m.

---

[108] British weekly magazine of humour and satire established in 1841.

16-5-16   Rode over at 11.0 to Suzanne & saw Diplock & Bretherton. Burn away with R.E. & C.C. Got back for lunch. Got a wire to say "Daughter all doing well" from Mr. Malcolm also a letter from Kaye. Wrote Kaye & Sammy. Went over to find Wyatt but went to Chipilly & he wasn't there so tried Etinehem & found he lived at Ecluse between Chipilly & Etinehem. Met Molesworth so went in & had tea. Hindle got his 3rd star[109] dated back to 14th - he came in late - a Maj. Of 18th Div. Art. was in & also a lot were signallers. Did nothing after dinner. The wire was dated 15th.

17-5-16   Went up to Suzanne in the morning via the road parties & saw Potter & Burn rode up there had a drink & then came back over the top with Diplock. We did not leave there till 1 o'clock & got here at 1.30. Had lunch & then rode up to the Div dug outs where Parsons was asking to see Panet - saw him about roads Bale was there & then returned - we got nothing very definite from him ..... what we should have to do up on the Peronne Rd. Going out in the morning I met I think Heap of the 24th or 23rd Manchesters but I don't remember which he used to be Adj. I rode up after tea to Etinehem & had mess & dinner with the Signallers - about 9 to mess & Hindle & Allen played a fellow called B....shaw I think & myself - we lost in 3 rubbers about 1000 points. Got back about 12.30 & just coming into from town picked up a South Stafford officer who was trying to find his billet - had a whiskey & soda & then got to bed about 1.30 a.m.

18-5-16   Craig & Diplock went on leave. I stayed in all the morning & was going up to Suzanne in the afternoon but Potter persuaded me not to & ultimately I went with him in the evening up to see the Div Dugouts which Parsons was working on. In evening at the mess I & Woods played Potter & C.C. ended all square. Early to bed. Wrote Kaye & Mrs Malcolm.

19-5-16   Rode up to Div. Dug out that Parsons was on & met Potter then after that went on to Trigger Wood & saw Dean there & then over to 'B' Co & had some refreshment with Garton & then I rode over to Suzanne & had lunch there - Bale turned up for lunch - rode back in afternoon with Burn & Bale for tea. Dixon turned up at tea then Potter & I saw a Brigadier about 35 he looked belonging to the Artillery up by G. Copse. Lieut W.G. Fletcher turned up about 8.30. Woods & I took 25 fr. Off C.C. & Potter - rash doubling by Potter.

---

[109] Rank of Captain.

20-5-16   Went up with C.C. to Suzanne - he went on to 'B' Co. I had lunch with Burn & left about 3.15. Went over the top & called in at Parson's Div Dug outs. Hindle came up & talked. He came over to see about his wires - he offered to take me & another into Amiens tomorrow. At tea I asked C.C. & Potter gave his leave. Got letters from Kaye - Mother Hilda & Pat & parcels from Mrs Malcolm. Wrote mother Kaye & Mrs Malcolm. Started Bridge with Woods v. Potter & C.C. & De Jong & Russell the Sussex Adj. & M.O. came in & we talked a bit & promised to go over. Eric rode over to Suzanne.

21-5-16   Rode over with C.C. to Suzanne to see Eric & C.O. I came back by Cappy Corner & saw the men working - C.C. came over the top. Both had lunch at 1.0 & got over to the Div Sig at Etinehem by 2 o'clock found the A.D.A.S. was there so we had to wait till he had gone before leaving. Got off at about 2.45 & got in to Amiens at 3.30. Tyre burst just as we were getting to the Place Gambetta. We went via Corbie & Daours. Hindle went off & C.C. & I went & had a bath & then some tea & bought a few magazines & chocolates & then the Hotel du Rhin & a champagne cocktail & then Hindle turned up at 7 o'clock & we got back. We came back by 7.55 & came in the French side of the Somme via Villers Bretonneux & Warfusee Abancourt & Chipilly. Stayed dinner at the Signallers & got back about 10.30. Found Dixon had found a cutting in the Times of Sonia's arrival & everyone knew it. Arranged with Potter to go bathing tomorrow.

22-5-16   Went off with Potter & C.C. to Chipilly to the Sussex to bath. Got there at 12 o'clock met Matthews at Chipilly & he showed us his cinema & we went in. De Jong was just off to Corbie to buy stuff so we had lunch without him. Doctor Russell turned up after & we went & bathed - bon - & then de Jong turned up just as we were leaving. We got home for tea & found letters from Edith, Kaye & Huggins!! & Rosalind. Wrote Kaye etc & went to bed soon after dinner. Bretherton & Dean came to B.H.Q. for leave next day.

23-5-16   Bretherton & Dean on leave. Left at 10.0 with Potter & went to see Parsons & then on to Suzanne - tried Callaghan - Potter did & gave him 7 days F.P. No 1. Then Eric bicycling & I riding we went up to Maricourt & went down Maricourt Avenue right along Diplock Trench & up Weston & from there along Mersey Avenue to Main Trench & so back. Had lunch at Suzanne. Simmons objected to Potter over the question of people getting their second leave. He wanted to see the General. So Potter & he had a row - before he got his first. Burn & I rode back & had tea with Parsons. Got back about 5.0. Letters from Kaye & Mrs Townsend. After dinner to which Burn stayed we played Bridge. Woods & I lost one rubber to C.C. & Burn. Slater dragged me out to see a dud Stoke's shell lying above the Q.M. Stores.

24-5-16   Rode over with C.C. to Parsons & then to Suzanne. When we got there it started to rain & we stayed for lunch & tea & played Bridge - he & E.O. v. Burn & I & had the gramophone. Left then in the pouring rain at about 5 & got back. No letters only a parcel of sweets. Wrote Kaye & Arthur ..... No one came back from leave although it was the right day. Leave was stopped for 24 hours. After dinner a M.O. from 21 Div wandered in. He was trying to find the D.L.I. Woods went to Trigger Valley[110].

25-5-16   Went up to Trigger Valley saw Woods up there - found Potter Dixon W.G. Fletcher. The Adj. also up there. Sent Thompson round with my horse from the ravine where I met H P..... who I believe was in the Northants & had a chat to 'B' Co. & walked up to the road to the 'U' Defences from Billon Wood (N). Then went round to 'B' Co & saw W.G. Walker Garton & Parr & then on to 'C' Co & saw & had lunch with that lot & then rode round the road parties & returned to tea. Found records & letters from mother (2) Kaye (2) & Dai. Wrote Kaye & others. Nothing doing after mess. Miller & A D Walker & the N.C.O.s returned from leave.

26-5-16   Rode over with C.C. to Suzanne & saw E.O. then came back via Cappy Corner & Parson's Dug outs. Got back for lunch. Did nothing all afternoon expecting Maj. Fenn to arrive. He came at 6.50 p.m.in the end. First impressions good. Got a letter from Kaye. Wrote Kaye Mother & Dai. Burn came to mess & went off after mess with A. D. Walker to Suzanne.

27-5-16   Rode over with Thompson to Parson's & picked Miller up there & then on to Trigger Wood. Saw C.O., Potter, Adj., Dixon & Woods then rode on to Suzanne. Later on the C.O. & Co came in there but did not stay long. I stayed to lunch & then returned about 3.0. On the way back I met Capt Ramsden of the Yorkshire Reg who was taking over Brig. Maj. To 95th Brig in place of Montgomery. He was at Flixecourt. After tea I had a talk to the C.O. & he asked me all about

---

[110] Near Carnoy.

officers etc. Potter came in after we had gone to bed & talked till 12 o'clock. Wrote Kaye & sent her £32. Got a letter from her.

28-5-16   The C.O. .....gged up here in the morning so I could not go out. Williams turned up from Corbie about midday. After lunch the C.O. having returned I got my horse & rode over to Suzanne by myself - looking in at Parson's place on the way, had tea & a talk to Burn & C.C. & then got back about 7.30. When we came to saddle the ..... up I found she had broken her head piece & was very frightened at the shelling & also almost throttled. Williams messed with 'A' Co. I wrote a note to Kaye but got only a letter from Brooks.

29-5-16   C.O. did not have my horse so I rode up to Trigger Valley & saw Woods, Fletcher & Miller there. Potter was there also. I rode on & had a look at the work from Billon Wood[111] up to the 'U' defences & then rode on to Suzanne. Had lunch there. C.C. was out with the C.O. I then rode over back with Burn & C.C. & got back for tea. Culshaw came down to H.Q. to go on leave with Williams tomorrow & Gardner came to H.Q. to go to Corbie on a course. Diplock returned from leave but Craig did not, presumably ill as he left in such a bad state.

30-5-16   Company started to move to Trigger Valley at 9.30 so got up to see them off. Saw most of the stuff away & then rode round the roads & back over the top from Suzanne. Saw Polly in Bray. Got back for lunch. Saw the rest of the Company out & then left about 3.30 myself with Diplock came over the top. Saw the C.O. on the way back. Got on to Trigger about 4.0 with Potter then - also met C.C. on the way there. He rode in after tea & said C.Co & A's two platoons had to move out from Suzanne tomorrow into Trigger. Played Bridge with Potter, Ward & Bacon in evening & wrote to Edith. C.R.E. said we should give up the roads on June 1st.

Missing page.

..... up his ..... General Rawlinson & dozens of Brigadiers etc were there. We all went back to Heilly for tea & then got back about 7.0 to Grovetown. Potter C.C. & I stayed to dinner with the C.O. & then came in to Trigger Wood about 10.30 & bed. Burn & 'C' Co & 2 platoons of 'A' had all come in. Headquarters still at Grovetown.

---

[111] Just south of Carnoy.

1-6-16   Rode over with Fletcher & saw the men left at Bray. On the way back Bab's horse shied at a motor lorry & came down - luckily it did the Bab no harm. We saw Parsons on the way there. Headquarters left Grovetown & came to Trigger Wood. In afternoon Bab & I walked up to road Billon Wood - 'U' defences & then went back & found the chalk quarry in the road on which Maj. Mellors Battery used to be. Later we were told that it was in French area so we could not use it. Col. Paul & Capt Wright O.C. 200 Field Co R.E. came to tea. I met Wright at Parson's place in the morning - he seemed a very nice fellow. He was going to take over Div Dug outs when Parson's went on leave. He told me he knew Martell very well - who had left 9 F.Co. R.E. - gone to G.H.Q. His company being mentioned in despatches by Haig. After dinner Burns & I went up to Trenches & saw the men in the trenches in front of Maricourt & the men on the road too. Got back about 11.15.

2-6-16   Stayed in all morning going through the orderly room stuff. In aft Burn & I walked round the road & saw work & also found place for a chalk quarry. In evening I examined both parties. No 1 & 2 were very dirty & No 3 & 4 were very clean. Bob very energetic all day. Fine but inclined to rain. Letter from Kaye.

3-6-16   After breakfast Burn & I went up to the trench & saw what had been done in Mersey street. Going up we found a poor little French man carrying a great bundle of props who had lost his way the French having just taken over this part of the line R hd side of Maricourt - so we took him along with us & carried a prop each. We found some French men at the far (east) end of Mersey street so we left him there & returned by way of Crater Avenue. We went up Castle Avenue. Had a drink & talked to G H Walker in 'B' Co's place on the way back & heard of the French Capt who commanded 4 - 75s a Col having 3 sets of 4 guns each - who had been here Dec 1914 & knew Bronfay Farm & all this district when the Bosch held Maricourt - then he had put 150 rounds into them at 400 yards laugh. He also said the French had used at Verdun only half the ammunition which their factories were turning out. He belonged to the 30 Reg of the 90th Corps - which was one of the French spot Corps & always meant a push. Also he had 1600 rounds to play with now. After lunch we did nothing but I made up a few more leaves. After tea Burn & I walked up to the road & sat & talked to a Maj in the Suffolks who came along & told us the Push was to be for 50 miles 25 miles north & 25 miles south of the Somme. Got back for dinner at 7 o'clock then Burn & I played C.O. & Potter at Bridge & lost badly though we got 800 above out of a rash double by Potter.

4-6-16   Rode over to Bray & saw parties on the road. Also went & found the transport place & saw where the men were billeted. Returned for lunch & after walked up with Burn to see Bab's road & round by Dixon via the quarry for tea. After tea Bretherton & Dean returned from leave. Played Bridge with C.C. v. Potter & C.O. & just won - 2 rubbers out of 4 & a few points. Walked up after & saw men on work in Bab's road. Came back with Bab & got in about 12.30. Had a letter from Kaye & wrote Kaye & mother. News through of great battle in North Sea.

5-6-16   Rode over in the morning to see men at work in Bray & went on to see Woolcock but as C.O. was there I left without seeing him & returned just in time for lunch & to escape the rain. After lunch Burn & I went up & saw the road. Letter from Kaye & wrote Kaye after dinner. C.O. & Potter played me & C.C. at Bridge they just won.

6-6-16   Beastly wet day - rained hard all morning. Burn & I were going up to trenches but owing to rain we put it off & only went up to the road. Met Fletcher halfway up & he told us he had seen the C.R.E. who told him he did not want the road made so wide & only wanted half the work done on it that we had done. At lunch the C.O. told us C.C., Maj. & Sec in Com of Batt. had come through & also leave was not down so no one would be going. C.C. appeared in orders at night. Also Beal took over 'C' Co., A D Walker came to 'A' & Diplock took over signallers. In afternoon Burn & I walked up to see the Roads - but in coming C.O. told us 'A' Co were to be taken off roads & 'C' Co put on entirely. Also the men of 'A' Co at the transport were to be recalled. C.C. & Burn were beaten by the C.O. & I at Bridge after mess. We sat up till about 12.0. Wrote Kaye.

7-6-16   Burn took party up to Maricourt. In the morning I walked up & saw the work & brought Burn back. A D Walker took 2 platoons 1 & 2 to Bath & brought Holmes & his party back. After lunch we had 1½ hours bombing & bayonet fighting for No 1 & 2 Platoons. Then at 5 o'clock we had kit inspection for the whole Company. That evening we were put in - No 1 & 2 to Grove Avenue & No 3 & 4 to Mersey Street after the camouflage was wiped out by the C.O. No Bridge. Potter rode over to transport to go on leave. Letter from Kaye.

8-6-16   Went up at 8.45 with C.S.M. Williams to the trenches. Burn Walker & Bretherton went up at 8.0. Started on Grove Avenue. I walked round with Burn & saw everyone at work. Got back to 'B' Co & had lunch with Dixon & G.H. Walker. Came back at 3.30 about. C.O. came in later & said they had found a dead man which stunk the place out. C.C. went on a Court martial on an officer in 18 Man. He was junior Off on the board. No letters & wrote none. Another pouring wet day especially at night. Bridge with C.O., C.C. & Bridge withC.O. v C.C. & Burn at night. Rice & Craig off the strength. C.O. told us Kitchener was dead[112].

9-6-16   Went round trenches in morning - walked up to Peronne Road with Woods & from there on & saw Walker in Grove Avnue - then went round to see Burn at the other end of Mersey Street. Came back for lunch at 2.0. In afternoon had bath & reported to C.O. ..... had no letters or parcels. Had orders to clear out of dug out as taken over by R.F.A. Had no bridge but went to bed early. Fine all day but shower at night.

10-6-16   Very wet in morning. Decided to go up in aft to trenches but then remembered I had promised to go out with C.C. to tea with Miller. So went up. When I was with Walker a thunderstorm started - after getting nearly wet through it seemed to have stopped - I set out for ..... & got absolutely wet through as it came down again in ..... - got back & changed & had lunch & then rode over with C.C. to Miller at Div Dug outs & had tea with him. He came over & had dinner with 'D' Co also 2 Sussex men. Culshaw came back after mess. Williams did return as he was doing business for the C.O. Letter from Kaye & wrote her.

11-6-16   Got up at 8.0 o'clock & took morning parade & went up & took A D Walker party - stopping up there all day. Got plenty of shells near but nothing much doing otherwise. Got back at about 5.45 very dirty. Saw Elstob, Worthington & Ramsden in the trenches. Burn better.

12-6-16   Went up with C.C. in the morning & went round the trenches. In the night some infantry had dug fire steps in Grove Av & Mersey St as the French had intercepted a Bosch message that they were going to attack us that night & someone had got the wind up about it. On the way through C..l..n St we saw Worthington shaving & had a chat with

---

[112] Lord Kitchener drowned on 5 June 1916 when HMS Hampshire hit a mine and sank west of the Orkney Islands. More than 600 were killed.

him. At Maricourt Av & Mersey St we met the C.O. & Adj. & had a talk to them. On the way back on the Peronne Road we met Panet. Going out we met Re....r & a Seaforth Sub in the Pioneers - they claim to be the first pioneers formed (1914 Nov). Panet said their C.O. had got rid of 25 officers. When we got back we found 6 Act Off R.G.A. having mess. They had brought up 6 6" Hows[113] & were putting them in at the bottom of the Valley in our old dug outs. Maj Arnott & a Capt were messing at 'A' Co table. In evening a draft of 39 turned up. Wrote to Kaye. Got letter from her.

13-6-16   Went up with Culshaw to trenches as he was taking the draft & 1 platoon of 'C' Co up to work there. I paraded the draft at 9.0 for C.O. but he put it off till 3.0 p.m. so I had a kit inspection & then went up. It rained most of the way. Cully left us at Grove Av West end & went round the rest of the trenches. Saw Bretherton but not A D Walker. Got back about 1.30 getting from Grove Av East & to Dug outs in 40 minutes. Changed & spent evening in. C.O. went to Div & dined with C.R.E. to talk over the Staff. C.C. & I played bridge with E.O. & Burn we won easily. Went to bed about 11.30. The Bosch started a Strafe & sent quite a quantity of shells over - ..... lachrymatory. Wounded 6 of 'B' Co. The draft got the wind up & ran into the ...per trench left a lot of tools & equipment & stuff standing in trench. Changed a lot of rifles & also equipment with a lot of 17th Manchester people & generally misbehaved themselves. Strafe ended about 12.15. Woods was sent to Hospital with nerves.

14-6-16   Did nothing much all morning - it rained a bit & I & C.C. talked to R.G.A. Capt. Had lunch early & then went over to trenches. Went all down Mersey Av & saw picks, tools & rifles & equipment etc left by draft. Saw Bretherton then on along Maricourt Av & along Seymour St & Hill St where 'B' Co were supposed to have been working. Fearfully dirty & tons of tools etc lying about. Back along Support Av which was also fearfully dirty. Saw camouflage on the way & then back very tired for tea & dinner. C.O. had us to a conflab at 5.0. Told the Company Commanders what we had to do in Strafe. 'B' Co's place for 5 days strafe from 20th then I had to assemble in 'U; defences & then go down in 2 parties to along Support Av, along front line to left, to A9/3 & A9/4. A. D. Walker taking furthest & myself nearer. He had 1 & 2 plat. I have 3 & 4. C.O. went out so Burn & I played C.C. & Williams & won easily.

[113] Howitzers

15-6-16 All off. staff to go to Corbie tomorrow so this is last entry for a bit. C.O. & C.C., M.O. Burn & I & C.S.M. Williams all went up to trenches in morning. Split at the camouflage & C.C., Burn, I & C.S.M. went on & saw the entrance to our Russian Sap[114] A9/4 & 9/3. C.C. & Burn went back & C.S.M. & I went along & up Maricourt Av & along Mersey Street & Grove Av. Saw A.D.W. Got back for lunch at 3 o'clock. Packed all evening. Letter from Kaye. C.O. told us 5 days Art Strafe - also they were going to blow up a communication trench so our work would be easier. Time was put on an hour[115] between 14th & 15th so that 11 p.m. of 14th became 12 midnight 14/15th. Changed into C.O.'s dug out. C.C. remained in the other.

16-6-16 Sent all superfluous luggage in the morning to Corbie. Wandered up with the C.O. to the trenches & had a look round. Saw Walker. The C.O. said I had to dig a trench 500 yds long to accommodate a Batt otherwise it would have to stay out in the open. So I said I could & then I had to wait for orders from Capt Wright as to when to dig it. Cully took the party out at 8.30 & just as I was going after him I intercepted a note to the C.O. from Wright so took it to him & found we had to dog the trench between Maricourt Av & Weston St. Overtook Cully & checked where to put it & when he came up put him on the job. Got back about 11.30 a.m. Found them playing Bridge. Went in & saw C.O. & Adj who were in bed reading.

17-6-16 Took up Piggott, Howden & Henshall to show them right along Support Av right up to the Russian Saps. went along them. They were about 270 ft long & 'T' shaped at end. Very hot & damp in them. Did not stay long. Then I let the other 3 return via West Av & I went along the front line to Machine Gun Wood & along Maricourt Av & up Grove Av. Had a look at Cully's work last night & back along Mersey Street & then Weston St & up through Downe's Redoubt & back to lunch at 3.0. After lunch went down with C.C. & saw the new 6 fire for the first time - twice. Letters from Mrs Townsend & Kaye. Wrote Kaye & mother.

18-6-16 Slept all morning had early lunch & went up to trenches with Karl & Willy. Left Willy at entrance to Support Av. Went on with C.C. along

---

[114] A trench dug towards the enemy on or close to the surface, but with some sort of cover on it.

[115] The introduction of British Summer Time (or Daylight Saving Time) which had come into force in the UK on 21 May 1916.

Camouflage to Maricourt Av. Found that Wright had taken Walker off trenches & put us on some more in Downes Redoubt. Went down to front line & saw AP3 & 4 which an entrance to Sap 3 & 4 it forms & returned for tea. Saw C.O. & then W.G. Hitchen & dean & Featherby. Then Dixon & Garton & finally an aeroplane strafe. After tea the C.O., C.C. & I went down & had drinks with Maj Arnott 28 Siege Batt R.G.A. The Strafes had apparently been put off. Saw Sim - a subaltern from A.S.D. after my time who was in another Batt. Arnott came in after dinner. No mail in.

19-6-16   Went up in morning with C.C. & Burn & saw Walker & Bretherton in Trenches in Downes Redoubt. Got back for lunch at 3.0. Hindle turned up for spades as he had a Batt of S.Africans on a wire line trench. Asked him to tea. Went & saw Arnott with the mad Doctor who had to leave including being relieved. Had some Revolver practice at Walker's tin hat. Put 2 through it. After dinner Burn & I just had one rubber v. C.C. & C.O. Fine day.

20-6-16   Went out in morning with Bretherton. Burn being late. Got up there & found C.O. & Adj. so came back with them via Maricourt & Peronne Road. After lunch felt rotten then lay down & went to sleep. Handle came & had lunch with C.O. Tea at 5.30. After tea we had stump cricket till dinner. Fine & hot day. Got letter from Kaye & photos of Sonia[116] with Kaye. Potter returned in the evening with wonderful rumours - leave etc starting again!!

21-6-16   Went up to trenches with C.C. & met C.O. & Panet up then returned for lunch at 2.15. Wrote letters in afternoon. Played stump cricket in evening. No post at all.

22-6-16   Went up to the trenches by myself as C.C. & Miller were late. Went up via Support Av. new & camouflage. Saw Panet & C.C. & Adj up there. Left C.O. at Grid & went round after & back by myself. Back to lunch at 3.0. Letter from Kaye. Wrote to her. Rode out with C.C. & saw D.W. Dug outs with Parsons too. Played bridge after dinner.

23-6-16   Got orders to trench board new Support Av trench. Needless to say orders from Payne are incorrect & A D walker had to hunt around before he could find any place to put them. Went down early & saw him. Then went on complete round of Grove Av. The Grid & Mersey St with Burn & got back for lunch at 3.0. Found the Batt had

---

[116] A. T. Champion's daughter.

to move from Trigger Valley at 10 a.m. On the way back from the trenches A. D. Walker's servant Richardson[117] was killed by shell in entrance to tunnel under Peronne Road. Company moved about 9.30. I saw Maj Arnott just before leaving & left about 10.15. Got in to Etinehem by 12.0. all men transport turned up by 1.0 a.m. 'A' & 'B' were in Etinehem 'C' & 'D' in Bray.

24-6-16   Did nothing all morning. Matthews turned up in morning & had lunch with us. If afternoon I went a ride with Bob to Ecluse & saw Wyatt & fixed dinner next night with him. Got back about 4.30 & found G.O.C. was to inspect the 2 Companies at 5.0. Got there & he addressed us very favourably. As usual the Adj. was very officious. After tea we went up to view the strafe from the mill but saw very little that being 'U' day the day the artillery started. After dinner we played vingt-et-un & other games of & with Matthews. He stayed & slept the night in the mess room. We fixed up a bed etc. Wrote Kaye.

25-6-16   Got up for going to service but a note came that the C.O. would take us to Amiens so Dixon C.C. the C.O. & I went to dinner & got there about 11.30. Through Corbie & Daours. Maj Arnott lent the C.O. his car. Had a bath & lunched at Rest. des Huites & then bought a lot of strawberries etc & came back via Villers Bocage having tea there with the Special Brig. R.E. Corp attached to the 4th Army. They seemed to be officers from Col Fenn's old Batt. We returned through Amiens & Corbie. Miller & A D Walker were also in Amiens & came up to Villers Bocage. Stopped at cabin for petrol & got back for dinner. With Keys. Found Matthews had cleared off & also we had to move tomorrow to Bray, bed very early. 'V' day.

26-6-16   Had a practice of the digging schemes in the "Push" up at the trenches above our Billet & then rode over to Bray with C.C. to see our billets. Burn brought the company along & we got in nicely before lunch 'A' & 'B' Co in the same hour as had the officers. 'W' day. Company & ..... in billets by 12.30. We had a house on the square opposite the church. Company towards Etinehem direction. Stayed in all afternoon. Bosch put in a few shells into Bray. Rode over to Etinehem about 7.0. Wyatt's car went over & I had dinner with Wyatt, Col Ainslie, Capt Bridges R.A.M.C. & Lt Parker A.S.C. Adj. Played cards with first 3 & stayed till 12. Motored back to Averfin ..... Bray, Corbie Hill & got in about 2.0 a.m. 'C' Co had had a shell into their officers mess & killed their cook Hill & wounded C.Q.M.S.

---

[117] Pte. 20572 Joseph Richardson.

Barton slightly. One came by our cooker & Booth collapsed with nerves.

27-6-16   'Y' day. Got up about 10.30. Went round to Bat. H.Q. Got orders to turn a platoon out to work on some saps in Billon Valley. Burn took No 2 out at 2 o'clock as he had to stay behind with C.C. & Struthers during the Strafe. I rode out with Parsons in the afternoon at 3 o'clock - he was going up to see Culshaw who had been found tight by Brig. Gen. Jack...ich-West the night before. Saw the men working - fearful din going on - Ginger very restless. Walked over to 'B' Co old place & got our eyes badly gassed. Came back & had tea with Maj. Arnott & Capt Gilpin & Burn. Got back about 6 o'clock. After dinner had bridge with Burn C.C. & the C.O. Lost 5 Francs. Bed at 12 o'clock.

28-6-16   Got up about 10 o'clock. 'Y' day. Made every preparation for going up to 'U' defences at 4.30. Got orders that had to be there at 7.30 so changed parades to 4.0. Was to inspect Gas Helmets at 2.0. At about 11.30 the C.O. came round & said the Push was postponed about 48 hours so everything was cancelled. Polly came to tea & Capt Bicker..... 18 Liverpools came in to see Burn just before dinner & stayed pretty late. After dinner we went round & played Bridge with the C.O. Warning came through about 7.0 that the Hun was going to strafe Bray at night & also the Town Major said the C.O. had to turn out of 123 men's billets - so he decided that he would send all men unable to find cellar accommodation to the Transport. The whole of 'A' Co. Walker & & Bretherton went over to the Transport to sleep.

29-6-16   Got up about 11.0 & went over on the ..... to the Transport. Saw Walker, Bretherton & Diplock ..... the ..... All the men seemed alright. I had them some ...... Got back for lunch. Played cards & wrote all afternoon. Got a letter from Kaye. Wrote to her. Had tea at H.Q. & then at 'A' Co & then back to billet. Burn went out mistakenly thinking he had to take a platoon out to the trenches & spent the day out there. Got back for dinner. After we went round & played bridge with C.O. & C.C. C.C. & I just lost. Featherby got a cushy wound in the leg & Struthers took his place.

30-6-16   'Y' day. Did nothing much all the morning. Went down to transport at 12 o'clock & saw to bayonet wire cutters & then after lunch went round & saw the C.O. Had parade at 3 o'clock & went up to Batt dumps & picked up tools etc & set off to "U" defences. Plat 1 & 2 went the right way via 'X' road& 3 & 4 went ..... via Bronfay Farm.

We all got to 'U'. Burn went back & got hold of No 3 & 4. Miller was in with M. G. Sect in U⁵. 'C' Co in Napier's Redoubt. ½ 'D' in Chateau Redoubt & ½ in Communication Trenches. ½ 'B' in reserve in ..... Valley & other ½ with 'C' Co. As 2nd Yorks were not in I had to wait till they came before arranging when we were to go over. We dug ourselves into the side of the trench so that we could lie down. Went down with A D Walker & saw Col. Young of the 2nd Yorks at about 12.30. he said not too soon & at any rate not before 20 mins after Zero. Heard Zero was at 7.30 a.m. M.O. & his lot were in 'U'. Bombardment quite intense but we got nothing back from the Bosch.

```
            PRELIMINARY ORDERS.

"A" COY.

No 3 party will consist of 2 platoons of "A" Coy under Capt Champio
No 4 party      ditto      ditto    ditto    under 2nd Lt A.D.
                                                       Walker.

Both parties will assemble in "U" works North of Peronne Road on a
day to be fixed later.

No 3 Party will open up Communication trench from Sap No 6 (A 9/3)
at head of Support Avenue to enemy's trenches and onwards into
enemy's lines.

No 4 Party will open communication trench from Sap No 5 (A 9/4)
(West Avenue) to enemy's trenches and onwards.

Both parties No 4 leading will move up SUPPORT AVENUE to our first
line trench as soon as the supporting battn of 21st Infy Brigade
has left its assembly trenches. On reaching the front line the
leading man will wheel to the left. Both parties will move along
the front trench until opposite their respective saps. They will
leave the front line trench over the top and get to work simul-
taneously on both ends of the communication trench as soon as the
supporting battalion 21st Infy Brigade has crossed enemy's
support line.
On completion of these trenches each party is to prolong its
trench into enemy's lines along existing trenches.

O.C. each party will reconnoitre enemy's trenches he has to deal
with while the party is completing its final task.

Each man will carry pick and shovel and 6 Sandbags.

O.C. "A" Coy is responsible that all Officers & Sergeants under
his command thoroughly understand what their parties have to do,
and that they study the ground and the map of the enemy's
trenches beforehand.
He will also be responsible for getting in touch with the support-
ing Battn 21st Infantry Brigade.

Detailed orders will be issued later.
```

1-7-16   'Z' day. Could not sleep owing to cold & noise. Bombardment started at 6.30 about. Very intense till 7.30 & then the front line went over. There was a very heavy mist so we could not see much except shells exploding. Beautiful day & plenty of sun. Aeroplanes by the dozen & sausages galore. Went down & met C.O. & Potter & orderly MacGorman. Platoons got rather messed up on the way down as we were going into H.Q. trench & out again but only No 1 & 2 did so they were right whereas we in 3 & 4 were wrong. Bretherton & I got a very hot shelling down at the bottom end of Support but somehow got through alright. We got No 1 & 2 out alright then C.O. ordered us out so we got & went over about 8.30. When I got out there was only 6 men with me. Got them started the Bosch end of the trench. Frodsham[118] was very cool & told his men to keep cool & got them to working alright. I went back towards the front trench & as our first 4 men got out a shell blew the lot into the air. They all got out though & got to work. Bob & Jackson doing very well & got them all posted out. I left Bob in charge & went on to reconnoitre the Bosch lines having no orderly or servant or anyone near me. I went on up Siberia Trench & then came back & had a look at the men. Found Fletcher had been wounded & Sergt Jackson & Small killed. We worked all that day with a lot of casualties. Found a very nice officer i/c of Sap who went out with the Oi/c other sap & pulled in heaps of wounded our stretcher bearers being absolutely napoo[119]. About 10.15 W G Fletcher & 2 platoons came & started removing the tops of the Russian Saps. I got a few minutes nap. The Adj. came round about 11.30 p.m. L/Sergt Williams[120] was v. good all day.

Our casualties are

Killed	Wounded
20070 Sgt Jackson T.	20079 Sgt Hunwick E.
21879 Sgt Small J.	20053 L/Sgt Holmes H.
20087 L/Cpl Allender B.	20128 L/Cpl Gosling F.
21316 Pte Ovens F.	20136 L/Cpl Birks W.
21054 Pte Oakes W.	20040 L/Cpl Shaw A.
20168 Pte Hodgins J.	20215 Pte Grace C.
21378 Pte Houghton T.	20228 Pte Turner R.
21240 Pte Beckett T.	20193 Pte Turner F.
21367 Pte McDonald J.	21921 Pte Stanley C.
21909 Pte Skelhorn J.	20196 Pte Rogerson J.
21803 Pte Montgomery T.	20000 Pte Galsworthy R.
21473 Pte Mullen J.	21354 Pte Kilshaw W.

---

[118] L/Cpl. John Frodsham was awarded the Military Medal for his actions on the day.
[119] Slang meaning 'used up', from the French "il n'y en a plus" meaning 'there is no more'.
[120] L/Sgt. John Williams was awarded the Military Medal for his actions on the day.

20057 Pte Bryan W.	20135 Pte Sowerbutts N.
13 killed	21980 Pte Malone A.
	20047 Pte O'Reilly H.
	20413 Pte Greenall T.
	20103 Pte Kiernan B.
	21627 Pte Dysart W.
	20108 Pte Cowley G.
	21576 Pte Smith A.
	21097 Pte Barclay T. S.
	20262 Pte Langton H.
	21884 Pte Ormesher H.
	20154 Pte Pennington T.
	21823 Pte Robinson T.
	20110 Pte Howden J.
	21600 Pte Ashton J.
	21629 Pte Glover H.
	21604 Pte Downey R.
	20176 Pte Alcock E.
	20094 Pte Cook F.
	20202 Pte Owen R.
	20148 Pte Crompton P.

21365 Pte Nolan J reported missing at first but found out after 14 days to be wounded. Parsons, Williams, J H Fletcher all wounded & Garton[121] killed.

2-7-16   About 3 a.m. I got orders to take the men back to rest in our Trenches. I got them into Dixons Ditch at last No 3 & 4 - No 1 & 2 proposed to sleep in their own trench. I could not get any sleep being too cold. Had a man shot when cleaning rifles next morning. About 10 a.m. I got them back on the job & started work again. Not half as much shelling & very much quieter all round. Saw the C.O. once or twice & Potter who came calling for a short time. That evening we went back to Dixons Ditch about 10 p.m. About 9 p.m. an officer from the Seaforth Pioneers 9th Div came along & I handed over to him. About 3 a.m. I got the following note from the C.O. "Your

3-7-16   two parties will be relieved tonight by ...afles (probably Seaforths) after resting for at least 6 hours please arrange with C.C.'s parties in Saps 3 & 4 to work shifts with them until tomorrow evening. The Platoon of B who was in reserve & the 2 platoons of D who were maintaining communication trenches will also assist. If possible work

---

[121] Lt. Reginald Garton, aged 19.

should be continued on the 2 new trenches i.e. Stanley & Maricourt avenues continued." I had been woken up by the Adj coming round at about 2.15 & had been unable to go to sleep again so had a walk round to Gully up West Av & into 'U' defences & then I met the orderly with the ..... I had some breakfast & went round to the place via Maricourt & M.O.'s place about 5 a.m. Saw Kettle & Dean & both said the two parties had gone back - presumably relieved. I met Lt Ra.....ttom of the Sp. R.E. & got back about 6.30 a.m. & I wrote the following note to Adj. "Have been all round by Saps 3 & 4 & find no signs of any S.L.R. except Mr Dean & the M.O.'s place. Cpl Kettle & Mr Dean both report that the two parties have left for H.Q. I went all round Faviere & Glatz Alley & find them quite good except in places & infantry are working on these places. The ...aples? are working on Sap 5 & Sap 15 the end of Siberia Alley & have practically finished that. Am waiting further orders which I hope to get by return & favourably!" We then waited & got the following reply from the Adj. "The C.O. wishes you to carry out the orders that you received last night please & to arrange with 'B' & 'C' Coys." I wrote back "Received note. Would like to know where 'B' & 'C' Coys are to be found as they are not at their ..... work. Would also like to know how I am to carry out work I know absolutely nothing about?" I got a note from the C.O. "B & C Coys are now at work on saps AP3 & 4. Capt Dixon is up there & knows what has to be done." So took the company round there. Found not enough work for the whole company so sent Walker & No 1 & 2 back to behind Gird Avenue. Bretherton & No 3 & 4 started on the sap from Ca.....t Trench towards Glatz Alley. Walker relieved Bretherton about 2.30. Was talking to Capt Shaw RAMC when they started straffing us - so had to run for it. Capt Shaw was from Glasgow & belonged to S.A.I. From there we got back to U defences where the company stayed tonight. Bretherton & I getting a good ..... of Capt the Rev Balla... in the dressing station. 'C' Co went & bivouacked about 47. We went into 'U'. D & B out digging. I slept at H.Q. in Sniper Valley.

4-7-16   Two companys came in about 11.0 a.m. & about 3.0 set off for Bois de Tailles calling in at the Transport just off the Bray Road on the way to Grovetown & had a meal & a fine drink of Beer. Got to Bois de Tailles about 10.0. Men very cheery & wearing all their souvenirs. Got to H.Q. about 1.30. C.C. rode with us & was very impressed by men being so cheery. Diplock became Adj. Payne C.O.2 of 'B' Co.

5-7-16   Had nothing to do all day. About 5.0 a.m. 'A' & 'C' Co had orders to "stand to" ready to move off at ¼ hours notice. At about 11 p.m. I had order to report to Gen Sackville West G.O.C. 21st Brig. He told me he wanted me to go up & cut 4 pathways through Bernafay Wood. Companies to go up that night to Cambridge Copse & sleep there. Burn took them up both companies & I slept the night at Bois de Tailles.

6-7-16 Got up at 4.30 & rode down to 'U' defences. Started at 5.10. Called in at RE dump Bray about bill hooks & got up to 'U' defences at 6.0 exactly. Hard going. Found companies at Cambridge Copse & proceeded up to Bernafay Wood. We set to work on the four paths. A D Walker & 1 & 3 Plat doing southern one. Bretherton & 2 & 4 Plat doing No 2. E.O.C. & 2 Plat doing No 3. Culshaw & 2 Plat doing No 4. we got all done in about 4 hours & then got back. Was not very satisfied with the job. It was very bad going as they shelled rather a lot. Got back to 'U' defences & had lunch. Cooh..... came up. C.C. & Mullen came up to see the work. I went back to camp early about 1.45. Company set off about 2.15. Got halfway back to between Bronfay & Bray & got orders to turn back & remain up there ready for next start. I got lunch & told the C.O. how tired the men were so he sent orders out to recall them & sent off 'B' & 'D' Cos. Cos got back to Cambridge Copse before they got the order. Ultimately they got back about 12 midnight. C.C. brought them back - most got rides in motor lorries. 'C' & 'D' got ready to go up but were put off 24 hours.

7-6-16 Rest all day. 'B' & 'D' Co set out to go up about 5.0. It poured with rain all day & was fearfully wet. Played bridge with C.O. Mullen & Burn. C.O.& I won. C.O. said I had been passed by the G.O.C. Div. for the M.C.!

8-6-16 Batt had orders for 'A' & 'C' Co to go to Talus Boise[122] & the H.Q. to go to Copse Valley so we started off at 3.0 & went via Bronfay Fram where I rode in to see about tools. Got the Companies down to Talus Boise & found only 50 shovels & 50 picks. Adj. had ordered a G.S. Wagon with 200 of each to come up to us. We found lots of Bosch prisoners there & also wounded all coming down from Trones Wood. The 2nd Yorks & 2nd Wilts 16 & 18 Man & 20 Liv all got cut up badly there taking the Wood. Rations & Tools came to Carnoy & got stuck there. Got transport about 5 a.m. We got orders about 10.30 p.m.to report to Glatz Redoubt at 9.30 p.m.so I sent off

---

[122] A thin line of woodland south of Montauban.

Simon[123] & 50 men & went along & drew Tools off 'B' Co. Got them & Simon came back & stated we were not needed - the 21st Brig at the Bricketerie had told him. It turned out that 'B' Co had had nothing to do but remained at Oxford Copse. 'D' Co had gone up & had to come back gradually nothing to do & shell fire too heavy. W G Fletcher got back injured & went to hospital.

9-7-16   Got order to return to Copse Valley. Rations & Tools having turned up we had breakfast & got to Copse Valley about 6.30 a.m. All asleep. The cooks lost a sack of mine containing mackintosh, mess tin, etc etc. I slept all afternoon & then got orders to report with B & D Co to Brig. H.Q. 95th Brig at Train Alley so we went up. Potter, Dixon & I & we had to dig a trench from S.E. area of Bernafay Wood to the Sunken trench from the Bricketerie to Maltz Horn Farm. We got to it about 11 p.m. & started 'B' Co at Bernafay end & 'A' Co at the other end. They shelled us pretty badly & we had 9 casualties in 'A' Co. We left about 1.30 & got back to Copse Valley via Maricourt at about 5.30 a.m.

          Killed   20189 Pte Webster C.
          Wounded   20194 Pte Rogerson J.
                        20201 Pte Wilkinson V.
                        21593 Pte Jackson T.
                        21366 Pte Millington C.
                        20160 Pte Brown J.
                        20118 Pte Parr J.
                        20204 Sgt. O'Brien J. Shell Shock
          Missing   20200 Pte Kay R.

10-7-16   Did nothing all day. Capt Wright R.E. turned up to tea & tried to get the Batt to dig trenches round S. End of Trones Wood in daylight after the infantry had finished but Col Panet came in & squashed all that. So 'B' "C" "D" Co went up & dug them that night. 'B' & 'C' did their work but 'D' did nothing - came back & reported Hun in Trones Wood & holding it. 'A' Co went out & dug a signal wire line towards the Bricketerie in two parties - 6 p.m.to 12 - 12.50 a.m. I stayed in & played bridge with Diplock & C.C. & C.O. Bed about 12.10 a.m.

11-7-16   Did nothing all day in evening Wright came in & gave us our work. 'B' & 'A' had to go up to the Hairpin & dig the trench from Maltz

---

[123] Probably Lt. Carril H. Symon.

Horn Farm Trench to Trones Wood & also from Maltz Horn Farm Trench to the farm itself. 'D' Co had to open out the trench from Bernafay Wood to Trones Wood. We set out about 8.30 p.m. & got up to Maricourt. Mullen came with 'A' to help. I put him on putting out the bombers. 'B' Co went in front but went wrong in Maricourt & we got in front, rested outside as it was still too light & then went up. Bosch was shelling very heavily & we had to cross a barrage but we got up safely to the hairpin & then found Col Cobham 20th Liv. He told us Bosch had retaken Trones Wood so I sent 'B' Co back under Dixon - keeping his bombers only. We waited up there about an hour hoping to hear further from the Brigade. We were heavily shelled about 12.0 just after 'B' Co had gone but had no casualties. We then heard from Col Cobham that the French had caught a prisoner in possession of a paper stating the Hun were going to attack Maltz Horn Farm at 2 a.m. in strength also he was only 60 yards from it - so the C.O. & I agreed it was better to get home. The Company got out easily & when Miller & I came with Ellison & Piggott about 5 min later we got about 50-100 Whizz Bangs at us but by extra speed in running we luckily got there. We could not believe the company had got away so quickly so we waited outside both ends of Maricourt for about 1 hour & then gave it up & got home to Copse Valley to find the Company had got in alright about 2 a.m. Maltz Horn Trench running up ..... Trones Wood & Maltz Horn Farm the Bosch could attack from other side. It was very humorous seeing the French who were fearfully excited near the lines looking both ways.

12-7-16   Did nothing all day expected order to do work undone the night before. But in the afternoon Col Glasgow C.O. of Sussex Pioneers came along & said he had order to relieve us. Later order came through from Div for our Company to remain. Dixon said he & his men were prepared to remain so 'B' Co remained - under orders of the 18th Div & the remainder to return to Grovetown & take over the Sussex old place near R.E. dump. We set out about 8.0 p.m. leaving Sussex in possession - saw Maj Walker their C.O.2 & Capt D. Jong their Adj. Horses did not turn up except the C.O.'s so had to walk all the way & got ..... about 11 p.m. with a hut to myself for the night. There was plenty of accommodation for all the men & officers under cover. The first since 'Y' day 30.6.16.

13-7-16   C.C. got Maj Arnott's car so C.C. Burn C.O. & myself went off about 11.0 to Amiens. The car had to take a spare part of a gun to Corbie & we wasted a bit of time there. But got to Amiens about 1.0. Had quite a good lunch at Rest. Godbert & a bath after that the other three got their hair cut. Tea at the chocolate shop & back via Corbie. Got in in time for dinner. Henshall got all my things from Corbie. I got some M.C. ribbon at Amiens. Lt Thompson Sp R.E. Brig came to dinner. He knew the C.O. & we had bridge after. C.O. & I lost to him & Potter.

14-7-16 Rained hard in the morning. Company went to bath; did not get up till about 11.0 a.m. Rode over with C.C. Burn & Culshaw to Bronfay Farm to look for .... Cavalry were there. Found part of the 2nd Ind Div Cav. Craig being in 3rd Hussars 2nd English Div was no ..... there. Burn went in by himself to Talus Boise & found 7th D.G. & Laurie Hastings who had been out on patrol with 4 men & ..... & had found it v. hard going, was going out again at night with whole Reg. Cully left us as we were going to Fricourt. C.C. & I saw Fricourt & returned for dinner. Bridge with C.C. & Burn & C.O. C.C. & I lost to Burn & C.O. Wrote Kaye.

15-7-16 Company inspected by the C.O. at 10. Not bad but had not all taken their equipment to bits. Had 2 hours drill & after lunch Burn & I rode out again for Craig. Went to Meault & then Dernancourt & found there that the 2nd Cav Div English was at Arras - also the raid for North Wood & 7th D.G. & Poona Farm was quite a success only 36 casualties. So rode on to Heilly via Ville & Treux & Buire. Had tea ..... & cakes between us & got back via Mericourt, Treux & Morlancourt. Found C.O. had gone to Amiens. Bridge with C.C. v. Burn & Mullen. Won 10 francs. Letter from Kaye & wrote Kaye.

16-7-16 Did nothing all day. Was going to Amiens but could not get the car. Karl & others went to Corbie. In afternoon 7 officers from the 12th Worcester Reg Pioneers turned up. Seemed a good set of fellows. Rained hard all afternoon. C.O., C.C., Burn & I played bridge. Burn & C.O. won. 'D' Co relieved 'B' Co at Copse Valley so Potter & Co went off & Dixon & Co came here. C.O. ..... for Amiens tomorrow. Letter & parcel from mother. Wrote Kaye.

Lieut C. Brackenbury C. Coy.
2nd Lt T. N. Bishop A. Coy.
2nd Lt S W. McLeod Braggins A. Coy.
2nd Lt W. Ridsdale B. Coy.
2nd Lt E. J. Coulson B. Coy.
2nd Lt C. T. Griffiths D. Coy.
2nd Lt A. W. Lewis D. Coy.

17-7-16   Going with C.O., C.C. & Burn to Amiens, car coming at 11.0. Did not turn up but a note to say it would again at 2.15. Had lunch doing nothing all morning. Company had one hour's drill. Car ultimately arrived about 4.15. Went round by Villers Bocage. The car having to leave two guns there & get 2 new ones. Rained most of the way. Got to Amiens about 6.30. Got a cocktail at an American Bar opp. Rest des Huites. Saw Basil Hall..... & another Robertson of 17th Liverpools who complemented me on M.C.! Had a terrific dinner of Hors d'oevre - Sole - L'inguste poulet - Strawberries & cream & peaches. Walked streets till 10.35. Got back about 12.30 a.m. rather an uncomfortable journey.

18-7-16   Rained hard in morning. In afternoon cleared a bit & Company had 1 hours drill. Burn C.C. & I rode over to Meaulte & picked up Laurie Hastings, R.....y Marsd..... & Aizlewood. First two in 7th D.G. & last in 4th D.G. All went to tea at Heilly & drank fizz. Got back about 8.0 p.m. Johnson Sp R.E.s to dinner. He & I lost to C.O. & C.C. at bridge. Bed about 11.30. Burn came in & talked till about 1.30 a.m.

19-7-16   Orders came through of G.O.C.'s inspection tomorrow. Had 2 hours drill in morning & cleaning equipment. Beautiful day. Burn & I rode out to bring in some Bosch Guns from Mametz Wood & then rode on to Heilly for tea. Came back by 7.0 & rode round by Sailly-le-Sec & Sailly Laurette & saw Wyatt & Col Ainslie at the latter place. Got back for dinner at 8.0. Laurie Hastings & Marsd..... turned up & we had a good rowdy dinner.

20-7-16   Orders came through for moving to Happy Valley[124]. Nothing about the inspection. In afternoon we moved. C.O., C.C. & Burn went off to Amiens with Thompson Sp R.E. & saw Laurie Hastings & Marsd..... then dined at Godbert. I stayed in all time & rode with Miller over & saw Fricourt. Got back for tea.

21-7-16   Drill in the morning for 2 hours. In afternoon Burn C.C. Mullen & I went over & saw Albert & then on to Heilly & had tea & then back. C.C. & Miller called in at Morlancourt & saw L..... who is an M.O. in 5th Div. Got back for dinner. Potter & Dixon went to Amiens. C.C. & I lost to C.O. & Burn at bridge.

---

[124] A valley which was used as the main supply route during the attempts to advance the line at High Wood near Bazentin-le-Petit.

22-7-16   Burn & I rode on to Heilly to tea via 7th D.G. Camp. Came back short cut over the top by Morlancourt happened to see Wyatt on the way in his car. At 5.0 moved to the Talus Boise. Got there at 10.0. in morning drill from 7.0 - 8.0 & from 9.30 - 11.30.

23-7-16   Spent all day getting the men into their billets & places so no work at night. I slept in pipe trench in the South end of Talus Boise with just a piece of tin over & some chalk on that & slept on a trench board.

24-7-16   Work at night. Batt mess started under a tarpaulin. Work was a cable trench from the dug outs in Sunken Road to Trones Wood. As 'D' had done least they took the Trones Wood end then 'C' 'B' & so 'A'. It was to be 1ft x 3ft 6". 'D' made a muck of the job & wanted me to send men up to help but as I got to work about 1 hour before I left as soon as I had done my work. Burn was hit & we had a few casualties.

25-7-16   Still on cable line. To be cut 2ft x 3ft. Heard Potter & Payne complained that 'A' did not do its share of work so I walked up with C.O. to D.H.Q. & he said he knew all about it & I need not trouble. We did not get it finished by a long way that night though we dug it down 2 or 3 places correctly. 'D' Co still had about 100 yds untouched up at their end & the rest was not really finished.

26-7-16   'C' & 'A' on cable line again. 'B' & 'D' on another towards Maltz Horn Farm as on previous nights 'D' Co lost itself also 'C'. There was a lot of gas about that night & Braggins & two platoons got held up in the Glatz Redoubt. But turned up 2 hours late & got to work. I think I must have got a dose of gas that night. Still more dropping into Montauban all the night. They made a very funny hissing sound going over. C.C. came up but went back early.

27-7-16   Feeling very queer all day thought it was flu. Potter went to Hospital with gas. I got worse as the day went on. But having been given some special dug out in the Sunken Road to do went up there with my orderlies in the evening & pegged them out. C.R.E. saw C.O. about them & Hall came to tea. Got them pegged out & then went to tea. Woke up in the middle of the night feeling rotten & sent for the doctor who gave me some pills & I got to sleep.

28-7-16   About 2 a.m. when I called the M.O. Henshall went off early in the morning to Happy Valley where Transport was & returned about 12 with mess cart for me. I heard we had no casualties the night before but C.S.M. Norbury 'D' Co was killed. I lay down in the bottom of the mess & cart & had a very rough, fearful & jerky ride to Happy Valley & got into bed in the canteen being sick while doing it. In the evening Woolcock got me a truck so they carried me over in the bed.

29-7-16   In bed with pretty high temperature as M.O. from RAMC att 21st Brig came to see me & gave me some pills. I had practically nothing to eat & felt pretty bad. Temp 102. M.O. said he would see me in the evening but he did not turn up. Very bad day. 'A' Co went up & dug a trench in front of Trones Wood for assembly of Brigade which is going to attack Guillemont. Had a very rough passage indeed. Miller took command. Only one man wounded & Sergt Green shell shock & Braggins who behaved rather .....ably I heard afterwards. He got his knee hurt by being ..... into a shell hole. Miller & Bretherton did very well I heard. Henshall was awfully bad all day. I told him to come every hour & he left for about 3 hours without any water or anything.

30-7-16   In bed all day. Temperature down but not quite normal. M.O. came to see me. I determined to sack Henshall as he seemed quite incapable of doing anything right. He asked to go so I sent him back with rations & got Watkins the C.O.'s old servant up. Kuny had had him but he had gone to hospital with gas having the end furthest from him in his dug out knocked in by a cart! I heard the Batt had orders to move back to Happy Valley. Had some rice & peaches to eat also some bread & milk. I was told the attack in Guillemont had failed badly. Later I learnt only 1 Brigade attacked.

31-7-16   Still in bed. The Batt returned & occupied the old huts as before. Later I heard the other 2 Brigades of the 35th & 1 Brig of the 55th & 2nd Div were attacking Guillemont this also failed. The 25th was now napoo. 21st Brig being wiped out at Trones & others at Guillemont.

1-8-16   Got up for the first time & got into the mess in my dressing gown. Felt very groggy & had to go back to bed pretty soon. Heard we are moving to another aera & had to move tomorrow to Hardencourt. Batt moving at 4.30 & entrain at Maricourt at 12.0 But had to be there by 8.0. All transport left that day for Hallencourt near Pont Remy. C.O. gave me leave to ride in mess cart leave at 8.0.

2-8-16   Batt cleared out at 5.0. I came in at 8.0. with mess cart. Rode into Heilly & found Batt resting in fields. Trains all went wrong so we did not entrain till 5.0. Went fearfully slow till the other side of Amiens &

got in to Longpré at 10.20. Luckily I got Tov..... & a car to take me to Hallencourt & Miller had all the billets so I got to bed early after an omelette but I felt very rotten & fearfully tired. Eric slept on the floor in my room.

3-8-16   Felt very rotten but got up after breakfast & heard we were moving on the next day at an unearthly hour - went to bed without any dinner or lunch but had breakfast about 11 o'clock.

4-8-16   Felt very rotten in bed so sent for the doctor & he told me I had far better go to hospital - so he sent for a lorry which took me to a C.C.S. in Hallencourt & there I stayed about half an hour & got shifted to Abbeville. I was in pyjamas & Watkins was looking after my kit - he could only get as far as Abbeville & then had to rejoin his unit. I went into No 2 Stationary Hospital No 14 Tent. Day nurses ..... Sisters & night ..... was ..... menu & the M.O. was Capt Gordon R.A.M.C.

5-8-16   In hospital at Abbeville. From 5th-8th. Lt Cardwell who lives at
to   Lancaster was in with a displaced cartlidge in his knee in the next bed
10-8-16   to mine. All the time Braggins was in also till the 8th when he left on 3 weeks sick leave to England. On the 8th Tancy Entwistle came in - he was in Liverpool Scottish & was shot through arms in an attack in Guillemont. A. Entwistle was in the other officers tent for a few days with his finger fractured & they left together for England on 10th. About the 7th the nurses changed & Sister Stratton came in place of Sister   for day duty & also the M.O.s Lieut Craig came in place of Capt   I got up into dressing gown on the 10th & lay on another bed & also had some of my blood taken to see if I had typhoid but proved negative. W. E. Wiggins O.R. Town 2nd Lt Worcester Yeomanry came in & left on the same date as Entwistle.

11-8-16   Got up into clothes. About 9.0 p.m. it came through we were leaving for 3 weeks leave at midnight so I had to pack everything up & we left Abbeville at 11.0 o'clock for the 12.0 train which did not arrive till 3 a.m.

12-8-16   Had breakfast at Boulogne when we arrived about 6 a.m. & caught the 11 o'clock boat getting on board at 10.30. Had a very good crossing & left Folkestone about 1.30. Got to Victoria about 3.30 & left about 4.0 in taxi - called at 4 Mount St & heard Roy was at Dieppe playing golf & Pat & W away at Stella's for week end. Went on to Euston & caught the 5.25 for Silverdale got in about 12 midnight.

13-8-16 to 20-8-16   At Silverdale. Did nothing all day all the time but Puzzle. Saw Sonia for the first time. In the big spare room. On the 15th we motored over with baby to Lancaster in Karl's car & saw them all there. Mary Callender & Miss Jones were stopping there. I saw Dr D..... having previously seen Dr Jackson. Followed Dr D..... advice & Dr Jacksons. On 16th mother had all the Tommies in from next door to tea & games. The Hawkins came over from Arnside where they were all staying the whole family including Mr Walker Edith's brother in law & a young nephew & also Mr Buddington (padre) & his daughter Ursula. Mrs Philpotts (..... Martin) who owns Lindeth Lodge also came. On 19th Hilda & Dai came up. Went over to Carnforth in 7 minutes to fetch them. Mistook took telegram for arriving Silv at 4.0 instead of leaving Wolv at 4.0. Roger & Mrs Bacon arrived on 17th & left on the 20th. Went over to Lancaster & a few runs with Roger. They came in his Singer.

21-8-16 to 24-8-16   Went over to Lancaster in my Singer & got in about 4.30 for tea.

25-8-16   Left by the 1.7 for Glasgow & got up there about 6.30. Raining hard. Kaye saw me off. Mr Townsend met me & we had a quiet dinner & early to bed. Mr Townsend had us invalids upstairs.

26-8-16   Breakfast at 8.0. Caught 9.35 to Troon with Mr Townsend. Did not seem very promising. Ronald met us at the house that Mr & Mrs Maclean had taken for the summer. Near Poldean. Hope was there too & Wallis. We went along to golf - it was raining hard so Ronald & I played it alone. I was playing v badly & we only did 16 holes owing to the rain. Had lunch at the Club & decided to play no more so returned to tea with the MacCleans. Mrs Townsend turned up & we saw Peggy & her new hat. Got back to dinner at Huntly Gardens. Ronald came with us.

27-8-16   Sunday so Ronald Mrs T & myself went to Kirk. Uncle Charlie (Capt Townsend) came in to lunch. We played billiards & music most of the day.

28-8-16   If fine was going to have golf at Troon. Looked very wet so decided to return now. Got the 10 o'clock. Had lunch at Carlisle & got in at

3.30. Kaye met me. We all except Mrs M & Miss Jones went to the Hippodrome - not a first class show.

29-8-16 Wet all day so stayed in & puzzled. Cleaned up & had a set of Tennis in the evening. Very exhausting. Sonia's hair growing fast. Started to sing top notes & blow bubble.

30-8-16 Went up to Barracks & saw Capt Morgan R.A.M.C. who gave me a fortnight extension. Sent it through to the D.M.S. War Office instead of the Secretary for War. Got no reply so simply took the leave. In the afternoon returned then all except Miss Jones to Preston & we saw the War Films. Thought nothing of them. Got back for late tea at 6.0.

31-8-16 Spent all day at Lancaster. Went down town every day in car.

1-9-16 We three went over to Standish.

2-9-16 Did nothing all day but puzzle. Karl phoned from Wolverhampton he was coming home on leave getting to Silv on monday.

3-9-16 Did nothing all day. At lunch mother lost her temper & departed & we saw nothing of her till tea when she made ..... remarks so Kaye & I decided to leave on first occasion on monday. So fixed up cart to take our things & packed up.

4-9-16 Left Silverdale for Lancaster at 10.0 in the morning, cart met us on the way & we got safely in & everything arrived about 2 p.m. Karl came through by the 1.7 so Kaye & I went down to see him. Told him & Mrs Malcolm about the row.

5-9-16
to
13-9-16
At Lancaster on the 6th a big fete on the cricket ground for Star & Garter fund. Realised about 600£s. Saw young Roper there. Only went for half an hour. Mrs M & Tancy & Mary all worked hard at it. Miss Jones left on 5/9/16. On the 8th we all went over & saw Betty at Morecambe. It was very good indeed considering. The Irvines were there too. On 12th got a letter from mother asking me to go over so I went over to tea. After that we all went over & saw N... War at Morecambe. It too was awfully good considering. On the 9th Mr Malcolm & I had golf. We played a four ball v Huntington & Grant Storey. Huntington gave Mr Malcolm a half & Storey gave him 3 strokes & I gave Storey a third. Storey ..... in about 4 & Huntingdon about 2 & Mr Malcolm 8! We had them 1 up on the last hole - it was

an awfully good match & we all enjoyed it very much. Had lunch & tea at the Club & then Mr Malcolm & I had a few holes after & got back to dinner. I went down town nearly every day in the Singer. Karl came over once or twice & he came up to lunch & I took him over to see the Works & to show the car off on the 13th & then we met Williams who came up from Town. Kaye came down too. He looked awfully bad. He was staying at Ocklia.

14-9-16 Went down town in morning - caught the 2.0 train to Wolverhampton. Went in Khaki. Kaye saw me off by Singer & changed at Crewe. Hilda & Flo met me at Wolverhampton & we went up by taxi leaving valise at station. Hilda had to go to class at 6.0 so I wrote to Kaye & walked to post & met Dai in car bringing Jack & Col. T.... home. Flo came to dinner & Jack came in after & we had a mad game or two & then bed.

15-9-16 Walked with Hilda up to town & sent some chocolates off to Kaye & bought a few things & then got back for lunch. Caught the 2.15 to town arriving at 4.50. Ronald met me & we went straight round to 4 Mount St. Found Roy & Stiller there. Also Piggy Malden. Waited while they all changed. P..... came in later & then dinner at the Savoy. Saw Jock Sampson (the elder) there also Camilla Clifford. Then went straight on to Bing Boys[125]. Very good indeed. Back to supper at Savoy. Ronald left then & we were joined by a Miss Grove commonly known as Stella & her brother in law Major   . We had quite a good supper party - saw J.C. Symmonds & wife there - bed about 2 a.m.

16-9-16 Caught the 11.30 train at Charing X - getting a cigarette case at Asprey's on the way. Pat Roy & Roddie all saw me off. Got Pullman & lunch on the way. Got through to Boulogne without any hitch. Met the M.O. 11th R.I.F.s with whom we were in at Mailly-Maillet on the boat. They told us at Boulogne to report to M.L.O. but I missed that & also the RTO Found the train for 30th Div. & Bethune was leaving at 7.30 - so had tea at Officer's club & 2 boiled eggs & then got to the train. Fearfully crammed. Got going about 8.0. No light hardly so all slept.

17-9-16 Got into Bethune about 2 a.m. Did not see the RTO officer but found my way to Gorre & found Batt. had left about Thursday last so

---

[125] A a series of reveus which played at the Alhambra Theatre in London, starring George Robey, Violet Lorraine and Alfred Lester; began in 1916 and ran for 378 performances.

trudged all the way back & found a train going to Aubigny at 11.30. Had omelette & then went up & wandered around Bethune found D.H.Q. 30th Div. So saw signals & found Hindle at Malpast. He told me all the Div. was moving to Doullens area & the billeting party was going by the 11.00 so I went with them. Found with them was Capt. Torry Staff Capt 89th Brig., Capt Fearnside D.S.O. Staff Capt 90th Brig., Capt. Torrence Staff Capt 21st Brig. Also 2nd Lt Knolls, brother of the M.C. commonly known as "he knowing the language". I picked up 2 men one in 'D' Co & one in 'C' Co who were returning from hospital & got them billets too. Bury was there billeting the Div. I slept in Hotel de Quatre Fils d'Aymond. Stan too was there so I managed to get on by borrowing 40 francs from Fearnside.

18-9-16   Rained all day. After lunch walked out towards Longuevillette where the Batt. Were to be billeted according to Bury but got wet through before getting there so returned. Slept that night at Hotel.

19-9-16   Got Hindle to lend us the car & went out to Longuevillette & saw the Billets for the Batt. Still raining but cleared about 12. Had lunch at 12 & got to the station as the Batt. Arrived. Saw them all including the new Q.M. Telford & the new Monmouth Officers. Capt Hodges, Lt O'Connor, 2nd Lt. Griffiths, Gorman & also Manning (Capt) had arrived. Batt. Marched out then & got into billets without any rain. C.O. had taken Ginger so I had the original C.O.2. old man. Miller finally arranged Billets & we got settled for the night.

Company's location & work
From 5/8/16 - 19/9/16

On 5/8/16 Entrained at Pont Remy for
Marched to Mollingham. There from 5/6/16 to 9/8/16. Night work at Bergutte. Filling in Shell Holes (M.G. Works)
On 10/8/16 Marched to Gorre. At Gorre from 10/8/16 to 9/9/16. Three days rest & Drill & then Work at Givenchy Sector. Clearing & repairing Trenches.
On 10/9/16 Marched to Bethune & entrained for Aubigny. Marched to Ecoivres to line between Neuville St Vaast & Carency. Clearing & repairing Trenches.
On 17/9/16 left for Aig. Left Aig on 18th for Sary & entrained for Doulens.

20-9-16   Rained most of the day. Rode in with C.O. to Doullens. Lunched at Quatre Fils saw Miller & Walker there & got back for tea. Watched footie match in evening.

21-9-16   Batt. moved in morning to Havernas. Supposed to be marching with 90th Brigade but their march all went wrong & we got in early.

22-9-16   Company drill morning & afternoon from 9-12 & 2-4. Football match played in evening - with platoon competition.

23-9-16   Drill in morning, football in afternoon. After tea, C.O., Dixon, Hodges, Woods & I all went in to Amiens & picked up Musgrave at Villers-Bocage. Met Oscar Winterbottom & Betts there & had dinner in private corner at the Savoy a new place only opened a week. Menu consisted of soup, m...ch lobster, veal cutlets, Duck, Piche melba, 6 magnums among the ....., 2 bott Brandy & coffee. C.O.s late transport officer now A.S.C. & his friend turned up for coffee - much fun & things broken. Got back about 12.0.

24-9-16   Ought to have taken church parade but did not know orders till 9.50 & church parade was 9.45. C.O. wanted "Reasons in writing". Thought it was result of night before. Got up about 10.30 & watched football in afternoon.

25-9-16   Company drill all day. Football - evening. Semi finals. M.G. Section drew with No. 6 - one all - very good & exciting game M.G.s shot their goal on the whistle.

26-9-16   Company drill C.C. arrived from leave (special extended by sick leave) at lunch time. Football in afternoon. M.G.s lost to No. 6 after playing ten minutes extra both ways by 4 to 2. C.O. got a car for Amiens & C.C., C.O., Ridsdale & I went in & had dinner at Godbert. Menu soup, eggs, lobster, ducklet, Piche Melba menu ..... so I had fresh fruit, 3 bottles fizz & coffee. Got back about 10.30 to find orders to move in motor buses on next day.

27-9-16   All got on busses at 12.30 for Albert, on way we were told we were going near Dernancourt. Transport went on to Allonville that day. Off. Valises on a bus. Fine when we started but when we got near our destination it poured. We went via Flesselles - Villers-Bocage - Amiens & Querrieu. We broke down in Amiens. As we were waiting 3 French officers came along & the band happened to strike up the Marseillaise. The officers stood to attention & saluted & then asked for it again & finally asked for God save the King. We got to camp 11 miles short of Albert into tents & huts about 5 p.m. Had a snatch meal in our tent & then bed on the floor.

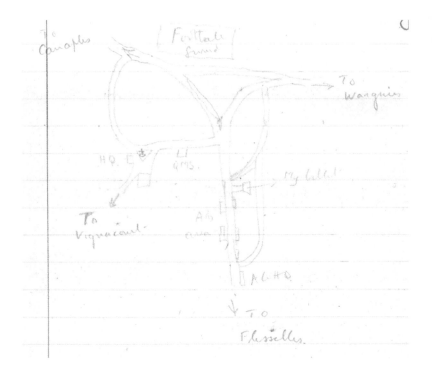

28-9-16   Orders to move at midday to Montauban. Transport just arrived as we departed & came straight in. We started by Cuerpeniers at 12.30 & came via Albert - Fricourt - Mametz & got in about 5.0 encamped N.W. of Montauban about 300 - 400 yards. Drew tents & all got into tents - very fine that day & there were plenty of Bosch balloons up. I got an old Bosch dug out as I would have had to sleep with O'Connor otherwise.

29-9-16   Tents were shelled in the night & one man killed in 'B' Co. So they all had to get out & make dug outs for themselves tons of material lying around. Had all day for doing that.

30-9-16   Batt. put on repairing road from Montauban to Bazentin. 'A' Co. at Bazentin & 'D' near Montauban. We had about 3 shells at us about 4.30 where I had left in the afternoon. Saw a tank for the first time. Four near Bazentin.

1-10-16   30 Div. R.E.s came along & 'A' Co had to hand over to them at 2 p.m. & take the road between 'D' Co & Montauban in the hollow of the road.

2-10-16   On Montauban road all day.

3-10-16   Pouring day. Still on road. Two companies had orders to be held in readiness for 41 Div stunt. C.O. decided on 'B' & 'D'.

4-10-16   'A' & 'C' still on road. 'B' & 'D' had to go up & work on Goose Alley & Fish Trench respectively. Found a lot of shelling going on up there & 'B' Co had two wounded but not badly. Both companies got into the wrong trenches.

5-10-16   'C' & half 'A' took over 'D' & 'B's work - I went up with 'A' (half) Walker & Braggins. We had a lot of shelling round up but only one man buried. 'C' Co had one killed & 5 wounded. O'Connor brought the other half company up at night. I waited for him & met him he carried on the wrong work. I got back about 7.45. We had 3 men wounded by shrapnel. Very hot up there.

6-10-16   Went up the whole company at 3 p.m. went via Longueval to pick up duck boards. Then down Fish Alley & across to Turk Alley & so on to men's work, which was parallel to the other job but further along Abbey Road. Found we had been working on Factory Trench. I sent A. D. Walker up first to make sure of the job. Got up there about 6.0 & did a good night's work & then got back about 12.30. Plenty of shelling round about the place but none actually in the trench until we left when they put one in but it did not do anyone any harm. They shelled very heavily from 6.0 to 7.0 so I decided to come down a bit later next night.

7-10-16   Left at four instead of three. Did not get up till 11.30 a.m. Then O'Connor & I went by Bazentin & Turk Alley other part of company went to pick up Trench Boards as before at Longueval. 41st Div doing a stunt for the 30th Div to jump off from so Bretherton went on ahead to see if it was fit to work down there. Got down there to find Turk Alley all blown in & a dickens of a strafe on. Waited a bit & sent a note to C.O. to say we were not working. But strafe cooled off so we went on & started work but half a Batt. of W. Kents came in & sat down in our trench to wait for other half so after waiting half an hour we decided to give it up as the rest of the Batt. had to come through also a Batt. of Queens. Got back about 11.30.

8-10-16   Went up as before. O'Connor & I got there early & sat down waited till 8.30 & then A. D. Walker came along & said company was stuck up by relieving Batts. No. 2 Plat. were on clearing Turk Alley where it had been blown in the day before. At 9.0 suddenly a strafe started & they started putting shrapnel & stuff on Abbey Road - so O'Connor & I decided to get back & stop the company coming up. Had a bad run for it & got into Turk Alley by side of Abbey Road to find an half Batt. of 23rd Middlesex lying in bottom of the trench & one platoon behind. Could not get along as Bosch was putting a barrage along Abbey Road so waited. Other platoons came along & waited. After waiting till 10.15 we decided to chuck it & dump the boards. So we left the boards & got back about 12.15 a.m.

9-10-16   Work at night as usual - got two letters from Kaye arrived. Work at night consisted in one platoon on Turk & one on Fish clearing up & two platoons working on the continuation of Fish under Payne. Went myself later & wandered round & saw them all. Got back about 10.30. Feeling rather rotten.

10-10-16   Work on Fish Alley with 'C' Co.

11-10-16   Had a complete day off as we had to stand by for the 35th stunt. Only a small one so as to get a jumping off place for the big one on Le Barque & Ligny-Thilloy. At first we thought we had to spend the night in the trenches but they could not find room for us so we had the night at camp & were to go up next day. Started a horrid cold.

Map for attack of 30th Div showing work for Pioneers 12.10.16.

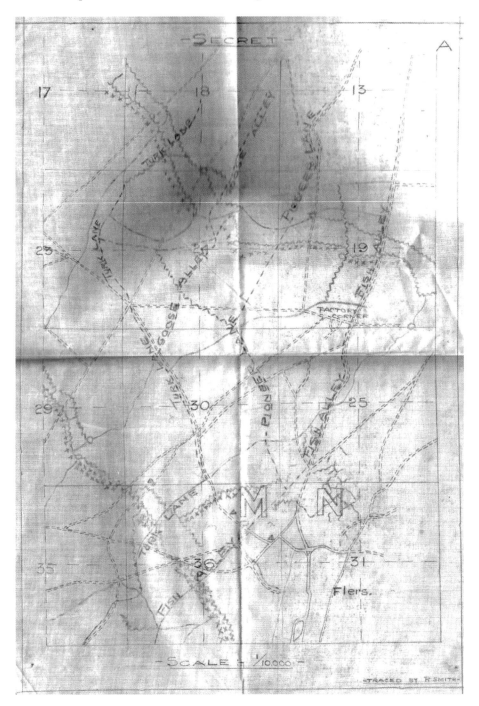

12-10-16 Zero was to be at 2-5 & we had to get into a nameless trench behind Cross Trench by 2.0 so left caves at 12.30 & was there by 2.30. 'A' & 'C' Co's were to join up the old front line with the new - a sort of continuation of Fish Alley & 'B' & 'D' the same sort of thing with Goose Alley. Strafe started & we left at 4.30. Payne going ahead to mark out when we got up to Fish Alley. I met Payne who said we had not got our objectives he thought so was waiting for orders from C.R.E. After a lot of contrary orders Payne went up & found we had not left an original front line. Meantime orders to continue on Fish Trench arrived so we continued till 2.30 a.m. & then came back to camp. Got back from 5 - 5.30 a.m.

13-10-16 The whole Batt had to go up & dig a trench from the junction of Turk & Goose up to the front line really the continuation of Turk along Abby Road. 'A' had along Abby Road & then 'B' 'C' & 'D' up to the front line. Did not get finished till about 3.30.a.m. Waited till the end as No 2 & 3 Platoons had not got finished. No 1 & 4 went ..... a lot first.

14-10-16 'C' Co had a rest - had hopes of 'A' getting one but in the end 'A' & 'B' were on Fish Alley & 'D' in Goose. So we had to go out after all. Quite a quiet night & we got a good bit done. Got back about 2 to 3 a.m.

15-10-16 'A' Co had a rest & did not go out. Other three companies went out as usual. Payne had 'C' Co on Fish Alley & of course said we had gone done most in our trench on the night before. Did not believe him at all. played Bridge with C.O., C.C. & Walker at night. Heard that on night of the Strafe Dixon had found the V. in our front line & cut ..... new & the old one as he thought. Also they thought it was leading to Bosch & so had never explored it but merely blocked it up. Letter & 2 Parcels from Kaye. Wrote her.

16-10-16 Company on work. 'B' & 'D' have a rest but go on roads the next day. Company split up in 21st Brig area. No 1 on Turk under Bishop. No 2 on new assembly trench off Turk under Braggins cutting steps out. No 3 on Goose under Bretherton half No 4 on Support Trench for 19th Man & the other half joining up some old Bosch trenches to Turk. Went out & saw them ..... the work & got back by 9.30. Called in at 21st B. office to see about work. Wrote K. Letter & Parcel from her.

17-10-16   Rested all day. 'A' & 'C' Cos doing nothing. 'B' & 'D' did nominal work on roads owing to 30th Div going to do a stunt on the morning of the 18th. We saw about 5 Tanks going up for the stunt. Started to rain in the evening about mess time pretty severely. Went to bed early no bridge. O'Connor left for Flixecourt 4th Army School of Instruction.

Map supplied showing 30th Div front in attack on 18.10.16.

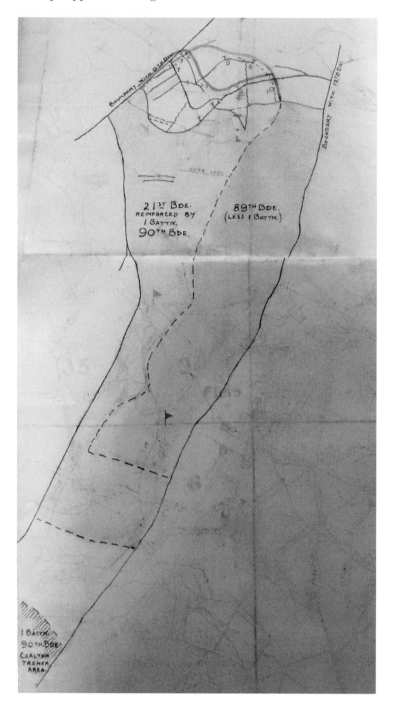

18-10-16 Went out to work at night. Job was a fire trench up behind the front line off Gorse. At first it being another 30th Div Stunt the Batt had to assemble in the same trench as before by 4.0 p.m.so all left at 2.0. We expected to have to dig Turk trench on to the new front line. But stunt which was at 3.30 a.m. failed in spite of one or two more efforts. 3 Tanks helped & one owing to the road stuck in no man's land. I believe the 30th Div did not distinguish themselves. We got orders that our original jobs were off when we got there & then had this fire trench to dig with 'A' & 'C' & half 'D'. Hodges & I were to go up Drivers Lane & start & join 'C' starting from Goose but Hodges & I could not determine our end so we started off all from 'C' Co end & dug a trench by all evidence it was in the right place but I am quite sure it was not. Very muddy & rained hard on the way back so we got in about 6.0 having started on job at 1.15 a.m. & left about 3.0 a.m. 'C' Co lost two platoons which never turned up at all. Very muddy & dirty & very tired when we got back. Rather a bad night for shells.

19-10-16 Had to finish the trench we were on the night before but 2 platoons of 'A' only had to go out so Walker took them. Rained all day & no one got up to the job owing to the mud & the trenches being full of water. Terrible night. Pethick turned up late. I got early to bed.

20-10-16 Expected a day's rest as the Div was to be relieved. But the 5th Australian Div could not get up in time owing to the heavy conditions of the road so the relief was put off & we had to go out. A scratch party went out under Pethick Bretherton & Braggins. Bretherton had a rotten time being ordered by C.O. 19 Man to make a strong point in front line & no one knew the place. Played bridge with C.O., C.C. & Diplock. Early to bed as I had to get up at 6 a.m. next morning for work with the Company in Fish Alley. Hard frost at night.

21-10-16 Got up at 6 o'clock. Freezing morning but quite fine. Had breakfast in bed. Took company with Walker or rather 66 of the company to Fish Alley North of Abbey Road - they had to get trench boards so I went straight there & Walker went via Longueval. Got down there with Payne who was also waiting in Fish Alley. Found 20th Div occupying front of the trench. Company had 1 killed (Hynes) & 3 wounded on the way up. Nice day but very cold. Orders came through at lunch. We were to go to Dernancourt tomorrow.

22-10-16   Received a wire from C.R.E. as follows:- "To CRE 30th Div. Must really congratulate pioneers on excellent work they have done in Fish Alley. Recommend as many trench boards being sent up as possible. The work is wonderful. From General Stanley 89th Brig. Forwarded to you. The C.R.E. wishes to add his congratulations & to thank you for the excellent work done. ..... Capt R.E. Batt moved off for Dernancourt at 7.0. Went via Albert to the same old camp. Got in about 3.30. Had company mess for the night.

23-10-16   Had an inspection at 11.0. Heard we are moving back to Montauban next day. C.C. A D Walker & I went in to Amiens in afternoon getting a lift in motor lorry to Querrieux & in R Flying Corps car from then on. Had tea & bought a few things & then dined at Godbert. Saw Dixon & Manning & Morgan in main street. Menu. Soup. ..... Oysters. Eggs Sole. Lobster Ducklet. Ice & cigar & coffee. Went back to Savoy to see if we could get a lift but failed. Pouring with rain - stood at the corner by the station for a long time & then walked to the Barrier & waited there. After many failures we got a lift in 30th Div General's car - Bury & Weber in it the latter merry & without his hat! C.C. got inside & Walker & I by the chauffeur. Got back to camp & in to bed about 12.45 with orders for 'A' Co to move at 5.30 to Montauban.

24-10-16   Orderlys came in all night long so I got no sleep & got up about 4.15. Company ought to have been on parade by 5.30 but was not on till 5.50. Had no breakfast - we half marched half doubled through Dernancourt to Meaulte L. Station & got there at 6.45. Waited half an hour & then had to go up the line about a mile & entrain there. Train left about 7.45 & took us to Fricourt where we had to get out & walk to rail head. McF..... Capt O.C. Coy R.E. Company left half got in the train & took us to our destination. A very nice fellow indeed & showed us the work. Making a 9 foot bank in a little valley about 100 yards across. We got into it & made it ship shape - only clearing up & marking it out. It rained mainly the whole time. We left then at 4.0 & marched back to Montauban to our old camp at about S.2.7.a.3.5. Found the battalion there less transport & nowhere to sleep. A few tents gradually turned up & by 9.0 I had one fixed for myself & got to sleep.

25-10-16   'A' Co dug themselves in all day & got messes & places all ready - half 'B' & half 'D' companies went out at 12.0 for work on the railway. Horrible day as it poured most of the day & we had no news or any kind of plan to go to.

26-10-16   'A' Co paraded at 5.15 for work on the railway to start at 6.0. a.m. Walker & myself took the platoons out. I rode out then about 10.0 saw the progress & then returned over the top by 11.30. Had to take the horse through wire entanglements & our trenches & all sorts of places. Met Dixon on the way back & got back for lunch. Played Bridge in aft with C.C. Hodges & A. D. Walker & in morning with C.O., Diplock & C.C.

27-10-16   Stayed in all day. Wet. Bretherton & Braggins took company out to work.

28-10-16   Braggins took the company out at 5.15. I got up late & did not turn up till 7.30 at the work. Stayed there till 12.0. Beautiful morning but had a shower towards evening though it did not rain while we were there. Bretherton to Amiens. A. D. Walker to Heilly to join in to R.F.C. Bridge with C.C. Adj & C.O.

29-10-16   Changed over times with 'B' Co. We worked from 12-6 & 'B' from 6-12. Braggins to Amiens & A. D. Walker & Bishop took party for R.F.C. work at 12.0. Voluntary service at work at 11.40. I stayed in. wet all day beastly.

30-10-16   Karl & Ridsdale to Amiens. Bretherton & I took the company out at 12.0 & had a very good lunch up there of sardines - sausages & tomatoes - peaches - coffee - coronas & stout & biscuits & cheese. Very satisfying. After lunch it started to pour with rain & rained incessantly all afternoon. Luckily it just stopped for us to come back. Returned over the top of the hill - very hard going. Bridge with C.O., Hodges & Diplock. It poured all night & I got very little sleep as the tent leaked very badly.

31-10-16   Stayed in all day & played bridge. Post fearfully bad these days. Fine day but did not seem to get the mud dried off much. Got a new tent & put it over my old one to help keep out the rain. Walker & Braggins took out company starting at 12.0 as usual. Told off Bishop for next day & because he was ill in bed. So Braggins went out again. Bridge with C.O., C.C. & Diplock in evening.

1-11-16   Bretherton & Braggins took company out to work. Started work at 8.30 a.m. instead of 12. Whole Batt in at same time. Rain started after lunch. Still no post in. bishop up & about but seemed to have a very bad cold. Played bridge after dinner with C.O., C.C. & Diplock. Heard we had to join the Div on the 6th.

2-11-16   Got up at 7. Rode out to the work & took charge with A D Walker. Told Piggott & Wilson to fetch our lunches up but they went all to the wrong place down to clearing station in Turk lane so did not turn up till 2.0. Left at 2.40. Rode back. No post as before. Played Bridge with C.O., C.C. & Woods.

3-11-16   Stayed in all day. Got up very late. Fine day. Got 6 letters 2 from K & 2 from mother. Played bridge with C.O., C.C. & Hodges in evening.

4-11-16   Went out to work in morning. Bretherton & Braggins went up early & I relieved Braggins at 8.0. Stayed till 1.30 & then was to be relieved by Walker we were to move next day or rather transport was & us the day after. Walker fell over with horse so I went back & left Bretherton to bring company back. Got everything fixed up for company to move & then heard all arrangements altered & we were to move also & spend night at Talmas bussing then from Ribemont & going on to Berles next day. Transport going that day also.

5-11-16   Got up at 5 a.m. as Valises had to go by Transport early. Moved off by Companies at 10.30 to Ribemont via Mametz Fricourt Albert. Had lunch just outside Albert & then to Ribemont got there at 4.0. Change of Officers, Bretherton taking over sec.-in-com. of 'B' Co as Manning went to 'C' Co. Eric also going to 'B' Co. Dixon living still with Div taking on the work. Bussed to Talmas via Corbie & Amiens. I slept on the floor of bus with a bit of grit in my eye. Transport went to Toutencourt. Got in about 8.30. 'A' Co billetted in a Café. I had quite a nice bed but Manning & Walker both had "strangers". 'C' Co could not get into their off. billets so came into ours.

6-11-16   Embussed at 9.15. Orders changed & instead of going to Berles busses had to go to Hamlincourt. C.O. had had no different orders so when we got there via Doulens & Beauval the Town Major had heard a batt of Lancs Fus might leave that day so C.O. took their billets. Quite nice & comfortable.

7-11-16   Did nothing all day but have rifle & gas helmet inspection. Rainy day. Went down at night & had music at H.Q. Mess. Hodges sang very well & Manning played. Diplock & Pethick also sang.

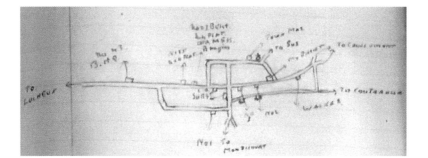

8-11-16   Got up so as to leave at 7.0 for Berles-au-Bois on horse back with Hodges, Manning & Ridsdale to take over work from Monmouths. Got over there at 11.0 going via Couturelle, Humbercamps, Pommier & Bienvillers-au-Bois. Went up without steel helmet & was stopped. Much surprised to find civilians in Berles & only 1500 yards about from Bosch. We passed 18 ... R.F.A. on the road up to Berles from Pommier. I was taking over from 'B' Co who have a Plat at Berles under 2nd Lieut Harris & two at La Cauchie under the C.O. Capt Bonycot. Settled up all work at Berles Strong Point T-12. Also question of manning it in case of an attack. Rode back with Diplock via La Cauchie having seen Bretherton & Dixon. Saw Bonycot at La Cauchie & saw about walls. Got back to Humbercamps about 3.0. Rained in showers most of the day.

9-11-16   Paraded at 3.30 for Batt to move to Berles. We're not to cross the Doulens-Arras road before 5.0 p.m. (dark). Saw the two platoons in at La Cauchie under Walker & then rode on to Berles & saw other two Platoons in. Got there as Batt arrived. 'C' Co went to Bailleval 'D' & 'B' Co coming to Berles. Got in about 8.0 & had a meal & got to bed about 12 o'clock. All 2 Platoons in one billet & very comfortable.

10-11-16   'A' Co did no work as our work was changed & I had to reconnoitre new work - "trenches 117-120 & culverts right sector" - having no map this was very difficult & Braggins & I did not set out till 3.0 about. We went down Farnborough trench & along the front line till we got to 120 & then up 121 & back by Renfrew road. Saw the work & got back about 6.0. Very muddy & tired. Front line was not so bad as support line. Communication trenches main area pretty good. No 4 Platoon under Bishop was to go off for work in right sector & billet in Bienvillers.

11-11-16   Started work. Bishop took his platoon off & Braggins went on 117-120. I rode over with C.C. to La Cauchie & saw Walker - his men were spread all over the roads so could not see all of them. Got back for lunch. Our position in case of attack being altered. I inspected my points A, D, H, & what I thought was 147. Got back very tired. Walked down to H.Q. & saw C.O. & C.C.

12-11-16   Walked over to Bienvillers in morning & found Bishop. He seemed to be doing very good work. Got back for lunch at 2.0. Went down to H.Q. C.O. said we were probably moving to La Cauchie 'A' Co. altogether. Nothing in orders about it. Got tea at 'D' Co mess. Had a warning about "Pelling" signifying gas being sent over by us from 7-10 p.m. "Napoo" signifies the attack off. Did not go to bed owing to expecting Pelling till 12.30. Got to bed & asleep & it started at 3.0. But no retaliation at all from Bosch so slept alright but rather late.

13-11-16   Got up rather late. Bishop came to lunch to see over his Strong Point 'A'. So I took him round it in morning & tried to find the short cut to Braggins down Farnborough & along 18th but could not find it. got back to lunch & spent afternoon making chair etc. Had dinner at H.Q. at 7.0 & played bridge after with C.O C.C. & Diplock. Got to bed about 12.30. Packer went on leave.

14-11-16   Rode over to La Cauchie & Bienvillers with ..... in morning. Met Hindle on the way. Saw Walker & Woolcock but not Bishop. C.C. had lunch with us & then we went down & saw Braggins work. More satisfied with it than I expected. Got back for tea. E.O. & Bretherton in to tea. Had bridge after & dinner alone with Braggins. Bed early.

15-11-16   Rode about in morning to Bienvillers & saw Bishop & his work. He was going to be stopped by material so we went & saw the R.E. Oi/c Detachment 2nd Lieut Lester. He said the Dump was being changed so no more was to be supplied. Later C.C. told us they were going to hand over that part to R.E.'s 49 Div. C.C. was to ride over next day & hand it over. Stayed all afternoon & made chair comfortable by covering it & upholstering it. went down after dinner & played bridge with C.O., C.C. & Diplock. Woods, C.S.M. Harrison & Sergt Jones on leave.

16-11-16   In morning went down & saw Braggins at his job. Met Diplock & Ridsdale. Bosch aeroplane brought down near Bienvillers in morning. Afternoon rode over to Walker & saw him & Woolcock. Rode back by Bienvillers but did not see any signs of the aeroplane. Went to bed early. Went down & played bridge with C.O., C.C. & Diplock having dinner there too.

17-11-16   Spent morning in orderly room getting things straight. Frosty & very cold. Walker came to lunch & we went round "A", "D", "H" Strong Points to Fort 147. He stayed to tea & E.O. & Bolton came in to tea. I sent Thompson over for a couple of chickens to Pommier & C.C. E.O. & Bolton came in to dinner & we had bridge after. Braggins went to bed sick. Orders came that Bishop was ..... & the whole company on roads.

18-11-16   Bishop came back from Bienvillers in the morning. I rode over to Bailleulmont to see Culshaw about taking over the roads. Found it very frosty & some snow had fallen & the roads were terribly hard & we slipped all over the place. Got there & saw the R.E. officer & about taking over roads. He motored us back to Batt H.Q. & then I went in to see Bretherton & fix up about handing over 117-120. After lunch Gorman & I walked down to 117-120 & saw it & got back for tea. Bishop returned & relieved Braggins so we saw him down there. Both turned up for tea & then Braggins went to bed.

19-11-16   All company on roads around La Cauchie & Bailleulmont No 4 Platoon seemed to have made a very good impression on General Stanley as he wrote Platt a note & sent him 2 stripes owing to him being a Corp & only wearing one. He said he could not get men out if CQMS & then the G.O.C. specially asked for No 4 to go on work on .....ls alley. I rode round in the morning & saw all the parties at work & stayed in all the afternoon. Had dinner & bridge at H.Q. Mess. Rainy day but no frost. High wind.

20-11-16   Company on roads. Rode round through Pommiers & Humbercamps, La Cauchie & saw Walker & back via Bailleulmont, La Buc du Sud & Bailleulval. Very nice round. Spent afternoon in orderly room. Dixon & Hodges went on leave & R.S.M. Harrison. Had dinner at H.Q. & played bridge after. Mess utensils & cutlery & stuff came from Lancaster.

21-11-16   Rode round to Bailleulval. Sent Lieut Waters R.E. over roads & McClaren. Had a huge row with Watson as he said my men did not take any interest in the work. We had a jolly good set to & in the end he cooled down & became very affable & we parted in a sort of armed neutrality. Had a row with H.Q. over parade state. My points were (1) Order as strong as possible. I had obeyed it to the letter. (2)

Any man on light duty capable of cutting up wood was capable of going on parade. I had a man with sprained ankle. (3) Next day any light duty men had to cut up wood for H.Q. mess. Also they said if companies did not parade strong enough Off. Servants would have to go on parade & yet they had 4 men at H.Q. mess not Off. Servants from the company. I wrote to H.Q. very strongly on it & finally all they could say was the C.O. wanted my letter & if he wanted to could do what he chose. Confay defence of Balyschum scheme altered.

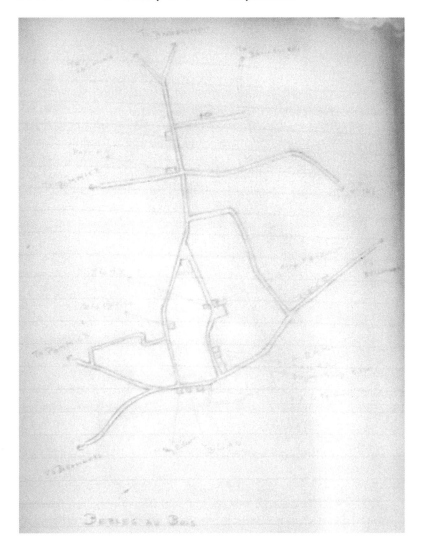

22-11-16 Rode round & saw RE officer at Bailleulval. He was very efficient & said the company was doing very good work & he was very satisfied. Quite a different town. Went round new defences scheme of Buleston afternoon with Bishop & nearly got picked off by a couple of 4.2. Spent the evening writing.

23-11-16 Rode round in morning via La Cauchie first & met Walton & McClaren both very gracious! Said we were going to change billets & all ..... at La Cauchie but we heard nothing about it in orders. Heard Bishop & 1 Sergt to go to Div school - although we had O'Connor away & other companies were sending 1 Corp & 'B' Co none.

24-11-16 Rode round. Heard O'Connor had turned up at La Cauchie saw him there & went round by Bailleulval. Saw Martin in 2nd Wilts. He was at Vickers with me & an O.R. Got back to lunch & found Walker's elder brother in to lunch. Spent afternoon putting lean question all right. Got 2 parades at night.

25-11-16 Rained hard all day so did not go round the roads. Diplock came in to take an officer round to some dug out that I had had to keep a section off duty for. We found what we thought was the place just in front of Batt H.Q. on the Ridge road when Renfrew came out. Got wet through & decided wanted further particulars. Woolcock & Simmons went on leave. Went round & had dinner with 'B' Co & played bridge with C.O. v. Bretherton & Gorman. Got to bed about 11.30.

26-11-16 Rained all morning so did not go out. Also company had small box respirators fitted in morning so did not go to work till 1 o'clock. Rode over & saw Walker at night. O'Connor went to 'C' Co while their off. on leave. Had dinner & bridge with C.O.

27-11-16 Had to meet RE officer from 7th Corps to find position of proposed dug out. He took me out in a side car to opposite Remp..... on the town road & we saw the job & got back. He was on a ..... & side car & its clutch slipped. Got back & took Braggins, Sergt Platt & Hill to the job to hand them it. Then rode round by La Cauchie & afternoon & saw all Walker's men at work but could not find Walker. left instructions with Servant as to moving hut etc. Stayed in at night going round to 'B' Co & having bridge with C.C. v. Diplock & Bolton.

28-11-16   Rode round all the work - Pommier - Humbercamps - La Cauchie - the hut on Arras road - Bailleulval - Baillemont & home. Afternoon I spent in orderly room. Woods came back from leave. Had the wind up about a gas attack on the 6th Corps the ..... north of us as the Bosch was keeping gaps in our wire & a tape was strung across to our line. All sorts of precautions taken & we played cut throat till 12.0 but nothing happened & nothing happened.

29-11-16   Rode round in the morning & saw Walker & the hut etc. Spent afternoon in. C.C. came up after to say Williams Jervyn was coming back in a fortnight or so. Had dinner at H.Q. played bridge with Diplock v. C.O. & C.C. C.O. was going on leave next day.

30-11-16   C.O., Bretherton & Culshaw on leave. Rode round work & went into Bavincourt to see Wyatt but he was out. Saw Linton Smith. Went round in evening after dinner to 'B' Co & Eric & I played Bolton & Gorman. About 10.0 orders came for us to take over from 'B' Co & the whole of 'D' to go to La Cauchie. Went round & saw Pethick & also Sergt Major & got to bed about 12.30. Went down 'Y' C..... in afternoon a huge big place dug out by French.

1-12-16   'D' Co went to La Cauchie & Walker brought his two platoons here & we took over 'D' Co billet. Spent morning looking over things. The Company went on to 'D' Co work. Spread out all over the country. Afternoon spent wandering round O.P. "A" "D" & "H" dugouts having spent squaring up matters. Bishop went off to Saulty for his Div course.

2-12-16   In morning rode over to La Cauchie to see Petharil & hand over to him. Found he was out with R.E. officer so I handed over to Wood. Rode back by Bailleulmont. After lunch went round BE 1 to 5.6. & 7. Also round new improvements in billets. Had dinner with C.C. A D Walker came to. Sparks flying on the fact that I brought up the question of indents & the light duty men & medium & duty men having such a slack time. As usual Diplock was up in arms, & as rude & ungentlemanly as ever. Came to the conclusion he has far too good an opinion of himself. Bishop started his course.

3-12-16   In morning went down to Lincoln Lane. 2 platoons under Jones Sergt were working for 'B' Co. Coming back saw O.P. H & D & met C.C. at end of Farnborough Lane & he & E.O. came back to lunch. After lunch visited B.E.5 & then the billet returned for tea. Had dinner at 'B' Co & played bridge with E.O., Gorman & Bolton. Piggott returned from leave. Dixon got extension. Hodges returned.

4-12-16 Ran round all day & had tea at 'B' Co with E.O., Gorman & Bolton. Walker's elder brother came in to dinner & had bridge & Ving-et-un. Gorman also came. C.O. & Bolton going to H.Q. The M.O. of Walker's Batt was coming but failed. Named Littlejohn.

5-12-16 Went round morning & afternoon. Rather a rainy day. Shelled over work at Farnborough Rd. BE 5 & 6. No casualties. E.O & Dean went on leave. Walker not at all fit all day so stayed in bed. Stayed up & wrote a lot by myself.

6-12-16 Went round work in morning along to A. D. & H. then B.E. 6-12 Strong Points. Saw Diplock in evening about C.O.s dugouts No 6 & 7. Afternoon went round again. Stayed in at night. Walker better - got up.

7-12-16 Rode over to Bavincourt in morning & got money for company. Changed messes midday. In afternoon Braggins & I went up to O.P. & measured up & found them going slightly wrong. Found new mess rather cold. But got a good fire going. Early to bed.

8-12-16 Went round A. D. & H. in morning. Afternoon billets & BE post. Rather a rainy looking day. We had C.C. Diplock Ridsdale - Doctor Giles & Walker's brother to tea. Managed all quite comfortably. C.C. stayed to dinner & we had bridge after. C.C. & I walked over A.D. & Braggins to start off with but they pulled up & won eventually. Bed at 12.0. Sergt West accidentally shot in billet.

9-12-16 Rainy day all day. Stayed in in the morning. Walker's brother & his M.O. came round in morning. Talked a lot. Pethick & McLaren also turned up for a few minutes. After lunch went round the BE works. In for tea. Walker to go on leave next day.

10-12-16 Went up in morning with Braggins & measured up the O.P. & had a look at the other dug outs. Wandered round work in afternoon. Stayed in for the evening playing bridge. A. D. Walker did not go on leave as the leave was postponed 24 hours owing to railway congestion.

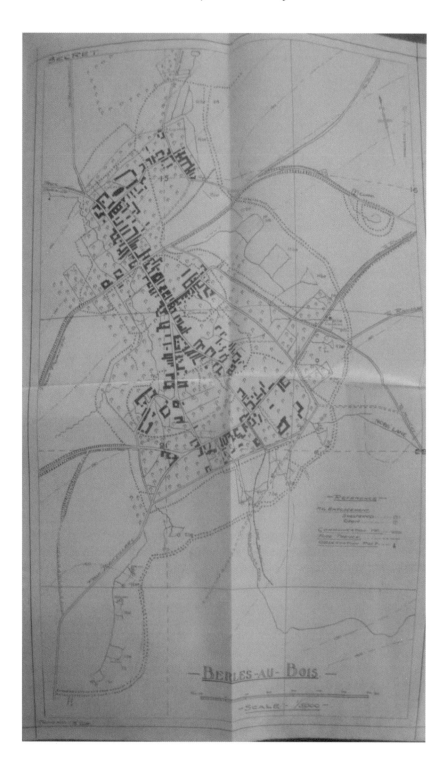

11-12-16   Went round Lincoln Lane & Farnborough Rd in morning. A. D. Walker & Boulton went on leave. Wandered round work in afternoon. Reported that O.P. sap had fallen in. Woods, Gorman & Griffiths came to dinner. Braggins & I played Woods & Gorman & drew at Bridge. A scare but the village should get shelled as we had had shelled a Bosch village.

12-12-16   Board in morning on Sergt West's accident. Ward & Ridsdale on it We sat all morning taking evidence. Ward stayed lunch & we sat all afternoon & they both stayed tea. I ..... in evening. Great excitement as we were going to shell heavily nearby & no work was to be done on our right & expecting back shelling all were to take to cellars from 10 - 3. This was for next day. Funny correspondence going on during 10 & 11th between Diplock & I - he got on his hind legs & tried to be very cutting over a facetious note of mine re candles. Think I squashed him by remarking his sense of humour was decreasing.

13-12-16   All work on 89th Brig area stopped as we had a strafe on - had to be in cellars from 10 a.m.to 3 p.m. As nothing came over we in officer's mess all stayed up & had meals as usual. 1 section of 'D' Co & Jones' Party in Lincoln Lane stayed on work. We sent over 58,000 shells. We were on the right of this show. All passed off quietly. C.O. returned from leave. Got a box of cigars from Wolverhampton. 'C' Co has gas over.

14-12-16   O'Connor turned up from Foursville. Had a wander round the works & found the O.P. had fallen in. L/Cpl Molloy was killed in B5 this morning. Woods & I walked round to see a new job with C.C. Support behind 116 to 112. They stayed to tea & Ward to dinner. C.C. had great stories about peace.

15-12-16   Lewis came along to take night party on the new job. Support from Farnborough to Fish St. R.E. officer called about O.P. which had fallen in - motored me up in Singer & we saw it, it had fallen in very badly. Afternoon I took Lewis & Braggins up to see Support line. Got back for tea. We played Cut-throat at night. C.R.E. very annoyed over A D & H's Monmouth's work but he blamed us.

16-12-16   O'Connor & Telford went on leave. RSM took over A D & H but seemed very lost in them. Went to O.P. hot & hard entirely. C.O. & C.C. came in in morning & C.C. stayed to lunch. French had a stunt at Verdun & got about 6 miles of trench. Final preparation being made about X was dinner for the men. I had dinner at 'B' Co &

Diplock was there. Bretherton & I played Wood & Diplock at bridge & just won.

17-12-16   Went up with Bretherton to Support from Fish to Farnborough. C.O. & C.C. were there. Got back about 12. Stayed in all afternoon reading. Bretherton Wood & Griffiths came to dinner & Braggins & Wood just had Bretherton & I at bridge after.

18-12-16   Rode over for way to Bavincourt. Returned through La,. Cauchie, La Herliere, Humbercamps & Pommier. Got back for lunch. Rode up to O.P. in afternoon. Also went round B.E.5. Paid at night.

19-12-16   Went up in morning to Support line with Bretherton. Bosch started putting heavy stuff in RE dump on Ridge Road in Berles. Killed Tierney ex 'A' Co. Bretherton's servant & wounded another 'B' Co man L/Cpl Gaskell. I paid at 2.0 & a hit came in through the window. Dined at night with C.C. & C.O. Ridsdale had gone on a course & Barton was ill in bed. C.O. said all leave was to be stopped after Jan 1 for officers as we were going in to training. After that Bishop Ridsdale, C.C. & Diplock were all going in front of me so I was not going to get any apparently. Freezing hard at night. Got note from Wyatt asking me to dinner.

20-12-16   Went up to O.P. at first - sent a wire to Wyatt in BAB code which went "Interim Tanks situation satisfactory". Nearly got into a row over it! Paid some more men after lunch & then rode over to Bavincourt in afternoon. Bosch shelled the R.E. dump again. Had tea & then played bridge with Wyatt v. MacIvor & another Capt in A.S.C. We won. Owing to slippery roads ..... the c.....al back & Wyatt promised to motor me back. Williamson an Irish Capt in the M..... Vit Sect came in & stayed dinner & he & I beat Parker & MacIvor again. D & C was in & the Cannon. Lynton Smith came in too. A jolly good evening & very cold drive back.

21-12-16   Raining hard & Bosch still shelling RE dump. Went up to see BE5 & found no one in it - wind up. Came back & saw Slater etc about a few things. In afternoon went up to Support & saw Braggins. C.C. went on leave. Lewis got a boil on his spine & was rather bad with it. night party knocked off. Thaw set in.

22-12-16   Wood came to the company. Lewis & Griffiths went on leave & Dean returned. Lewis in great difficulty & pain with his boils which had increased to three. They went off at about 12.45. In afternoon went up to O.P. Found Platt carrying on quite alright. Also saw RSM at B with Wood. Went in morning down to Batt Ord Room over a question of transport. At night Braggins had to go over to Bavincourt to see Col Platt A A & D.M.G. over the tramway up to the trenches. Got back for dinner. Horrid wet day.

23-12-16   Frightful day. Wood took party up & I went up in morning to see him & met the C.O. coming back. There was to be a strafe on in afternoon so the party all got back by 1 o'clock. Frightful afternoon. Came down in torrents most of the time & a very high wind. Braggins started his duties as O/C Tramways. Diplock said he was going on leave on the 27th but no hopes yet of mine coming along but only possibilities.

24-12-16   Spent morning in orderly room & BE5 arranging Xmas dinner etc. Afternoon Braggins & I went round to O.P. & found the same side fallen in again owing to rain. As we left they started shelling the ..... Cutting by H.Q. Put over about 200 shells. Heavy over as well. We also had a look at 'D' post & found it had had a slip as well. Got back to find H.Q. had been pretty well bashed about & had had to evacuate. They came up & made one mess. Everything had to be taken out & was brought up to our mess. Said it was only a temporary move as they were going to find another H.Q. Very windy & rather a rainy day. Only casualties from shelling were 1 R.G.A. killed & 2 wounded.

25-12-16   Christmas day. Rode over in morning to Bavincourt for money. Got back for lunch. Spent afternoon in mess. Men's dinner started at 5.0. Went up to that till 6.45. Their menu was 1lb pork each potatoes turnip carrots onions & apple sauce. Sergts had a dinner after that & we had ours at 8.0. Menu soup fish duck plum pudding & fruit. The men also had ½lb plum pudding each with rum on it & then smokes & 2 litres of beer each. Quite a good dinner. Wood & Bretherton went to La Cauchie to 'D' Co.

26-12-16   Went up to see Simon at Support line in morning found him thick in mud. Afternoon spent paying men & went round to B.E.5 as well. Bosch shelled village - Church end again hard. Wood took over Adj job & S..... came from 7s & took over the Support line.

27-12-16   Rode on to Barrincourt in morning to see Wyatt. Saw him - he said he was going on leave on the 1st so we arranged if he could get off to go together. Saw Paten & Parker. Got back for lunch. Bosch started shelling as I left village & I had a near 'do' by the church. Came back via La Cauchie & saw Pethick. Went along to O.P. in afternoon. Diplock & Ridsdale on leave in morning. Ridsdale going straight from his course.

28-12-16   Went along in morning to Support - found Simon doing nothing very much. Got things moving. Quite foggy so went along to O.O. & had a look on top & saw work getting on alright there & also in A D & H. After went round billets & also to B.E.5. A lot of water there. But getting on alright with the job. Dixon in to tea. Bretherton came in after dinner. Bit of a Strafe on in early morning. Heard Bosch had been over at Gommecourt & got S Staffs knapping. Note from Wyatt to say unable to take me by car to St Pol owing to 3 more Train people going. Comic Cut very optimistic about peace.

29-12-16   Stayed in all day & did not visit any other place but O.P. in evening & B.E.5. Got a note from Wyatt to say he would motor me to St Pol if he could possibly manage it. party taken off Farnborough Shelters & put in Support lines. Struthers came over from 'C' Co. To keep Sinon on Support.

30-12-16   Went along to Farnborough Rd & found it too deep in mud so went along to O.P. & then back to B.E.5. In afternoon went into support by Knobbs Lane & along ravine. Got shelled on coming out. Saw Struthers at work draining trench into Farnborough lane!! When returning from O.P. to bottom of village they dropped a shell quite close to the field by sick ..... but did no damage. O.P. full up with water. C.O. said Allevet was long full up with water - a dug out 40 feet deep was full to the brim. All due to the rain the night before. O'Connor returned from base.

31-12-16   Spent whole morning getting out special work returns of work done since we had come to the area. Capt Clancey R.E. O.C. 20 F.C. R.E. came in to lunch. All changed round as regards work. All now on communications trenches. Had to switch over about midday. Quite a muddle on as to when people are working. Ultimately Synon had to go out with 'B' Co at night on Newark Street. Berry came into tea & a friend of C.O.'s out of old Batt now in 2nd Wilts came to dinner 2nd Lieut. Martin had gone to Tanks. Braggins ill.

1917

1-1-17   Rode on in morning to Bavincourt for money saw Parker-Allen in
          Pay Office - got back for lunch spent afternoon in fixing things up all
          round.

2-1-17   Mess cart left with my things about 10 for Bavincourt. I rode over
          about 12 for lunch with Col. Ainslie, Wyatt, Bridges, M.O. & Parker.
          Left in car about 3.0 for St Pol then for tea & rubber of Bridge & left
          at 6.30. Got to Etaples about 11.0 & left straight away for Calais got
          in after midnight. Capt Hinch A.S.C. also came with us as a four.

3-1-17   Slept in Train in station & at 7.0 a.m. walked down to the quay about
          1½ miles & after waiting about had a very bad breakfast at the
          Terminus. Got on board about 9.0 & left soon after. Hinch being on
          duty in another boat. I ran & so escaped it. Pretty rough crossing.
          Got over about 11.0 & left about 11.45. I got off the boat first &
          bagged 4 seats in Pulman. Got in about 2.15. Went round to 4 Mount
          Street & had a bath etc & then tea at Ri.....s with Roy - L..... Hastings
          T.... ? & Monchit & Miss Constable his fiancee. Had dinner all of us
          at Savoy & then went to Theodore & Co ..... a ..... & a bit of a squash.
          Mr Burn was not there not being very well. Had supper at Savoy &
          then back to M Street. I left about 2.30 a.m. & went round to the
          Euston.

4-1-17   Got up at 6.0 & caught the 6.45 to Lancaster & got in just in time for
          lunch - No-one knew I was arriving. Unplanned surprise! Had no
          breakfast except cup of tea & bread & butter at Euston - No change.
          Slept most of the way. Found Enid very much bigger.

5-1-17   Did nothing all day but went down town in morning for shopping.
          Singer running very well indeed. W..... Holmes very ill. Went to Oh I
          Say after dinner at theatre. Motored there & back. Quite good. Had
          seats in dress circle round at left of stage.

6-1-17   Nothing all morning but go down town. Eric ~~phoned from Carnforth~~
          ~~for me to go rescue him as radiator had frozen.~~ came over to golf &
          had lunch at the club - he & Frank Storey beat Mr Malcolm & myself
          7&5. Eric went out in 37. Played just as well coming back but lost a
          ball at 16 so had no score. Mr Malcolm had a meeting so Eric went
          straight back to The ..... for tea. I brought Mr Malcolm along later.
          Eric got back after tea.

7-1-17　　Kaye & I went to St Helens - not a very nice day. We started at 10.5 & went via Preston & Ormskirk. 55 miles & got there at 5 to 12. No stop at all . Found Aunty ..... & Uncle Bert in. He & I went to see Col Thomas now a commissioner or something in Boy Scouts! Got back for lunch - Gwen & Evelyn came home for lunch but had to return to Rainhill hospital later in evening. Went round to Slater's wife & saw her & told her Slater was alright. Gwen came along to show me the places. Got back leaving at 3.10 about 5.15. Tyre burst just as I was coming in the gate of The ......

8-1-17　　Had a slack day & did nothing but shop in the morning.

9-1-17　　Golf in afternoon. Went down Town & Eric phoned up to say his car had broken down at Carnforth - the radiator having frozen & all water ran out. So I went off & found Dr Jackson had brought him along to Slyne. Took him up & after lunch we went along in Belsize & he & Frank Storey beat us again 2 & 1. Far too cold to play well. Eric came back to dinner & after we all went to Find the Lady - fearful show. Mrs Malcolm did not come. Dr Bury & Mrs Stanton there & we walked back with them. Good day & quite a day.

10-1-17　　Took Eric as far as Carnforth & then we found his car alright so I left him there & got back - went down town & back for lunch spent afternoon doing a puzzle. Kaye packing. Billiards at night.

11-1-17　　Caught 9.5 to Wolverhampton. Train did not turn up so we had to rush off in the Belsize. Just caught train. Changed at Acton Bridge, Crewe & Stafford. Taxi to meet us & we got in for lunch. He & Jack came to dinner & Johnson & Mrs Johnson came round afterwards. Dinner needless to say being very late - about 7.15

12-1-17　　Caught 11.55 Low Level to London had no lunch. Rather a slow train. Long wait at Wolverhampton & also at Paddington to get a taxi. Got to Savoy Hotel & then rang Burn up & could not get on to anyone. Got round after to Mount Street - saw Pat, Laurie Hastings & Roy - took him round to see Pilkingtons at 12 Hyde Park Place. Mrs Pilkington ill in bed so we only saw the ..... & children. Burns all came to Vanity Fair & dinner at Savoy. Also Laurie Hastings but Nelson Keys[126] not being in it made it very flat only spectacular. We were separated 3 hours there. Then had supper after & then to bed.

---

[126] Successful British actor [1886-1939] who appeared in movies and co-founded the British and Dominions Film Corporation at Elstree Studios.

13-1-17 Breakfast about 10.0. Then we went shopping Kaye to Peter Robinsons. I went to Benson & Hedges & then both to Harrods. Just ..... then but ultimately got out & went in to Toussauds. Found Mrs Mary McLean & Fran Stevens there. Had lunch & then went to the see Ronald play footer at Richmond. Hope put us into the .... & we went round by Putney & did not get there till 3.30. Back for tea - then to Savoy to dinner. Roy had to go on duty at Epsom on Sat. Had good dinner & then to the Girl from Ciro's not frightfully good. Good acting but not much of a piece. Back to supper & bed.

14-1-17 Breakfast at 10. Caught staff train at 1.0 from Charing X. Questioned about rank but said acting Major. Quite a good crossing. Got to Calais about 5.0. Nasty accident - lady's foot being cut off by tram opposite terminus. Got a bed at Victoria Hotel left by a ..... man called Henderson. Clean bed. Glad to get to bed. Went round after breakfast to Ronald to cadge £5 off him as Hotel bill too big!

15-1-17 Breakfast at 7.30 caught 8.30 from F...t..... about 5 miles out of Calais. C.C. Watson O.R. W.S.M. were in the same carriage. Spent all day getting to Doulais about 9.45 p.m. Nothing to eat. Got a bed & dinner there. Bed was in another house.

16-1-17 Took a motor lorry to .....icourt & then an ambulance to Lucheux & went to B. H.Q. Found Diplock & C.O. & Maj. Beal away at Doullens. Had lunch found 6 new officers ..... Beal had arrived. Lieut Taylor - McCreary - Glover - Weatherley - McKenzie - Howes. Came up to company at La Foutain Farm in afternoon. Found the place in a terrible mess. So started putting things straight. Pethick was O.C. company & O'Connor & Walker & Braggins also there.

17-1-17 Wandered out & saw the work. Also found the billets. Went down to B.H.Q. about mess & saw the C.O. & Maj. Beal. Had tea with Hodges & then went on to the Blue Bird with Hodges, Pethick, Walker, Weatherley & McKenzie. McCreary & Glover attached to mess. Braggins went on leave also M.O.

18-1-17 Thick snow. Wandered round work in morning. O'Connor went to H.Q. to pay them. Stayed in all afternoon & evening. O'Connor, Gl.... & McCreary went to Blue Birds. 2nd Lt Joliffe joined Batt.

19-1-17 Wandered round with Pethick in the morning. Spent afternoon in writing letters etc. Pethick went down to practice match for next day.

Band had a practice in afternoon. Played Bridge at night with Pethick, Walker & O'Connor. C.O. & Hodges went to Amiens.

20-1-17   Went up to work in the morning. After lunch Pethick & I went down to football match v 35th Div Artillery. He was playing. When we got down there we heard that 'A' Co was moving on Monday to Dainville just W of Arras & that ultimately the Batt. was all going to Agny. Later in the day we heard we were to go straight to Agny. We were going by Motor Bus. Watched the match with Matthews. C.O. & new M.O. were there. Also Ormerod & B O Moore - the latter was playing for the Artillery. We won 14-0. Good game but ground was very hard & a lot of caked snow on it. Got back for tea. ..... of H.Q. had gone to Amiens.

21-1-17   Walked with Pethick to lunch at H.Q. Got back to tea.

22-1-17   Buses to take us to Agny turned up at 9.15 - we were a long time embarking owing to only sending 6 buses instead of 7. A M.M.P. who would send them into the ditch at the side of road to let cars etc pass. At 9.45 another bus turned up. Ours got going about 10.30 leaving Pethick going on leave. Came through Ivergny - Sus St Leger - Warluzel - Sombrin - Barly -Fossaux - Wanquetin to Warlus where we debussed & marched on to Dainville. Then saw 42 Brig Staff Capt who supplied a guide. Stanly & Staff & Col Wilson were all there. Came to Agny found Slater had been wounded & Walker had gone to Simencourt to billet Transport. Were given shocking billets - only cellars available & officers were distributed among other Batt. in the village - I did not take any of them but slept in cellars. O'Connor & I slept together in a cellar. Frightfully cold & not much sleep.

23-1-17   No work. We moved into new mess & men's quarters. Men worked on clearing out the chalk & stuff in them. Saw Hall, Woolley & Armstrong. Hall told me the work we & R.E.s had to do. Mainly preparing rabbit wire for camouflage & 2 sets of dug outs. Still very severe frost. No post.

24-1-17   Walker, McCreary & Gleave on work the latter two for instructions. O'Connor had to walk over to Simencourt to inspect & generally see how the transport was getting on. Still frightfully cold & the mess still progressing. No post.

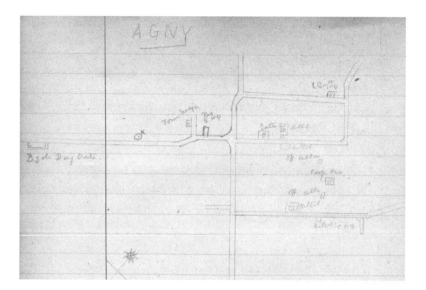

25-1-17   Glover took working party. Went round work & called in at R.E.s. Men going strong. Windows pulled up mainly. Got a very small post in. Frost still continuing.

26-1-17   McCreary with working party. Went round work. Frost still continuing. No post in. Heard C.C. was very seady. Got a note from him. Mess still progessing.

27-1-17   A D Walker took party. O'Connor went to Wailly to get money. Went out wrong time so could not get money. Rations fearfully late owing to Bosch shelling Saulté. Arrived about 2.40. Men going strong. Day acrid & cold as about starting work on dug outs next morning. Post in. Not good.

28-1-17   Gleave taking party. We started on dug outs. Brigade H.Q. remainder on camouflage. Frost still continuing. Day & Woolly came round but did not stay long. Two Liverpool Officers were asked round to dinner so we worked hard all day & practically finished it & got a coat of whitewash on. They did not come up having forgotten about it. Walker went to see them but they had had dinner.

29-1-17   McCreary with party started on Brigade dugouts. No post. Frost still going strong. No news on camouflage. Day & Wooley to dinner. No post.

30-1-17   A D Walker on duty. C.O. turned up for lunch in jolly good form. Said C.C. was better & we could stay. Rather impressed by the mess. Walked on to Achincourt with him where Bury now D.A.A. & Q.M.G. had his car & took him back. Bury said he could lunch with us on 1st. Two Liverpools were to come to dinner but heard nothing about them. Day said clay outreached water level. No post. Frost still going strong.

31-1-17   Woolley giving up his work & taking on tramways. So 200th who had come into attachment - took over & Hill came round at tea time to see me. Most of company on camouflage. A.D.W. & McCreary went into Arras to arrange about. Billeting H.Q. but could do nothing for them. Mess about finished. My cellar almost done. No post. Frost still going strong. Snowed a lot.

1-2-17   Went round work - on getting back found Torey Staff Capt 89th Brig & Stephenson the new Town Major. He had come about a detachment of 'D' Co & M.G.S. who are coming to build a new Batt. H.Q. & put ..... in state of panic. Torey stayed to lunch. In the evening the detachment turned up 39 of them. Also a large Post. Frost still hard.

2-2-17   Put Gleave on the job of building cellars etc. Started work but lacked tools etc. Town Mayor seemed a very shifty sort of fellow & wanted to alter everything. Had another Post in at night. Still hard frost. My cellar practically finished all but 6ft of canvas. Got a lot of parcels in. saw Clavering.

3-2-17   Carried on work as usual. Saw T.M. who had another scheme for Billetting. Poor fellow did not know if he was on his head or his hands. Braggins turned up at night back from leave. Frost still continuing. No Post as usual.

4-2-17   Carried on in morning & saw Town Major about Billets but he had to see Brig Maj 89th at 7.20 so left him as usual undecided. Walker & I walked in to Arras & saw Town Major's assistant - a Capt Clark - late 16th Man. Then went in to the cathedral. A simply immense ruin. Got back for tea. T..... ..... into tea. Heard Batt were moving into Simencourt & to Arras on 6th.

5-2-17   Batt moved into Dainville & did not get to Arras. Walked round the work. Frost still continuing. In the evening O'Connor & I walked in to Achicourt & saw Hodges & Strachan & Griffiths & Weatherley. Got back for dinner & found ..... Walker's brother.

6-2-17   C.O. & C.C. turned up shortly after breakfast. Beal came in later. Walked round our work & then came in to lunch. Bishop came in for tea. After lunch we all & Walker went up with him to see the Russian Saps. They went off after tea back to Dainville.

7-2-17   Had a beastly throat so got up late. C.C. Dixon & Bretherton came in to lunch. Lt West - late Sergt West 'A' Co who went to Altcar as musketry instructor came in - he was in the 20th Liv. Did not stay long. All went back for tea. Bretherton came in after but did not stay. Pethick returned from leave.

8-2-17   C.O., C.C. & Struthers came into mess - first two stayed to lunch. Bretherton came in to tea. Stayed in most of the day. Pethick, A D Walker & ..... went to Arras. Gagnall, Bishop's understudy Byrne from 17th Liverpools came in to dinner. After dinner Walker Boulton & West came in. walker, Bagnall, O'Connor & I plated Bridge.

9-2-17   Usual work but C.O. came to lunch with C.C. & made a large fuss of us working under REs. We heard no more but I got a note to say be in at 12 next day. Not feeling very fit so went to bed very early after dinner. Frost still going. Started some T2 Mortar Emps 4. No 2,3,4 & 17

10-2-17   C.O., Beal & Riddick came in to lunch & Maj Clavering O.C. R.E. came in at 12 o'clock to talk things over. Decided to have our own work entirely & so we have to start on a dug out next day off Girl Street between support & front lines. Pethick & I went up with A D Walker up to T.M. Emp & then to the new dug out. Stopped work on Brig H.Q. Dug outs. Asked out to dinner by Walker's brother to 20th King's H.Q. But not feeling fit so did not go. Played Bridge after dinner with Pethick, B..... & Gleave. Pethick & I saw 'D' Co & Adj. 20th about Agny Defences. Capt E.....y was Adj.

11-2-17   Pethick & I went round Agny defences in morning & found CC in to lunch. Hindley called in just before we set out. Started work on dug out off Girl St. Pethick & I walked round to dug out in afternoon. ADW was asked out to dinner at 20th Liv but felt he did not want to go but went in the end. C.O. & Adj & half Batt had gone to Div school. Played Bridge & bed early.

12-2-17   C.O. & CC to lunch. Pethick & I wandered round trenches in morning. Found R.E.s working in T.M. Emp. So sent Pethick to find Clavering & tell him we were taking men off. C.O. held orderly room in afternoon. We all walked up to H.Q. Dainville - called in at 'D' Co & found Hodges had gone up too. When we got there we found 2 new officers Lidgett & Baines & a draft of 8 men. Had tea - Ridsdale & M.O. there & then Hodges & I walked back. Got in for dinner. Saw preliminary orders for push.

13-2-17   Hindle called in & I went with him & Lt Cotteral R.E. & explored a long chalk passage for cable purposes. After lunch went round with O'Connor round billets. A D Walker & Pethick went up to H.Q. for tea. Bishop called in at tea. Pethick went up in morning to Dug out. Did not go up myself. Bishop & Bagnall came in to dinner & bridge.

14-2-17   McCreary had to go up to see the C.O. I suppose about the report I sent in of him which was not good. Pethick & I went up to dug out. Met Beal & Sinon up there & then C.O. & CC on the way back also Struthers. C.C., C.O., & C.R.E. came in to lunch. C.O. did not have any. Bretherton came in after to tea & stopped tea. At dinner G.S.O.3 Capt J. H. Brockholes came in, a very nice fellow who had been in before to see us about some camouflage stuff to be drawn evening for a cable line. A subaltern came in after by name Lt Baker R.E. Signals. Orders McCreary to go to 'C' Co.

15-2-17   McCreary reported to 'C' Co. went up twice to dug out - morning & afternoon with Pethick. C.O. & C.C. to lunch. Bolton in to tea. Hinder & Alana R.E. signals also in to lunch. After dinner Most..... R.E. signals also came in to see about camouflage. Talked for about an hour.

16-2-17   C.O. & CC in to lunch. They brought J.E. Mercer in to join the company. Rest of company on camouflage. No-one in to tea. Started to rain in afternoon. Bosches had sausages up with the result that the village got shelled slightly with shrapnel. Culshaw came back from Hospital to 'C' Co. Shaw turned up too & went to 'C' Co. Mortimer came in at dinner time & stayed dinner.

17-2-17   Went round work early. O'Connor started on the tunnel under Agny - Agny Chateau road but had to stop as we should not have been able to get it in water level being only 4ft below side of road. About 6 ft below road surface level. C.O. Ridsdale, C.R.E. Beal, Culshaw & Atkinson the R.E.'s Adj came in to lunch. Went round again in the afternoon, saw Bishop & Bagnall in the morning. Bishop & Bagnall came in to dinner - very uproarious. Pethick had a bath in the ...ath.

11th (S). Bn. South Lancashire Regt.(Pioneers).

PRELIMINARY OPERATION ORDERS.

The Battalion will be employed during the forthcoming
offensive on work as shown below.
These orders are liable to alteration.

"A" COY.

1 Platoon will be engaged on the upkeep of roads in the
area to the rear of AGNY.

1 Platoon will be engaged on the upkeep of Communication
Trenches.

1 Platoon will be engaged on the upkeep of the Denaville
Track. MILES @ MiLES

(The above mentioned work will begin at the same time as
the preliminary bombardment).

1 Platoon will be engaged on the forward Tramways along
the Sunken Road, Near G.16. *g 20 (C R E 10-3-17)*

"B" COY.   2 Platoons will be engaged clearing forward roads.

2 Platoons will be in Reserve.

"C" COY.   This Company will be in Reserve.

"D" COY.   2 Platoons will dig forward Communication Trench from the
Sap at about the junction of Trenches at G.7 & G.8 to the
German Sap marked Y.8 on the 1/10,000 Map.

2 Platoons will dig a Trench from G.11 to the German Sap
marked Y.11 on the 1/10,000 Map.

These Trenches will be Fire-stepped and traversed for fire
in a South Westerly direction.

Full details of all the proposed work will be issued later.

In the meantime, Officers Commanding Coy's will,as far as
possible,detail their Officers for their prospective work, so
that they may have an opportunity of reconnoitring the work,
and the best means of getting to it.

"D" Coy will probably be in Assembly Trenches South East of
AGNY.
Remainder of the Battalion will be in the Assembly Trenches
in the rear of AGNY CHATEAU.

H + ...

Lt.Colonel.

17th Feb.1917.   Comdg 11th S.Lancs.Regt.(Pioneers).

Copy. to O.C. "A" Coy.
             "B" Coy.
             "C" Coy.
             "D" Coy.

18-2-17   Received preliminary orders for push among other things. Also orders for the two new jobs. Took Piggott up with me to locate them. Went round by Girl St & saw that job. Got back for lunch - No-one in to lunch. Sent O'Connor up to measure up the two new jobs. Went up to Girl St Tunnels mortar stunt on the part of the Bosch. O'Connor could not get along to two new jobs. Bretherton came in to tea. Quiet night. A D Walker went to Bath early returned & played Bridge till about 2 a.m. We went to bed early. Got invitation from Bing Boys to dinner Monday night. O'Connor went up to jobs again after tea.

19-2-17   Went up with C.C. to new jobs. Quite a bad Trench Mortar Strafe on. Grouse St & Gun St & Support were quite knocked about. O'Connor was up. Went round all the jobs. C.O., C.R.E. & CC in to lunch. Went up with Pethick to new jobs again in the afternoon & saw jobs. Lidgett came in to tea. Pethick & I went to the Bing Boys to dinner & bridge - had quite a good evening there though Bishop had a slight attack of flu & did not get up to much. They had a priceless menu. New jobs were at M.15.a.6.5 Grouse St Bomb stores & M.15.a.25.1.5 Aid Post.

20-2-17   Dragged Pethick round the trenches in the morning & saw all their dug outs - Gleave was on the job. No-one came in to lunch. Raining slightly all day. Beckett 19 K.L.R. came into dinner. Had a bath after dinner about 12.30.

21-2-17   Went round in morning with Pethick. C.C. came in to lunch. C.O. not well. Pethick & I walked back to Dainville with him, calling in at 'D' Co & new M.O. & Ridsdale to tea. Got back to find Bretherton & Hindle had been in to tea. No one in 15 Division.

22-2-17   Went round by myself in morning. Got back to find C.C. waiting for Hodges - who was supposed to be in 11.30. He did not come in till 1.0. H..... was with C.C. & all 3 stayed to lunch. Met Hindle in morning who said he would come in to tea but did not turn up till about 7.15

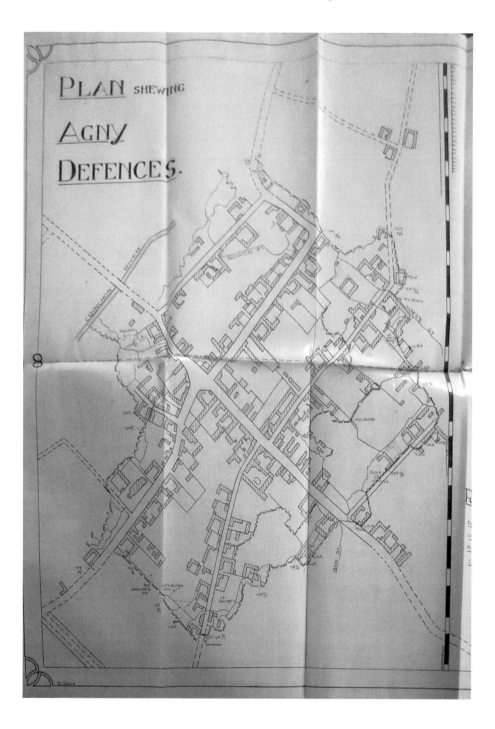

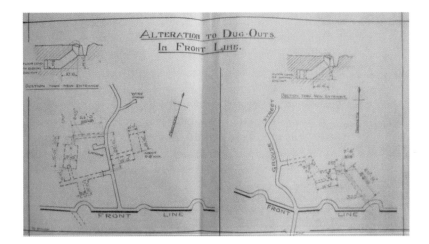

23-2-17   Went round in morning with Pethick - saw C.C. & Maj Beal up there. Heard a rumour that Bosch was using Russian & French prisoners in Support lines & some gave themselves up but it was contradicted. Got back to lunch. Saw Bretherton & Dixon early. C.C. & Dean came in to tea. & stayed the whole afternoon .... to tea. Bagnall came to dinner - Bishop still indisposed so could not come so we asked Bethel round to take his place - he came but was not very fit & finally just before he left was ill. Bretherton came along too & we had a very ..... party. Broke up about 1.30 a.m. Hodges came in about 11 p.m. but did not stay long.

24-2-17   Went round in the morning. C.C. to lunch. Nothing doing in afternoon. A. D. Walker went round & borrowed the piano from Batt H.Q. in the village & we had much music & singing in the evening. Capt B.R. Delbs M.G.C. came to dinner he was A.D.'s music master at Private school. Quite a good sort & humorous. More singing & bed fairly early about 1 a.m. Played bridge after he left. Bishop in bed. Still in with Dugouts in front line. C.O. still unwell. A new officer called Ramsbotham reported & 4 men came to the Battalion. S.T.E. Clench to 'C'. W J Owen to 'D'. R L Leake to 'B'. J R Cole to 'D'.

25-2-17   Went up in morning round jobs. C.C. to lunch. Went up again in afternoon with Dixon round the jobs. Had a quiet evening. Nothing doing at dinner or tea. Bit of a raid by Bosch on our right about dinner time. Also at night there was a good ..... strafe on our right. Ramsbottom was unharmed. P..... : He came round the work in the morning & was a very slow walker indeed. Hodges came in but did not stay to a meal. He was leaving .....incourt but had orders to come to Agny & also to go to Arras so was not quite sure what was going to happen to him & was generally in a despondent state. He came in after dinner.

26-2-17   Went round work in morning. C.O. & C.C. came to lunch also C.R.E. Spent the afternoon on a board with Dean & Lewis to decide if it was reasonable to consider Pte Maloney who was missing from July by Trones Wood. Could not decide till heard from Fairclough (Ration man) so they stayed to dinner & tea. Heard 'D' Co was coming in to Agny not Arras.

27-2-17   C.O. & C.C. to lunch. Went round in morning. Board finished soon after lunch. 'D' Co came in to Agny for billets. Had night work in Trans line. Went out at night in slacks & got thoroughly muddy all over. Lot of bullets flying round but not much else doing. Got a few letters so sat up late answering them.

28-2-17   Went round in morning with Piggott found Mercer up there & he came too. Came back via the railway very dirty. C.C. came in just for a minute before lunch but did not stop. Hodges came in for lunch. Had hair cut in afternoon. W. Walker & their Padré Preston came in after tea & had some. Saw C.R.E. & Hall in the morning. West came in to dinner & had bridge after. Had a few whizzbangs in just after dinner. Only a few. Went out after dinner & saw Walker & Gleave on the tramways. Had a bath about 12 o'clock. Very good indeed.

1-3-17   Went round in morning with Pethick & saw all the work. Went up again in afternoon & saw Grouse St & Green St jobs. As we were returning in morning they started to shell round about our cooker so we waited a bit & got in just for lunch. C.C. had been round but left & did not stay lunch. No-one in to tea. Wood came in to dinner & had bridge after.

2-3-17   Waited for C.C. to come in & went round with him - Pethick & Ridsdale. C.C. came to lunch but Ridsdale did not. Went up in afternoon & saw Grouse & Green St jobs. No-one in to tea or dinner. Want fairly early to bed. Fine day but a bit for post at night. C.O. went on leave & Maj Beal had to leave for the Fusiliers. Some of the ..... last left on 3rd or 2nd but believe 2nd.

3-3-17   Went round in morning & started new entrance in Girl St job. C.C. & Harvey came in to lunch & Pethick & I went out after & saw Girl St job. Quite a stunt going on by our artillery from 3 p.m.to 5 p.m. Very little retaliation. No-one in to dinner or tea - quiet night playing bridge. No Post.

4-3-17   Went up with Pethick in morning. No-one in to lunch or tea. Had mess whitewashed in morning & we put up the mirror & painted all woodwork white & generally titivated up the mess. Looked quite nice when we had finished it. Bolton came in after dinner & played bridge. We had a service at 3.0 to which 3 or 4 of the officers went. Bosch supposed to have let off gas opposite Wailly about dinner time - did not smell anything of it here. O'Connor thought he did when going to his dug out. Very poor post. Made the band chair.

5-3-17   Went round in morning with Piggott & found they had broken through at Frown St Aignet. Not perfect but can make a good job of it I think. Found we had had 2 or 3 inches of snow before breakfast. Nippy day. No-one in to dinner. Had a horrible sore throat - went to bed early - no-one in to tea or dinner. Wandered out to Gird St in afternoon.

6-3-17   Horrid sore throat. Went up with Pethick in morning & saw all the jobs. Got back for lunch. Stayed in all afternoon. No-one in to lunch. Saw 'B' Co. No-one else. Bosch aeroplanes fearfully cheeky in morning & came right down on the village. Saw Ridsdale in afternoon. Trench mortared a bit in afternoon & morning.

7-3-17   Went round in morning by myself. Snow on the ground in the morning. Nothing doing in morning. Saw Ramsbottom on the road Agny to Beauvain - quite by the village. Saw Woolly on job in afternoon - he seemed rather windy. Had an argument with him about who was in charge of the job. No-one in the mess for any meals. In afternoon we had another walk up to work - nothing doing. Pethick & I were in to dinner - had most awful luck at bridge at night.

8-3-17   Went round in morning with Pethick & found C.C. was up - he had been indisposed with diahorea so had not been up lately. He & C.R.E. came in to lunch. Saw Ward again in afternoon nothing doing. Bretherton in to dinner. Stayed fairly late - had bridge.

9-3-17   Went round in morning with Braggins - went up in afternoon to road. C.C. came in to lunch. Got Pia..... round in afternoon. Gorman came in to dinner & played the piano & stayed till 1.30 a.m.as he was on duty at 3.0 had bridge & sing song.

10-3-17   Went round work in evening with Braggins - things seemed to be going on alright. Went round again in afternoon. Rather busy all day making arrangements for the concert in the evening. Two Bedfords came in to dinner also Dixon & Foreman. Bedfords were 2nd Lt Methuen & Hobbs. Concert started at 8.0. We were a bit late in starting. Two Bedfords came to help. Sgt Tebbott & Pte Adams.

Programme was
1. Gorman Selections
2. Quartet Sgt Queen Sgt Pendlebury & Pte Booth. The Vacant Chair.
3. Pte Adams Bedfords Song & 2 encores
4. Pte Rowe When you come home dear
5. Pethick On the day on which peace is declared - 1 encore
7. Sgt Tebbott Piano sketch 1 encore
6. Pte Judges Annie Laurie
8. Duet L/Cpl Swift & Pte Roberts The Karl...rd Watch
9. L/Cpl Knockton Casey - 1 encore
10. Pte Flynn 'B' Co a song
We had a rum issue before starting & another one at half time.
Second half.
1. Pethick - Keep on carrying on - 2 encores
2. Pte Adams Irish songs - 2 encores
3. Pte Atherton 1 song & Isobel as encore
4. Sgt Tebbott sketch on piano - 1 encore
5. Pte Flynn impromptu
6. Ramsbottom meitatum of sa...ly ...o
7. Knockton song & 1 encore
God save the King

The whole show went off awfully well - I think everyone enjoyed it. Dixon could not stand the fug & smoke & had duties long before half time. The items which went off best where Pethick's especially the Keep on carrying on which he had added to by 5 extra verses on bathing, Pit Props & things up to dug outs - another rations & one on Braggins collecting souvenirs. He had a Lancashire chorus to end up with when Glover, Burn, Mercer & Walker acted the fool as the beauty chorus. The two Bedfords were very good & got a lot of encores. Knockton's Carey was very funny & applauded all round. He had no idea of time. Then another turn got quite a reception for singing topical songs. We came back & got a drink & then bed. I heard the Division had sent for the piano. I think the Bedfords thoroughly enjoyed themselves.

11-3-17   Went round the dug outs in the morning. C.C. came to lunch in afternoon. Pethick & Mercer who had come along in the morning came round with us to see the new line - we went down Guy St to the road & walked up the Reserve line then went along the Discus line - a fearful sweat & very much fallen in so much so as were walking up from it our waists above ground. Got back about 3.20 & found Woolly. Had a little argument with him & put things on the correct footing. Went out after dinner & saw Mercer at work on the road everything going off all right. Got back about 10.30 & had a bath & went straight to bed.

12-3-17   Started out early with Piggott - went up Hope St - it had rained hard in the night & the trench was in a fearful state. Then up Haig St & saw the work. Walked down it to Hope St & found a tree had been blown down which had been down since Mercer left - there was a stunt early on the brickstacks to our left & they had been putting a bit of stuff on Hope St & the road - hence the tree. We sweated right up Hope St fearfully dirty & right along the front line - the 49th Div Front was awfully dirty. After a lot of struggling we got along to our front & found the Wilts all with their gas helmets on - found it was only a practice so did not mind - got along to Grouse St & found that alright but unable to get any stuff up the trenches were so bad our front line was infinitely better than the 49th. Met C.C. with A D Walker but no orderly. Walker came back & we went in & found the other two jobs going on alright. Got back for lunch. Padre Thompson came in after lunch & had a game of chess with Bunny Walker. Woolly, Dean, Wood & Bagnall turned up for tea. Bagnall stayed on for dinner others all went. Pethick went up to see Mercer at night - early to bed.

13-3-17   Woolly came in just after breakfast & he & I went up to view the road. As we were going up Fritz was shelling the road by Grey St - so we cut along the reserve line - very dirty & saw the road - all was well but a bit more work to be done on the reserve line - left Woolly & went back by way of reserve - the loop - Granger - Reserve into Gravel - the support & the Glich & along the front line to Grouse - found they had had a nasty fall then at the corner & it would put us back about 3 days. Sent the afternoon shift to carry up material & put Ashcroft & his party who were on the afternoon shift in Green St in the evening. Green St & Girl St both going on well. Came back to Grouse before lunch. Bagnall & Bishop came in to tea. Bishop was going off to hospital tomorrow generally bad with neuralgia - toothache - impetigo etc. Went up at night along Gravel St to Grouse

St & found getting on very slowly. On the way back up Gravel St the Bosch was putting 5.9s over & nearly got Piggott & I more than once. Braggins & O'Connor went along to the Bing Boys & dinner. Played bridge with Pethick Burns & Gleave. Early to bed.

14-3-17   Went round with Pethick in the morning & saw road. The were dropping them on Guy Street but they stopped as we got up there & we struggled along the front line which was pretty bad till we got to the job & found Grouse St was looking very well considering & then round - saw ...tham All the jobs looked going on alright. Girl St practically finished. Stayed in all afternoon & evening. Had bridge & a bath before going to bed.

15-3-17   Went round with Pethick in the morning only round the dugout. Being very wet we gave the road a slip. Got back for lunch & found C.O. & C.C. in for lunch. Fine day. Heard a big raid was to take place at 10.30 p.m.by Bedfords & 18 Liv. Heard later that Bedfords part was off as the night before a patrol reported that their saps & front line had been filled with wire & mines etc so it was no use going over tonight. Heard the bombardment etc but very poor show of retaliation etc. Got to bed fairly easily. No material owing to bad weather conditions.

16-3-17   Went round with Piggott in morning to road & then along front line to dug outs. Met Pethick on our way round. Finished the round. All jobs nearly stopped for want of material. Went along to road & had a look at what the work required. Back up for lunch. No-one in for lunch. Went round the dug outs in afternoon with Pethick & also showed Ghan the work he had to do to Brighton road. Went out after dinner & saw Glover on the road. Later on we got whiz banged & gas over lunch J.T. Pennington c.....ded.

17-3-17   Went round with Pethick in the morning. C.O., Diplock & C.R.E. to lunch. Small party on Grantham St owing to shortages of material. Saw that party at work & saw work in wood at Petit Chateau. Lewis & St..... in to dinner. Refused to have any men carrying for REs but heard later they had to. At any rate we had no-one tonight. Wrote to Kaye but did not play bridge. Walker got orders to go to the RFC at Hendon. We painted the Reg ..... in green paint on his back to send him off with.

18-3-17   Started work as usual & then heard Bosch had retaliated - the 20th & 18 KLR went over the top about 10 a.m. found no-one & followed up past Beaumains. By the night we heard they had gone about 3 miles. We were all stopped work & started on the Agny Beaurain road clearing it. a lot of very indiscriminate heavy shelling on the Bosches part but nothing else - nothing seemed known & every thing very uncertain. We finished our job but told we had to do & Lorry us in & out again after dinner. We are to be relieved by 'C' Co. Nothing known at night. Started again at 9 a.m. & worked till 11.30 & got back at midnight & were told to start work again at 8.30 next morning.

19-3-17   Started work at 8.30. C.O. came up about 10.0 & he & Diplock & I walked to Mercatel. C.R.E. came up & saw the road. Walked all afternoon till 4.30 & got back for tea. News still very uncertain. Reserves of Cavalry being in action & taking St Leger. Started to rain when we came in very windy so aeroplane observation impossible. O'Connor went sick. I went to bed about 10.0 but was woken up at 11.0 & 12.0 again with notes from orderly room.

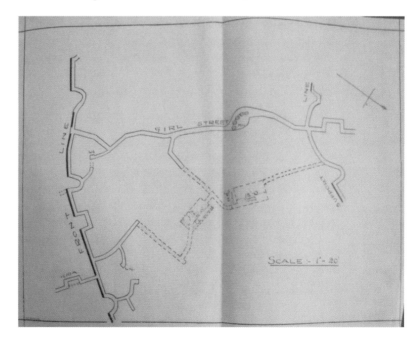

20-3-17   Pethick took the company out at 2.0 & Cooke was up again. I got up at 5.0 & had breakfast & got on to the job about 6.15 got back about 8.30. Snowed & rained while we were on the job. Played cards all the evening with Burn, Ghan & Mercer. C.R.E. came in to lunch. No news. C.C. came in just before & then later on for lunch he had been round the road. Told us what he wanted done tonight. Got out again at 6.0 having paraded the company at 4.30. went out with Pethick & Burn. Company came along later & set them out & then returned for dinner. O'Connor still sick. Saw the Doc in the morning & he said he might send him to hospital.

21-3-17 Got up late had a jolly good night. C.O. & C.C. came in about 11.0 & said there was no work at all today & that Batt was moving it was behind to Ficheux on the 23rd. also that Struthers had told Col Poyntz[127] of the Bedfords that Neuville Vitasse was empty. Struthers had not been there at all really he had been to Boiry or Bosleux. Played bridge all afternoon & then after tea C.C. sent his man for me & I rode up to Dainville. C.C. in good form had a lot of new records - had dinner & some bridge. Lost to C.O. & C.C. with Diplock. Went back. Very hard in the dark as the whole road was one long line of transport. Got back & had a bath. Snowing when I went to bed.

22-3-17 Went out onto Ficheux-Mercatel road. Got the men spread & they started shelling us. Perfect marvel how no-one was hit - they put 2 into the middle of us. Braggins & Gleave were out with Pethick. Burn & Mercer relieved us at 7.0. Walker came in after lunch & told us that ..... Struthers after 1 officer 1 Sergt 2 L/Cpl & 2 men had been scuppered in Neuville Vitasse. Spent afternoon packing up after tea. Evening after dinner we played bridge.

23-3-17 Company set off at 9.0 for Blairville. Went rather a long way round by Wailly & then across the trenches & got rather tied up. When we got there we found the R.A. & R.E.s had got everywhere & we were given a totally insufficient place for our quarters & men's. Left Burn behind to clean up & put everything into the wagons. No transport could get or out of Blairville owing to state of roads over Bosch front line. Village in much better state of affairs than we expected. Got to work straight away at 11 o'clock. Made the road passable. Presumed all water poisoned - a horse having died in 2 hours after drinking it. Managed to get a comfortable night as all beds etc came up. Pethick & I slept in the mess. Burn arrived just before dark. All transport got through or dumped in no man's land. Beautiful fine day but frost at night.

24-3-17 No officers on parade so I had to take it out myself & get the men out. Had a party on the front from Shrapnel Corner to Bethencourt

---

[127] Commanding Officer of 2nd Battalionfrom 10 Nov 1915 until 28 Feb 1918.

Corner. Came back across the fields. Saw an aeroplane come down. Also 4 or 5 balloons came over from the Bosch with papers attached to them which they either dropped or all came down together. I got one of them. Gazette des Ardennes. There seemed nothing in it but the War from a captured Frenchman's point of view. Had dinner at HW & played Bridge with the C.O., C.C. & Hodges. The time changed to Summer time & 11 p.m. became midnight. Beautiful day frost at night.

25-3-17 Officers again late on parade. I got out & found no parade. The Cpl of the guard apparently found no-one would take him seriously when he woke them up. Rode round to Shrapnel Corner in the morning. Saw Stevenson at Bethencourt on the way back to lunch early & relieved Pethick on the job in the afternoon. Walked round with the C.O. morning round Panet's Posts afternoon on the job. He seemed in very good humour. Maj Beal turned up again at night & a Capt Dunthorne who was posted to 'B' Co. went to bed early. Beautiful day but clouded over a bit in afternoon.

26-3-17 Got up at 7.0 found it was raining. Beastly day. Subalterns not too punctual again. Pethick took the company out as I had to leave & be at Orderly Room over man who had been caught taking things off dead French men. Took afternoon party. At night Gleave Mercer & myself went to H.Q. Mess & saw a cinema show G.C.O. quite a good show. Mess getting more comfortable. Started to snow in afternoon. Had a great time on the work with an A.A. gun lorry which got stuck on the corduroy. O'Connor returned from Hospital. ..... Sergt Brown blew a finger off with nose cap.

27-3-17 Got up at 7.15 again. Beautiful fine day. Pethick went on work. Rode round in the morning but started to snow so did not do any more riding. Saw Hindle in afternoon. C.C. came to tea. Turned into a horrid wet day & snowed hard. Quite a good post at night except for me. My shanty not nearly finished.

28-3-17 Went round roads twice in the morning. Put on two first jobs so rode round in the afternoon through Bethencourt - Shrapnel Corner then old ridge round to Allouette & back by Ransart. A very bad road from Allouette to Ransart. Fine & frosty day. Buildings getting on well. Still sleeping in the mess.

29-3-17 Had to sit on board of enquiry on how A S S Brown A.O.C. lost his hand. Taylor & Lewis were members. Apparently Brown had a nose of which he had got from a shell C.C. was taking to bits & it went off. We spent all day as at first there was no evidence & then we gradually got quite a lot. The thing was we did not want to implicate C.C. as it might seem as if Brown was taking it to bits by C.C.'s orders. It took all morning & afternoon & they both stayed to lunch. Bridge at night. Still sleeping in the mess.

30-3-17   Had to sit or rather as Prisoner's Friend on a F.G.C. martial at Bellacourt on Pte Hart for looting the dead. So rode on with Diplock. President was Maj Roberts 16 Man & Diplock was Prosecutor. Went off alright. My opinion was it was Brockholes evidence against the Prisoner & no other witnesses. I should have given in favour of the Prisoner. Needless to say I don't know the result. After went round to our company H.Q. & had a drink. Found 2 or 3 of the old ones who had been to Suzanne. Then went on to H.Q. & had lunch with Elstob - just the same only a bit older. Met a few more Thomas, Gibbon etc. Lawton Smith & Ballag..... were both there. Got back after lunch. At 5 'B' Co officers were playing 'C' Co. 'C' won 3-2. Bridge & then slept in my new shanty. Pethick still in the mess.

31-3-17   Spent morning riding round ..... whole company in Bult...court wood except for No 1. who are erecting a screen on the railway embankment. Walked up with C.C. to the screen & they were getting on with the job. Mercer was up there. Afternoon went along the road. In afternoon I went up to the screen & when there found Gorman & just caught Mercer. They started shelling & rather frightened the old man, so when one had landed quite close we got off. Then never stopped going till in our ..... Got back alright. C.O. had a talk to O.C. Companys about men getting slack. Told off Platoon officers. Heard that Hart had got 1 years imprisonment. Had a soccer match v 18 Man. They beat us 4-0. Bridge & bed. Clench, Sgt Ledwith & Cpl Barclay went to Batt Depot somewhere to train drafts.

1-4-17   Rode round in morning spent most of my time improving the mess etc & my billet. Mess was whitewashed. Hodges & Lewis came to tea. Raining all day. Hill went in & got my spurs from the dump. Had tea at H.Q. Bridge at night.

2-4-17   Tuned on to putting up Nissen Huts in the quarry for the new Div H.Q. Great fun in morning trying to make them out but luckily we had a scotch joiner from H.Q. called Grey who knew all about them. Braggins started on clearing out old Bosch Dug outs for Battn H.Q. & C.R.E. when push started. Also still on roads to Bretencourt - rode all round both morning & afternoon. Walking back at night from Quarry a bad snow storm started & we were caught. Postponed the company soccer match we were playing 'D' Co. Mess & my room leaked very badly.

3-4-17   Went round to Batt H.Q. & read a lot of frightfulness. Then on to Nissen Huts. Getting on fairly well. Bishop & Bagnall turned up for lunch & had come to stay. Asked them to mess with us. Had tea in H.Q. Mcr & then another in my own. 'D' Co beat A 4-2 at night. Very bad affair as A were 1-2 at half time & had the wind second half. Should have easily won. Lost 100 francs to C.O. by buying the ticket. Mercer returned very late at night got anxious about him.

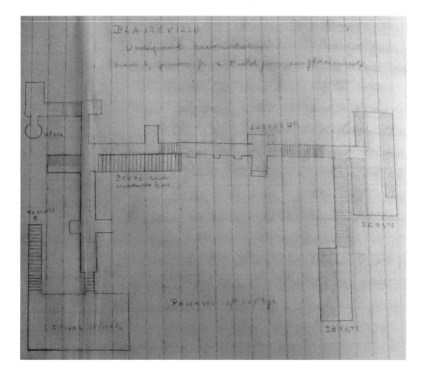

4-4-17   Went round the work in the morning. Huts getting on well. Div fussing on the possibility of us getting them up. Put canvas on mess in afternoon. At night orders came to cease work on screen & carry on erecting a new A.....ing Hut for Gen Lloyd 90th Brig in morning. Woolcock came in very excited in evening about some Pack Mules harness.

5-4-17   Rode about the hut but could not find anyone who knew where it had to go. Found Nissen Huts etc going on very well. Also saw Huns being buried too near the work. Spent afternoon erecting A.....y for General - very dilapidated & in a very bad state but with wood & nails we got it up. After tea played a soccer match. Batt beat Bedfords 5-1. All goals shot by Evans of 'B' Co. Ripping fine day all day.

6-4-17   Good day in morning. Walked round to quarry in morning & afternoon but stayed in most of time. We were told definitely we should not assemble in the dug out Braggins was in so reached mine. In evening 'B' Co played 'C' & 'C' won against expectations 2-1. Rained very hard mainly all the match & also most of the night. Dixon found some Spandau case Batteries & Braggins found a lot of souvenirs including an electric Bell so we rigged it up in the mess after Bridge.

7-4-17   Rode round the work. 2 Platoons still on Div Camp & 2 on Ficheux-Boiry road. Div not coming in. Rode out again in afternoon & met C.C. going out so went the extent of our work with him. Hindle caught us up & we had a chat with him. After C.C. came in to tea. Quite an uninteresting day. Rather inclined to rain. Quite a lot of shelling going on, on our part.

11th South Lancashire Regt.(Pioneers).
....
OPERATION ORDER

No. 40

by Lt.Col. H.F. Fenn, D.S.O., Comdg.

INSTRUCTIONS FOR O.C. No.1.ROAD PARTY.

The party will consist of "C" Coy under the Command of Major G.F. Beal, and will assemble at Billets in BLAIRVILLE ready to move off at ½ hours notice from 1 p.m. "Z" day.

OBJECTIVE.

To open for Wheeled traffic the following roads:-

(A) Road running from BOIRY BECQUERELLE at T 7.a.9.8 via Cross Roads at T.1.c.7.2. HENIN sur COJEUL, MARTIN sur COJEUL, HENINEL, WANCOURT.

(B) HENIN - St.MARTIN - N.28.c.3.2. N.27.b.3.7. N 22.a.7.5.-WANCOURT Road.
Should Road between N.28.c.3.3. & N 27 b 3.7. be in a bad condition O.C. "C" Coy will use either the alternative roads at N.33.a.3.2. or N.32.d.5.1. to the road running approximately parallel to the HENIN -HENINEL Road.

In the event of both roads requiring much work you will open a road through to WANCOURT first.

RECONNAISANCE.

O.C. "C" Coy will detail 2 Officers and 4 Other Ranks to reconnoitre "A" & "B" Roads respectively. These Officers will report to Batt.Headquarters at 12 noon "Z" day and will move on receipt of orders. .... reaching these roads to await arrival of "C" Coy at T.7.a.9.8.

INSTRUCTIONS FOR O.C. No. 2 ROAD PARTY.

The party will consist of "D" Coy under the Command of Captain H.A.Hodges, and will assemble at Billets in BLAIRVILLE ready to move off at ½ hours notice from 1 p.m. "Z" day.

OBJECTIVE.

To open up road for Wheeled Traffic from MERCATEL through NEUVILLE VITASSE to WANCOURT.
The 56th Divisional Pioneers will be working from N.19.c.1.8. as far as WANCOURT. It is probable that "D" Coy will open the road from MERCATEL to this point first. "D" Coy will then take over the road from WANCOURT back to junction with 56th Divisional Pioneers.

RECONNAISANCE.

O.C. "D" Coy will detail 1 Officer and 2 Other Ranks to reconnoitre the road. The Officer will report (with 2 Other Ranks) at Batta Headquarters at 12 noon "Z" Day and will move on receipt of orders. He will send a report on state of the road to await arrival of "D" Company at N.28.d.7.6.

DIVISIONAL RESERVE.

"A" & "B" Coys will be in Reserve,and will be held in readiness to move at one hour's notice,from BLAIRVILLE.

-2-.

EQUIPMENT. Each man will carry a shovel and every 4th man a pick. 6 Sandbags, 50 rounds of S.A.A., unconsumed portion of "Z" days ration, iron rations & Full Water Bottle., Waterproof Sheet and Haversack will be worn on pack straps.

TOOLS. To be Taken by each Coy. 4 Axes, 2 Cross Cut Saws, Wire Cutters (as many as possible), Notice Boards for Roads, Rope for moving trees, and 6 Heavy Hammers for breaking bricks or stone for roads

R.E. STORES. R.E. Stores are available at Field Coy dumps situated at- S.12.a.1.7. and M.35 d.3.6.

REPORTS. O.C. "C" & "D" Coys will report as soon as possible as to state of the roads. Progress will also be reported every 3 hours and when either of the roads are open for wheeled traffic to WANCOURT.

ESTIMATED CASUALTIES. Will be sent when the number exceeds fifty. In the case of any casualty occurring to an Officer, his name must be stated on the return. Actual Casualty Return to be sent with full details, made up to midnight, if possible each day.

TIMING OF MESSAGES. All messages must be accurately timed. O.C. each Coy will detail an Officer to report at Bn. Headquarters at 9 a.m. on "Z" day to synchronize watches.

SIGNALS. Messages will be sent by runner. 8 Cyclists will be detailed for this purpose.

BATTN.HEADQUARTERS. Battn Headquarters for the present will be at BLAIRVILLE.

MEDICAL. Regimental Aid Post will be close to Bn. Headquarters. Advanced Dressing Station will be established at S.3.a.0.5 Collecting Stations will be at S.5.d.5.1 and M.35.a.2.8. Walking Wounded will be directed to the Corps Walking Wounded Collecting Station at M.8.b.8.0.

Aid Posts will also be at approx the following places. M.34.c.7.5., M.34.d.9.4., M.35.d.3.5., M.35.d.4.7. S.4.c. 9.2.,S.5.d.7.5.,S.6.b.9.2., T.1.a.1.3.,

Lieut.Colonel,

7.4.1917. Comdg 11th S. Lancashire Regt.(Pioneers).

Copy No 1. File.
     2. O.C. "A"
     3. O.C. "B"
     4. O.C. "C"
     5. O.C. "D"
     6. Major O.C.Champion.
     7. Medical Officer.

8-4-17   Supposed to be no work but we had to send out 1 section on Div Camp & 2 Platoon to the Ficheux-Boiry road. Mercer had to take 12 men & bury a horse at the Bridge between Boiry au Mont & Boiry St Marc. I rode up there in the morning & saw the job. Rather bad getting the old mare passed the guns. Got to the job & saw the horse right under the bridge. Bosch started shelling so I came back for lunch just in time for lunch. Did not go out after lunch. 'C' & 'D' company's resting. At night there was the final of the football company match. Great excitement. 'C' beat 'D' 2-1. 'D' scored the first goal against the ..... & wind & 'C' got their two after half time. Beautiful fine day. Just like Spring. Not sure what our work are but just appreciative orders to be in reserve.

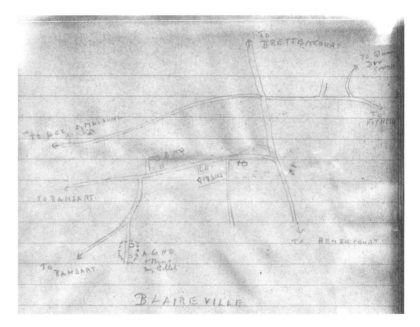

9-4-17   Woke up to find a horrid wet night & morning. Court Martial in my mess at 10 o'clock on Cpl Thorpe who had been Cpl of the guard at Newlingham & had not woken the Batt at the right time. Major Watson 20 KLR was President. I was Pres of a court of enquiry with Bretherton & Braggins on Gaskell 'B' Co who had disappeared at Agny. 'D' Co went out to do their work at 12.30. I went about 2.0. At lunch news very good about 2900 prisoners & the blue line got all objectives secured obtained up to time. Also Cuba & America & Bolivia had declared war & Brazil was thinking of it. Bosch seemed well on the run. Went round to H.Q. after mess & had bridge till 12.30. Had orders to turn the Company out at 6.30. Apparently the

35th Div had not done very well - the wire was not cut & although some got through their work not enough to withstand the counter attack & so had to fall back behind the Hindenburg Road.

10-4-17 Got up for breakfast at 7.0. Company left at 6.30. O'Connor left at 6.0 to reconnoitre road to Neuville Vitasse. Got up there about 8.20 & reported that it was not safe seeing the Bosch were still in the Hindenberg line. There was a general attack at 12 o'clock & we sent Braggins up & half a Platoon to mend crater between Mercatel & Neuville Vitasse. Frightful day snowed every hour hard & a very freezing wind. Left there about 4.0 had tea at H.Q. & they told me the Bosch was retreating fast all along. A good many prisoners. Reached over 6000. went round to H.Q. for Bridge after dinner. Finished the Board of Enquiry just before dinner. Heard we were probably going to move up to St Martin sur Cojeul. Heard that 30th Div was not advancing as they hoped the 21st & 56th would cut off the Bosch in front of the 35th. Later I heard we were probably not moving as the 35th had not advanced. 'D' was going out to work on the Neuville Vitasse road.

11-4-17 Stayed in all morning. Got up late. Very windy indeed. No news except 3rd Army had taken over 1200 prisoners & 50 guns. Company had to go up after tea to work on Fricheux - Neuville Vitasse Road. Snowing hard all the evening well up & round myself. Fearful night & freezing cold. 33 Div going up to relieve 25th. Awful lot of prisoners etc going up to Neuville Vitasse. Got back at 7 o'clock.

12-4-17 Had orders to pack up & get ready to move. Had lunch & then heard we were moving at 4 o'clock. Heard later we were not moving till after tea so went round to H.Q. & had tea. Found Maj I Spiers who was in the S.H. when I was there. Good fellow he was in the Scottish Rifles. Cameronians. Also Maj Goldthorpe a brother of the C.O. friend. Finally we left at about 5.30 & marched to Buddeux. Supposed to be billeting there but no room so we went on to Bailleulval - 2 company's there & 'A' & H.Q. & 'D' went on to Bailleulcourt & slept there. Fed in a café for dinner & had a good bed for sleeping. A very hard march as it rained a lot & the roads were frightfully congested.

13-4-17 Paraded at 9.45 & marched to St Amand Had breakfast in same café. Cold but fine day. Marched through Berles, Bienvillers & then St Amand. A few showers but band played & it was a very much better march. We expected to stay a few nights at Amand. Had quite a good mess & sleeping quarters were all in the old school. Got to bed early. Woken up at 1.50 to say Batt moving back to Boisleux. Much cursing.

14-4-17   Luckily I woke early. We were not called till an hour later. Got a frightful bussle on & manage to get off on train. Marched to Boisleux au Mont. Good march as we had packs carried. Went through Pommier, Bienvillers, Monchy, Adinfer & then Boiry. Had lunch on the way. Monchy seemed very knocked about by shell fire. Got in about 3.0 to find no tents or anything. Men had to dig in. found a hut for Pethick & myself luckily. Went in & played bridge at H.Q. after dinner.

15-4-17   Filthy day. Slow rain all day made everything most frightfully muddy & dirty & in a disgusting state. We went out on roads making towards Boiry. Went in & played Bridge with H.Q. after dinner. Got men & things started but not completed. Very uncomfortable all day. In the evening Parsons returned & a new officer called Miles. Parsons went as C.O.2 to 'D' Co & Miles came to A. Seemed rather to think a lot of himself & made rather a noise generally. Did not like him to start off with.

16-4-17   Went out in morning to start on works & as I was going out met Gleave who said the C.O. was sending 'A' Co back to billets as we have to go out at night. I just went to see Burn finish bringing us back & then returned. Company had to go out at 7 p.m. to mend the Henin Croisilles road. Braggins took them out. A fearful night as poured with rain the whole time. Pethick & I stayed in. Burn had a very hard time getting to Croisilles as he went to St Leger & lost his way. Back about 3 a.m.

17-4-17   Stood too all evening expecting to go out but did not have to. Mercer, Gorman & McCreary went to Div School at Bouquemaison to relieve 21st Brig officers. Howes to A.P.M. & Peters to G.M.B. Did nothing all day. Very doubtful day. Showery. Men's march very much better. Braggins & I reached later & finally O'Connor & Braggins slept there making it draftless with some bags. Draft turned up about 3.0 Sergt Abberley among them. He went to 'D' Co.

18-4-17   Company went out in morning to mend the crater or rather the company went round the crater on Henin Croisilles road. O'Connor took them out. Pethick & I walked out then in the morning got on motor lorry to Boisleux. Got back for lunch. Stayed in afternoon &

wrote letter. In evening heard from C.O. we are moving to near Neuville Vitasse. Started packing up.

19-4-17   Moved at 10 a.m. via Mercatel. Got in about 12.30. Braggins had taken over from the 1/5 Cheshires. We are in Trenches. They left us very uncomfortable & dirty. Men are alright so we set about making a mess. We are in an old Bosch dug out. Very dirty & not half enough accommodation for all. Burn & Miles went to another cubby hole. Spent aft & evening trying to make ourselves comfortable. Rather a doubtful sort of day.

20-4-17   Company out on the Road from Henin to Heninel South of the Cojeul. I went round billets in the morning. Took me 2½ hors. In afternoon I strolled up to the job & saw them working on it. evening spent working on the mess. Finer day. But not too warm.

21-4-17   Company on the Henin to Neuville Vitasse & St Martin to Neuville Vitasse roads. Wandered round the jobs in the morning. Afternoon spent in the mess. In the evening No 1 Plat played No 4. The ground was very rough & the game very funny. I watched with C.C. After the full time no score so they played five minutes each way. We went off to the cinema. When we came out we found No 4 won 1-0. Had mess in the mess. Very cold in there with no doors.

22-4-17   Stayed in all day. No 4 Plat on Nissen Huts under Gleave. Bosch brought a balloon down. Rest on Neuville Vitesse to Wancourt road. Beautiful sunny day but I did not go out at all. In evening No 16 Plat played No 15. No 16 Plat won 2-0. Company are going to stand to for the next day's stunt.

23-4-17   Had orders to go up at 7 a.m. & work on the road running between Wancourt & Heninel from N.22.a.0.9. to the Cojeul & as far on after that as possible. I took the Company up. Pethick coming up to relieve me at 11.0. when we up there we found things pretty warm. But got going on the road. Sent Burn & Hughes to reconnoitre. They said it was too warm to work on further. Dean came along & talked a lot of rot. Pethick & C.C. came up at 12.0 & I left about 12.20. Came back to lunch feeling a little rotten. Went in to see the M.O. Dean was then reporting on the roads. It struck me his merely going up & coming back as soon as possible gives no idea of the danger. Just got to bed & orders came along to draw 100 more rounds of ammo & stand to. Bosch supposed to have broken through. 'B' Co & 2 Plat of 'D' went up under Atkinson R.E. Adj. An hour later came through we could go to bed & be ready to leave at half an hours notice. I felt very rotten at dinner & went straight to bed. Same thing as on the Somme.

24-4-17   Braggins & 3 Platoons went up to the same road. Burn & his Platoon on Nissen Huts. I was not feeling very well so I did not go up to the road. Pethick went up & I went along & saw the Nissen Huts both morning & afternoon. An aeroplane came down about lunch time half way between 'D' H.Q. & Telegraph Hill so I went over & had a look at it. it was burned to bits. The man had had 6 bullets through his leg while fighting 3 Bosch on their front line & had ..... back as his gun jammed & feeling dizzy had tried to land in doing so the plane turned turtle & threw him out breaking his leg in 2 places & .....ing his other one. He seemed alright otherwise & was quite cheerful. Plane seemed to be very small & frail. Either a Spad[128] or Morain[129] probably the latter. Heard at night that E.O. was going to the 2/4 SLR & Williams returning to us. Got a letter from E.O. C.O. told me he wanted an officer to go to P. of W.[130] cage at Ficheux, so Miles whose nerve has completely gone was detailed. I told him at night & he seemed very bucked about it. Went to bed early. Braggins fainted at night & we had to carry him to bed. M.O. came to see him.

25-4-17   Had a bad attack of diarrhoea all day so did not move from the ..... Braggins was in also all day. Working on the same road Pethick went out to see them. A Capt Parkin who was at B.N.C.[131] with Pethick & Sinon came in to see them. A Capt Parkin told us that the guns on the Hill opp where we were working were his & had been captured by Bosch on the day we were up there & held for half an hour. Felt better towards evening & went to bed early. Fine but colder day.

26-4-17   Company on the same road & also from the X roads to St Martin. O'Connor took them out. Got very heavily shelled. I had considered going out but was not feeling very OK so I stayed in. Pethick went out. We had 3 casualties 2 killed & one wounded. O'Reilly & Bailey killed &   wounded. I heard after that O'Reilly's uncle had been in 'D' Co & was killed in July & that O'Reilly had been living with him & his aunt & had afterwards married his aunt. O'Connor brought

---

[128] Probably a Spad S VII, introduced in 1916.
[129] A Morane-Saulnier
[130] Prisoner of War
[131] Bangor Normal College. A teacher training college now part of the University of Bangor.

them back. They got back about 1.45. Reported to C.O. Wrote letters all the afternoon. Heard we were moving between the 27th & 29th. Went into dinner at H.Q. Had quite a good dinner. Got back about 10.35 & had a jolly good bath. Football match H.Q. beat

27-4-17   Company did nothing all day but bath & wash up generally. Heard we were definitely moving the next day & somewhere in the St Pol area. Not seen where. Watched football match in evening. Off servants beat No 7 Plat. Lieut   att 18 Middlesex from 2nd Monmouths came to dinner. He was a good friend of O'Connor & had been with him in the 2nd Monmouths. His Batt seemed to do nothing but have confabs. Officers pow-wow at 9.30 every evening. Platoon pow-wow every day etc & all the officers had to have their hair practically shaved off. Got across to parade at 11.0 & entrain at Arras.

28-4-17   All ready & moved off at 11.0 & went to squares MG at 1.0. Sat down there & then at 1.10 we marched to Arras & entrained almost immediately. Sat in the train till about 4.30 before it moved. The Hun was shelling Arras in the vicinity with a heavy H.V. Gun. Quite a nice day for weather. Bishop & Bagnall came into our carriage. Went by train to St Pol & then on to Pt Houvin detrained there about 8.30. Saw Bury & then marched to Beauvois - 'D' Co dropping off at Haricourt. Got in about 12 o'clock midnight & found the Billet awfully badly dour. Ridsdale supposed to have allotted them & did not show us when & Braggins who had come by lorry from the station did not know. We all had to bumble too in the mess & slept there for the night. Jolly glad to get down.

29-4-17   Did nothing all day but get the men settled in billets & cleaned up a bit. A beautiful day lovely & hot & everything seemed at its best. Had a real slack day. Wrote to Kaye & that was all. Company doing nothing.

30-4-17   Company doing drill etc. P.T. from 7.15 - 7.45. Drill in morning from 9.15 - 12.0 & in afternoon the C.O. inspected us. Not badly clean but kits very poor indeed. Rather a row on with the section commanders. I had orderly room in the morning with the C.O. At night listened to the band. Heard the Div Gen was leaving for the sack generally thought for a bad show on the 9th.

1-5-17   Beautiful day again. Went on parade in morning & afternoon. Heard the new Div Gen was a fellow called Williams, a late R.E. Also the C.O. seemed to think he was a bit of a blood & thunder fellow. Had a pretty slack day on the whole. Subaltern out before breakfast under Diplock - rather a mess made of the show alround Nothing much doing at all.

2-5-17   Beautiful day again. Did company drills in the morning - tried a bit of ceremonial had to change fields as the old woman objected to us using the field. Nothing much doing all day. Heard we had to reorganise the company to new method.

3-5-17   Beautiful day had ordinary duty in the morning & then Batt Drill in the afternoon. C.O. very pleased with the performance. Had a conference with company commanders on the new training all Platoons had to be reformed with 7 bombers, 7 Lewis guns (in No 1 & 3) & 9 Rifle Bombers & the rest riflemen. Having so few Officers the C.O. decided to join us more. He thought Pethick did not look after things & young subs enough so gave us Dunthorne. Then he thought O'Connor had a bad influence on younger subs so took him away. Gave me Williams as an active officer & also Clench so now the company ran myself & Dunthorne
No 1 Braggins & Myles
No 2 Ramsbottom
No 3 Williams & Mercer
No 4 Clench & Gleave

We had a farewell dinner in which we got rid of 4 bottles of Fizz, 1 of Port. Pethick & O'Connor were very funny & did nothing but give speeches. Dunthorne & Ridsdale came in - then when they left we all went down to 'B' Co & pitched up absolute Hades there. Bretherton & Co being rather merry. Dean was there so on the way back I met the C.O.. Gleave got rid of about 1½ glasses of rum neat & was very tight. Had to be put to bed. Heard that Diplock had got leave starting from the 6th.

4-5-17   Rode over in morning & got money from Blanqueval - ripping morning got back about 12-0. Dunthorne & Williams reported & O'Connor & Pethick left. Afternoon spent time reorganising & paying the company. After tea Mercer & Clench turned up to report to company. Had dinner at H.Q. & played with C.O. & Diplock & C.C. Nothing in it. Got back about 7 to find them all playing bridge. C.C. went to St Pol for a bathe.

5-5-17   Started the new training. Bombing & Lewis Gunners going strong - left the company very weak. Gorman & Mercer were changed in companies. Williams & Braggins on Lewis Gun. Ramsbottom, Clench & Gleave on bombing so it only left Gorman to take the company out. Dunthorne was also on parade. General Williams came round & found him& asked him some questions & then wandered over to the transport. In the afternoon we had Ridsdale on the Lewis Gun. Went to bridge at H.Q. after dinner. 'B' Co went to bathe at 8 p.m. Heard rumours that we were moving in the week for Hazebrooke area.

6-5-17   Sunday beautiful day. No padre turned up so no church parade except for NonCon & R.C. G.O. turned up & was posted back to the Batt & to 'C' Co. After 11, all companies could send 50% of the men into St Pol. C.C., C.O & I went on walk to the Bois de la Chapelle - a very pretty wood near Humieres where the tanks were. C.O. seemed very fit & it was very nice but somewhat hot. Had tea at Headquarters.

7-5-17   After general ord. room I rode over to Blanqueval to get some money - found the Field Cashier had flitted, so returned. Spent afternoon on the range. Very bad as we had no notice & could not get anything up. Shooting was awful. Saw Hindle on the way in the morning also called in & saw Busby Camp. Went for ..... whiskey chit. The Blue Birds came down in the evening & gave a most awfully good show at which everyone turned up.

8-5-17   Company paraded as usual for musketry in the morning & I rode out with Shaw to Flers to get the money - got it alright this time & got back for lunch. Afternoon company went over to St Pol to bath & Williams & I rode over & had a bath. Raining hard in the morning but cleared up for the afternoon & was very nice. ..... had a ripping bathe. We all except Gorman went into St Pol & had a very nice tea & then did some shopping. Pethick came in at 6.30 & after a bit more shopping had dinner at the Mikado a very poor show. There was Dunthorne, Pethick, Williams, Braggins & myself there. Got back about 11 p.m. The baths were most excellent & the band came & played & made it very much nice.

9-5-17   Usual company drill etc in the morning & afternoon - fearfully hot day. Spent most of the day wandering around. After tea I rode over to Oef & had dinner with Hindle at Signals mess. Maj Howarth, Dados & 3 others were there & after dinner Dados & Hindle took 5 francs off Baker & myself. Got back at about 11.30. Very nice night ride back. They seemed very ferocious at that mess & I bet Dados £10 that war was over before the end of year.

10-5-17   Company running round in morning as usual - in afternoon we were on the range all afternoon. I heard we were better than the other companies but we were precious bad after tea which I had at H.Q. I rode up with C.O. & saw race between Woolcock & Beal getting 200 yards start over 500 yards. Beal easily won. After Hodges & I went a ride round Siracourt, Croisette & Oeuf. Got back for dinner - bridge with Williams, Burn & Gleave.

11-5-17   Messed around all morning with musketry returns - spent afternoon having kit inspection & fixing up the platoon in their new formations. Hindle came in to dinner & we played bridge after. He & I played Willy & Dunthorne & won a bit. Cleared off about 11.0 as we had an early morning parade owing to the C.O. having the Batt on parade next morning at 8.0 a.m.

12-5-17   Batt parade after a short bit of arms drill we went on a route march through Oeuf, Noyelles & Humieres & got back about 11.30. A very tiring morning. Sports in the afternoon but owing to the morning march very few went in for it. Started at 2.0 & went on till after tea. What events there was were very good. Had bridge after at the H.Q. & halfway through orders came that the general would expect us on Monday.

The events won in the sports

Mile	Hughes 'A' Co M.G.S.
½ mile	Hughes 'A' Co M.G.S.
¼ mile	
270 yards	
Tug of War	H.Q. & 'A' Co
Obstacle	Atherton 'B' Co (ex 'A')
High jump	Pike 'A' Co M.G.S.
Long jump	C.S.M. Williams 'A' & J Harrison 'B' Co
3 Legged Race	Cpl Burley & Pte Goodman 'A' Co,
100 yards	Bardsley 'A' Co
100 yards Officers	Braggins, Williams
Blindfold Drill	Funny in the extreme

The officers put in a team, ended all over the place. C.O., Beal & Dixon had a race. Dixon won easily - then Beal. C.O. fell but would have been second.

13-5-17   Had a practice parade in the morning for the inspection by G.O.C. on Monday. Very hot but rather fun as we had a lot of new formations. Nothing doing after parade. Spent afternoon reading & writing. Nothing doing most of day.

14-5-17   General inspection in morning. He said we were the finest out of men in the Div. Gave the S.M. the MC. Very quick inspection. Spent the afternoon watching Bowling. Rained & we got a bit wet. Bishop returned to the company.

15-5-17   Spent morning drilling. Afternoon we went to Oeuf & stayed there, very comfortable billet. We had the old Signal billet rooms. Rode over in morning & saw all was straight. Fine day but rained at night.

16-5-17   Heard we were moving. Rode over to St Pol to get money but found indent unsigned. Came back to lunch. Saw E.O. then rode over & had a nice bath in afternoon with Williams & the company. Had tea in St Pol & got back for dinner. Rained on the way back. Played bridge fairly late.

17-5-17   Got up early for the move. At first were embussing near Hummier but later heard buses were coming to Oeuf. Got in by about 10.30 to 11.0 & bussed to St Hilairs. Rained early but cleared up during journey. I went to sleep inside the bus most of the way. Got there about 3.0. Ripping mess & billet & had a jolly nice tea. Had a most pleasant walk round with Dunthorn & then we had a very fizzy & hilarious dinner. After many bottles Dunthorne dressed up as a woman & Willy as a very good Spaniard & we went up for a musical evening at H.Q. but no one else turned up so it fell rather flat. M.O. had billeted there before joining the 11th SLR

18-5-17   Move to Hazebrouk. Embussed about 11.30 for Hazelwink. Ripping day so all rode on top. Came through Aire. Got in about 4.0. Billeted men alright but no officers billets so had tea - then given billets - found Dunthorne & mine in a hour also the mess but they wanted 15 or 12 francs for the mess so we decided to have the mess in the Trois Chevaux quite close - had a jolly dinner & then Braggins & Willy played bridge in my room. Bed about 11 p.m. At 12.30 the orderly turned up

19-5-17   Move at 11.40. We had breakfast at the Trois Chevaux. Then heard that 'A' Co was to be attached to the C.R.A. 10 Corps & the rest of

Batt to C.R.E. so we went on ahead through Steenvoorde & Abele & Poperinghe to a place N of Brandhoek.

No 17 H.A.G. Very nice set of officers

C.O. Col Brownlow, Maj. Barrington

Adj Lt Straun

M.O. Cpt Bliss

Sig. & Lt Gro..... Webb

Ord Off & Lt Roberts

Then the company was split up round various signal battalions & H.A.G.s

Party	No. of H.A.G.	No. of Batt.	officers	N.C.O.s Men	Officer's names
1	19HAG		1	19	ATC Williams
2	19HAG	39SB	2	66	Gleave
3	19HAG	197SB	1	33	Gorman
4	19HAG	298SB	2	34	Clench Myles
5	5HAG	188SB	1	20	}Braggins
6	68HAG	128SB	1	20	}Burn
7	69HAG	325SB	1	20	}Bishop

Took an awful lot of arranging & we were not certain of everyone's location or No of battery that night. Got things pretty straight though. Transport turned up at 7.0 o'clock. Orderly arrived from H.Q. & told us Batt were coming up about two miles or one mile off us. Got back about 11 p.m.

20-5-17 Messed about all morning waiting for parties to report that they had got to their right destinations. Rode over at about 3 p.m. & saw the C.O. & Batt which had just arrived. Saw Williams & Braggins & Dunthorne & went over & found where Williams & Braggins were billeted. Quite comfortably situated bivouacing & Braggins practically in a farm. Heard the location of billet & work of all parties. Just after dinner I heard that leave had opened & Bishop & one man from 'A' Co are to go. Sent Corp. Scott. Got to bed about 11.30. Sat talking for ages

21-5-17 Spent morning walking round seeing the parties. Saw Clench, Foreman & Williams. Found Braggins had flitted elsewhere frightfully hot. Found the O.C. of Gorman's Battery was a fellow called

Coombe Johnson whom C.C. knew & was at Clifton[132] with. Went over & had lunch at H.Q. found them all fit. Rode on & saw Burn's party but no one there except Sergt Green. Got a good post in at night.

22-5-17   Poured with rain in the morning so I did not go out. Williams & Dunthorne came in & the former went for money at H.A. H.Q. & got back for lunch. After lunch I walked over to Williams' plan & then on till I found Braggins on Dickebusch lake. Great excitement as some Canadian R.E. who was building a railway had dammed the lake & so was flooding the gun emplacements. Got back for tea & wrote letters all evening. Had my first sight of Ypres.

23-5-17   Started at about 11.0 for Myles who was south of Kemmel. Had to go via Hallecourt corner, La Clytte, Loker & Dranouter & it was about 2¼ miles further on than that. Total distance about 9 miles. Got back for lunch at H.Q. about 1.45. Had lunch there & sat & talked to CC. Got back to tea. Nice ride but too much main road. Saw Haig's car at Locre. Wrote letters in the evening. Bed fairly early. Saw Willy & Braggins at night.

24-5-17   Rode over to H.Q. in morning & picked up C.C. & we rode over to No 197 S.B. & saw Coombe Johnson. Got back to lunch as there was some talk of Doc going over to Poperinghe to the EFC. We could not go owing to C.O. wanting the car. So I stayed in all the afternoon & slept. Beautiful day still.

25-5-17   D. & I went over to E.F.C. Poperinghe. They had put some shells in & blown a lot of the place to bits. We got all our purchases & had lunch at Cyrals or however they spell it. Got quite a good lunch. Then wandered round & had tea to end up at the Officers club & then walked most of the way back. We called in going at the H.A.H.Q. & also at Camp No 2 & saw some A.S.C. fellows. Doc's dog Lump - captured from 6 Jaeger Reg as a Red X dog at Beaumont-Hamel came with us as far as No 2 camp & then we lost him but picked him up on the way back. Diplock returned.

26-5-17   Rode over to H.Q. & saw C.O. etc. He told me Batt moving to Ypres on night of 28th. Rode to Poperinghe with C.C. & Hodges & had lunch there - they had to leave in the middle as they were going on leave & wanted to catch the leave train. Rode back by myself & got

---

[132] Clifton College, Bristol. Established in 1862.

back about 2.30. Rode all the way there & back. Wrote all the afternoon - got no post in at all.

27-5-17 Set off with Williams at 10.0 to go to see Bunny Walker at Bailleul. Called at H.Q. & also saw Dean on the way. Went via Hallebast Corner - La Clytte - Loker - & then on to Bailleul. Found out he had just gone up as we landed there so went into the town & had lunch. Went back after & saw Bury who had had a very successful days shoot. Just the same as ever. Left about 3.30 & went to Loker & saw Miller, Betts & Winterbottom s.p. brig. R.E. Had tea there & then returned via Ouderndom. Went to H.Q. & saw C.O. just before Betts & Winterbottom arrived. C.O. warned us about gas attack. Bosch started shelling us when we had got back about 9.0 p.m. & we had to return to the Dug outs. After various scares etc we finally slept in ours. Roberts & I had a very short & uncomfortable owing to shelling & false alarms about gas. Gas shell landed within 5 yards of my tent & ruined my British Warm Mackintosh twice & breeches luckily all old and so it was not very much loss.

28-5-17 Walked round parties in morning. Williams, Clench & Gorman to see if any casualties - none at all. After lunch rode over to H.Q. & saw C.O. Told us probably moving at night to Ypres. Went on & saw Dunthorne & Ramsbottom no casualties then Batt had 8 casualties working in roads. Fine day. Batt had 1 shell land in road to the farm about 12 yards from the Off House they had all to turn out of their camp. We slept in our cubby holes again. Things went over but no damage to us personally though a lot done in the neighbourhood.

29-5-17 No work as we were expecting to move at night. Stayed in all day doing nothing but just rode over in morning to see H.Q. Quiet day but at night again things began again & we had to sleep in. 'A' Co again had no casualties though the Batt was shelled again & had one man killed & one wounded. C.O. seemed rather upset when I saw him. Myles came up early in the morning & camped his men on us & Myles went down & had his place with Dunthorne. Slept in Cubby hole at night.

30-5-17 Still standing by ready to move at night but got orders about 5 p.m. to say we were not moving but probably would move the next day. Stayed in camp all the day. Nothing doing. A few came over after dinner so I slept in cubby hole. A new man called Dewsbury came - or some such name & before going on to the battery spent the night there he slept in my hole & Roberts slept in his tent.

31-5-17   Orders came about midday we were to move up - I rode over about 10 a.m. & saw C.O. he had just sent for me. I found we were going to The Ecole[133]. We decided to move about 7.0. Later orders came 7.45 & finally 8.15. I had tea there & then Dunthorne came along & we wound up with Slater, Wilson, Piggott & as Hill had to go on leave Goodwin. In the morning I saw Beal who had returned from leave & Mercer & Hill & Lidgett were going on leave. Got up via Krommestraat & the south of Ypres. Got in about 8.30. Company turned up at 11 p.m. having gone various ways up. Later at night we found it a pretty hot place - fearful row went on all night. We let gas off & practiced barrage .... & all round was pretty warm. We relieved the 5th K.O.R.L.R. T C Outram & Roper & Joe Preston were in it. Though I did not see any of them. We were in cubicles - more like a prison than a school. Locks, bars & everything outside horrid place & in ruins.

1-6-17   Had to stay in all day so slept till about 12 & got up for lunch. Did not go out at night. Dunthorne did. Gleave Ord. Off & Gorman next day - Williams had a night off so Braggins took the road party - Burn the Trench & Clench went for sand bags. No casualties - quite a quiet night for them only pretty rowdy back here. Bretherton & Dixon were on leave. Changed my room.

2-6-17   Did not get up till 12.0. Bridge etc in evening. Parties taken by Dunthorne & Williams, Braggins road, Clench & Gleave taking out to Krommestraat for sand bags for tomorrow night. About 11 o'clock went out along Menin Road to Hell Fire Corner[134] & along Zillebeke down China Wall, Oxford St. to West St. Saw Dunthorne & Williams on the work & then went on along Bond St. & saw No man's land where we had to dig the next night. Got back & saw Woolley & the transport - had a cup of tea with C.O. & then to bed. Saw Boshell up in front line. Came back by China Corner & across the .....

3-6-17   Did nothing much but have a conference about work at night. Had a row with C.S.M. Started out about 9.30 to the work. Bosch shelling a bit & put off a dump just to our right so we went the way I did last night. Got up to the job by 10.45. 'B' Co seemed to be rather mixed

---

[133] Ecole de Bienfaisance, a school on the Menin Road.

[134] Considered 'the most dangerous corner on earth'. Intersecting with the Menin Road it was an important route junction under constant observation and fire by Germans on the high ground.

up & stopped up a lot. Braggins had gone forward to see the trench marked out. We got onto the job & all was quiet for the first hour or so then they tried machine guns & a lot of shrapnel & hit Pte Hesketh but no more. We had to construct trench about 200 yards in front of our front line like this - 3 ft deep & 3 ft - 2 ft 6 across. Got it mainly all done including fair amount of work on the traverses.
Got off the job about 2 a.m. Left Braggins to bring the company back & I went in with Taylor & the orderlies. Gorman got past Hell Fire Corner & found they were plastering the Ecole with gas shells. I tried the railway cutting that was full of gas. Got up on top & was so fed up I made a B-line for the Ecole. Shells dropped all round us but we managed to get through & found everyone rather the worse for gas & the place full of it. Williams & Doc & Taylor were pretty bad. All the men were affected & we had 3 casualties by hits from gas shells. Several of the men were so gassed that they had to go to hospital next day. Finally got to bed about 6.30 a.m. but eyes were so sore from not wearing goggles I could not get to sleep for a bit. Stinking night but men stuck it very well indeed.

4-6-17 Got up for lunch felt quite alright. Did nothing all day owing to men having to have 24 hours rest before working again. About 12 men altogether went off gassed. Did nothing all day but played bridge - bed about 12-1 a.m. No gas or shelling to speak of. D. Lucas the Div Burial Officer joined the mess. Bishop also returned from leave late at night. Had dinner at H.Q.

5-6-17 Nothing doing all day - but company had to go out & dig a communication tunnel & finish fire loops etc. Dunthorne, Braggins, Bishop, Clench & Gleave went up. I went to H.Q. & saw the cinema show. Later on the Bosch started shelling & putting gas over - not the usual phosgene a musty smelling sort of gas. I stayed at H.Q. till the company returned - everything accomplished well according to reports. So went to bed - just as I got into bed they sent a few more over but then light a fire & went to sleep. Williams' men having gone he went down to Transport in the morning.

6-6-17 Was getting up at lunch time when C.O. sent for me - C.O. said C.R.E. had sent to say that G.O.C. having reported that trench was too straight - ordered us to redig the trench. Joliffe went up & with Smith took accurate bearings of trench & sent it to C.R.E. Orders were cancelled & we went up to finish it off. All but No. 1 Platoon. I went up early to see the trench - it was quite alright. Saw Dixon up there. Saw Bishop up there when he arrived & left him to finish off the trench. Came back & went into H.Q. Dixon got the MC birthday honours. All quiet up there - had to come away early owing to strafe commencing next day at 3.10 a.m. We stayed up & saw the beginning of the strafes. Hill 60 went into the air about 3.7 a.m. Supposed to be 2000 tons of explosive under it. Went to bed about 4.0 a.m.

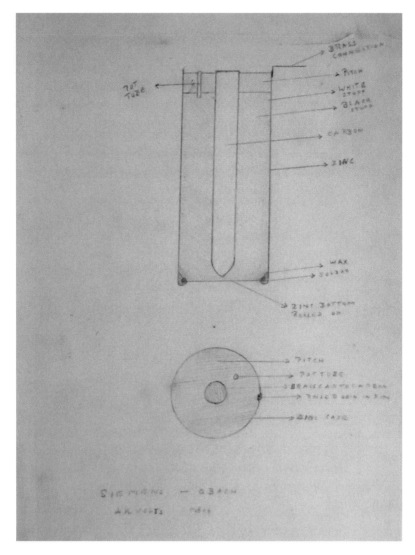

7-6-17   Got up about 12 midday - Company had to stand to owing to strafe. Got a few reports in apparently by night we had cut off the whole of the Wijtschate Salient. On a front of about 9½ miles. Stood to all day but had no work only 50 men of B went out. Had bridge at night at

H.Q. with C.O., Diplock & Taylor. Hodges returned from leave & Dean went on leave. Went to bed about 1.30 a.m. & slept the best sleep since coming up here, did not wake till 12.30 p.m.

8-6-17 Did nothing all day. Nothing was done apparently in the push - had to send the company out on work. Braggins - Ypres Menin road. Gleave Zillebeke - Hell Fire corner. Bishop with 'B' Co. & Gorman on West Trench. I stayed in all night & played bridge at H.Q. C.C. did not turn up but wired he would be turning up the next day.

9-6-17 Stayed in all day - at night we had one platoon working for 'C' Co - & 10 men on each of the roads & the rest under Burn on the West Trench. I was going out but the C.O. stopped me & told me to go & play bridge so I stayed in. C.C. turned up with the transport at night from leave.

10-6-17 Stopped in all day - at night the whole company was working on St Peters St. I went up early to reconnoitre & just as I was coming back the Bosch set up a barrage & it came over pretty hot. There were 3 Batt moving in the trench they all flopped down & the company could not get up. Finally things cooled down & they turned up about 12 & worked till 1.15. I left about 1.0 & on the way back ran into gas. I stopped all the company I could but Braggins remained with a few & Clench & Gorman went back & did no work owing to a message coming down when the company was halted in the trench. I saw Taylor & all 'D', 'C' & 'B' Co so we waited till nearly light in hopes of the gas stopping but it didn't & we made a run for it & got down with about 5 casualties. E.O. & his party on screens[135] got caught & E.O. & his Sergt was killed.

11-6-17 Did nothing all day. E.O.'s funeral at night. Maj. Beal, C.C., Culshaw & myself present. Only about 30 men out. Rest resting. We had a shell in the billet which wounded Chisnall, Smith & 2 others & shocked. Played bridge with C.O., C.C. & Diplock. Parties had quiet night on the work. Got to bed about midnight.

12-6-17 About midday he put quite a lot into the place & a lot of gas too. One shell knocked in one of the billets killed Willetts & sent 4 to hospital. Another one put out 20 of 'C' Co. Gas made us feel very

---

[135] Canvas screens were erected beside the road in the area of Hellfire Corner in an attempt to conceal movement, much of which took place under cover of darkness, when the junction thronged with activity.

rotten - C.O. went to C.R.E. to see if we could change billets. Later we heard owing to the change of Div. cover we were changing to Railway Dug Outs next day. 8th Div relieving us. Only sent very small parties out at night. Roads - Screen & the track north of Zillebeke Lake. Had a quiet time & got back alright. More gas came early next morning.

13-6-17   Changed billets at night to the Railway Dug Outs. Just SE of Zillebeke lake. We were to be relieved by the 2nd Northants. Very nice night & the change affected very satisfactorily. Braggins went ahead to billet. The burial Officer came with us. Just as we left the church in Ypres of St Jacques was blazing & gutted absolutely I should say. The spire fell just as we left.

14-6-17   Started early in the day nets & about 9 a.m. M.O.'s & Ridsdale was knocked in back end & C.O.'s dug out was hit - so they all turned out. 90th Brig. were coming then but advance Officer report so adversely that they did not come. So Braggins, Boshell & Clench took over. C.O. & C.C. slept in Officers mess. Later on about tea time they started passing the Dug outs up & down. We had 7 men hurt 1 killed S. Woods & 7 wounded all the guard room was knocked out. Piggott was wounded all over the face - doubtful if he would lose his eye. They did not stop all night till about 4 a.m. pasting us up & down. Did not send out many working parties - Braggins took out some men for Vince St - Gorman & Clench on Boarder Lane - Burn on screens. Got back about 3 a.m. I had a rubber of bridge.

15-6-17   Company went out to work as usual. Burn & Gorman on screen - Bishop on Vince - Clench & Glover on Border Lane. Dunthorne went to bridge at H.Q. I took Hill out & we went round the lot. I went south of the lake & shot the road south of Zillebeke. 'D' Co were working there filling in a colossal shell hole in the road. Got back about 12.30 & then started playing bridge. Bed about 4 a.m. Came back N. of Zillebeke lake. Quite quiet.

16-6-17   Got up late on & weather still very grand. Just as the parties were moving off Bosch started on us & we had to desist. Parties were Burn on screens, Bishop on Border & Lovers Lane, Gorman on Crater Crawl, Gleave on road. I played bridge at H.Q. with C.O. v C.C. & A.B.D.[136] Had several journeys to find both & back again. Got back about 1a.m. Found Glover had got back very early & had not worked

---

[136] Lt. Alfred B. Diplock.

on the right road at all. Dunthorne had gone up with Gorman & they had not got to the job owing to starting late & as the Bosch had come over at night & were sent back again & the trenches were very blocked in consequence. Bishop & Burn seemed to have done a v.g. job. Clench was off & Braggins O.O. Midday I heard from C.O. that G.O.C. was stopping all officers leave so Culshaw was going instead of me. Also the push was off for 30th & 8th Div.

17-6-17   Got up late. Bosch had quite a strafe on nearly all day. Being Sunday I suppose. G.O.C. recommended 24 hours rest for us all owing to the continual work we had been on. At night Bishop & Clench had to go up & reconnoitre a trench to be dug so as to do away with Lovers Walk. Remainder stayed in. Went to bed early. A lot of shelling going on all day. I had diarrhoea at night & had an awful job running out in between the strafes & then stopped up as usual very late. During the day one shell landed in the end of the mess & caused much trouble & another blocked up the entrance to Gorman's & C.O.'s dug out. Got in at night to them but

18-6-17   Got up usual hour. Rained in aft. Bosch still busy all day. Parties at night Clench & Glover & 2 platoons with 'B' & 'C' on a new trench. Burn & 1 platoon on Vince & Zillebeke & Braggins with 1 Platoon on Gap. 'A' with Dunthorne & myself went out at night stayed in & played bridge. Officer from 2nd Wilts came in for some time he was in charge of burial fatigue for Lucas.

19-6-17   Stayed in all day. Owing to us going to throw over gas at night over Trench where Bishop marked out could not be dug. Braggins was in Sap A, Bishop Vince St, Clench Zillebeke St & Gorman on the Screen. Dunthorne went out to see trench, I stayed in. Bishop told me that gas was not going over but probably the next night.

20-6-17   Stayed in all night. Parties on work as night before. Braggins in Sap A, Bishop in Vince St, Clench in Zillebeke St & Burn on Screen. Gas went off at 12.15 so they had to come back. Braggins had a bad time as the Bosch had a raid on our left. They managed to get back alright no casualties & our gas went over. 900 drums in 90 secs. The Intelligence had informed them a Div. had come from Russia & had no gas respirators. There seemed to be a lot of discontent in the Mess started by Dunthorne.

21-6-17   Got up as usual for lunch. Dunthorne very rude at lunch in the mess. Did not say much too him as I thought perhaps he had lost his temper or something. But later on in the day he was very rude & so I determined to have a mess mutiny & have it out. I did not go out at night. Dunthorne went out also Braggins on Sap A Bishop on Vince St & Gowan on Zillebeke - Burn on screen but he had to go out to see the Corps Camouflage Officer at Vlammertinghe he could not see him so went to Reninghelst & back for dinner. Lucas went with him. After they were all in at night we had the meeting - it was absolute farce as they had no complaints to make against the mess or rules but only that Dunthorne said it was much too much like a parade. Needless to say nothing came of the mess but a little rude talking in which only Dunthorne Gorman & Clench took part & Dunthorne had obviously been rattling a grievance for a long time. Gorman only argued for the sake of arguing & Clench did not know what he was talking about & was only officious.

22-6-17   Stayed in all day - very quiet day indeed - only ominously quiet. Burn & Dunthorne went to Vlammertinghe in afternoon. Parties were Gorman - Sap A Bishop Vince St & Gleave Zillebeke St. Burn just visited his party on screen. Heard we were going to change places with 'D' Co. I went out at night & Lucas came too. & Hill. Went up & reported at Downy house & then along Vince St to Sap A saw Gorman & came back crossing over to Zillebeke St - did not see Gleave at all. They were Straffing Zillebeke so that party was rather disorganised but we ran for it & got safely across. Went & came back by south of lake. Parties got very strafed. GHV gun on south side of lake when returning. E.O. was in the casualty list of the 21st.

23-6-17   Went out to work as usual only that the Vince St party worked on Zillebeke T2 as well - we changed own with 'D' Co. I went up to Chateau Segard early & Dunthorne stayed till the Company had come in. Braggins went over first with party in advance. I got clean away & the Company got onto the work & then they started on Railway dugouts all sorts & sizes of shell & gas shell. Gave them the worst time they had had. 'B' had lots of casualties & 'A' had 3 missing 'C' also had a few casualties. Ultimately the Companies got here about 4 a.m. Clench took Zillebeke St Gleave took Sap A Dunthorne & Gorman turned up about 3.30 a.m. Bishop was gassed & had to stop up at H.Q. 'B' Co. Mess was blown in & Pethick's dug out absolutely l....ered! 'D' Co got in alright.

24-6-17   Got up for lunch. C.O. came over - he had had to run for it & was very puffed. He was off on leave. Parties at night were Biggins on

Zillebeke roads, Gleave on Transport Farm works & Gorman on screens. Very quiet day & spent our time digging ourselves in

25-6-17   Nothing doing all day. Dunthorne arranged to go next day to Reninghelst after camouflage stuff. Parties at night work. Clench & Gleave on roads - also had one platoon of 'C' Cos. Rained hard at night & the men were rather swamped out. Lt/Col Walker & Maj. De Jong of 9th Sussex turned up. They had one company attached to us & did not know where to find them. I went on with De Jong & found them - lumps flying about & I had only soft hat & no gas bag. They determined to shift.

26-6-17   Quiet day. Got a new roof on mess. Started canteen about 6 p.m. with 500 Frs worth of stuff & sold over 400 Frs that night! Parties were Bishop on Sap A Braggins on Roads. All this time Burn was on Screens. Gorman & Mercer went to dig Practice trenches for Div. near St Omer.

27-6-17   At night the whole Batt came to Chateau Segard. We put up the H.Q. & 'D' Co at our mess. They were all very keen on getting away from Dug outs. they had had a terrible time all told. We had a good night - C.C. sleeping in my hut. I had made all preparations for leave next day & got my ticket & everything ready. Bishop went on roads & Clench on Sap 'A'. 17 KLR came to billet men so I saw Bagnall. Dunthorne started a wet canteen.

28-6-17   Left Chateau Segard on leave by horse at 10 a.m. Poured with rain early in morning but just cleared up for me in time. Saw Bagnall before leaving. Got to Poperinghe about 11.30. Saw Myles & then had lunch with him. Caught the 1.26 - had to change at Hazebrouke. Got in with Turnbull - played a lot of piquet with him. Train stopped just before the station at Boulogne so we hopped out & got to the Hotels before the others. Folkestone full so we went to Paris, quite clean. Turnbull was Padre of the Bedfords & I heard a lot from him of them & the 89th Brig. Quite a good fellow & I thoroughly enjoyed going with him.

29-6-17   Got up at 7.15 for breakfast. Got to the boat by rowing boat across the Liane[137] about 8.0. Boat left about 9.45. Got to Folkestone about 11.45 - 12.0. We for no apparent reason did a complete circle about mid ocean. Got to town about 2.30. Went to 4 Mount St after ..gging

---

[137] The River Liane flows through Boulogne and into the English Channel.

room at the Savoy & saw Roy. Sat & talked & then caught 5.20 to Lancaster. They did not get my wire sent by Roy till next morning so I only found Mother & Kaye at the house & no one to meet me.

29-6-17[138] Had breakfast about 8.0 got to boat about 9.0 & left Boulogne at 9.40 with Turnbull. Stopped in mid channel & did a circle & then went on. Got in about 12.15 & town about 2.30. Got the first train up. Called in at the Savoy & found C.O. out ordered rooms & went on to 4 Mount St found Burn there & had a talk & tea. Caught 5.30 North. Turnbull came as far as Crewe Roy sent off a wire home about 5.30 but it never got there so I found room to wait in & had to lug all my stuff up to the ...ms found Kaye & Marie in by themselves. She had just returned from her honeymoon.

30-6-17 Went to Silo did some shopping in the morning on the way. Found Mother & Mabel in. Had lunch there & the gramophone & got back for tea. Mr & Mrs Malcolm arrived at Carnforth at 9.0 so we motored over there Kaye & I to meet them great excitement Miss Parrish also returned by that train. Singer stuck going to Silo. Clutch worn I think Took Karl's back.

1-7-17 Stayed in & lunch at the ...ms & with baby on to Silverdale in afternoon & stayed tea. Came back after tea still using Karl's car.

2-7-17 Intended going to Glasgow with Kaye immediately & so we went down to catch the 11.35. They had had a smash at Galgate & could not get the train through - after having lunch at the County & waiting till 2.30 we came home & gave it up for the day. Went round & called on Mrs Hel..... but she was in town getting Weno's flat ready then went round & saw Marie & ..... George - a funny couple.

3-7-17 Caught the 11.35. Train absolutely packed could not get into Glasgow part so found seat in a Perth part & changed at Penrith into Glasgow part had empty carriage from there. Baby was rather a nuisance after that. Mr Townsend met us - talked all evening bed about 12 o'clock.

4-7-17 Went round in morning & saw Aunt Maggie Townsend. Mr T & I missed Kaye on the way out & went to meet her & were caught by aunt. Caught the 1.0 train. Had carriage to ourselves to Lancaster - very good journey. Tommy met us.

---

[138] The date is repeated in the diary.

5-7-17   Caught the 9.5 to Wolverhampton. Just got to station as train came in. Mother travelled to Warrington by the same train. Uncle Os met her at Warrington first time I had seen him since he had his hand off. K & I had to change at Acton Bridge - Crewe & Stafford but we had not long to wait anywhere. No one met us at Wolv. Got in about 2.15. Hilda sent a taxi for us. Sankeys & Elsie Hunt came in after dinner & we had a very jovial evening of it. George Sankey was very funny.

6-7-17   Went into town in the morning & caught the 2.0 to town, had comfortable journey to town. Hilda did not see us off. Got to Savoy & found C.O. had left the day before - as a matter of fact he had only gone to a hospital in Jermyn St but I naturally concluded he had gone back to France. Had wired Norman from Wolv to meet us & have dinner but he never turned up. Egerton came & had dinner with us. & Burn joined us at the theatre we had a box at Th.... & Co. Back to supper at Savoy.

7-7-17   Had breakfast about 10.30. Air raid at 11.0. Watched planes from balcony & heard guns & bombs but nothing anywhere near us. Went shopping. Afterwards seemed huge excitement all over town over it all. Met Norman as we went out. He had to go to his board so we arranged to meet at lunch at Prima's. Had lunch there & saw the Burn family - Board gave Norman 3 weeks leave so he went straight off north. Arranged to have dinner at Prima's with Pat & Roy before theatre & then went to call on Houghtons. Luckily they were out so returned for tea at Savoy. Egerton came to dinner with us at Prima's & then we 5 went to Bu..... - saw a lot of Burn's friends in the Guards there - had a jolly good time & returned for supper at Savoy. Bed about 12.30.

8-7-17   Got up late & had lunch at Waldorf with Egerton, Mrs Helm & Gladys - but first they called for us & all went round & saw Weno's flat - a ripping place. George - Weno's husband was A.D. of T.F. & I hoped to get a home job from him but he would do nothing for me unless I was on light duty. After lunch got Kaye White or rather Edina round to tea - called for her & sat & talked then got Egerton & Gladys out to dinner & had a jolly good time. Bed early.

9-7-17   Shopped in town all the morning caught aft train to P..... In evening went & saw Dr Kidd but he could find nothing wrong with me at all Hope had a very nice place indeed in P..... & a very nice mess. Stayed to tea. Returned in time for dinner at Savoy. Kaye & I went to

General Post at night at the Royal Haymarket. It was very good indeed.

10-7-17   Spent the morning doing nothing bought a few things went for the staff train but they would not let us go so caught the 5.15 from H.Y. with Kaye to Herne Bay. Had a very good journey down. Eileen & Capt Bates Eileen's father met us & we had dinner & then a walk out. He was O.C. of a company on coast defence training etc.

11-7-17   Breakfast at 7.15. I caught the 8.20 to Whitstable - changed & went to Canterbury West & then to Folkestone. Caught the 12.50 boat to Boulogne - picked up Rev S..... padre to the 2nd Guards Brigade & travelled to Pop[139] with him. Train left Boulogne at midnight - so we had our meal in the Officer's Rest camp & went for a stroll along the front to pass the time.

12-7-17   Got to Pop about 7.30. Wash & breakfast at Officers rest & then got a lorry to Ouderdom & on to Reninghelst & walked to transport lines from then I rode to camp & had lunch at H.Q. tea at Company & Dunthorne & I dinner at H.Q. when I heard that I had to go off on a railway stunt - practice for the push - to E.16.d.9.9. the next day. Cully was to come with me & Braggins (for leave) & Clench to stop behind.

13-7-17   Company started at 9.a.m. I waited till the end & then rode to Brandhoek. I understood it was quite plain that we all assembled there but only Dunthorne & his party & the transport came there - Burn took a round about route to Pop. We went right through & could not find him so went back for lunch in Pop & met him struggling through on the way. Finally all men but 12 turned up. Had 2 or 3 hours rest on the road. Got to E.16.9.9. about 6.0 & found 7th Can Rail Const Co Major Alan Main Jackson & Col Turner 11th Leicester Reg - both very nice. Found our patch & found 'B' Co 8th Sussex there too. No accommodation. Col Turner lent us 8 Biv sheets, 3 tents & 1 huge sheet. I got under a Bivy sheet & the other off slept in a café at the town which was marked out of bounds. I went over to Piovre & saw our area for tents. No good. Rang up Army Corps 2nd & 14th & they said Div had to supply!

14-7-17   Got a note early in morning to say we were in the wrong field & had to change to E.10.d.9.9 so as get there quickly & found a company of

---

Welsh Reg. then O.C. ..... Culshaw. Dunthorne went on to Pioneers & get the loan of 91 tents from the area commandant & we got those & put them up & was very comfortable. In the field were

19th Welsh Reg	Maj Burn Harkness & Capt. Austin	38th Div
8th R Sussex	Capt Hill	18th Div
22nd DLI	Capt White	18th Div
6th S.W.B's	Capt James	25th Div
& ourselves.		

15-7-17   All officers & NCO's senior went up & saw work O.S. companies had to see Col Martin in morning but he did not turn up so we went back & had to see him in afternoon at 2.0. Seemed a very nice & business like fellow & we all thought most excellently of him. Got back to base & settled down. Batt sent up 21 Biv sheets & 70 sheets of corrugated iron.

16-7-17   Men started work at 7.30 - 12.30. They were just removing some ballast from under a track which had been put down by someone else & had to be taken up again. Went up & had a look at them in the morning. Heard the Area Comm wanted his tents back next day at 7.0 a.m. Sent most urgent messages off to Batt. But got no further than Div being out they could not supply us with anything & the Batt had sent us all they could. Cpl Marsh. got some more tents for us & several Bivy sheets. Cully, Burn & Bish on work only.

17-7-17   Went up in morning & saw the work Company on grading. Handed over 22 tents as required & had 3 left which Marsh got so we were quite comfortable. It rained hard at night but everyone managed to get under cover. C.C. & Diplock came over to lunch. Roaring hard day & they rode over for lunch & tea - very thankful we had some beer in for them - they seemed very fit. Heard the C.O. was due back that day. In evening went & saw a footer match of the composite Batt -v- Leicesters - we were 2 all at half time & they won in end 5-2. First time I had heard Beal was so unpopular. Bish & Burn on work only. Col Martin came round & looked us up at night.

18-7-17   Went off to work in morning. Company again on grading. Cully & Burn on work they went off straight from work to Pop & returned about midnight - Leicesters left to go up somewhere by Bilge Corner a Chateau. In the morning Brig-Gen May (?) of Corp came down with Col Martin to see O.C. Companys & talked to us & asked us what we wanted & also said he proposed putting an O.C. in charge of the four composite companies. He seemed a very nice fellow. McAlister came around in evening to tell me of next day's work.

19-7-17 Welsh Reg left the field early in the morning. Went up in morning to see the work. We started work at 8.0 & left at 1.0. owing to them wanting to mark off new work. Got back for lunch. Payed company in afternoon. In evening got a note from 14th Corps saying I was to command the composite Batt of 4 companies without acting rank or pay! Went round to Sussex & played bridge. Fishwick & I v Maj MacAlister & Kean. Got 20 francs off them. Two Gloucesters to dinner. Came back after bridge to find them V. merry with plenty of beer especially Dunthorne.

Captain A.T. CHAMPION,
11th. South Lancashire Regiment. (Pioneers).
A.D.L.R. (S). - (For information).

With reference to II Corps G.T. 1998
dated 11/7/17.

You will hand over the command of your Company to your 2nd-in-Command, and will take over the command of the four Companies of Pioneers from 11th. South Lancashire Regiment - 8th. South Wales Borderers - 8th. Royal Sussex Regiment, and 22nd. Durham Light Infantry.

On taking over this command you will not be entitled to any increase of pay or temporary promotion.

H.Q., II Corps, "A".   Captain,
18th. July, 1917.   D.A.A.G., II Corps.

20-7-17 Work in morning. Went up & saw the work we were on taking up rails. Saw the chinks (chinamen) up there horrible looking around. Two Canadians & their officers from the Comp Batt went to Dunkirk, one officer from SWBs, 2nd in C of the D.L.I. & Kean from the Sussex. Did not return till very late. Maj McAlistair came in for bridge at night. He & Fishwick played Dunthorne & I & beat us by about 15 Frcs. Did not get to bed till about midnight.

21-7-17　Went up onto the work. We were on grading. About 12 I saw Maj & he said we were not going to Dunkirk till about 1.0 so Burn & I who wre going had some lunch & we started about 1.15 Burn, Hill & I & the Maj & Gillon (?) 11th Canadians. We got there about 2.10 & the Maj & Gillon went off to see No 1 Can R Const Co who were near them & Hill & I went off & Burn went off by himself to get a tunic. We walked about a bit & then went up to Malo le Bains & sat on the shore & watched some monitors doing firing practice at a target about 5-7 miles away. Returned & had tea at Dunkirk after failing to get any in Malo. After tea we went out again to Malo - saw 2 very decent Australians riding a motor cycle on the way out - perfectly marvellous how they stuck on & fell off & never seemed to hurt themselves. Stopped there till about 6.30 & then returned & had dinner at the Arcades. Not much of a dinner. Went & got some stuff for the men & ready to return at 9 p.m. Gilles came along & said he was going back about 10 & the Maj. was stopping the night. Later we saw the Maj. who said he was stopping set off about 10.0 & came round all over the place via Bergues, Wormhout, Herzeele then up to Hondshoote via Rexpoede & Killem I think then back via Oost-Cappel & Roesbrugge-Haringe & home about 11.30. Awful way round. Maj told us we were probably moving about Tue evening or Wed morning to about Pioneer Camp.

22-7-17　Got up very late. Three officers - White & his second in command & James & a Canadian went to fetch Maj. Slept all afternoon. I stayed in camp all day but went a short ride in evening. Got back for dinner.

23-7-17　Went out to work as usual. Only two platoons in morning. At lunch we got order to send one platoon in afternoon under Lt Jarrett to work on a new Siding to the 62 & 63 CCS. One platoon from each company. About 2 p.m. we got orders to send 2 companies on a special stunt as a sort of test & demonstration - there were some big wigs coming down to watch the progress of the rail work. We went out but although they turned up & saw the others work they did not come as far as the grading so we all returned. Col Martin said we were not going to move tomorrow he thought.

S E C R E T

11th (S) Bn. S. Lancashire Regt.(Pioneers).

POSITIONS AND LOCATIONS OF R.E. DUMPS.
AMMUNITION DUMPS, MEDICAL DRESSING STATIONS
AND AID POSTS.DURING OPERATIONS.

1.AMMUNITION DUMPS.

Ammunition Dumps are situated at :-
Right Brigade,   I.34.d.10.51.,   I.34.d.40.78.
Battalion dumps,   I.34.b.25.66.

Left Brigade,   I.34.b.15.90.,   I.34.b.40.66.
Battalion dumps,

The Right Brigade Dump at I.34.c.35.40.

New Left Brigade Dump at I.33.b.9.8.

The Divisional Reserve Ammunition Dump is situated at
WIDFORD HOUSE.

Main Divisional Bomb Store at H.26.b.7.6.

The following may be drawn from any of the Battn, Brigade,
& Divisional Dumps :-

S.A.A.   Mills Hand Grenades, No.24 Rifle Grenades,
Mills Rifle Grenades, Stokes Bombs, Green Cartridges
for Stokes Bombs. Rings, Flares, V.P.A. 1° S.I.
V.P.A. 1° Red (or S.O.S. colour), V.P.A. 1½° S.I.
V.P.A. 1½° Red (Or S.O.S. Colour), Pistol Ammunition.
Petrol Tins.(from Battn & Bde Dumps only)

2.R.E. DUMPS.

The main 30th Division R.E.Park will be at E.27.d.0.4.
The advanced Divisional Dump is located at INDISDDAY at
H.19.d.4.6.
The main BATTLE DUMP (SUNKEN LANE DUMP) will be located at
I.34.d.5.5. This dump will be connected to a Pack Transport
Track, that will be opened shortly after Zero, which will
run to CLAPHAM JUNCTION and then on to FITZHARDINGE FARM.
Stores this Dump will contain are shown on attached Table A.
A Small Battle DUMP, Stores as on attached Table B will be
located at VALLEY COTTAGES, I.33.d.1.6. This dump will be
on the track which will be opened as soon after Zero as
possible through I.34.d.5.5., I.19.a.4.2., I.13.d.0.6.
to CLAPHAM JUNCTION.

Any of these dumps will issue on demand to any Battalion
or Battery immediately after Zero.
There will be a small supply of timber, explosives &c. at
the SUNKEN LANE DUMP for use by the TECHNICAL TROOPS only.

It is hoped that a Stone Dump will be opened about I.21.a.
on Z day.

3.MEDICAL DRESSING STATIONS &c.

Regimental Aid Posts will be established at :- I.34.d.5.7.
I.34.a. 7.4.,   I.34.a.5.4.,   I.34.c.3.9.
During the earlier part of the action wounded will be cleared
to these by regimental stretcher bearers.

From the Regimental Aid Posts etc wounded will be cleared
by hand and down the Tramway by R.A.M.C. bearers to Collecting
Stations at   I.33.d.6.8.   DEREY.
I.33.c.3.6. VALLEY COTTAGE.
The Advanced Dressing Station will be at FOXGOATE HOUSE,
I.26.c.4.8.

The various routes will be "flagged" for Walking Wounded to
collect them at SMITHIES I.19.d.0.8. from which place they
will be conveyed in busses and lorries to the Corps Main Dge

-2-

-ing Station.(Lightly Wounded) 25th Field Ambulance
at H.27.c.1.9.

Walking Wounded of the 8th Division will be collected
at KRUISSTRAAT (H.15.d.8.6.) where such men of the
30th Division as go down that way will be attended to.

A.T. Champion

Lieut & Adjt.,

24.7.17.   11th S.Lancs Regt.[?].

O.C. "A" COY.
        " "B" "
        " "C" "
        " "D" "
        M.G.
        File.

TABLE A.

SOMME LANE BATTLE DUMP.

Sandbags.	50,000.
Barbed wire,rolls.	400.
Plain wire, rolls.	17.
French Wire, coils.	250.
Screw Pickets,Long.	750.
Screw Pickets,Short.	1500.
Picks.	500.
Shovels.	1200.

TABLE B.

Sandbags.	25,000.
Barbed Wire,rolls.	200.
Plain Wire,rolls.	8.
French Wire,coils.	124.
Screw Pickets,Long.	500.
Screw Pickets,Short.	750.
Picks.	100.
Shovels.	200.

24-7-17 Went out to work No platoons on C.C.S. siding. Watched hospital train in & all available NCOs on a test job to see if they knew what they were doing. Some were taking readingson pegs as inches not tenths of feet. About 5 p.m. Wire came "Twenry four lorries reporting G.16.d.99 at four p.m. today to convey Four companies pioneers to new camp at H.23.c.3.3. a.a.a. urgent" Took it down to Maj McAllister & he said he thought it was a mistake & they had forgot to cancel lorries. I went to Adj 7 CRT & he said it was OK & we had to move. Lorries arrived about 5.45 & we actually got all aboard by 10 p.m. Hill had to return to his unit to take command of another company. Col Fenn was struck off the strength. We got 26 lorries so we filled 2 with bivouac sheets etc & they came right through to new camp with Hill & I - dropped Hill at Pioneers Camp. Arrived about 12. Rest came on & dropped the men about H.14.b.4.8. We came via Abele & Reninghelst. The others all split up & some came that way & others via Pop. When I got there I could not locate camp owing to thinking the 7 CRT would be there - but after struggling round for about 2 hours I found them & Maj Jackson was awfully kind & came out & showed us the place. I had actually been over the ground but did not notice it was the spot.

25-7-17 Companies came in in bits & we unloaded the two lorries & sent them home. Wilson got my tent up by about 4 a.m. I toddled off to bed. Companies waited till daylight to fix up. I had put Kean J 2nd Lt R Sussex as T.O. & he & transport came in about 6 a.m. Jolly good work. Got up about 11.30. McAllister came round & said work at 3 p.m. I said very hard on men so he said he would try to get us off. Martin turned up & said we must work - then McAllister came along & said all off so we did not go out. C.C. & Diplock came over at lunch time both very fit. Doc came later. I went over later & saw them at H.Q. DLI & SWB going out at 3 a.m. Saw our Batt Op Orders for start.

26-7-17 Parties went out at 3 a.m. & 3 p.m. on the work. In the afternoon ..... called & he, I & Jarrett went up to see the work - it was rather hot up there. We only went as far as Railway Dugouts & waited for parties to come up. RS were working up by Zillebeke Lake & we were on V.7 by Bedford House & Woodcote Farm. Very warm round there & they had to wait a bit before gettinh on with the work. Got back with ..... about tea time.

All that I am I give to England
In great layers I lay upon the altar of her need
My youth, the middle years I lost to the evening days
That should be milestoned by success.

I pin my dreams, my hopes - & who shall know
The stories of luxury homes this means to me?
I give her all the things that I have done,
And all those vortex things I should have striven too,
And more.

The quiet hours that should be waiting me
Sunset that should gild the future win
The sweet June rains, the crisp & cleanly air
Of winter days. The moonlight on the singing water of ships
That would have carried us to other romantic lands
The kiss of lips, the cling of hands
My friendship then are hardest given.

The million words to write the thousand songs to sing
I give the rush of birds wings ~~to~~ in the sun
The glance of rain upon the clustered trees
The velvet pall of silence near the sea
The lilt of speed.

And Sabbath morning chimes the chime of home
That warms the faces of the choir boys with glee
The long held fascination of the dusty road
Between the hedges of the home place
And friendly paws of dogs I'm loved.

Lazy hours upon the edge of sleep
And joyous struggles in the hearts of men
Clear thoughts deep hope & big endearment
I'm the swift sting of failure & the laugh
I learned to hurt ~~with~~ them with
These I leave behind - and more!
Dear eyes of her I love, dear hands, dear hair
And all the untold beauties of our bliss.

The hallowed hours which troubled with the stir
Of our unspoken thoughts & prayers
I give myself & her more than myself
Dream sweeter greater with her smile
For disappointment & the uplifted gleam
Of comradeship to most accomplishment.

The life of her, the sanctuary
She gives when efforts robbed of triumph
The warmth of her, the silk of her
Her dear reserve & her abandonments

England, England, England!
All these I give not only but without regret
Because you ask them with a clamorous voice
Your very being prompts. And in return
I too must make request of you.

I pray I may be worthy of your task
But pray I more insistent you be worthy of me
And thousands other of your sons who pass
Down the grey road of duty - to the dawn!

Shine on resplendent in your might
Be you exemplar of the eternal right
Be tender too that you may give your strength
When the dull agony of war be done
Find cleansed and vivified your nations soul
And fling your hands across the seven seas
And be a mother to the troubled world.

26.7.1917

27-7-17   Did not go out though we sent 2 platoons out as usual on the work. Went over & saw H.Q. CC & Diplock came & saw us. They were only a few hundred yards away nearer Café Belges. Aeroplanes over at night.

28-7-17   Did not go up. Sent parties as usual in day. Went over & had tea at H.Q. At night an aeroplane came over & also a bit of gas but by having tent tight up no gas came in but of course I had to wake up.

29-7-17   Breakfast at 7.0 Maj McA took White Jones Lewis & myself over in his car to a conference at 7 CRT H.Q. where Col Martin told us in the main particulars of the work etc & told us that Tues was Z day. Very funny sort of meeting altogether but we got on alright. Huge thunderstorm came on in middle. We went to Picture Trenches by Outersteene & saw them. Gave us quite a good idea of the many trenches etc to go over & then got back for lunch without really getting wet. Afternoon spent arranging matters & I then went & had dinner at H.Q. Hodges came in after & played bridge. Got back about 1.30. Another Aeroplane over. Braggins returned from leave.

30-7-17   Very busy day indeed. Saw H.W. in morning & spent rest of day writing orders in my tent - a lot to consider. Got up very late. Went round & had dinner with Col Turner of 11th Leicesters. He was awfully nice & we had a great joke with him around. He got rather merry after dinner & we went over to see McAllister. He had a row with a sentry (7 CRT) on the way. The adjutant Capt. Raleigh came too. Sec in Com Rawson or something like it had put his shoulder out. Met the Doc Capt Scott who was to look after the grading party in ..... Saw McAllister & then went over & saw Capt Stone. Got back about 1.30 a.m.

SECRET.

OPERATION ORDER No. 42.

By Major C.C. Champion, Commanding,

11th (S) Bn. South Lancashire Reg.(Pioneers).

1.	The 30th Division will assault the enemy's position on our front on "Z" day, which will be notified later. The 8th Division will be on our Left, and the 24th Division on our Right.

2.	The Battalion will work in parties as follows:-

(a)	Three Platoons "B" Coy, will work on STRONG POINTS under Major E.W. RAPIER-LAVOISIER, D.S.O., R.E., 200th Field Coy R.E., Each Strong Point will be for a garrison of 2 Platoons and they will be for situated at : J.13.a.40.15, J.13.c.40.65, J.21.a.95.95.
	The Commanders of these Platoons will acquaint themselves with the ground by means of the MODEL TRENCHES at J.28.b.6.4.

(b)	1 Platoon "D" Coy, will maintain the Artillery Track from MILLERAND,past YEOMANRY POST to about I.24.a.8.6 and back to MILLERAND.
	This Platoon will leave ASSEMBLY AREA(present Billets) at ZERO minus 3 hours, and will move to site of work by Track No.1.

(c)	"D" Company will prepare a Track for Artillery from CARNAVON LINE and at I.26.d.5.0. through J.19.a.1.0. J.19.a.4.0. J.18.a.2.0. to J.19.b.1.5.
	A reconnoitring party will start out an hour before the Company to find the best way. It is believed that "No man's Land" about J.13.a. is water logged. The track should be kept below the sky line.
	This Company will leave ASSEMBLY AREA(Present Billets) at ZERO plus 1 HOUR and will move forward to site of work by TRACK No.1.

(d)	2nd Lieut: E.W.Gorman and 2nd Lieut: J.H.Mercer, along with Pte Longworth J. "B" Coy Pte Thompson J. "B" Coy, Pte Henderson J. "C" Coy, Pte Firney K "D" Coy,Pte Martin J "B" Coy and Pte Johnson J "D" Coy, will signpost the German trenches under Lieut. Mc.Callum R.E.,
	This party, along with Lieut. Mc.Callum R.E. will assemble at Battn Hd.Qrs. in present area at ZERO plus 1 hour and move forward by Track No.1 to the site of the work.

(e)	"A" Company will work on Light Railways under the orders of A.D.L.R. Fifth Army.

(f)	"C" Company will be in Divisional Reserve.

(g)	1 Platoon of Infantry under 2nd Lieut. WEATHERLY will keep in repair road from WINCHER COMMON to KILLICK inclusive.
	This party will leave ASSEMBLY AREA,(Present Area) at ZERO plus 3 hours.

S E C R E T. (Continuation of Operation Order No 44.)

3.   Picks and shovels will be carried by parties (a) (b) (c)
(f) (g) in the proportion of 1 pick to 4 shovels.
Party (c) will carry a proportion of Wire cutters & MAULS
in addition.
All parties will carry 5 sandbags per man.
Party (a) will also carry 2 Mills Grenades per man.

4.   DRESS. Battle Order. Officers will wear Privates tunics
with piece of red ribbon placed on shoulder strap as per
previous orders sent to O.C. Coys.

5.   Companies will turn out for work at Full Strength, only the
following will be left behind.
(a) C.Q.M.S., (b) Assistant to C.Q.M.S. (c) 1 Shoemaker per
Company (d) 2 Cooks per Company. (e) Those mentioned in
letter No.O.P. 100/3 dated 22nd instant.

6.   O.C.s parties not working under the R.E.s will report progress
every 3 hours. In the case of party (c) a report will be sent
in every 2 hours, and in addition a report will be sent as
soon as the Track opened for Artillery.
All messages must be timed.

7.   Messages will be sent by the Relay system of Runners, advnd
B.H.Q.(Runners Post) will be established at I.25.b.2.4
A relay post will be established in Railway Dugouts, in Sap
near by the late Batln Headquarters, and near the Report Centre
of a Brigade.
Messages will may be handed in at these posts.

8.   R.E. Stores, including Pickets, may be obtained at Advanced
Dump at I.24.c.8.3.(BORDER LANE DUMP) and at VALLEY COTTAGES
I.23.d.1.6. Details as to these dumps and what may be obtained
from them sent out to Coys under this office No.119/12.

9.   Advanced Dressing Stations will be situated at I.24.d.6.7.
I.24.c.7.4., I.24.a.8.4., I.24.c.5.9., I.23.a.6.6. DONEY.,
I.23.c.9.6. (VALLEY COTTAGE). Advanced Dressing Station also
at WOODCOTE HOUSE. I.30.c.4.2. Details re these Advanced
Dressing Stations also issued in letter No. O.P.319/12.

Water Points in the forward area are situated at KILBURN LANE
MAPLE COPSE and wells at CRAB ORAWL Dugouts. Full details
issued under this Office No.O.P. 119/11.

Ammunition Dumps and Bomb Stores are at I.24.d.10.31., I.24.d.45
73., I.24.b.23.60., I.24.b.15.60., I.24.b.40.80., I.24.a.35.40
and at I.23.b.9.8. Divisional Reserve Ammunition Dump is at
BEDFORD HOUSE. Main Divisional Bomb Store at R.29.b.7.6.

10.   Casualties will be reported to Bn.Bd.Qrs. not later than
8 p.m. each day, made up to and including 18 noon each day.
Return 12noon to 12 noon. Estimated casualties over 50 will
be rendered at once to B.H.Q.,

11.   The following Officers will not go in to Action, but proceed
to Advnd Corps Reinforcement Camp at a time to be notified
later.

    Major. G.F. Beal. 2nd in Command.
    Captain C.J.Dixon. M.C., O.C. "B" Coy.
    Captain H.A.Hodges. O.C. "D" Coy.
    2nd Lt. J. Ridsdale. Lewis Gun Officer.

C. C. Champion Major,
Commdg.11th A.Issex

31-7-17   Zero day. Company went up in four trains all supposed to start about 4.30. Got Capt Barry Jones P 22nd DLI as Adj. He was very keen to be & I had more work than I could manage. We went up at 7.0 a.m. & got up there about 8.30 & found every one just on the work. We were all working on the C3 job. Saw Martin & McAllister up there. We found a H.Q. for ourselves & then went round the work. Got up to far end & then Strafe started. Had to run for it & just got out in time & returned to H.Q. where we stayed for the rest of afternoon. They got very little work done on the Zillebeke end owing to being shelled off it continuously. The idea was to turn up there but our forces not advancing & also the Bosch straffing prevented all that & had to come back. Got back about 5.0 by doing a forced march & so managed to stop our ration train just in time. Got all bivouac sheets etc out. Had tea & dinner at H.Q. & back about 9.30 with orders for 2 companies (SWB RS) at 4.0 & 2 at 8 a.m. for tomorrow. Very little new though - none official but we did not get all our objectives.

1-8-17   Two companies as arranged went out at 4 a.m. & 2 at 8. Fearful day - poured with rain since about midnight all day Weather had really had a turn for the bad. Got the following report in about 10 a.m. & went over to H.Q. & saw them in morning & got the report. Had copies of report circulated to everyone. Was going to up to work after lunch in hopes of weather having improved but Lewis came back & said they were returning so I did not go up. Went over to H.Q. again after tea & got another report as orders circulated that to all as wwll. C.R.E. at H.Q. he said push had been put off 2 or 3 days. After dinner McAllister came over & talked about next days work. Wanted 2 companies out in morning at 4 & 1 at 12 Cut for it & the R.S.P. stayed at home. S.L. & D.L.I. went out in morning & SWB at 12. Went to bed early. No post. McAllister said he did not want many out all at once on the work owing to shelling. They had been shelled off the work today.

From Adjutant.
To   O.C. " /M " Coy.

          Following Copy forwarded:-

"Fifth Army wire begins aaa Situation up to about 10 am
14th Corps captured GREEN LINE to time and were in touch
on both flanks aaa They have since captured passages of
STEENBECK except on Left Flank where situation unclear aaa
A counter attack against the junction of the Two Armies
was reported bythe First French Army to have been
repulsed aaa F.O.O. reports 3rd Guard Fusiliers BERLIN
COCKCHAFERS smashed by them aaa Opposition on this Corps
front does not appear to have been severe aaa 18th Corps
reports left div. on GREEN LINE with post across STEEN-
BECK and bridgehead at M---- BERASTA and intouch with
right div. which has also reached the stream ... This
Div. reported to have taken ST JULIEN aaa 19th Corps left
Div. established advanced post BORDER HOUSE and
POND FARM rest of Div and whole of Right Div on BLACK
LINE Right Div. met with considerable opposition
about SQUARE FARM FREZENBERG and STATION BUILDINGS aaa
2nd Corps situation still obscure on centre and right aaa
Left Div gained BLACK LINE and commenced to advance to
GREEN LINE on time aaa Centre Div. was held up in front
on GLENCORSE WOOD and INVERNESS COPSE where heavy fighting has been going on aaa Left and right of right Div
believed to have reached BLACK LINE but centre held up
by post about J.25.central aaa Considerable enemy
movement in front of 2nd Corps and several counter attacks
reported unconfirmed forward movement field artillery
being successfully carried out on 14th 19th 18th Corps
fronts aaa Tanks everywhere reported moving forward aaa
Enemy reported heavily shelling J.7 from S.E. and enfil-
ading BLACK LINE W. of POMMERN REDOUBT from direction
of BROODSEINDE CRoss roads rough estimate of prisoners
to date 1750 have reached Corps cages aaa ends aaa

              A.B. DIPLOCK, Lieut & Adjt.

To O.C.
"A" "B" "C" "D" COY.
~~TRANSPORT LINES.~~
....

     Following is copy of wire received from
Division for your information.

Fifth Army Wire timed 10 p.m 31/7/17 begins aaa
Situation 14th Corps line runs U.20.d.0.6. PINSON
FARM RUISFAU FARM U.27.cent. with Posts E of
STEENBECK U.27.cent AU BON GITE REGINA CROSS
counter attacks on AU BON GITE dispersed by Arty
M.G. and rifle fire with heavy casualties to enemy
aaa 18th Corps U.28.b.3.3. FERDINAND FARM REGINA
CROSS to STEENBECK West of ST JULIEN with posts
at U.26.d.4.2. and D.91 aaa 19th Corps BORDER HOUSE
POMMERN CASTLE DEENA FARM VAMPIRE POTSDAM and
Heavy counterattack on POMMERN CASTLE from HILL
33 in progress 2nd Corps D.26.d.2.2 WESTHOEK
CROSS ROADS J.7.d.6.7. J.14.c.2.5. J.19.b.5.2.
J.23.a.3.4. J.31.a.8.8. aaa 1st French Army
lines runs T.11.c.8.1. T.11.d.8.4. BIXSCHOOTS
CUIRASSIER FARM SCOTTISH HOUSE REDMILL KORTEKEEG
CABBET U.20.b.4.7. aaa Second Army captured HOLLE-
BEKE VILLAGE and LA BASSE VILLE and report capture
8 Officers 340 O.R. aaa Fifth Army captured 71
Officers 3080 O.R. aaa 4 field guns and 1 How.
brought in.

30th Division 2 p.m.

                (S) a.B.Dyplock

                                Lt & Adjt.,
1.8.1917.   11th S.Lancs Reg.(Pioneers).

2-8-17   Sent out two companies in morning & one in afternoon. SLR & DLI morning & SWBs in afternoon. RSR had a rest all day. Went round in afternoon & saw Leicesters & Maj McAllister but he was not in. went over to H.Q. & had dinner there. After dinner Hodges & I won 10 Fcs[140] off C.O. & Diplock. Saw C.R.E. in afternoon & he said the push was put off for some time. No more news in except heavy Bosch shelling & counterattacks all of which failed - we were consolidating all our line all along & not trying to push in any more.

3-8-17   Was going to have a conference at 11th Leicesters with Col. Martin over returns required by Maj. Watts but at the last moment Col. Martin could not come along so he sent his car over & the C.O., C.O.2 & Adj of Leicesters & myself all went along to 7 CRT H.Q. Furious driver & we got shot up to Heaven more than once. The Col. of Labour Batt came in his car. After a furious conference when we got everything straightened up we stayed there to lunch. They had a ripping H.Q. & we were very comfortably done. Got back to tea. Two companies RSR & S.L. went out in morning & other two in afternoon. The afternoon party was cancelled but not in time - they got out on the work & then got order & returned. Had camp commanders meeting in evening & straightened things up. Got mess for men - fixed up Batt stores (QM) & everything. My cigars turned up at night.

4-8-17   Only two companies reached our work. S.W.B. & R.S.P. went out & got a jolly good days work done. Cleared up a lot in morning & we actually had a bit of sun but afternoon was again very wet. C.C. came in in the morning & told us the Div was going out & we had to go too. The Div was going to Second Army & was leaving area altogether. I went over in afternoon & told Maj. McAllister & then got on to Martin - who got very excited & rang up corps & said he would let me know results. Later he came along & got hold of Karl & we went in & got onto Gen. May D.A. & Q.M.G. 2nd Corps. He said we were not to move until we got orders. So Karl got onto Div. & about midnight they said we were to stay till we were relieved. Had bridge in evening with Fishwick & Kean & White. Won by a little.

5-8-17   Nothing doing in morning. DLI & SLR went out & practically finished the C3 Jobs. Batt moved out at 11 a.m. & were to entrain at Reninghelst about 1.30 & were to go to camp in billets between Godewaersvelde & Steenvoorde.

---

[140] Francs

6-8-17   R.S.Ps & SWBs out in the morning early on C2. I went straight off after getting up with Kean to Pop. Got there for lunch at Skindles[141]. Jolly rotten. Huge wait & food. Lumsden, Fishwick & Boyes went to Officers' Club. After lunch we rode down to Corps & fixed up with Field Cashier about having imprest accout book. Then went back to Pop & had a late tea at Cyril's[142] with Lumsden & Boyes. Fishwick gone home. Tried to get my hair cut but all places full & closing. Went to W.....y W..... at Y.M.C.A. Boyes & Lumsden came. Saw Martin O.R. S.H. there late 2 Wilts - now in Tanks. Ratcliffe from Queens Hall. Court Jardin etc sang The Trumpeter - a little thing ...zith - & Until - he was very good indeed. Other things went bad. Dinner at Cyrils - quite good & got back about 10.0. Barry Jones had had some difficulty with Dunthorne over orders. Dunthorne as usual frightfully hot headed. So I went into matter & the orders held good. As we rode into camp they put 2 or 3 shells over & later on at night very close to our transport but did no damage. I could not get to sleep. Got a bit of a chill which developed later. Saw Miles & Dean at Tea in Cyrils. Dean just going to rejoin his Batt. next morning. Sent ..... for post & it reported Batt moving next day on 5 days trek.

7-8-17   SLR & DLI went out to work. I borrowed car for 3.0 from McAllister. No Canadian officers turned up at work in the morning so with that & the shelling Dunthorne came away & did no work. I saw McAllister about it. Dunthorne & Gorman came in & we went to 2nd Corps & got away & then went to O.C. Troops & tried to find out about the company being relieved. Also about leave. The officer covering for O.C. troop was a Lieut from 2nd Beds I met at Blaireville. Went on from there with no success to canteen Pop & I got my hair cut. Awful tea at Cyrils & then home again after dinner. McAllister came in & He & I lost 20 Frcs to Bishop & Gorman. Really we had no cards at all. Feeling pretty rotten owing to chill I think. Batt. had Baths.

8-8-17   Got orders that C3 & C4 must be finished that day - sent up RSP & SWB & in morning DLI relieved RSPs on C4. SWB finished C3. DLI went up about 12.0. S.L. had to go up about 3 p.m.in case of need

---

[141] A popular officers' club in Poperinghe. Originally called 'Café à la Bourse de Houblon' it was nicknamed it 'Skindles' after a member of the Rifle Brigade declared the place was just as good as Skindles at Maidenhead.

[142] 'Hotel Cyrille' ('Cyrils"), an officers-only establishment in Poperinghe run by Cyrille Vermeulen.. It was struck by a shell in 1918 and the Vermeulens and their four maids were killed.

under Braggins. Maj. Watts up there fussing round. About 6.0 it started to rain in torrents - a real bad thunderstorm. Found out the 7th CRT were handing over to the 9th CRTs - under Col. Moody, Maj. Meredith & Capt. White. O.C. D 9th CRTs came in & had a chat at night & we arranged to wait till Canadians had looked at the work before going out next day. Also told me then location of main line was damaged a lot. Braggins & his party wet through.

9-8-17   No one went out in morning owing to Canadians not knowing job. Capt. White & ..... Little came in in morning & afternoon & told me they wanted my company out at 3 p.m. Train would be provided - they went up & did not have a very hard time. The balloon went up about midday & a hun came over in an English Nieuport & brought the balloon down both occupants got off alright & landed safely in their parachutes. Brought another balloon along & got it ready to go up. Orders were to send out 2 companies in morning & afternoon. Dunthorne behaved very badly & made a huge fuss about going up - although he had no casualties - he said it was murder going up there etc. etc.

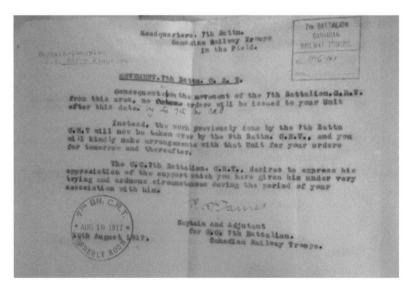

10-8-17   In the morning I heard Dunthorne making some very rude remarks to Lumsden - subaltern in the R.S.F.s - outside my tent in a very loud voice - so I called him in - he said he had not meant them to be so that I could hear but he felt very strongly about it. I put the matter i.e. about going up there to him as best I could & asked him if he thought that he would like to see Capt White about it - if he thought that would do him & us any good - he hum & harred about it & finally voiced that it was not the work he was objecting to but he disliked me - I told him that if that was all it was not the way to show it by being rude to me outside my tent, & at last he said he would see Capt White - & said he thought that the fact I did not go up to see the work more often was a sign I practically funked it & all that sort of twoddle - he made a huge fuss & boast about he not being afraid etc of going up & put it down to his not like visiting the men up there. Personally I put it down to him bossing the men a bit & being excited & feeling the strain of the work up there. I told him I quite realised the situation was beastly & he asked me to go up that afternoon so I said I would with pleasure if he thought was going to do him any good or the men. I think he behaved very childishly & is really only a troublemaker especially with the subalterns. I went up in the afternoon - meeting Col. Moody & his C.O.2 by the Bund - he wanted to see me when I got back after tea. I went out with Cameron & the train took us just short of the Shrapnel Corner - Voormezele road when 4 tractors off the rail delayed us & we had to walk. Cameron & I went on ahead & finding a balloon up stopped the party below the crest & went in & marked out all the stakes. Got back & put the Canadians on to the side facing Bosch in small parties & the two companies on the other slope - I came back along the rail - & walked all the way - picked up a man trying to get to Dickebusch & guided him in. Went on to see Col. Moody & all he wanted was to tell me the Leicesters were finding a company so we had one day per company per 5 days off. RSP & SWBs in morning. SLR & DLI in aft.

11-8-17 At 11 o'clock Maj. MacAllister came in & demanded his two tents so I arranged to keep them till tomorrow while I got two more. Order came in from Corps to say I was to take orders in future from 9 CRT & not 7 CRT as the 9th had relieved the 7th. After lunch Kean & I rode over to II Corps & saw Capt. Gable ? & he got a Col. Henrick to grant us 3 more tents from the O.O. Corps Troops. It took us about ½ an hour to find him as he was about 1½ miles away & no one knew where he lived. He turned out to be a Capt. Sig.... (?) & on principle refused all new units everything but we talked him round & got all we wanted i.e. to get ordnance & ..... off him. He gave us tea & we got back about 7.15. Rained hard on the way & at night. Cully still inebriated ever since landing.

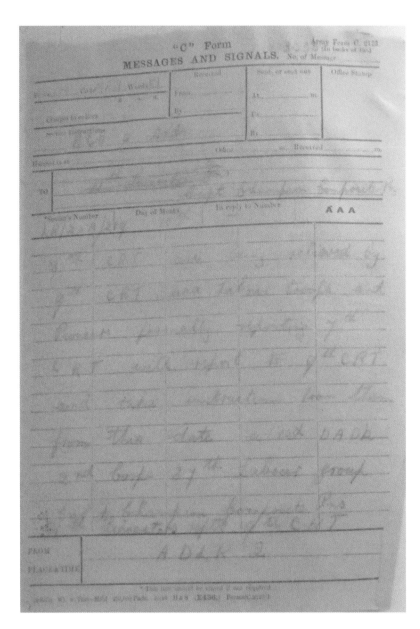

12-8-17   S.L. had a day off. In the morning I got a note from Diplock saying the Batt. was at Westoutre. I had meant to ride over to see MacAllister but Kean & I rode over to tea at Westoutre instead. Found they had a ripping good camp & were very comfortable - got back for dinner - got a good shower on the way back. Found we were moving at 10 a.m. next day to rejoin our unit. Went on & saw Col. Moody 9 CRT about it.

13-8-17   Took Capt. James SWBs who were taking over from us round & introduced him to Col. Moody & Col. Turner . Got 10 lorries to take the company over at 10.30. Got all our stuff & men aboard by 11.30 & set off. Got in to camp for lunch. Dunthorne & I had lunch at H.Q. & then got things rigged up for tea etc. Got an invitation in morning from Col. Martin to dine with him in Pop. Rode over there & got there by 7. Found party consisted of:
Lt. Col. Martin 7 CRT
Lt. Col. Turner 11th Leicesters.
Lt. Col. Bodwell A.D.L.R.2.
Maj. Watts 7 CRT
Maj. Mendith 7 CRT
& myself. We had dinner at Skindles & had a good dinner but an awful mixture of drinks - Cherry, Port, Chablis, Fizz,. Port & then went over to the Club & sat in the old Major Oi/c. Off. Club's room & drank Curacao . Had a ripping evening & Col. Martin was most awfully nice. I thoroughly enjoyed myself. Took over the C.O.2 Chestnut. Got back on her in fine style. Bury came over in afternoon to see us.

14-8-17   Had inspections all day. Morning I inspected the company. In afternoon I rode over with C.C. to Bethune & heard a lecture on Wood fighting by Capt. Montgomery who was Brig Maj at Bangor now G.S.O.2 of 9th Corps. Quite a good lecture. Got back & Bunny dropped a ..... & a letter saying he was going on leave the next day. So C.C. & I went over & had dinner with him & had a concert - quite good. He sent us back by tender at Bailleul. Got back about 1.30 a.m.

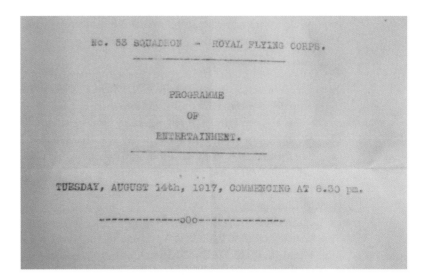

15-8-17   Started doing drill. 3 hours in morning & 2 hours in afternoon. I stayed in camp & got things fairly straightened up after disorganisation. Heard that the Batt. was moving to Vierstraat next day so afternoon parades were cancelled. Had a concert at 5.30. Got an awful piano & owing to no one having any music things did not go as well as they might have. Elstob came in to dinner & told some very interesting things about the stunt. From him the 30th did very well considering. Holding a Court of Inquiry owing to other Divs blaming the 30th.

16-8-17   Got up about 6 a.m. Ready to move at 9 a.m. Got going alright. Marched through La Clytte & Kemmel. Got into new camp at about 11.45. Found a few tents & huts there already. Got in very comfortably indeed. We are working for 35th Div R.E.s. 'A' Co for 200th. Major Clavering. We heard no news that day of our work so spent the day settling down. Pethick, Doc & Clench left behind to go on leave.

17-8-17 No news of work all day till Clavering came round about 5.30 p.m. Spent the day making tables & things for myself & generally getting in comfortably. Braggins & I & Piggott went up to see the work on the near slope of the Hill from Wijtschaete. Saw the work & got back for dinner. Ripping day & very quiet. Nothing doing up there at all. Heard Hodges had got a months' leave so Dunthorne took over 'D' Co. work & all. & thank goodness I got rid of him.

18-8-17 Got up at 5 a.m. & rode up to see the work. Got up there to find it nearly done. Draining a fine trench it consisted of a drain about 160 yards long & about 6 ft to nothing. Water let through as I was there - so 3 platoons came home & No 1 stayed & cleaned up a bit after. Company got in about 7.30 & No 1 about 9 a.m. Went over in ambulance with C.C., Hodges & Doc, Capt. Cameron, to Bailleul. Had lunch at Off. Club. Met Watson 20 Kings there. After lunch went to station & found Hodges had missed leave train from there & would have to go to Caestre 2 a.m. next morning to catch it. Then went to 53 S.G. & C.C. went up with Lieut from S. Staffs for ..... over Ypres & Pop & our camp. Meantime Hodges & I went to cemetery where a lot of his friends in 3rd Mon were buried & looked round there got caught in the rain. Then went on to Off. Club & had tea. Padre O'Shaughnessy joined us at tea. Just as we finished C.C. came in & had tea. After tea we sat in lounge upstairs & read till 6.45. Then had a stroll & Hodges wanted to buy a Baby's hat! Had dinner at Off. Club. Quite a warm ..... considering. Doc called for us after dinner in another ambulance & we got back about 11.0 p.m. just missing all the bombing stunts. Quite a big post in for us. Bretherton returned from Rest Camp near Boulogne.

19-8-17 Being Sunday there was no work at all. Padre had service in the morning - I was not there. Got up very late & spent all day reading on my bed. Evening we had some most energetic cricket. Wrote about six letters.

20-8-17 Working in 2 shifts. Bishop took the first shift starting work at 7.0 a.m. Parade at 5.0 & they got back for lunch. Braggins took the afternoon shift starting work at 2.0 p.m. I walked back with C.C. in the morning. He was very unfit so sat down at X.roads Wijtschaete while I went on to the work. Found Clavering there & went round the work. He seemed very satisfied indeed. Got back for lunch. Read

& wrote all the afternoon & played cricket in the evening. Very bad pitch & all that but quite good fun. Heard in the evening that we were moving south about 4 miles or so & taking over just north of the 2 Anzac Corps.

21-8-17   Rode over in morning with Beal, other 3 company commanders & Walcock to take over from the 4 Australian Pioneer Batt. at Spy Farm just to front of Lindenhoek. Got up there about 10 a.m. C.C. was too unfit to take over. I found we were only taking over about half their work so did not take over by companies but made notes of all the work & sort of took over in place of Beal. Lucky as he knew very little about it when the time came. Got back to lunch. In afternoon I rode over to see the Leicesters & Composite Batt. Saw them all. The Leicesters were very fed up with 9th CRT, Sussex & DLIs were going to be relieved. They had been bombed since I left & lost about 6 horses & BQMS & a batman. Got back for tea.

22-8-17   Moved to Spy Farm. Companies moved at 1 p.m. at 200 yards intervals under our arrangements. I rode over in morning & saw all was straight & then rode over after lunch with Diplock leaving Culshaw to bring the company. Got in about 2.15 p.m. & started to make our camp. The Australians had left nothing so we brought all our stuff with us. We got in fairly successfully & erected our camp. Found it very comfortably situated. Found we were on Trench Railways. O'Connor & McKenzie on leave.

23-8-17   Had to send out 1 Platoon under Burn on trying to close in some railway from Metres to Decimal. Rather useless work. Braggins went out to reconnoitre Anzac Farm road. I stayed in all day & got camp more ship shape. Had dinner with H.Q. Played bridge with Taylor v C.C. & Diplock. Lost to them fairly lightly about 1 Fr!

24-8-17   Culshaw went out to reconnoitre & peg out rest of task but apparently did not do it. Burn & Gorman stayed in all night & Bishop took out one platoon to work on railway. Braggins had to reconnoitre the next line. I wanted to try & find the line from the Enfu Wood end with Piggott but I never got there & lost my bearings altogether so came back for tea. Apparently a message had come just after I had left saying all work on railways was to cease & to recall Bishop & party. They returned very shortly after me. At night Burn & Gorman went out with 3 Platoon & worked on a trench - Manchester Avenue under Dunthorne. Got back about 1.30 a.m. Went out at 7.45 p.m.

25-8-17   Sunday & no work to do. Spent morning in bed & writing letters. Afternoon we had a game of cricket in the Pitch Braggins made. I then rode over to 16th Man to see Elstob but found he was acting Brigadier to 90th Brig. Brig being on leave. I rode on to try & find 90th Brig but could not find it so returned for tea. After tea we had another game of cricket. C.C. came down & we had pretty good fun. Rained a lot towards the end & hard all night. Went to H.Q. for bridge but did not have any after all.

26-8-17   Stayed in all day & played cricket in afternoon. At night I took the company out with Bishop to work on Manchester trench. I had two platoons & was working up as far as the road & he was working the other side of the road. I got my bit of trench down & would not allow them to go till they had made the trench absolutely to a template. I took up Bishop but his party go early & told me that his was alright when I went to try it you could not get the template down at all. Awfully bad work. Got back about 1a.m.

27-8-17   Did not go out at all. Rain started & also a terrific storm of wind - nearly removed all the tents. Bain & Culshaw went out at night on the trench - they could not do any work actually in the trench much but spent their energies on carrying stuff up there. I went over for Bridge to H.Q. but they did not have any after all. Woods came too but we talked instead.

28-8-17   I got a message to go & take over work from the 4th Australian Pioneers just south of Neuve Église so rode over there early & saw the C.O. & C.O.2 about 10 a.m. Got back to lunch. Only two trenches to take over Fanny's C.T. & also Cross Avenue. Latter was so near the River Le Da..... which is Div boundary that we did not think Div would own it so Gorman & I went up in afternoon & just saw Fanny's trench. Went via Messines & came back just skirting Wytschaete. Half an hour after leaving a note came to me to say R.E.s were taking over trenches & I must go on roads. So Braggins & one platoon went on Huns Walk. Bishop went off in early morning to Rest Camp.

29-8-17   Did not go out. Arranged with Dixon which roads we were to take over & we fixed on Fanny's, Dover & Huns Walk. So sent out Bain & Gorman on Huns Walk & Fanny's. They had one casualty - from machine gun. Not a quiet night though. Straffing Fanny's C.T. I did not go out. Still damp & windy.

30-8-17   C.C., Doc & I were going to ride over early to Bailleul but C.R.E. came so I had lunch at H.Q. & went after lunch. We had tea at the officers club. Then C.C. went off & saw Panet - Doc & I went to 52 Sq RFC & heard Bunny was staying in England to have pilot work. So we returned & did a little shopping & went to Off Club for dinner. C.C. joined us about 7.15. After dinner we went to get our horses & found that C.C.'s stirrup leathers & stirrup had gone altogether & mine had been half cut through. Doc's were untouched. Managed to get home safely. Cully reported road nearly finished.

31-8-17   Late up. Played cricket in afternoon. Gorman took party at night. Went up shortly after him onto the work. Found there was heaps of work to do on the road. Cully was all out of it. Coming back had a lucky escape - cut off the Railway Dump & they put 8 shells into it - just as we were level with it. Braggins with one platoon on Special Corps light railway work. Giles returned from leave.

1-9-17   Braggins taken off railway work. Doc Cameron left us as Giles had returned. Braggins went out on same roads. I had to go round & take over work from Pioneers 37 Div as the Div was moving up on Brig front.

2-9-17   Sunday so no work. I rode over to 37th Div Pioneers to take over roads in new area. Found they were N Staffs. New roads were Estaminet Corner to Rose Wood, St Eloi to Oosttaverne .... Got there about 11 a.m. Found they were just south of our old camp by Vierstraat. Played cricket in afternoon.

3-9-17   Was going round new work with C.C. but they decided to have a Sergts cricket match so I did not go. Sergts made 56 & we made about 80 for 7 or 8 wickets. I took about 3 wickets & made about 3 runs. Burn went on the new work & Cully went out to see it. Got a bit of shelling so decided to send out by day times if possible.

4-9-17   Rode up with C.C. & walked round roasd. Estaminet to In de Sterkte to Oosttaverne & back by 15" corner. A bit rowdy but nothing very much doing. Got back to lunch. Very hot indeed. Played cricket all afternoon & evening. Braggins took party out 3 a.m.

5-9-17   Did nothing all day. Braggins had a bit of gas shelling going up & nothing while up there though Bosch did some heavy shelling of Back areas early in the morning. Beautiful day. No post again. Played cricket at night but did not feel very fit so did not do much all day but lie up. Huge thunderstorms at night.

6-9-17   Burn went on leave. Cally went up in morning to consider the drainage of the new road. So I stayed in. Gorman took party up. Braggins went off to Bailleul. Played cricket at night but rain again interrupted. Though not much. Little ..... Ridsdale to dinner. Had bath at night.

7-9-17   Went up at 6 a.m. to work. Rode up to Wytschaete & then walked to Estaminet corner. Met Braggins & walked with him to Rose Wood & back & then went on & saw railway location to Anzac Farm. Got back about 9.30 a.m. Spent rest of day messing around & playing cricket. Had bridge at night with Bolton, Gorman & Cully. Braggins to Bailleul.

8-9-17   Stayed in all day. Had a bit of cricket in afternoon. Bridge at night with Dunthorne, Braggins & Bishop who returned from Rest Camp Boulogne about 3 a.m. that morning. Very nice day. Cully & Gorman to Bailleul. Came back v. late.

9-9-17   Sunday - no work. We had arranged to play IX Corps H.Q. at cricket. Montgomery was getting it up but although he said he would send lorries for us none turned up & so we did not go but played the Sergts of the Batt instead. Beat them by an innings & 4 runs. We made thru ns for no wickets in first innings. I retired at 26 having wrenched a muscle in my thigh. Sergts had made 32. Taylor in. Did not play after tea. Bishop to take Miles' place as Disbursing Off to 30th Div. Hughes going on leave. He came & had dinner with us & stayed the night. I got sort of impetigo & had a horrid face.

10-9-17   Stayed in bed till 9.0 but had to get up for C.O.'s orderly room over 2 ASC drivers who had refused to take another load of bricks. Leg rather rickety. 'A' Co Off & Sergts played the men at cricket & won twice - in aft & after tea. Got 100 cigars from Bunny. Got orders to put up some Nissen Huts. Work now 1 Plat with 'D' 2 Plat on road & 1 on Nissen Huts starting on 12th. Bishop to Bailleul.

11-9-17   Did not go up to work owing to leg. Cully went up. After we went along to site for Nissen Huts & saw the place. Stayed in all rest of day. Watched cricket. Braggins on road.

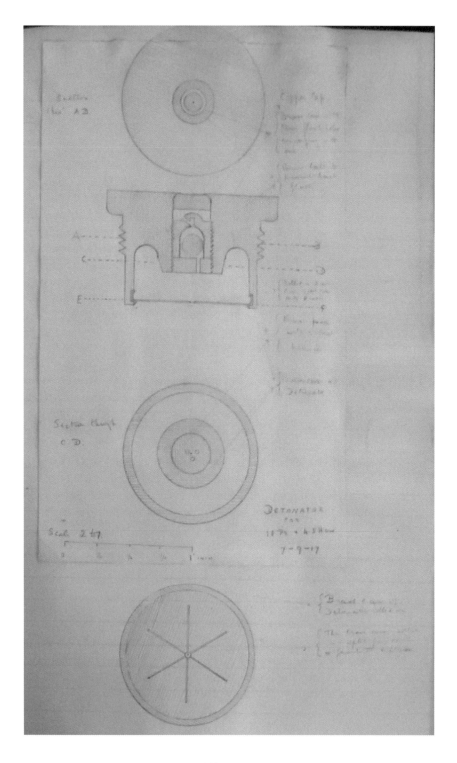

12-9-17   C.C. went on leave with Wood & Col. C.C. got a car to Boulogne from Bailleul from Bury. Started on Huts. Braggins started & Cully. I went up to see work early morning then went to see the Huts - going on very slowly. Gorman on road.

13-9-17   Got up late & went round to Huts. Getting on very slowly. Braggins on road. Gorman on Huts. Got orders to build more huts by Kemmel & take over Duckboard tracks over up to Deny's Wood & over by Canal north E of St Eloi. Got huts going strong. Went to see 200th F.C. R.E. & saw Hill about Duck board tracks. Spent afternoon on carrying. Got that dug out at night to 3 ft deep.

14-9-17   Rode over early to see duck board track. Met Cpl Fletcher up there & walked along track to B.H.Q. Douglas asleep so arranged to ration men & returned. Spent afternoon on Huts by Kemmel. Played bridge with Dixon Braggins & Cully. Just won. Bath at night. Had one platoon of 'B' Co attached for work on roads. Bury came just after tea.

15-9-17   Got up at 6.0 a.m. & rode out to road. Met Bolton about 7 a.m. He had put in the box chain across the road. Went on along duck board track & saw S...art in Deny's Wood. Got back about 9.0. Rode out to Kemmel camp. Had a few men working there to unload Hut coming by lorry. Sunday 20 more ..... was working. Dixon had Sports in afternoon in field Gun cricket field so went out to see that after working all afternoon. Payne returned in afternoon so Taylor was coming to me on 18th as C.O.2 Payne taking over 'C' Co. Dixon had Blue Birds[143] at night. They were very good indeed. Bridge at night. Saw Stanley Clark, Corfield & Mellor at Kemmel in morning. D.....ra episode! Went round after & saw new job at Daylight Corner.

16-9-17   Rode round huts in morning & afternoon. Bolton was taking party on roads so Gorman showed him the road & then returned. Braggins at Kemmel. Cully at 'S' Camp getting on famously. Bridge at night.

17-9-17   Lidgett & 2 platoons of 'C' started on Daylight Corner job. Braggins helped Lidgett in morning. I went round in morning & picked up Chippendale at Daylight Corner. He took me round to 'S' Camp & Kemmel & then back to Spy Farm. Saw something going wrong at Kemmel so rode round again. Had a party in there in afternoon to unload lorries so went round again in afternoon. Lidgett merely

---

[143] 30th Division's Concert Party.

putting in piles. They knew nothing about the job when they started. Chaippendale seemed a pretty good sort & thoroughly enjoying his job as acting C.R.E. All huts delivered at Kemmel job.

18-9-17   Took Taylor round the job in the morning. Joiners delivering pit props split for planking at Kemmel. Spent most of morning erecting a hut for Lidgett in about 1 we got floor & ribs put on. Got back for lunch. Gorman went on leave & C.S.M. Williams. Bain returned at night. Also Pethick & Weatherley. Spent all afternoon & most of evening working at returns & details of jobs.

19-9-17   Rode round work in morning - seemed to be getting on v. well. Taylor went up - saw L/Cpl Fletcher & his party - they were having rather a rotten time up there hoped to finish their job in 2 days. In afternoon we had a sort of scratch cricket match Off & Sergts 'A' Co v men. We just won. Though we started with a very bad rot. Pethick & Bretherton played for us. Bridge at night. Taylor & I beat Burn & Culley.

20-9-17   Stunt north & south of us - heard very little about result but what Chippendale told us was that things went very well. Rode round with Taylor in morning things seem to be going very well indeed. Had cricket match in afternoon. 'A' & 'B' Off v. 'C' & 'D' we very easily won - made over 100 for about 7 wickets & got them all out for 5 1 bye & 1 wide. Dull in morning but fine day later.

21-9-17   Went round work morning. Got a chit to say all men to work 8 hours. Had more working parties. 30 on Daylight Corner[144] & 15 on Kemmel. Got round in afternoon as well. Job going on very well. Beal down in the evening. Taylor came round too.

22-9-17   Went round work morning & afternoon. Work progressing as usual. Taylor came round in the morning & he & Cully went off to Bailleul in the afternoon for whiskey etc. Orders - owing to Dunthorne going on leave - Taylor to take over 'D' Co next day & Hughes was coming to 'A'. Cully & Taylor had a huge argument at night with being fairly merry. O'Connor came in - grousing about Payne.

23-9-17   Sunday - had an appointment with CRE at 3 p.m. Cricket match v 19 Kings. So could play as it was timed for 3 p.m. Rode round by myself as Taylor had gone to 'D' Co. In afternoon rode round with

---

[144] Near Mount Kemmel

Clavering over all the work & got a lot of questions settled. We beat Kings badly. We made 69 & they got 35. Cully bowled arm over in second innings! Forced five. Waters came to tea. O'Connor. Had Beal, Dippy & Ridsdale who was v. drunk in after dinner.

24-9-17 Dippy, Dunthorne & Ridsdale all went on leave. They put the wind up Ridsdale by saying the Div wanted to see him over a spy he had been supposed to know something about - he & the padre - but after writing a huge letter of 10 sheets home to his wife for Dippy to take they told him so all was well. I went round the work morning & afternoon - it seemed to be getting on very well. Apparently the G.O.C. Div was round the camp in the aft & got hold of Beal & cursed him over a lot of things one of which was not leaving everything about the jobs. So he tried to get on to me. Wilson my servant went on leave.

25-9-17 Dean started his paper tactics & things became distinctly strained - couldn't leave well alone & tried to push his nose into things. But I told him pretty straight & he shut up. Got a summons at night by a note from C.R.E. that our camp was going to be changed - the RFA camp. Braggins went at midday. Played Bridge at night with Cully Burn & Bishop ended all square. Very hot day indeed.

26-9-17 Met Clavering as CRE in morning. They told us only one Brig RFA at Daylight Corner & the other ones at Kemmel. Went round with him round to new sights & also round jobs. Beal came down to Kemmel job. Rode round again in afternoon & then got back to play in match v. 17 Kings. They made 55 & we made 69. I got 14. Top score & one wicket for no runs in my first call. Walker Capt Bea..... round from 25th Kings. Dean still muddling along.

27-9-17 Went round both morning & afternoon. Lidgett started Sergt Moore on ..... camp at Kemmel. Putting up 6 huts there - transport lines not decided. Heard Col Fenn coming back this month. C.C. got extension till 1st Oct. Had bridge at night with Cully, Burn & Bishop.

28-9-17 Went round in morning. Beal came down to Kemmel so rode round with him. Went round again in afternoon. Sgt Moore getting on with 2 huts. Let company off early to go to a show of the Blue Birds at Beacon Hall - 20th Kings. Went myself & stayed there to dinner with Walker, Beaver & Capt Henderson of the 149 RFA. Didn't get back till about 1.30 a.m. Rather the worse for wear.

29-9-17   Went round both morning & afternoon. CE ? Corps was down in morning at Kemmel. At night we had a Batt event bad show too cold. Had no bridge at night. Myles came to dinner & stayed the night in good form.

30-9-17   Bishop went on leave about 5.30 a.m.to catch the civilian train to Boulogne. I went round in morning. Gotman turned up from leave midday. Went round in afternoon. Beal said something about putting a hundred of 'A' Co onto railway job in Railway Wood off huts. We had Walker & Watson to dinner. Cully & I played bridge with them. 2nd Lt Smith 2nd RSFs turned up after dinner to live & mess with us. He had a party of infantry working for us. Seemed quite a harmless youth. Gorman to Bailleul. C.S.M. Williams returned.

1-10-17   Round morning & afternoon. Burn went to Bailleul in afternoon. Heard C.C. was returning on the 2nd & also that Fenn was going to the Fusiliers. Spent evening writing. Hodges returned.

2-10-17   Went both morning & afternoon. C.C. returned midday. Symons & Miles came in to dinner. Symon & I lost badly to Gorman & Burn. Orders for Cully & 200 men of 'A' Co to go onto railway work in Ravens Wood. Paid men at night. Beautiful day.

3-10-17   Went round as usual morning & afternoon. Cully had to see RE Officer in morning & go out on work at 2 a.m. next morning. Job going on well. Got 55 men infantry for working parties. Of course it made the job very much slower but we managed to carry on alright.

4-10-17   C.C. came round the work with Beal in the morning. Beal knew nothing about the job. Also went round in afternoon. All going well. After dinner went in & played bridge with C.C. v Hodges & Dean & lost 15 francs! 2nd Lt Potts from 18th Man joined the mess.

5-10-17   Went up early in the morning about 6 a.m. & saw Cully's job. Not too good work. Saw Waters on roads on the way up. Went round the jobs in the morning - stayed in all afternoon as I was pretty tired. Played bridge with Cully v Burn & Gorman & won about 25 francs. Early to bed. Cole took Cully's party at night. Split up & 30 worked next morning.

6-10-17   First bad morning for months. Rained hard all the morning. Went round jobs. 18th Man H.Q. had come into 'S' camp. Officers & Lt W Lembeter the C.O. wanted to change everything. Got through to

Atkinson & he said they were not to alter anything without permission from D.H.Q. Stayed in all afternoon weather so obnoxious. No bridge.

7-10-17   Went round in morning. Poured with rain after I had got a short way round. Nothing much doing as the jobs were all getting on well. Left the 18th Man to their own devices & simply went on doing trench board tracks & railways. Stayed in afternoon & read most of the time. Had tea at 4.0. Rain cleared off at night.

8-10-17   Fine morning. Went round. Met Strang-Clark at Kemmel R.F.A. Went up to Kemmel to see the Strafe. Nothing much doing as it was over but a splendid view. Stayed in all afternoon as it started to pour with rain again. All evening. Cully brought a fellow called Barnes out of 20th Kings in to tea.

9-10-17   Went round in morning. Very wet so did not go round in afternoon but walked round to the Theatre with C.C. after lunch. Saw the General there then walked on with C.C. & saw the Soccer Match v 17 Kings. We won 2-1. They had never been beaten before. Heard Fenn was coming back crossing on the 10th. Huge attack in morning, seems Fifth & French armies A.C.C. attacked, no news.

10-10-17   Went up & saw railway job in morning. Not at all satisfied - they the Corps R.E.s did not seem to know the first thing about it some making an awful hash of it. The track was a huge quagmire. Rained on the way back so I did not go out for the rest of the morning. Went round in afternoon, saw Henderson on the way back. Job getting on alright. Manchester men relieved by 2nd Yorks in afternoon so Potts poor little devil had to go. Payne got O.C. Corps School job back. Going next day - got majority etc. Didn't play bridge or anything.

11-10-17   Went round both morning & afternoon. Found Sergt Moore was making rather a hash of things at Kemmel R 2 A. So spent quite a long time there in the afternoon. Scotte Smith was relieved by 2Lt Wile so he had to go - left about middle of the morning. At night Cully stayed in & Gorman went out on Railway. Played bridge & Burn & I won fairly well v Cully & Gorman. Payne left for Corps School. Taylor took over 'C' Co. C.C. told me I was going on leave on 18th.

12-10-17   Went round in morning. Everything going on better. Rained hard at night. Rained again in afternoon so I stayed in & wrote letters. Cully got orders to go on the 16th to Div reinforcement camp to train pioneers who came along. Sent to Bury to ask for a car. He wrote back that only one going on the 16th not 17th or 18th. Had bridge at night with Cully, Gorman & Bishop. My ..... last turn before going to bed. Saw a practice Rugger match at night.

13-10-17   Went round in morning - raining in afternoon so did not go round. Lt Saxton & Earlding from 18th KLR in charge of working party & also Lt Hayes 2 Yorks came to mess & we put them up also. Bishop returned from leave. All seemed quite good sorts. Did not go round owing to bad weather but stayed in & wrote. Dean trying to swap me for 17th instead of 18th so I could car it. C.C. decided Burn was to take over 'A' Co while I was away.

14-10-17   Went round in morning with C.C. & Wooly. Went ..... including Theatre but did not fix much up. Then in afternoon went round with Burn & handed over things to Burn. Went to theatre too. Ripping day but very cold.

25-10-17   Rode round in the morning & handed over to Burn. Expected to go
to   on 16th if I could get a car but could not manage it so it was put off
4-11-17   till 18th.

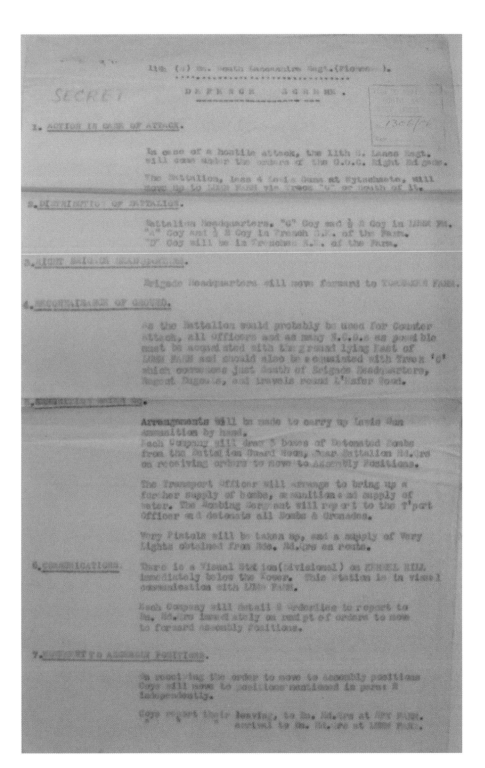

11th (s) Bn. South Lancashire Regt.(Pioneers).

SECRET

DEFENCE SCHEME.

1308/74

1. ACTION IN CASE OF ATTACK.

In case of a hostile attack, the 11th S. Lancs Regt. will come under the orders of the G.O.C. Right Brigade.

The Battalion, less 4 Lewis Guns at Wytschaete, will move up to LEEB FARM via Track "G" or South of it.

2. DISTRIBUTION OF BATTALION.

Battalion Headquarters. "C" Coy and ½ B Coy in LEEB Ft.
"A" Coy and ½ B Coy in Trench S.E. of the Farm.
"D" Coy will be in Trenches N.E. of the Farm.

3. RIGHT BRIGADE HEADQUARTERS.

Brigade Headquarters will move forward to TORREKEN FARM.

4. RECONNAISANCE OF GROUND.

As the Battalion would probably be used for Counter attack, all Officers and as many N.C.O.s as possible must be acquainted with the ground lying East of LEEB FARM and should also be acquainted with Track 'G' which commences just South of Brigade Headquarters, Rupret Dugouts, and travels round L'Enfer Road.

5. AMMUNITION AND BOMBS.

Arrangements will be made to carry up Lewis Gun ammunition by hand.
Each Company will draw 5 boxes of Detonated Bombs from the Battalion Guard Room, near Battalion Hd.Qrs on receiving orders to move to Assembly Positions.

The Transport Officer will arrange to bring up a further supply of bombs, ammunition and supply of water. The Bombing Sergeant will report to the T'port Officer and detonate all Bombs & Grenades.

Very Pistols will be taken up, and a supply of Very Lights obtained from Bde. Hd.Qrs en route.

6. COMMUNICATIONS.

There is a Visual Station(Divisional) on HUSSEL HILL immediately below the Tower. This Station is in visual communication with LEEB FARM.

Each Company will detail 2 Orderlies to report to Bn. Hd.Qrs immediately on receipt of orders to move to forward Assembly Positions.

7. MOVEMENT TO ASSEMBLY POSITIONS.

On receiving the order to move to Assembly positions Coys will move to positions mentioned in para. 2 independently.

Coys report their leaving, to Bn. Hd.Qrs at DRY FARM.
Arrival to Bn. Hd.Qrs at LEEB FARM.

S.O.S. SIGNAL. (1) The S.O.S. Signal will be sent up by order of any Officer.

The signal will be repeated until our artillery barrage opens fire. The message will also be sent by telephone to Brigade Headquarters in the following form :-

RIGHT (or Left) SUBSECTOR S.O.S.

(2) The following S.O.S. signals are available :-

In use (Night)   Rifle Grenade Signal - parachute - with 3 colours - red over green over yellow.

(Day).   Mortar Signal loosing red smoke.

First Change. (If necessary).
Rifle Grenade Signal - parachute - light changing from white to green.

Second Change. (If necessary).
1½" very Light - parachute - light changing from white to red.

As circumstances permit, this last will also be made into a Rifle Grenade Signal.

[signature]

Lt. Col.
15/10/1917.   Comdg. 11th S. Lancs Regt. (Pioneers).

DISTRIBUTION.

Officer Commanding "A" Coy.
"   "   "B" "
"   "   "C" "
"   "   "D" "

Lewis Gun Officer.
Transport Officer.

18-10-17   Left camp at 6.30 with luggage going by horse cart. Met Naylor at Bailleul & caught 8.30 Civy train. Got to Boulogne at 2.0. Did not try to catch boat but stayed at officers club & had a comfortable night in. Padré slept in my room so I finished the journey with him.

19-10-17   Boat left at 9.30. Got to town at about 2.0 p.m. very surprised to find Kaye had come all the way down to meet me & had a taxi ready so we went off to Mount St. Found Burns at Prima's so had tea there with Pat & Stella. They had a Red Cross thing on so we spent much money on that. Also went round & saw Weno & George. Caught 5.20 to Lancaster. Met Malcolm & Thomas met us.

20-10-17   Lancaster. Stayed in & pottered about getting Xmas presents & things. Met West down Town later in morning. Took cab to golf course & called for Mr Malcolm. Lunch there. Played golf with W Sharp v Mr Malcolm & Mr Storey & we won.

21-10-17   Rainy day so stayed in all day.

22-10-17   Town in morning. Went on to Oaklea. Roger Bacon & his Fiancée were there. Dull performance. Stayed the night.

23-10-17   Back to Lancaster this morning. Packed up for Hilda & Tom in afternoon.

24-10-17   All off including Baby & Nurse for Wolverhampton. Caught 9.20 train. Had carriage to ourselves to Crewe & full up from there. Raining when we got in & nothing to meet us. Went into town & collared a cab coming to station. Got to Hilda's for tea.

25-10-17
to
4-11-17   Stayed at Ash Hill. Played golf with Dai on Sat 27.10.17 Halved with him giving him a half. We had tea at ...andwin. Applied to J Winterton 26th for an extension & he gave me a fortnight. Got his extension till 12th Nov so stayed on at Ash Hill. Got a letter to say I had to report in writing to the W.O. on 5th so I stayed at Ash Hill till 5th then Kaye & I caught 11.0 up to London. Got a taxi to Savoy fairly easily, went back to Euston & met Thomas by 4.20. After dinner we all went & saw Chu Chin Chow[145].

6-11-17   Saw Lo..... in morning. Lunch at Prima's & then dinner with Weno & George. Rather a rush but got in nice time to Cubitts.

---

[145] A musical comedy based on *Ali Baba and the 40 Thieves* premiered on 3 August 1916.

7-11-17   Bunny arrived on the scene & took a room at the Savoy near ours. Had a large dinner ..... before going to Maid of the Mountains. Egerton & Gladys Pat Mr & Mrs Roxhill & Bunny & we 3 & had supper after. Had lunch midday with Wa..... & Flo - huge scream.

8-11-17   Lunch with Bury at Princes & Dinner with Garton & Gladys at Romanos & then all went to The Boy ripping thing.

9-11-17   Back to Ash Hill by morning train. Toma stayed on at a friend's near
to   town & went home on Sat with Weno. We went to church on Sunday
13-11-17   & then on Sat Dai & I played & Tim Adams. I beat them ..... all giving Dai a half. All had tea after with Baby & Kaye & Hilda at Franchines's.

14-11-17   Returned to Lancaster by morning train. Got in for lunch. Very good journey after Stafford had an empty carriage. No changes all the way.

15-11-17   Golf on 17th with Mr Sharp v Mr Malcolm & Jerry Sharp. Beat them
to   very badly. Went to Hippodrome & also Dinner at Helens though the
25-11-17   ..... Also went down after dinner & had cards with ..... & Teddy Marsh & Mrs & Capt Eels. Went over to Oakham on Friday 23rd. No one there but Mother & Mabel - Mother to lunch on Monday 19th with the ..... Coming back on Friday from Silverdale we were an hour late at Carnforth. Long wait on station. Got orders first to go to Bungay 68th Div then they sent me on to Lowestoft to report to 205th Brig.

26-11-17   Caught 7.50 to London. Got the 3.10 from Liverpool St. Saw Dixon on the train so travelled with him. Bretherton met us at Lowestoft & we got particulars from RTO reported to Major Lloyd Griffiths 52nd Welch Reg (C.O.2) & spent the night at the Royal. I am told to take over 'C' Co & Dixon 'D' Co.

27-11-17   Reported for Work. Cooper in charge of 'C' Co. agreed to wait & not take over till the end of the month so as to get account right.

28-11-17   Gradually took over the company but ordered no certificates on 7th
to   12 17. Kaye came down & stayed at the Royal ordinarily I was
21-12-17   sleeping at Kin..... & messing in mess. Kaye went back on Monday & I went up to Town with her - saw Egerton & Gladys also Weno. Kaye caught 5.20 north & I caught 7.45 back. On 18th mother came down for a few days. On 15th Lt Col Tudor Fitz John Worcester Reg took over command of Batt & things started to hum. Fireworks alround especially to people who had not been out. He was very nice

to me all through everything. He transferred Hackett to me to help train.

22-12-17　Got leave for Xmas. Caught 12.30 to Town. Just missed 5.40 owing to train being late. Hackett came with me so had dinner at Euston & caught 9.50 to Lancaster.

23-12-17　Ought to have got to Lancaster at 3.50 did not get in till 5.40. Freezing journey all the way. Kaye met me with Belsize. Went to bed for 3 hours. Did not go to church. Spent rest of day indoors.

24-12-17　Went down town. Mother still at Lowestoft so did not go to Silverdale. Didn't do much all day.

25-12-17　Xmas day. Mr & Mrs Malcolm had a single at golf & I played with Dr Bailing, Wolsenholme & Warbreck & later Mr Malcolm joined us. We halved both matches. Golf bad owing to frozen ground. Huge dinner at night. Us four Mrs Stirling Capt & Mrs Stirling Dr Bury Mr & Mrs Gil..... Mrs Austin & Mr Wilson & Mr Duncan.

26-12-17　Played golf v the Vicar in morning beat him hollow, in afternoon Mr Malcolm (a half) & Mr Storey (a third) beat Mr Sharp & myself 2 & 1.

27-11-17　Nothing oing much but went down town. I asked for an extension
&　　　of leave & got it till the Sunday night instead of Sat.
28-11-17

29-12-17　Played Mr Malcolm & Mr St..... & Mr Sharp & myself & they were up again. I caught the 5.45 to town & got in at 10.45. Slept night at Euston.

30-12-17　Caught 9.15 from Liverpool St. At Euston found Capt Henderson O.R. W.P.B. looking for taxi so shared his. He was at Munich with RFA. Got in to Lowestoft midday lunched with mother & reported for duty.

31-12-17　Started work again with company.

1918

1-1-18   Karl on leave so mother rushed up to Town by 5.34 train.

2-1-18   Carried on training as before. Company going strong. Hackett away
to   on course so Williams & myself ran it almost entirely. Kaye came
16-1-18   down on 16th so we lived at the Royal.. Baby & nurse also came.

17-1-18   Still training our Coy. Leslie Evans of Blackheath turned up - at
to   Admiralty had a chat. Uncle Fred came from Farnworth[146] where he
25-1-18   was with an advance party to billet his Batt which were coming from
          Newmarket.

26-1-18   To go on a course to Bisley. Kaye & I went up as Mother & Karl
          were both in town so stayed at Euston. Had Edith Hawkins, Uncle
          Fred & Norman to dinner. Mother & Karl coming up late. We all
          went to a Little Bit of Fluff & enjoyed it much.

27-1-18   Went up in afternoon to Bisley to report & returned to town. Jennie
          Watson to dinner - had quite a good day & returned at night to
          Bisley.

28-1-18   Senior officers course commenced. Very cold but a ripping course.
          Nothing to do but ..... refresher N.C.O.s course going on. Found
          H.A.C. Goodwin was down there as an instructor in Revolver
          shooting. Also Richardson WNW O.R. was adjutant. Caught 4.30 to
          town. All went to Arleth after dinner - great success. Air raid going
          on but I caught 9.30 p.m.at 12.15 so was not very late. Bed about
          2.30 a.m.

29-1-18   Caught 4.30 to town & dinner at Euston & all saw Dear Brutus. Very
          good show. Another raid on caught 12.15 at 2.30 a.m. Bed about
          4.15.

30-1-18   Karl crossed over. Caught 4.30 to town & went up with Norman We
          saw The Beauty Spot - a ripping show. No raid but train rather late
          came in about 1.30. Bed about 3 a.m.

---

[146] A village in south Lancashire between Prescot and Penketh.

31-1-18   Came up by 4.30 with Norman & had dinner at H.A.C.[147] mess in the Tower[148]. Billiards to follow. Had much too much to drink so went to sleep on Waterloo platform. Train about 2.30. Bed about 4.0.

1-2-18   Wa..... till 12. Caught 12.30 to town & then lunch at Liverpool St & caught 3.13 back. Reported about 7.30 at orderly room.

2-2-18   Changed from Billets to top floor of the Empire. Dixon & his crowd taking over my Billets. CQMS Davies got the sack & I got CQMS Beatty instead. A good exchange.

3-2-18 to 10-3-18   Thomas came down to be confirmed on the 8th also to recuperate after his attack of swollen glands. Went to various dances. I didn't go. Also to the Palace cinema once or twice. Weather poor.

11-3-18   All there went up to town by the 8.25. Had lunch at Euston & went & reported to Chelsea Barracks. Put on No 1 squad. We booked rooms at the Grosvenor. Kaye & I went to Paunch at night.

12-3-18   Kaye returned to Lowestoft. Found a fellow called Bet...y also S. Lancs so he & I went to a Battn 'Ole having dinner at the Grosvenor.

13-3-18   Bet.....y again to dinner & he & I went to Arleth.

14-3-18   Stayed in & did nothing but write out note book.

15-3-18   Kaye came back from Lowestoft & we went round & had dinner at Wenos. George & she were going to Eltham for a few weeks while their house was being done up etc.

16-3-18   Caught the 2 p.m. from Paddington to Wolverhampton & got to Hilda's for tea. Dai & Hilda in good form.

17-3-18   Went over to works with Dai in morning instead of church & got back to lunch. Caught the 5 something back to London. Got in for supper about 9 p.m.

18-3-18   Went to Yes Uncle & liked it very much. First time we had a cab.

---

[147] Honourable Artillery Company.
[148] Tower of London.

19-3-18   Kaye returned to Lowestoft. Took Norman to dinner & Yes Uncle again. Enjoyed it more than before.

20-3-18
to
21-3-18   Stayed in & wrote notes & read.

22-3-18   Kaye returned from Lowestoft. Went to the Beauty Spa. Quite a good show. Had map reading exam.

23-3-18   Caught the 2.10 to Bedford & got in about 3.30. Edith met us & we had a very jolly evening. Music & much fun. Mrs Hawkins, Amy & C..... were there besides Edith.

24-3-18   Went a walk in the morning. So hot we sat out all the afternoon & caught the 9.0 train back to Town. Got in about 12 o'clock.

25-3-18   Mr Price came to dinner & sat & talked after. Started Barrack square exam.

26-3-18   Had the two Irvins to dinner at the Grosvenor & then went with them to the Savoy Theatre. Nothing but the Truth. Funny piece but Teddy was talking so much about himself I did not see much of the piece. Got a brougham there & back.

27-3-18   Was to have Burn, Pat & Norman to dinner at the Savoy & then Alhambra but Norman forgot to remind Bunny. Roy did not turn up either - had had order to go out & was very busy at Camp. So Pat Bunny & us two went & had supper at Savoy afterwards. Saw Bing Boys on Broadway[149] there. Quite a good show but Pat was anxious about Roy. Saw Norman for a few minutes before the ..... also a fellow Lt Savoy in R.N.A.S.

28-3-18   Last day's work. Passed off square. Had Miss Wright to dinner & then went to Lilac Domino pretty music but poor actors. She was quite nice.

29-3-18   Last day at Barracks. Left about 11.0 & determined to catch 5.45 to Crewe & stop there the night. Got to Euston hotel for tea & met Joliffe there. On the train met Chance (Major) Border Reg. He went

---

[149] A musical hit of the London stage during World War I.

with me up to Crewe & stayed the night. Quite comfortable & good supper. Being Good Friday trains were as on Sundays.

30-3-18   Caught 9.11 on to Lancaster & got in about 11.35. Chance came up with me all the way he was going to Grasmere. In afternoon I played golf with George Sharp against Threlfall & ..... Sharp & we won but did not go the proper round - though we played 19 holes! Had 9 holes with Mr Malcolm after tea,.

31-3-18   Had 27 holes with Mr Malcolm, Mr Sharp & Jerry. Did not go to church.

1-4-18   Had 45 holes of golf. Morning I played with Mr Malcolm for competition. Played v. badly. 94. Afternoon I & Mr Sharp played Mr Malcolm & Mr Storey & they won 1 up. Final 9 holes with Mr Malcolm afterwards after tea.

2-4-18   Went over to Silverdale to church. Mr & Mrs Bacon & Hilda there. Played Bridge & Billiards & had much music.

3-4-18   Returned in afternoon to Lancaster - had a walk in evening. Billiards also with Mr Bacon. Played 300 up. First hundred I was 98. Second 100 he was 199. Third I was 298 & he ran out for 282. Florie Rolands came round to see us. She was staying at Thorton's.

4-4-18   Caught 5.45 to Euston. Played Jerry Bardely in morning gave him ½. Played awfully badly & halved with him. Got 18th both times with spoon.

5-4-18   Spent morning going to Grafton Galleries & caught 3.13 to Lowestoft. Got in at 6.13 & reported to mess. Told we were shifting on Tuesday under canvas at Henham Park[150] Camp. Went out to sing at ..... after dinner.

6-4-18   Went to work in morning. Found it was true about Henham. C.O. off to France. Dance on but Kaye did not go to it. Went over in afternoon pouring rain with Ashton's by motor to try & find a spot to live in at Henham. Found nothing - got to know the Hickling at the ..... Frostenden, W Wangford Pouring all afternoon. Tried the Swan Hotel Southwold but no good. C.O. went on leave.

---

[150] An estate just north of Blythburgh in Suffolk. Originally the seat of the Earls of Suffolk, later the seat of the Earls of Stradbroke.

7-4-18   Went on to Southwold & tried the Grand Hotel fixed on that took Mrs Ashton over with us. Then heard of the Hermitage Frostenden from Mrs Gilbert so took motor over again after tea & fixed on that - with Mrs Jeffey. After dinner went into the Co..... & sang.

8-4-18   Spent all day packing etc. Spent the evening up to dinner with the commodore. C.O. still on leave. Kaye was stopping behind a bit.

9-4-18   Took Batt (about 50 strong!) over to Henham & saw them into camp. Started to rain. I brought the C.O.'s jaunty car[151] so used that to & from the Hermitage. Kaye still at Lowestoft. Messed in camp.

10-4-18   Poured with rain. Messed in camp all day. Slept at the Hermitage.

11-4-18   Kaye & family came over. All got in safe - had a lumber from Bill & they ..... to B..... it. Had dinner at Hermitage. Messed the rest at camp.

12-4-18   At camp. Getting settled.

13-4-18   Went over to Lowestoft to lunch & gathered last of our belongings. Spent the afternoon shopping & had just time to get back to tea. Put the cab up at the old stables. Saw Commandant Ashton.

14-4-18   At camp. Rained hard 15, 16, 17 so that camp was nearly under water. Took church parade on 14th. Fine then but looked like rain. Only heard at 8.20 so missed breakfast. G.O.C. inspected some gangs at work on 15th & had sort of lecture exam of senior officers in afternoon 18th. Ma....., Ch..... & Wynne for overseas on 21st.

15-4-18
to
24-4-18   At Camp. Weather cleared so had a better time. Had a scheme to do so Hackett, Cowper & I rove round & the subalterns did also. Bretherton had to cross on the 20th so I calculated I was crossing on the 6th so & I applied for leave & got it.

25-4-18   With family caught the 1.55 to Liverpool Street. Luckily a fine day so drove in jaunty car to Brompton. Stayed the night at the Euston. Quite a good journey.

26-4-18   Ellen came to see Kaye in the morning. We all caught the 1.0 p.m.to Lancaster. Had a very comfortable journey getting a coupé at Euston to meet us. Thomas met us.

---

[151] A light two-wheeled carriage for a single horse.

27-4-18   Played golf with Mr Sharp v Mr Frank Storey & Mr Malcolm & Carl. Had nine holes v Mr Hardshaw after & halved.

28-4-18   Played with Mr Sharp v Mr Malcolm, Jerry Sharp & Mr Farnen & won after being 3 & 4 down we won 1 up. Mr Sharp did 15th in 4 16th in 3 & I did 17th & 18th in 3 each. Caught 6.12 to Carlisle & stayed night at Hotel there.

29-4-18   Caught 7.10 to Glasgow. Saw Townsend & got 3.45 back to Lancaster at 7.0. Kaye & Thomas met us. Karl landed 3 a.m. & went to Royal Free Hospital Grays Inn Road for DSO.

30-4-18   Played golf with Eric Bardely & Eric. Fly played then ..... ball & lost 2 & 1. Thomas's 21st birthday. Played with Eric Bardely & Warbeck beat them rather easily. Neome joined in but did not ..... in. Thomas playing in aft. We gave her a scratch ..... Huge dinner of 10 at night Greta, Bunny & others & then we all went to see the Silver King done by the Munition Workers. V. good!

1-5-18   Caught the 11.40 to Silverdale. Babba came too. Aunty Edie ..... & Miss Rowlands to tea. Mabel stayed to see us & then went home to see Norman.

2-5-18   Caught 9.15 back to Lancaster. Carl had landed & was in Hospital so mother caught 3.0 down to Town. Played with Mr Sharp v Mr Malcolm Mr Storey & Jenny & beat them 2 & 1. Did about 36 good golf.

3-5-18   Caught 10.30 to Wolverhampton. Got there for dinner. Idea was to go back to Wangford till got orders. Wired for active service till ..... & got it. Mrs Clarence Smith to tea with Baby.

4-5-18   Got orders by wire to cross to France on Tuesday. Mr & Mrs Sanderson to tea. Decided to go up on Sunday. Mr Rider Smith in after tea & Mr Joliffe after dinner. Played croquet with Dai & he won v excited putting in ...tator.

5-5-18   Caught 10.50 to Town. Arrived at 4.40. Awful slow train. Saw Karl & had tea & he was staying at Euston.

6-5-18   Shopped with Karl in morning. Took luggage to Grosvenor in afternoon. Saw Dixon after tea. Slept at Grosvenor at night.

SECRET.   No.O.P.100/4.

11th (S) Bn. 5th Lancashire Regt.(Pioneers).

INSTRUCTIONS FOR OFFENSIVE
OPERATIONS.

Number of O.R. to take part in Action.

Further to my O.P.100/3 dated 22nd inst., the following
will also be left behind with the Company Hd.Qrs.,
and will not move forward without instructions.

C.Q.M.S.   1.
Assistant. 1.

Cooks.   2.

all other ranks employed on Coy Duties &c will parade
with their Companies, who should be as strong as possible
in all cases.

O.C. Coys will send in to Orderly Room by 8 p.m. on
Y night the strength of their Parties for Work, and
give details in the case of a company sending out more
than 1 party on any one task. i.e. If a company has been
allotted 2 or 3 different tasks for the operations,
2 or 3 different sets of figures will be required.

                                        Lieut & Adjt.,
                                   11th S.Lancs Reg.(Pioneers).

24.7.17.

A.B.C.D. 11th (S) Bn. S. Lancashire Regt.(Pioneers).

POSITIONS AND LOCATIONS OF R.E. DUMPS.
AMMUNITION DUMPS. MEDICAL DRESSING STATIONS
AND AID POSTS.DURING OPERATIONS.

1.AMMUNITION
DUMPS.

Ammunition Dumps are situated at :-
    Right Brigade.   I.24.d.10.51.,   I.24.d.40.75.
    Battalion dumps.   I.24.b.25.60.

    Left Brigade.   I.24.b.15.80.,   I.24.b.40.55.
    Battalion dumps.

    The Right Brigade Dump at I.24.a.55.40.

    The Left Brigade Dump at I.23.b.9.8.

The Divisional Reserve Ammunition Dump is situated at
BEDFORD HOUSE.

Main Divisional Bomb Store at H.26.b.7.6.

The following may be drawn from any of the Battn. Brigade,
& Divisional Dumps :-

S.A.A.   Mills Hand Grenades.   No.24 Rifle Grenades.
Mills Rifle Grenades.   Stokes Bombs.   Green Cartridges
for Stokes Bombs.   Rings.   Flares.   V.F.A. 1" D.I.
V.F.A. 1" Red (or S.O.S. colour).   V.F.A. 1½" D.I.
V.F.A. 1½" Red (Or S.O.S. Colour). Pistol Ammunition.
Petrol Tins.(from Battn & Bde Dumps only)

2.R.E. DUMPS.   The main 30th Division R.E.Park will be at H.27.d.0.4.
The advanced Divisional Dump is located at ZILLEBEKE at
H.18.d.4.2.
The main BATTLE DUMP (BOMBER LANE DUMP) will be located at
I.24.a.8.3. This dump will be connected to a Pack Transport
track, that will be opened shortly after Zero, which will
run to CLAPHAM JUNCTION and then on to FITZCLARENCE FARM.
Stores this Dump will contain are shown in Attached Table A.
A Small Battle DUMP, Stores in an attached Table B will be
located at VALLEY COTTAGES, I.23.d.1.6. This dump will be
on the track which will be opened as soon after Zero as
possible through I.24.d.8.2., I.18.a.4.3., I.18.d.0.4,
to CLAPHAM JUNCTION.

Any of these dumps will issue on demand to any Battalion
or Battery immediately after Zero.
There will be a small supply of timber, explosives &c. at
the BOMBER LANE DUMP for use by the TECHNICAL TROOPS only.

It is hoped that a Stone Dump will be opened about I.21.a.
on S day.

3.MEDICAL   Regimental Aid Posts will be established at :- I.24.d.6.7.,
DRESSING STATIONS   I.24.a. 7.4.,   I.24.a.2.4.,   I.24.c.5.9.
&C.   During the earlier part of the action wounded will be cleared
to these by regimental stretcher bearers.

From the Regimental Aid Posts etc wounded will be cleared
by hand and down the Tramway by R.A.M.C. bearers to Collecting
Stations at   I.23.a.6.6.   DORMY.
               I.23.a.9.6.   VALLEY COTTAGE.
The Advanced Dressing Station will be at VOORMEZEELE HOUSE,
I.20.c.4.2.

The various routes will be "flagged" for Walking Wounded to
collect them at WHITEPITS I.18.d.0.5. from which place they
will be conveyed in buses and lorries to the Corps Main Dr[...]

-5-

-ing Station, (Lightly Wounded) 26th Field Ambulance
at H.27.c.1.9.

Walking Wounded of the 8th Division will be collected
at KRUISSTRAAT (H.19.d.9.5.) where such men of the
30th Division as go down that way will be attended to.

A.B.Derbeck

Lieut & Adjt.,

11th S.Lancs Regt.(Pioneers).

O.C. "A" COY.
     "B" "
     "C" "
     "D" "

M.O.
File.

T A B L E A.

BORDER LANE BATTLE DUMP.

Sandbags.	50,000.
Barbed wire, rolls.	400.
Plain wire, rolls.	10.
French Wire, coils.	250.
Screw Pickets, Long.	750.
Screw Pickets, Short.	1500.
Picks.	800.
Shovels.	1500.

T A B L E B.

Sandbags.	25,000.
Barbed Wire, rolls.	200.
Plain Wire, rolls.	5.
Plain Wire, rolls.	100.
French wire, coils.	250.
Screw Pickets, long.	750.
Screw Pickets, short.	100.
Picks.	800.
Shovels.	

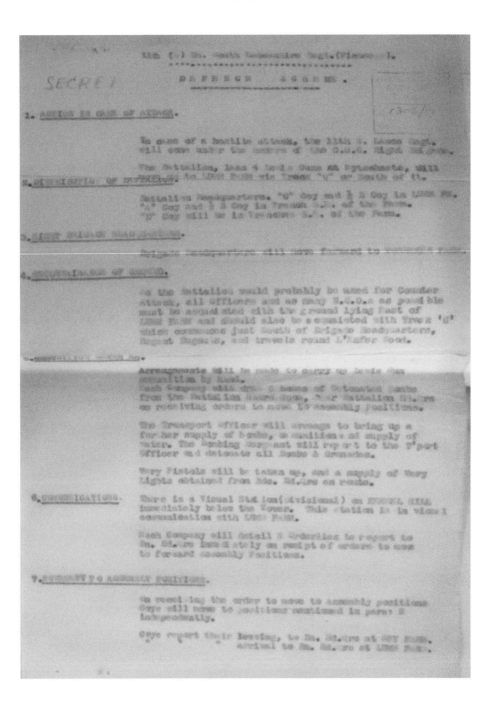

-2-

S.O.S. SIGNAL. (1) The S.O.S. Signal will be sent up by order of any Officer.

The signal will be repeated until our artillery barrage opens fire. The message will also be sent by telephone to Brigade Headquarters in the following form :-

RIGHT (or Left) SUBSECTOR S.O.S.

(2) The following S.O.S. signals are available :-

In use. (Night)   Rifle Grenade Signal - parachute - with 3 colours - red over green over yellow.

(Day).   Mortar Signal issuing red smoke.

First Change. (If necessary).
Rifle Grenade Signal - parachute - light changing from white to green.

Second Change. (If necessary).
1½" Very Light - parachute - light changing from white to red.

As circumstances permit, this last will also be made into a Rifle Grenade Signal.

Albert Dean
Lt r/qft

for Lt.Colonel.
13/10/1917.   Comdg.11th S. Lancs Regt.(Pioneers).

DISTRIBUTION.

Officer Commanding "A" Coy.
  "   "   "B" "
  "   "   "C" "
  "   "   "D" "
Lewis Gun Officer.
Transport Officer.

HERTFORDSHIRE DEFENCE SCHEME "Z"

Div.Com.R.741/17

205th Infantry Brigade Group.

SPECIAL ORDER No 6

Herringfleet Camp
Gt Yarmouth.   22nd September 1917.

The attached extracts of Northern Army letter
N.A./9518 (Q) dated 6.9.17 enclosing copy of Northern Army Defence
Scheme "Z" is forwarded for your information.

Headquarters R.A. Brigades will accompany one
of their Batteries.

The General Instructions issued under this officers
Secret letter No S.12 dated 6.9.17. will apply in this case.

The officers detailed to act as Entraining and
Detraining officers under that scheme will also act in the same
capacity under northern Army Defence "Z".

Herringfleet Camp.
22.9.17.

Copy No 1.   to O.C. "A" Company.
Copy No 2.   to O.C. "B" Company.
Copy No.3.   to O.C. "C" Company.
Copy No.4.   to O.C. "D" Company.
Copy No 5.   to O.C. "E" Company
Copy No.6.   to The Quartermaster.
Copy No 7.   to The Transport Officer.
Copies 8 to 10 Retained.

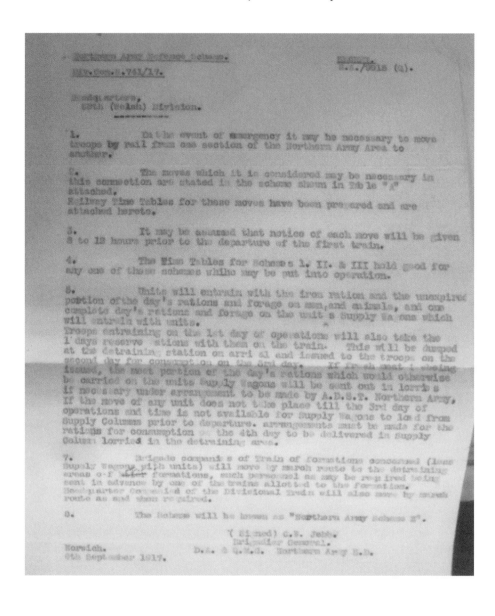

Northern Army Defence Scheme.

Div.Com.G.741/17.

N.A.S./8918 (a).

Headquarters,
38th (Welsh) Division.

1. In the event of emergency it may be necessary to move troops by rail from one section of the Northern Army Area to another.

2. The moves which it is considered may be necessary in this connection are stated in the scheme shown in Table "A" attached.
Railway Time Tables for these moves have been prepared and are attached hereto.

3. It may be assumed that notice of each move will be given 8 to 12 hours prior to the departure of the first train.

4. The Time Tables for Schemes I. II. & III hold good for any one of these schemes which may be put into operation.

5. Units will entrain with the iron ration and the unexpired portion of the day's rations and forage on men, and animals, and one complete day's rations and forage on the unit s Supply Wagons which will entrain with units.
Troops entraining on the 1st day of operations will also take the 1 days reserve rations with them on the train. This will be dumped at the detraining station on arrival and issued to the troops on the second day for consumption on the 3rd day.   If fresh meat is being issued, the meat portion of the day's rations which would otherwise be carried on the units Supply Wagons will be sent out in lorries if necessary under arrangement to be made by A.D.S.T. Northern Army.
If the move of any unit does not take place till the 3rd day of operations and time is not available for Supply Wagons to load from Supply Columns prior to departure, arrangements must be made for the rations for consumption on the 4th day to be delivered in Supply Column lorries in the detraining area.

7. Brigade companies of Train of formations concerned (less Supply Wagons with units) will move by march route to the detraining areas of their formations, such personnel as may be required being sent in advance by one of the trains allotted to the formation.
Headquarter Companies of the Divisional Train will also move by march route as and when required.

8. The Scheme will be known as "Northern Army Scheme E".

(Signed) G.N. Jebb,
Brigadier General,
D.A. & Q.M.G. Northern Army H.Q.

Norwich.
8th September 1917.

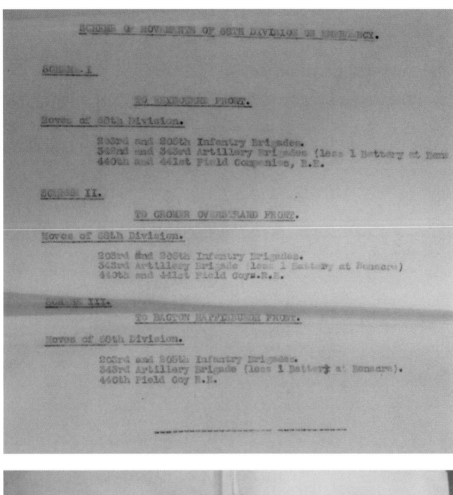

SCHEME OF MOVEMENT OF 68TH DIVISION ON EMERGENCY.

SCHEME I.

NO MUNDESLEY FRONT.

Moves of 68th Division.

    203rd and 205th Infantry Brigades.
    342nd and 343rd Artillery Brigades (less 1 Battery at Dene
    440th and 441st Field Companies, R.E.

SCHEME II.

TO CROMER OVERSTRAND FRONT.

Moves of 68th Division.

    203rd and 205th Infantry Brigades.
    343rd Artillery Brigade (less 1 Battery at Bonacre)
    440th and 441st Field Coys. R.E.

SCHEME III.

TO BACTON HAPPISBURGH FRONT.

Moves of 68th Division.

    203rd and 205th Infantry Brigades.
    343rd Artillery Brigade (less 1 Battery at Bonacre).
    440th Field Coy R.E.

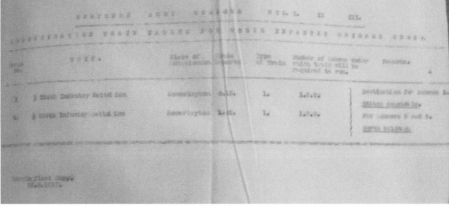

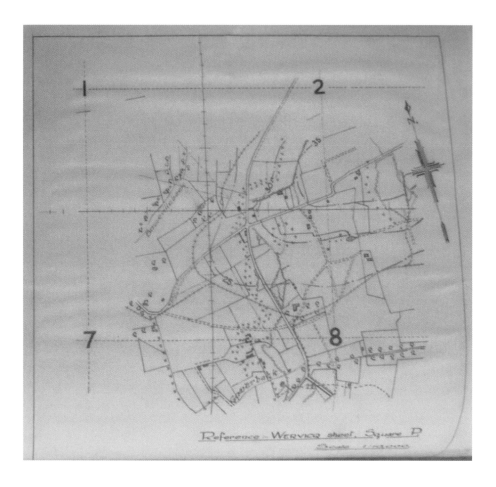

Points for an attack.

Information	from Brigade order
Intentions	from Brigade order
Assembly	Route up — Company lines
Objectives	Boundaries Company frontage Blue
Barrage	Rate, Lifts, Waits.
Dress & Equipment	Dress fighting order
Communications	Telephones Rockets, lamps, runners Relay Posts. Pigeons. Dogs. Power Buzzer
Prisoners	[illegible] also wounded returning carrying parties
Stragglers	R. Police
Counter Attack	
Consolidation	
Arrangements	Relay Post [illegible] carrying

Liaison.

Zero.

Barrage Wire

Contact
Aeroplane

Two sniper land on parapet out of
sight of trench population ...

Documents

Documents letter marked maps
envelopes with addresses already marked
Officers garden etc.

Tapping out

Compass bearing. Sound officers ...
Defensive marks & detail from Covering Party

Covering Party

Yellow armlet

Attached Troops

TMBs M.G.C etc.

Mopping up

Dumps

750 Sand bags 30 coils Barbed wire
50 Long Pickets   50 Short Pickets
... ...
50 Picks 30 Bombs SAA. 1 French ...
Very light ... 5 SOS

Rations.

Water.

Advanced H.Q.

Platoon carry.   Per Platoon   25 × N23.   170 S.A.A.
                 3 Smoke Bombs   9 very lights   18VS.
                 3 Sandbags for men   4 contact straps.
                 12 hw 2 B. Wire cutters.

HQ moved before
    Starting.

Synchronisation.

Battle dislocated

Reinforcements &   Ration. Carrying party. Ammunition &
    Rations   Rations   Carried by Troops

7-5-18 Left Victoria at 7.45 having slept the night at the Grosvenor. Kaye & mother came to see me off. Dixon & Hackett were on the same train. We had breakfast together & then on getting to Folkestone had to cross by the 3.15 boat. Went to the Hotel & played billiards. Pouring wet day but cleared up for the crossing. Saw H.H. Hardy on the boat. He was reporting to GH.Q. Reserve Army. Got orders to proceed to St Martins Rest Camp when we arrived at Boulogne. Left valises at the station & drove up in a cab. Not allowed to go out so had dinner there & turned in. Had to sleep in Tent boards with 9 blankets.

8-5-18 Spent the morning by going through gas & being fitted with a box respirator. Had lunch then I caught the 4.15 to St Omer reporting at RTO at 3.10. Got to St Omer about 7.15. found Ward was near there so Dixon rung him up & sent a light engine down for us & we had a splendid dinner & slept the night there. He was near Arques. I met a fellow called Sam & also the late Town Major of Hazebruck. We left there about 11.0 by box car to find the XIth but could not find them at the spot the 30th Div gave us so went to the 33rd for where they were working & found them near St Jean de Biezen on the Watou Pop road. Found Pethick with MC & a Major! Bolton, Dean MC & a lot of new men. Bretherton & Symon also just returned. Spent one night with them. Padre & doc there too. Mercer ill with gas.

10-5-18 Whole Batt moved by lorry at 4.30 to near Rubrouck which was 10 miles North of St Omer. Got in about 10 p.m. After marching & motor lorrying quite a lot. Had to sleep on the stone floor on a lot of straw quite comfortable though. In between C.O. & Pethick. Padré Ward & Taylor at our feet.

11-5-18 C.O. showed me a letter from the Div allowing me to wear Majority & Bolton to be a Captain. Rained most of the day so stayed in all the time.

12-5-18 Bretherton & I had to take the remains of the XI SLR to the 49th Div 19th L. Fus Reg[152] to swap them for a new draft they had got of 200 men whom we were going to take on to send to the Batt. The Div G.O.C. inspected the Batt at 7.45 & gave out the Ribbons to the new people. C.S.M. Harrison[153] getting D.C.M. & about 4 M.M.s & then we took the people off at 4.0. Got up to near Pop & saw Div

---

[152] 19th Bn. Lancashire Fusiliers, another Pioneer battalion.
[153] Actually R.S.M. 20581 Joseph Harrison M.C. D.C.M.

H.Q. CRE's Adj. He said nothing doing so we got back about 9.30. C.O. told me I might have to go to Base but probably not..

13-5-18 Pouring day. Went out ratting in afternoon. At evening C.O. told me I would have to go to the Base. Dixon probably going as Div Information Officer! Played bridge at night & let him down!

14-5-18 Left about 10.0 for Watten station in lorry with Bretherton to go to Base at Etaples. Got there & had quite a nice lunch & caught the train at 2.30 to Etaples. A very comfortable journey as we only had four in the carriage & it was a very comfortable 1st class compartment. Got in about 9.0. Found I was very comfortably settled.

15-5-18 Stayed in camp all morning. Went down in afternoon to Etaples & did a lot of shopping. Then took the train in about 3.30 to Paris Plage[154]. Had tea there of Lobster & Stout & then strawberries & cream with Bretherton & Dunthorne. Got back in time for dinner. Had a bath before tea.

16-5-18 Went over with Dunthorne & Bretherton, Symon & Mackenzie to Paris Plage & had lunch at the Continental. We thought we might be moving on to Rouen in the evening so got back for tea. Dunthorne went to Hospital in the evening. Called at Duchess of Westminster Hospital to see Bishop but he had gone to England at 2 a.m.

17-5-18 Went over with Bretherton to golf & found it closed in the morning so went on & had lunch at the Excelsior Restaurant with Bretherton, Symon & Mackenzie. Then went on & had golf. Awful clubs greens bad & pretty awful. I should say it was always a very monstrous course. I played pretty well considering everything & quite easily beat him. Got back again for tea as we thought we might be moving.

18-5-18 Detailed to sit on 5 FGCMs. Took all day. Met a fellow Capt Hatton who was C.M. expert attached to the court. He had been tagged on to the 30th Div & the 21st Brig. Came in to tea. Rather an ass but not so bad.

19-5-18 Went on with Bretherton to Paris Plage & had tea. Craig past the shop so we called him in & had some tea. He was stopping down there for three days rest with one or two other officers. Fixed up the

[154] An area of Le Touquet.

following day with him. Golf in the morning. Bretherton if possible. But a note came out to say no one allowed out before 2.30 p.m. Had a pretty heavy air raid at night from about 10.30 to 12.30. Managed to get to bed just before the raid so missed a bit of it. Had about 200-300 casualties round about.

20-5-18   Went over in morning & met Craig at the golf club. Had a round & beat him badly. Had lunch at the Continental. Drove out to golf club to meet Bretherton but he was not there so returned for tea & met him on the way back. Also Williams arranged to meet Williams at 12 on Wednesday. Came back by tram with Maxwell. Had to take the whole camp out after dinner & slept out in the woods.

21-5-18   Caught the 11.30 tram to Paris Plage. Met Craig & his lot & had lunch with them. Caught a motor which took ages to start as we had had to mend a puncture & arrived at the golf club about 4.30. I played with Chevalier brother to Pro at Dinard[155] & gave Keller & a fellow Ronald 2 up. Played awfully badly & lost 6 & 5. Couldn't play at all. Got a lift back & got just in time for dinner. Played bridge after & lost. No air raid though one flew over. Got back in morning from wood about 5.30 & had 2 hours sleep. Saw Seymour in the Continental.

22-5-18   Went over to Paris Plage about 12 o'clock to meet Williams. He did not turn up so I picked up Craig & Dalrymple & we had lunch at the Criterion. From there we went & had about 6 sets of Tennis. Tea at Criterion again & then I went & saw them off. Saw Rollo in Paris-Plage. Thunderstorm came up as I was going back - it rained a lot while I was at dinner. So we had not to go out into the woods. When I got back a message was given me that Manning was at the Officers Club & would I dine with him. So I spent the evening with him. He was going to the 2nd SLR as his 2/5 Lines had been broken up too.

23-5-18   Detailed again for Courts Martial. Sat from 10 to 1 & 2 to 5.10. Capt Harnett was again on the court so I think all went well. Got rid of 5 cases. I was to have played golf with Keller but did not finish early enough. Went to lunch with Harnett & saw Milestones - quite a good show. Played bridge at night with Keller. I & Jackson v Keller & L.G. We won 4 Francs. Frightful windy day & much colder. Only about 1 or 2 showers though.

---

[155] Golf course at Saint-Briac-sur-Mer.

24-5-18   Very cold & windy day & quite a lot of rain at night & in morning. McKenzie returned from draft duty & said he met Diplock at Rouen who was posted to 72 Div in England! Also he had great difficulty getting away like Symon had at Havre - or rather was having.

25-5-18   Paper full of air raid on Hospital. Making out deliberate. The one we had on Sunday night. I had to sit on a Court of Enquiry with a 9th R.S. Captain & MacKenzie at No 3 Base Employment Depot to enquire why 46 men were missing from that Depot. Lasted all afternoon. Went on walk at night with Evans.

26-5-18   Sunday. Papers full of Irish Plot. Did nothing all day. Went on walk at night with Evans. Played Picquet with Maxwell at night. MacIntyre who was in my room went up to 6th R.S.

27-5-18   Got my first letters through - one from Kaye, Hilda & Dai. Nothing doing all day. Went over afternoon to Paris Plage with Bretherton for tea. Had a concert at night - quite good show the acting was very good but the musical items were not up to much. At night there was bogus air raid warning but although nearly all the others got up I stayed in bed & slept through it. Third offensive started on the Aisne.

GRAND VARIETY CONCERT TO BE HELD IN No 1.Dining Hall

By kind permission
of
Major R.H.Keller DSO.
Commanding "G" I.B.Depot.

May 27th.1918.
Commencing 6-10.Pm.
Curtain Rised 6-15pm.

Accompanist..L/Cpl Leeming W.

Sergt Malcolm..Light Comedian.

Sergt Clive..Entertainer.

Pte   Perrin...Character Comedian.

CQMS Morgan...Barritone.

2/Lt.W.Cheetham..Character Burlesque
                                                          Impressionist.

I N T E R V A L

L/Cpl Collins..Duds Comedian

Pte   Bass...Tenor.

Pte   Guerdon..Pattor Comedian.

Sketch.
The TOUCH of TRUTH.
Richard Cumberland (An Actor)..............................Staff Sgt Leeming W.S.

Jim Bray (A Journalist)....................................Cpl Sturgeon G.E.

Scene. DINNING ROOM OF CUMBERLAND FLAT.

Orchestal Quartette under the direction of Pte Jackson
Organized by 2/Lt. W.Cheetham assisted by A/CSM. Thompson.

GOD   SAVE   THE   KING.

28-5-18   On sinking tents all day. 2 Majors turned up - one was Major Boyle
          who was with me at Flixecourt. MacKenzie & Hurley posted to 11
          East Lancs Reg. To go next morning.

29-5-18   Went over after lunch & had nine holes with Major Gracie & had
          him 1 up - he is a scratch man. Had tea & played a 3 ball with Keller.
          He beat us both & I beat Gracie. Finally played piquet at night. News
          through Chemis des Dames was lost.

30-5-18   Had golf in the afternoon - a single v Gracie. He won 2 & 1 stayed
          tea & got back for dinner. Keller & Hudson were out after. An air
          raid at night. Had to turn out. They hit the railway bridge & also the
          road to Paris Plage. Got a wire from Kaye asking if it was right

address. Archer-Shee[156] M.P. L/Col turned up & took half my cubicle.

31-5-18   Went over to golf. Gracie & I played Poyser Maj. D.S.O. D.L.I & Hudson. We won 3 & 1. Went down in morning & saw damage & town pretty extreme. Was superintending digging trenches & tunnels etc in ramps. Big air raid at night again on Hospital & the Railway. Kept us up till 2.30 a.m.

1-6-18   Stayed in all morning, working on Camp defences! Afternoon Maxwell, Gracie & I went over to Paris Plage in afternoon & had tea & returned. In the morning we walked round Etaples & saw the damage done by the air raid. Pretty considerably knocked in the Railway bridge last arch also dropped one in the middle of the road to Paris Plage.

2-6-18   Working all the morning. In the afternoon Gracie & I went over to golf & played 14 holes, huge squash on & we kept on cutting in & out. I just beat him.

3-6-18   Went over & had lunch with Archer-Shee at the Continental after played 6 sets of tennis with him. Byked out on the Padre's byke & rode back on a ..... Bridge & much argument at night.

4-6-18   Went over to golf in afternoon played threesome with Keller & Gracie. He beat us both & I beat Keller. Maxwell walked round with us. Ripping day. Had tea there by squash. Lady Sinclair then played behind us. Air raid scare but nothing dropped.

5-6-18   Went over & played tennis. Had lunch at Paris Plage. Archer-Shee, Stockforth & Maxwell Hudson met us at tennis courts Played about 6 sets & then Shee & I played with the cavalry subalterns. They were both a bit off. Bridge at night. No raid. Lady Sinclair to lunch.

6-6-18   Went over after lunch to tennis, Archer-Shee, Hudson & Stockforth. After tea we played again with 2 cavalry subalterns. Quite good tennis. Got back just in time for dinner. Bridge after with Gracie Keller & Hudson.

---

[156] Lt. Col. Sir Martin Archer-Shee D.S.O., M.P. for Finsbury Central. His half-brother was George Archer-Shee, whose expulsion from Osborne Naval College inspired the play *The Winslow Boy*.

7-6-18	Stayed in all morning & had lunch in camp. Went over with Gracie & Hudson to golf in afternoon & beat them both on the last green giving Hudson a third though he said his handicap was 5. Bridge at night, no air raid.
8-6-18	Went over & had lunch at Paris Plage with Archer-Shee & Boyle & spent afternoon playing golf. Maxwell was transferred from the depot to H depot so left us. G depot became Garrison Batt Depot & nearly all officers of Garrison Batt came in. Heard they were leaving on Monday. Got back to dinner & bridge after. Found out names of the Cavalry Officers we played with were Lt Byass 19th Hussars & Lt Porter 9th Lancers who was my partner.
9-6-18	Had arranged to go over & play tennis with Archer-Shee but he cleared off so I decided to play golf with Keller & Hudson & Gracie. But when we arrived it began to rain so Gracie did not play. We then set out & had a very good game. I beat Hudson 7&5 won the bye from him & then also Keller & halved the bye. I went out in 38 but did not come back so well. Bridge at night. It rained coming in & Gracie who walked got wet! Hudson & I cabbed.
10-6-18	Archer-Shee, Hudson, Boyle, Gracie, .Stopporth, Grogan[157], Ov...m & the rest went off in the morning at 7.50. I went over in the afternoon & played Hudson a single. Evans caddied for me & Lloyd going for Keller. I was 1 up at the 16th at edge of green & he was 3 missed one & he had ..... a stymie so I led. Lost the 17th & then won the 18th. Tried to rain but failed
11-6-18	Did nothing all day but stay in & play cards. Went a walk after tea with Evans. Bridge at night.
12-6-18	Went round work in morning. Golf v Keller in afternoon. Beat him 5&4 & also the bye. Byked out & back. As I got back Padre's byke gave out. Pedal axle broke. Good night. Col. Kirkwood & Major Wheatly to dinner. Huge argument with Padré & Lloyd ..... after about religion.
13-6-18	Nothing doing so I walked over with Lloyd going to Paris Plage. Met Mrs Dixon & got my flannels & came back by train. Bridge at night.

---

[157] Maj. & Bt. Lt.-Col. (temp. Brig.-Gen.) George William St. George Grogan V.C. C.B. C.M.G. D.S.O., G.O.C. 23rd Infantry Brigade.. Also referred to later as 'Groggy'.

14-6-18   Golf in afternoon with Keller. Borrowed Wainright's byke. Gave him 2 starters went out in 39 beat him 3&2. Bridge at night. Maxwell came over in the morning. Major Clark LF att. R.E's came in at night.

15-6-18   Got orders just after lunch that I was off to Rouen with Bretherton Symon, Harpur & about 70 other officers. We were ultimately going to join 2nd East Lancs. 8th Div. 6th French army. Train left at 6.20. I had to report at 5.40 .Went off at 3.0 with Maxwell to Paris Plage & got my tennis things what was left of them & bought some Razor Blades & got the train. Found Harry Cross was on it going to 15th D.L.I's. Slept in train all that night. Spent about 3 hours at Abbeville. Came via Amiens which they were shelling

16-6-18   Got in to Rouen about 12.30 Sent to '7' Depot & then on to the Cyclists Depot where we finally settled down, found Pulman of Lancaster was in charge. Filthy place. Messing awful & other things, no hot water etc. though I had quite a decent sized bed to myself. Found Diplock there when we arrived & Mercer & Owen in the next Depot. Had some tennis with Bretherton & Dippy against another fellow & I. They beat us badly so very badly indeed. Bridge with Dippy & Bretherton & Symon & won 20 francs.

17-6-18   Did nothing in morning. Tennis after & then went down to Rouen for tea & a huge dinner at Hotel which cost us 180 Frcs. Got a very good dinner indeed & got back very ..... Got orders on returning to join 2nd East Lancs next day. Bretherton, Symon & Harpur also moving.

18-6-18   Saw Struthers in morning he had just landed. Just as mad as ever. Had orders to leave by about 9.0 at night. Saw Palmer for a bit & also Cross he was coming too. We were all to join 8th Div. I was O.C. train. Had dinner at Brasserie & joined train at 8.45. O.C. train. Left about 10.30. Slept all night.

19-6-18   Landed at Orsinmont behind Longpré about 8.0. Detrained & reported to 2nd East Lancs. Found I was temporary O.C. though they expected a C.O. & C.O.2. Major (Acting) Ramsbottom also had reported but being only Acting had to ..... Bridge at night.

20-6-18   G.O.C. Div General Hawker to inspect us. Batt was awful. Companys late & then when drawn up the square was much too big. Still we managed to do it in the end & only got two observations - unpunctuability & the present was given too soon. He spoke to the old men who come through & also to the new draft. Did nothing all afternoon & evening.

21-6-18 Notification by G.O.C. Brigade Gen Pollock-McCall. He had a lot of fault to find but agreed that we could not help it owing to the new draft being so badly clothed. Had the Mayor & Mayoress & two daughters to dinner at night. Very jolly uproarious evening - played games including 'Up Jenkins'![158] Padre Hamilton & Ramsbottom very much in evidence. Orders to move next day.

22-6-18 Started to pass starting point at 10.0. Got Brigadier there so Reynolds & I stayed & watched march past with him. Russell & the Batt went wrong in the village & we found they found they had lost their way entirely. Got them going so that R.Bs did not have to wait. Just got the Batt past the transport & in good order again when past the G.O.C. Div marching past the 70 men to the town. Ticked us off about it but after halting them we had made up to the Brig so all was well. Got in to Fouquieres about 5.30. V. G. billets. Huge argument between Padre & Ramsbottom on House Rules. Had lunch on the way. Just before starting Major Brown turned up but not having his kit did not come along, went back to Reinforcements.

23-6-18 Marched to Onival near Ault never met a soul. Got in about 12.30. Brown turned up soon after getting there. Found we were mostly in tents. Not good billet at all. Had bridge at night with Ramsbottom v Reynolds & Brown & won Brown took me but I kept on C.O.'s billet.

24-6-18 Had inspection in morning. Brig conference in afternoon. ..... wet afternoon.

25-6-18 Training hard. Supposed to have a court martial in afternoon but the Corps Expert did not turn up so I did not hold it. No signs of C.O. Had Ramsbottom & Paton to dinner.

26-6-18 Brown down with malaria. C.O. turned up after tea. Col. Green D.S.O. late of 1st East Lancs I stayed on temporarily in H.Q. He was a bit lame from a twist getting out of train. I turned out into a tent & had to get two beds down from church one for self & one for Shaw.

---

[158] A game in which players conceal a small coin in their palm as they slap it on a table with their bare hands. The goal is for players to guess which hand the coin is under, often with alcoholic drinks as a forfeit.

27-6-18   Brown still in bed. Spent day going round with Green. C.O. asked Brigadier what to do with me & he said wait for Div. G.O.C. to return from leave.

28-6-18   Went round all morning with C.O. Had concert in evening. Courts martial all afternoon. Got through seven all told was late for dinner. Brigadier at dinner. Good concert & shoe in the church.

29-6-18   Round with C.O. in morning afternoon we played the Berks at soccer & beat them 1 nil. Bad soccer as the grass was too long & the ground pretty rough. Went out with Brown & had dinner at Hotel de Paris Ault & got back late. Huge success & Brown was very nice.

30-6-18   Church parade at 10.0. Padré had to leave us & go to 25th Field Ambulance & we got a horrid man called Hicky. Went out in afternoon & had to give up night march for tomorrow & in evening the flags for the Batt Attack next morning. All seemed to be c.....d.

1-7-18   Went out at 7.30 to see if Flags were alright but found them all wrong so set about & put them right just in time for the attack - missed breakfast. Show went off quite O.K. Bathed in afternoon with Reynolds. Paton, Heggs & another there. Had night march at night. Found the Rangefinder 75% out - all markers were 3/4 the length we had put them. This was found by Sig. Corpl. when he was checking them. Brown at a G.C.M. all morning. A D & C were alright but B was ..... out. Got to bed about 7.30 a.m.

2-7-18   Rode over to Dargnies with Brown to see training area. Riley on leave. Had lunch with 1st Worcesters Lt Col Roberts V.C. DSO MC was commanding. Very pleasant ride got back about 4.0 for tea. New M.O. Capt Connelly turned up about 5.30. All went down at night & saw the 5/7th - 8th Div Troupe quite a good show. Supper after.

3-7-18   Lt Smith 1st Worcesters came over & I spent most of the time showing him the camp. Also watched 'D' Co wiring & digging & some range work. In afternoon we had a committee meeting to decide about sports & boxing.

4-7-18   Battalion moved to Dargnies & I & Shaw rode over the short cut & got there early. Passed the 1st Worcesters & 5th Sherwood Foresters on the way & Saw Boxer   'A' company XIth S Lancs. By ..... rumour he was a stretcher bearer in them. Spent afternoon watching Boxing. Wonderful billets. H.Q. mess most palatial. I made billet in same house as Burn also most palatial. Electric lights & dressing rooms.

5-7-18   Rode round in morning with C.O. to ranges. 30 yd. 100yd & 600yd. Spent afternoon writing letters.

6-7-18   Rode round with C.O. in morning. In afternoon acted as judge to 'B' Co sports. Spent whole afternoon & evening down there. Evening went to a bad company concert with 'D' Co. Somewhat tired after all. W.... ..... a two .... Heard from Dixon, 30th[159] being made up again & going up to Westoutre way.

7-7-18   Church Service in morning. Spent afternoon in my room. Brigade sports on Wednesday so had to pin all that up.

8-7-18   Fixed up Company sports for morning & Batt. sports for Tues. coming. Rode into Treport & met Brown then had lunch & then rode to Eu. Looked round & returned for tea. Brown had another attack of malaria - he went by mess cart all the way.

9-7-18   Spent all the morning getting the sports ground ready. Sports all the afternoon rained a bit but not much till evening. Brown in bed all day. General down for a few minutes. Good show but few men turned up.

---

[159] 30th Division.

2nd Battalion East Lancashire Regiment.
==

Battalion Sports, on "B" Company Sports Ground,
3-7-1918,
commencing at 2 p.m.

Referee.

Lieut-Colonel J.E.Green. D.S.O.

Judges.
Major L.K.Vallentine Brown.
Major A.W.Champion.
Major J. Shaw. M.C.
Captain R.D.Reynolds. M.C.
Captain J.E.Ramsbottom.
Captain S.Y.Paton. M.C.
Captain G.V.Baxter.
Captain D.Meggs.

Starters.
Major A. T. Champion.
2/Lieut. H.R.Richmond.
2/Lieut. E.R.Noble.

Clerk of the Course.
R.S.M. S.E.Price. M.C. D.C.M.

PROGRAMME OF EVENTS

No.	Time.	Event.
1.	2.15 p.m.	Throwing Cricket Ball.
2.	2.15 p.m.	High Jump.
3.	2.30 p.m.	Hurdle. Heat I & II.
4.	2.30 p.m.	Putting the shot.
5.	2.30 p.m.	Sack Race.
6.	2.45 p.m.	100 yards flat (other ranks) Heats I & II.
7.		100 yards flat (officers) Heats I & II.
8.	3.15 p.m.	1 Mile.
9.	3.15 p.m.	Long Jump.
10.	3.30 p.m.	Veterans Race. Heats I & II.
11.	3.30 p.m.	¼ Mile. Heats I & II.
12.	3.45 p.m.	4 legged Race.
13.	4 p.m.	Slow cycle Race.
14.	4 p.m.	¼ Mile (Final)

INTERVAL FOR TEA.

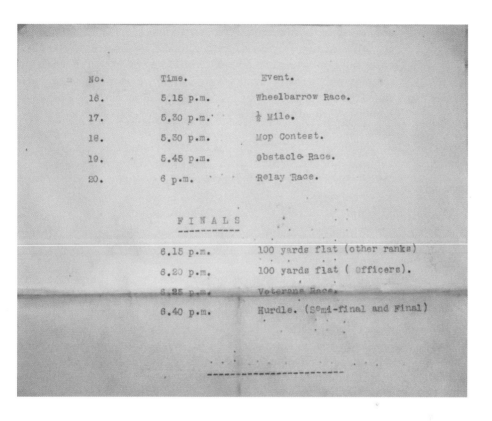

No.	Time.	Event.
16.	5.15 p.m.	Wheelbarrow Race.
17.	5.30 p.m.	½ Mile.
18.	5.30 p.m.	Mop Contest.
19.	5.45 p.m.	Obstacle Race.
20.	6 p.m.	Relay Race.

FINALS

	6.15 p.m.	100 yards flat (other ranks)
	6.20 p.m.	100 yards flat (officers).
	6.25 p.m.	Veterans Race.
	6.40 p.m.	Hurdle. (Semi-final and Final)

10-7-18   Rode round in morning. Met General Hennecker[160] with 'C' Co. He was pretty excited over musketry. Ultimately he went in to the C.O. & was quite amusing. Shaw went on leave. Sports of Brigade all afternoon. Showers but nothing very bad till we were returning when it came down in sheets. Bridge at night. With C.O. v Brown & Reynolds. 1200 up. We won quite a lot of events including 3rd Cricket .....

2nd High Jump	1st &2nd in Hurdles
1st Putting Shot?	2-1st & 3rd in 100 yds
1-1st &1-2nd Officer 100yds	1st Long Jump
1st Veterans	1st &3rd Sack race
1st Quarter	1st Wheelbarrow & 3rd
1st Obstacle?	4th mile
.... of heavy Tug of War	2nd Relay Race

11-7-18   Company's at the baths- so spent morning riding round & seeing them at the baths etc. Afternoon with officers of the Brigade & a lecture at G.O.C. General Hennecker. Awful rot about washing & shaving. C.O's very fed up. Finals of Brigade Sports afterwards. We won all the boxing contests. Did very well considering. Beastly rainy & blowy day. C.O. talked to all officers after. Dinner 9.20 p.m.

12-7-18   Raining most of the day. Spent morning with 'B' & 'A' Companies & the afternoon arranging for Revolver practice at night. At 5 o'clock all officers shot & then a lecture from Ramsbottom, a repetition of one from the C.R.A. some time previous. Not up to much really but very well repeated I should say

13-7-18   Battalion in attack with RFA & MGC co-operation. G Browne was O.C. enemy & I was acting C.O. In afternoon I should have shown Dublin in the Div. Horse show but was too late & did not get the notice till on parade. Major Moon was their RFA Officer in co-operation, Col Leyland C.O. 2nd R.B. was in to lunch. Saw Col. Isaacs of 2nd R.Berks at horse show. Maj Warr C.O.2 R.B. was about in morning. Orders to move to Garnache on Monday early.

14-7-18   Rode over to Horse Show was to get there by 11 a.m. for Dublin to go in for V.I. race. Owing to few entries ..... off for final. Richmond did nothing for jumping a bit ..... Came in 4th for VI race. Saw Col. Myers now ..... C.O.2 2nd Middlesex. Had lunch there sat next to

---

[160] General Sir Charles G. Heneker, commander of 8th Infantry Division from December 1916 until the end of the war.

him. Also saw Hamilton & Padre there. Hennecker came over & spoke to me. C.O. over then. Nevin also got back for tea

15-7-18   Moved out of Daguies at 7.35 a.m. & to Garnache. Huge excitement as there was an intense bombardment all night & morning. I went independently & got there first. Lunched at Hotel de Paris.

16-7-18   Went out with C.O. in the morning & watched having lunch out in the field. Got back to tea & dinner.

17-7-18   Went out training in morning. If afternoon firing competition. Got a wire from Brigade. Report to Berks as a company commander. Wrote out a letter explaining & got Col. Green to write an addenda to it & sent it in to Brigade.

To Adjutant,
2nd Bn. East Lancashire Regt.

Sir,

Reference 25th Inf: Brigade wire S.C. 452
dated 17/7/18 ordering me to report to 2nd Royal Berks
Regt for duty as Company Commander, I have the honour
to request that my case may be laid before the competent
authority for consideration.
I have been Company Commander for nearly 3½ years of which
2 years has been in France except for periods when I have
been acting Second in Command of the Battalion and for
about 6 weeks when I commanded a Composite Battn during
the operations at Ypres in July and August 1917.
I was promised my majority by my Commanding Officer in
May 1916 and my name was again sent forward twice in
1917 but was refused in every case owing to no vacancy.
I was sent to England for 6 months tour of
light duty at the beginning of this year, and on rejoining
I acted as Second in Command till the Battalion was
disbanded.   Altogether, I have acted in the capacity for
periods approximately amounting to three months.   On
the battalion with which I had been since September 1914
being disbanded I was sent to the Base, from where I was
posted to the 2nd East Lancashires, which Regiment I
commanded on joining till the Second in Command arrived.
To the best of my knowledge my services with my various
Commanding officers have been satisfactory, of which I
can produce documentary evidence.   I therefore request
that I might be considered for a senior appointment
to that of Company Commander.   Failing any appointment
in the Division being available might my name be sent
to the Senior officers pool at the Base, for consideration
for further appointment.

                    I have the honour
                         Sir,
                    to be,

                    Your obedient Servant,

17-7-1918.   Major.

[handwritten note, largely illegible]

18-7-18   Went out in morning & lunched with the Brigade & put my case to Brigadier Pollock McCall. He was very nice but said I had to report to Berks. Watched the shooting competition first & then went & reported to the Royal Berks. Put O.C. 'A' Co again. Heard Potter was in Garnache so I rode over & had dinner with East Lancs. Potter came in after. Just the same. He was O.C. 19 Div Transport taking it down to Dieppe. Got back to Tilloy[161] & spent the night there. Had orders that Div was moving up next day & I was entraining officer at Fouquiere with Gutteran.

19-7-18   Went off with Gutteran at 10.30 & rode to Fouquiere. Aldis accompanied us a short way. Spent the rest of the day entraining the Brigade which went in 7 trains every 3 hours. First three trains up to turn next ones late owing to (i) French guard not having had his supper (ii) Engine driver had a ..... & refused to run the train. Slept the night there. ..... as from 11 - 1.15 & Gutteran took over after.

20-7-18   Caught 9 a.m. train which went at 10.45. Gutteran & I had carriage to ourselves. Got to Pernes about 9.0 p.m. had dinner with Ramsbottom & his lot & then stayed the night at the Hotel Lo...ord Quite a good night.

21-7-18   Lorry jumped to Bois d'Ohlain near Baillieul & got there just before lunch. Had various inspections. Lancs & RB[162] next door to us. Went round & had a look at them. Sleeping six in a bed. Went & had tea with Brigadier. Heard Bill Bailey Transport Off, Gunning Staff Capt, Rix Intelligence Off. All got the ..... Saw Brigadier and he said I had to stay to ..... till a vacancy occurred. We hid up with Rice - very nice .....

22-7-18   Marched to Mount St Eloy. Col Isaacs very rusty on march discipline & cursed furiously - took no notice & went in to see him afterwards. Cooled down considerably & almost apologised for everything he ..... etc.

23-7-18   C.O. inspected Company, very pleased & congratulated wagons. Poured with rain in afternoon my company flooded out so changed huts.

---

[161] Ligny-Thilloy near Bapaume.
[162] Royal Berkshire Regiment.

24-7-18   Battn in attack. Battn had far too far an objective which was all crooked to line of advance. Battn attacked on a 3 company front & companys on a 3 platoon front. My front too short so I pulled ours out. Platoon attacked on equilateral triangle Apex leading ..... gun Sect acted as Lewis gun. Hunter Bunter (Weston[163]) Corps commander came along with Hennecker etc & was not pleased with the formation but pleased with the telling off of sections & their commanders. Asked me why I commanded a company etc. After getting halfway stopped & a powwow 'C' Company but 'A' Company praised. After lunch - lecture on formations by C.O. Stick to formation.

25-7-18   Company doing musketry to start with then Battalion drill awful show! No movement but marching backwards & forwards & marking time. Afternoon the subalterns & NCOs had communicating drill & men company drill. RBs had packed a ..... for limber & Brig had ordered all to pack the same. I tried it & found it bad so drew C.O.'s attention to it & he came & saw it & ..... did to ..... ours.

26-7-18   Battn in attack again. Four companys in the front line. Objective far too long & far too undefined. Still very pleased with 'A' Co & 'B' Co. 'C' & 'D' bad. Had to do a skeleton retreat & then back to lunch. Afternoon spent getting ready for sports tomorrow being Maiwand Day.

27-7-18   Maiwand Day the great day in the Royal Berkshire Reg. Apparently they were very highly praised for their actions at Maiwand in Afghanistan 27.7.1879. Extract from despatch from C in C states "History records no finer instance of devotion to Queen & country than that displayed by the Berkshire Regiment at the Battle of Maiwand. Day given to sports. Huge preparations but rained all day. Hennecker turned up & also Pollock McCall & Col Brown. Poured and so damped the proceedings. Night in the 4 camp ..... had dinner at H.Q. Fizz etc good dinner.

---

[163] Sir Aylmer Gould Hunter-Weston. Nicknamed "Hunter-Bunter", he was seen as a classic example of a "donkey general". Described by Haig as a "rank amateur". Served at Gallipoli and the early stages of the Somme. Elected as Unionist M.P. for North Ayrshire in 1917.

-- 2nd Battalion Royal Berkshire Regiment --
Conditions of Maiwand Sports 27th July 1918

---- Committee ----

Judges.
Lt Colonel A. G. T. Spence M.C.
Major A. T. Champion
Capt. W. M. Guttman M.C.
Major R. H. Tautz M.C.

Starter.
Capt. A. H. Saunderson

Treasurer.
2/Lieut T. R. Strange

Members.
Capt. H. I. W. Bird M.C.
2/Lieut M. C. Winter M.C.
1 Officer and 1 N.C.O. per Company.

N°.	EVENT	CONDITIONS
3.	Cleanest Soldier Competition	Dress Marching Order. 1 man per Platoon, and 1 man Battalion Head Quarters.
4.	Inter Company Guard Competition	Dress Marching Order. Officer Drill Dress.
5.	Inter Platoon Drill Competition	Dress Drill Order.
6.	High Jump.	Limit 3'6"
8.	Tug of War.	Each Weight 12 stone. Teams of 8. Best 2 pulls out of 3. One team per Company. Employed men pull with their company. Teams will pull as follows B. v D. A. v C.
12.	Sack Race	Competitors will retain their hold of sack.
17.	Bicycle Race.	Competitors will be disqualified for not keeping to their own Bicycle. 6 Entries will be allowed only per Company, to include employed men.
18.	Potato Race	16 and 18 Potatoes. 3 yds between potatoes.
28.	Alarm Race	Winners must be properly dressed
29.	Relay Race	Companies, Battalion Head Quarters, Quarter Master Stores, and Transport will furnish one Team each, consisting of 1 Officer, 1 Sergeant, 1 Corporal or L/Corporal and 1 Private. Distance for each Competitor 220 yards.

28-7-18   Church parade in morning & a bit of work. Heard we had to go up to the line all company commanders next day & also we are moving across the road to the East Lancashire Camp. They were going to Neuville St Vaast. Major Alloway went to Trouville for 10 days! Had tea at East Lancs. Then held a court of enquiry on a missing man with Sanderson & Tautz. Dinner in & bridge.

29-7-18   Did a trench to trench attack but a bad show Lasted all the morning. Afternoon Officers played v No 9 Platoon. Also lecture by Brigadier on his time out in the East. Not bad at all. Forgot it was anniversary of wedding.

30-7-18   Went up with motor bus to the Canadian Memorial Vimy ridge & then walked up through Vimy to Batt H.Q. with Major Walker there & then went on to 'A' Co H.Q. Lunch with Darcy & went round the line. Got back to B.H.Q. at 4.30 & caught bus back to camp at 6.0. All O.C. Companies went, Strange & Lawson quite quiet all the time. Frightfully hot all day exhausting.

31-7-18   Morning practising new artillery formation & silent patrol. Afternoon lecture by C.O. on both. Frightfully hot. Shelling at night. The RBs had a few casualties & we had one.

1-8-18   Companies at disposal of O.C. Company for first half of morning. We had three platoons practicing their silent patrol schemes & one platoon being inspected by C.O. for cleanest platoon. Second half of morning Battalion drill, acted as C.O.2 so had a soft time riding up & down. Lecture in afternoon on trench standing orders & matters in the trenches.

2-8-18   Sergeants field day. Started to rain on the way out & did not stop all morning. Everyone got ringing wet through. Heard nothing about schemes went wrong as the RBs refused to withdraw in front of the enemy (Richardson & his company). Afternoon lecture by Major Carr G.C.O. of Corps on Training. Talked a lot of rot about being able to train in trenches. Showed how far away from the Batt the army staff office is.

3-8-18   Company inspection. Bad sent a lot of men back also barrack inspection also bad so had that again. Spent afternoon doing that & a lecture by Capt Smythe G.S.O.3 of Div on Intelligence quite good. After men had a huge scare - had to go out & man Battle formations in case of attack by the Bosch. Started the whole Batt at 9.35 p.m. &

went along an awful track of mud taking them 1 hour per mile & got to the ridge above Vimy about 2.5 a.m. C.O. so fed up we returned. Huge jumble up with East Lancs & RBs. Got back to camp at 4.15 by the road. Padré Hamilton & a USA M.O. to tea & then watched Officers v Sergts. Officers beaten 0 - 2.

4-8-18   Got up about 10.35. Church parade. I took as C.O. was away at 11.30. Slept all afternoon. Conference in evening. Early to bed. Orders to move next day.

5-8-18   Orders to move at 3.0. Company at O.C. Company's disposal in morning. Started from Mt St Eloy at 3.30 p.m.by buses to Neuville St Vaast. Then we walked to the other end & had tea then went by Platoons to Hunter trench - Red Trail - Peggy Tr & along front line near B...ich T2 to 'A' Co H.Q. in the quarry. Took over from 2nd West Yorks. Got going & sent Oswell out with a small patrol he had a scrap with the Bosch & being the smaller party he came back. He did very good work as it afterwards transpired as he got us the possession of no man's land. Got back about 1.30 p.m.

6-8-18   Got a little sleep. Went round at stand to & then had a snooze till 10 a.m. Went round in the morning before lunch & down to the support line in afternoon. Nothing doing at night. Stayed in most of the evening. Matthews reported sick with Varicose Veins.

7-8-18   Very quiet day - did get some sleep as Gosling did returns. Went round at Stand to evening & morning. Brigadier supposed to be around in afternoon but did not turn up. He went round outposts but cut back across country. Had no letters. Had many rows with subalterns. Sent a patrol out under Maurice for scuppering Bosch but they did nothing. Went out at 9.45 p.m.

8-8-18   All quiet in morning spent afternoon taking an RE officer round the lines. Went down support line No 3 & 4 & then on to B.H.Q. Saw the C.O. who was very nice & insistent on me staying to dinner though he went to 'B' Co. Major Williams, Francis & I took a company of RBs back to dig new trench afterwards. Heard Allen T2 'B' Co went out to take a Bosch M.G. near Acheville but failed.

9-8-18   Went round at Stand To. G.O.C. Div supposed to be coming round but he only went round the support line. Very pleased but I did not see him. Went down at night & as No 3 platoon was away there were only 2 sections there. 'B' Co expecting Hun raid of night before as it was such a fiasco. Nothing doing this time either. They are supposed to have got into Acheviille Tr but everyone knew it was empty.

10-8-18   Missed Stand to owing to not being called. Went down & had lunch at B.H.Q. to discuss Patrol with C.O. No 4 under Whittaker was going to do. Morgan & Hopkins went to R.A.F. Heard Gosling was going to a course. Got back & made all arrangements for the Patrol. The C.O., Barnet Strange, MacGeorge, RB officer cousin of Rugby[164] MacGeorge & Whitaker were to dinner. Went out with Patrol after. C.O. also out then. Had great fun. The platoon of A got into Pioneer Way & then came out with a rush & I had to reorganise & go at it again & they machine gunned & ..... us so we cleared. They were supposed to go only to Totnes but over stepped the mark - C.O. thought they had only got to Totnes so sent us back but I persuaded him & all was well. Came back in pretty good disorder. Found Col Leyland in our mess & Francis. Later very nice indeed

11-8-18   Quiet all day nothing doing. Went round in morning & had orderly room & then went down to the Black line in afternoon. Saw M.O. & returned. Whittaker sent out again on patrol as his last was so bad. Ordered to go into Acheville Tr but they saw no one & returned after a fruitless journey. He only had 3 men with him. Stayed in myself

12-8-18   Relief day. Got up at usual time. Whittaker did not report to me although not on patrol. RBs relieving us started dribbling in after lunch. I actually got to the Brown line at 5 p.m. Had tea & dinner at B.H.Q. Stood to in the Brown line as usual.

13-8-18   Up at midday. Went round in afternoon & saw O.C. C & B & Rifle Brigade about work in evening. Went up at night & worked on new trench (named Allen afterwards) from 10 p.m. to 2 a.m. Got back for Stand to in morning.

14-8-18   Stayed in bed all morning. Went over to be B.H.Q. for tea & dinner. Right on top of ridge in a wood. Doc up there for dinner. V. hilarious. Quick & Weston also to dinner. Returned after dinner. Great walk back with Doc. Saunders took the digging party.

15-8-18   Stood to in morning as usual. As all O.C. companies had to go to a lecture by General Ma..... We went to B.H.Q. to dinner & Allaway took the digging party. I slept in Allaway's bed & pyjamas. I went up

---

[164] Rugby School.

about 7 p.m. C.O. & Barritt came to the company for lunch at the embankment on the Brown line.

16-8-18 Were going to catch an RAF lorry to the leacture but when we got there Col. Leyland was just going at 8:30 a.m. so he gave Allaway, Richardson & myself a lift. Lecture was as H..... about 20-25 miles away. We got there about 10 a.m. Saw there Spider Lynott of the 1st R.I.Fs. Kentish (Brig. now) & Col Taylor who was at Etaples with us. Had an excellent lunch with Richardson of omelette & chips & coffee. Lecture by M..... was very good but rather aiming too much at the ideal for practical purposes. We also had a demonstration by Col Levy of the ..... ex RSM guardsman. He acted as platoon officer to a platoon of H.A.C. General Howe was there & a dickens of a lot of staff. Levy's show was an excellent bit of historical work. Allaway, Barrett & I came back by the same car. Got back to tea & dinner at B.H.Q. C.O. out on the work. Saunders & Wedge had to walk all the way back. Richards got a lift. Just as I got back to the Brown line they dropped a shell on some of 'B' Co. places & laid out 10 men

17-8-18 Did nothing all morning. Working Party at night. I had to take it. Fritz shelled the embankment during the day. I managed to get out alright. Called in & saw RB's at the Quarry. Not as damaged as we thought it was. Met Leyland & Bennett out on the party. Left at 7 a.m. C.O. complimented us next day on our work. Maurice & his platoon returned from Div. school

18-8-18 Fritz shelled the embankment pretty well all day. Did not go up at night. Allaway took the party. Fidler & Maurice out on the work. Got orders to go to Mt St Eloi at 8.30 a.m. the next day at Canadian Monument.

19-8-18 Trundled off to Canadian Monument at 8.30 a.m. All O.C. companys, Col Green & Leyland there. Heard Capt Davies of East Lancs had returned after 3 days absence in the Bosch lines. Heard Div General at La Lytte camp Mount St Eloi talk about training Plat ..... the most awful rot imagineable. Got back to lunch at Batt. H.Q. also tea. Got back for dinner feeling awfully rotten. Did not go out at night.

20-8-18 Day off for cleaning up before going into the line again. Played bridge at night with Saunders & Aldis. RBs H.Q. shelled badly at dinnertime.

21-8-18   Started off for front line at 9.15 a.m. & took over from Bennett O.C. 'C' Co RBs. a friend of Richardson by lunch time. Went round after lunch all O.K. 'A' Co holding all the front line & outpost line about 2200 yds each line. Six points & two platoon points in the Blue line. Wind up at night about the Bosch raiding as they had the previous night lower down. All sorts of precautions taken but nothing happened. C.O. came up. Patrol of 'D' Co. out.

22-8-18   All quiet. C.O. & Brigadier round in morning found many faults. D..... reported very early in the morning. Nothing doing. Mathers went out on a patrol to Pioneer Way & got no distance. Bad show.

23-8-18   As Mathers show had been so bad he had to go out again. Went round in afternoon with Shepherd & showed the whole line & work to be done at night to him. Went & saw Mathers off at night on his patrol. Just before got shelled a bit at Acheville. Post nothing very heavy. He went all night but again did nothing. Said they had got into Acheville trench but I did not believe them.

24-8-18   Last day in the front line. Spent the morning in bed went round to the new dug out area or town in which Camp H.Q. was going to be in & then up to tea. Went round the line nothing doing. Patrol II D supposed to go out but did not go owing to order so late.

25-8-18   Changed over with 'D' Co. They came to Quarry & we went to their section in the Black Line. H.Q. in Poppy Tr. Bad show so we immediately started improving them. Cut a doorway & two windows in. Actually handed over about 3 p.m. Whittaker reported back to Batt H.Q. from Gas Corner but did not return to the company. Stood to at night. - bad night's the rest.

26-8-18   Got up early & got the working parties on the go. Special job started in Peggy & the Black Line. Day went up at night to Maud Alley.

27-8-18   Orders at 7 a.m. we were going to move & be relieved. Were relieved about 2.30 p.m. by 6th K.S.L.I. 20th Div. Marched to Canadian Monument & found lorries there for us. I waited till the last & saw everyone in. They took us to Balmoral Camp Ecurie. We stayed there for tea & cinner & then left at 8.15 p.m. in the rain & marched up & into the line by Bailleul. 7th A&SH were there when we returned. Awful muddle the whole thing. We did not know who was relieving us - where or when we were going (it was changed in the middle) When we got in the A&SH had advanced that morning & did not know where their people were so no relief when I got in all night. We were in the Rescue line. Put the H.Q. in 4 Pill boxes in front of Bailleul. Filthy dirty place worst I have been into but we cleaned up alright. At Canadian Monument saw Major Nickleson late C.G.S. Rugby. Belonged to 33rd Brig 55th Batt.

28-8-18   Stayed in all day & got the mess etc into working order. Went up to B.H.Q. for a very short time. Went round the men at stand to & once by day. All OK.

29-8-18   'B' & 'D' Co doing a stunt. Trying to pinch the rest of the trenches in front of them by creeping up trenches. So I had to move up to 'C' Co as 'C' Co only had 3 platoons 1 doing left flank & 1 carrying for TMBs. Burnett REs Company took my place more or less in front here though instead of Port Tr. took over 'C' H.Q. & slept there the night. Show failed badly as Bosch was strong & infilade M.G.'s from Oppy. Total casualties about 49 in Battalion. Nothing much gained.

30-8-18   Went up in morning & saw Sanderson & Richardson sent up by C.O. to test how 'B' Co had really got on in the show. Had to report to the C.O. about it. He seemed horribly depressed & rotten - so much so I think it affected all his men & reported accordingly. Went to B.H.Q. & had lunch at 3.0 p.m. Got back for tea at 5.0. C.O. came back with me. Took over from 'D' Co in the front line at night in North Tyne Alley. All quiet at night. Dug out big place a bit hard to make it comfortable but we started.

31-8-18   Went round after stand to & found Mathers all wrong so showed him exactly where to go - he did not even then go right. Fidler had to ultimately put him right! C.O. came round at evening. Met Beyn Steen Brig Major in 'B' Co lines. C.O. told me he was giving him Sanderson as he was taking the company away from him. Bosch started shelling heavy at 10.10 p.m. & kept it up all night.

1-9-18   Shelling continued all night. I did not get round as we were being relieved by the RBs at night. Fidler took the RB officer MacClean round in the morning. McGregor turned up just before tea. Relief was by 11 p.m. Walked to Chanticlu corner & got swiped by 8" on the way going down the trench. Went up Reubur C T Got a lorry from Chanticlu corner & got to Roberts camp by 2 p.m. & bed!

2-9-18   Did nothing all day but inspections & baths. C.O. straffed about cleaning up but agreed 'A' Co could not do it. Dinner at R.H.Q. with Richardson. Saunderson reported to me & Maurice went to 'D' Co.

3-9-18   Spent the whole day clearing up & inspecting the men. At night there was a concert. Saw Col Fielding AAQMG about lousy shirts but he said he could do nothing for them. I was very rude to him. Doc & Aldis to dinner & talk. Late to bed.

4-9-18   Batt parade at 6.55 a.m. then breakfast then we lorried to a so called ceremonial parade. Presentation of medals etc by the Corp commander General Hunter Weston 8th R Berks got highly complimented by the General. Back for lunch at 2 p.m. Spent the afternoon working, evening at C.O.'s orders Al..... in after dinner & bridge. Lost 1 franc!

5-9-18   Wet in morning. Parades from 9-12 & also 2-3. Company conference at evening lasted from 7-8.30. Talk at night. Orders very late.

6-9-18   Company at O.C. Companies disposal all day. Very hot day. Day well spent. Spent afternoon cleaning up for C.O.'s parade next day. Took senior N.C.O.s & officers in afternoon.

7-9-18   Company at my disposal for first three hours then C.O.'s Inspection in marching order. Got patted on the back very much for it. Played 'B' Co at football & frew after a replay 'C' beat 'D'. At night a concert in the YMCA. Quite good. Rained hard in afternoon.

8-9-18   Church parade. Col Green as Brigadier presented medals to No 8 plat as the plat which won the A.R.A. competition for firing & bayonet fighting in the Brigade. Got wet through marching back to huts. In afternoon baths. Fidler up to trenches to take over from East Lancs. Played 'B' Co again & halved. Richardson came in to dinner & Fidler & I took 5 francs off him & Saunders.

9-9-18   Day of Relief. Comp Com conference at 9 a.m. Prepared for moving by lorry at 6.30 p.m. to relieve East Lancs. Idea of going in for 16 days. 'A' in support & then front line & then back for good leaving Day & his platoon for the Platoon School & Oswald out for a rest. Left camp by bus at 6.30 p.m. Got to Lens Area road where guides met us. I & runners went on without guides. Got to Batt H.Q. & saw Brown, Reynolds etc. Then came on & got to Coy H.Q. all OK just as it got dark. Platoons taken all way by guides but finally landed up

OK about 1 a.m. All in Support Line. Took over from Capt Chapman D.C.M. & South African Queens Medal. Higgs in front line. C.O. took over from him. Started getting mens quarters comfortable straight away Platoon for rations went all wrong & did not get in till 7 a.m.

10-9-18   Spent morning wandering round the line & seeing everyone. Made quarters very comfortable with help of a Pioneer. Felt rotten at night & went to bed early. Slept all night.

11-9-18   Got up late feeling much better. Went up after lunch to Batt H.Q. & had conflab. Tautz back. C.O. told us there were 3 alternatives.

1. Push north of here going East
2. Push on where we were. Bosch going back voluntarily.
3. Attack north west & then turn due north for Lens etc.

Had a very bad tea & got back with Brown & had a second tea. Had to shift mortars. Stayed in all evening feeling better. Great things up at night from Oswell.

12-9-18   Stayed in all day as it was raining very hard. Got smoked out by my fire for my bath. C.O. came in at night & altered mortars then & ordered me to Transport lines next day.

13-9-18   Stayed in till lunch. Had that at B.H.Q. Felt very rotten & stayed till tea & then out with C.O. & Strange to spy out the land. Strange knew nothing about it. Left them & walked back to Transport lines - never a lift. Had dinner & went to bed.

14-9-18   Rode up with Alloway to B.H.Q. in Barrett's house. C. Commander conference on push. After walked with Richardson & Lawson to 24th Brig H.Q. & looked from an Art. O.P. & saw over ground to offense over! Then walked back & picked up Horn & rode in for some lunch.

15-9-18   Went up in morning with Richardson & found 19 Lanc Fus & had lunch with Dippy. Fenn out & their adjutant Wade going. Then went on saw Fenn on the way. Went up & pointed out the push to Oswall & 4 N.C.O.s Got back walking all the way by team time.

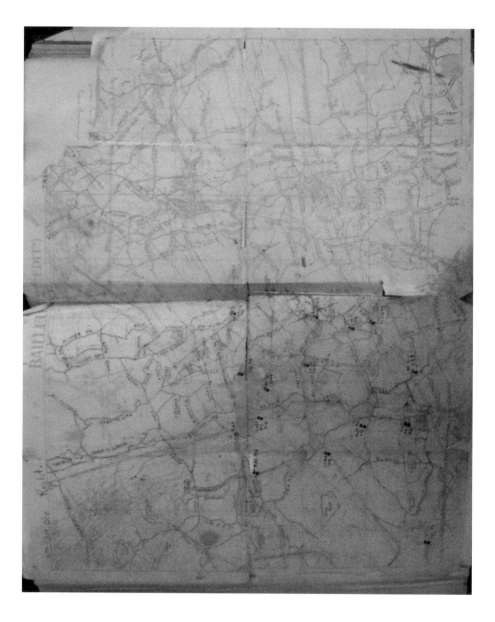

16-9-18   Woke up to receive orders to report to second West Yorks as C.O.2. Stopped in all day to see the C.O. He came in for tea & said some awfully kind words to me about taking it also well & helping him. I returned the compliment then left & found the 2nd West Yorks were all over the place. Batt. in the line 1 company in Cubitt camp Neuville St Vaast. Details in Downfoot camp & Transport in Fort George. Finally settled down at Cubitt Camp with Captain Green a very good sort of fellow. 'D' Co just came out of the line for 2 days (each company in turn). Got wire to say C.O. was coming to lunch.

17-9-18   Got up early & saw a Tank Demonstration near St Eloi with one company of Sherwood Foresters. Got back to lunch at Transport with Pearce the T.O. & Hinchcliffe the Q.M. No C.O. Rode up to B.H.Q. in afternoon & saw Adjutant but C.O. just gone up the line so missed him. Went back & went & saw the 5/7th. Early to bed.

18-9-18   Went up to Batt H.Q. & saw the C.O. Col A. Lowry D.S.O. M.C. He seemed very nice indeed & we seemed to agree as well. He is only about 25. Major Moore R.F.A. was also to lunch. Left there about 3 p.m. & got back to tea & change & then went again to 5/7th with Green.

19-9-18   Got up early & went along to Details camp. A..... was at Tank Demonstration so I got R.S.M.. Whole place was shockingly bad. Badly turned out. Bad Drill & bad huts. Kicked up hell & then returned to lunch. After lunch walked up to Transport & saw Hinchcliffe & Pearce & spent the afternoon with them. 'A' Co bathed etc. Stayed in all evening

20-9-18   Rode over & saw canteen at St Eloy about Champagne. Went round to details, they were cleaner but not too good. 'A' Co went off in afternoon & I heard 'B' Co were not coming out. Rode over to Transport & they did not know very much about the move except the 4th Company had to go in. Rode over to Ecurie & had tea there with Richardson, Isaac on leave. Leyland & Green at a conference. Richardson going up as the 4 companys were in. Came back for dinner by myself at Cubitt Camp. Slept there also.

21-9-18   Rode over & inspected the details. V. bad indeed. Made them parade again & still not up to much. Had my quarters transferred to Transport lines & lived with Q.M., T.O. & Padré Weeks. Rode round in afternoon & saw various Area Commandants about getting more huts but nothing doing.

22-9-18   Went to Detail Camp & had various inspections. Men awfully bad. Huts not too clean either. Had to see L.G. Section again. Rode on to Chautrelin corner & saw Fenn. Had lunch with him & got back just in time to inspect L.G. again. Had to wait for lunch as the groom's mare pulled a shoe off. Spent evening writing & playing petunia. Got a cross Q.M. as I gave him what I thought of the mens clothes.

23-9-18   Woke to hear Lt Col Lowry D.S.O. M.C. was killed. I went up & got there for lunch. Everyone very gloomy. After lunch I went round to Company H.Q. but no further as I hadn't been. Spent all evening & night in orderly room. Got to bed about 5 a.m. & up again at 7 a.m.

24-9-18   Spent morning at Brigade conference. Met Prior there also Toye[165] of the Middlesex. V.C. man. Also old Groggy a very great man. Like him immensely. Got back to lunch with the Div Water Officer a rotten dunce. After lunch spent afternoon in office then went & saw rear two companies. Spent evening up to 3 a.m.in office after that wrote battn diary.

25-9-18   Did nothing much all morning. Went up after lunch to Col Lowry D.S.O. M.C. funeral. G.O.C. Henecker, Brig Grogan, & Lowry the Gre.... General Col Nicholson 1st Army Staff. 2nd West Yorks & many others attended. Gun carriage etc provided. Big show. Got back after tea then had dinner at Brigade & returned about 10 p.m. & bed.

26-9-18   Went round the lines in the morning. The trench discipline etc was like nothing on earth. Made copious notes & decided pull all O.C. Ccompanys oover the coals about it. Spent afternoon hunting rats. At night the other two Battalions were doing a show. Taking Brittania & Brandy Tr. The Show started at midnight. We had a bit to do in it only from the support line though. Up to 1 a.m. all seemed to go swimmingly.

27-9-18   Expected to move but waited till midday then got orders to wait in till tomorrow. Went round the line & saw all the company commanders. Took the .....z with me. Went to bed early & then the SOS went up about 2 a.m. Took 40 minutes to get properly through to Companys.

---

[165] Acting Major Alfred M. Toye, 2nd Bn. Middlesex Regiment, awarded the V.C. for gallantry at Eterpigny Ridge, 25 March 1918.

28-9-18 Batt moved to Hill Camp. Started in middle of the day & we left at about 6.30. Had row with M.O. butthat cleared off. All had supper at Hills Camp about 8 p.m. Batt mess very comfortable all through.

29-9-18 Went round camp & spent morning trying to fire things up. Had a church parade No time to get to it. Had a long O.C. Companys conference in afternoon. Brig Grogan to tea. Worked all evening.

30-9-18 Worked all evening. O.C. Companys conference & Orderly Room. Afternoon lecture by Intelligence Officer & went to tea with Isaac & R Berks. Got back for Batt concert & dinner. Orders to move came in late at night. Played bridge till late & then worked till 2 a.m. Had Batt ...... at 6.0 p.m. v.g. Got up by North. Bulgaria[166] gave in.

1-10-18 Started off with advance party to new trenches at 9.30. Got to Brig H.Q. No 154 37th Div via St Nicolas, St Laurent, Blagny, Athies & Fampoux. Walked from there up to trenches. Batt H.Q. at I.7.d.1.5. Took over from the 7th Argyle & Sutherlands. Stayed there all day. Batt came in at night relief complete about 11.30 p.m. I went up & saw 'B', 'D' & 'C' Companys & got back about 3 a.m. All O.R. R.B.s came in on our right.

2-10-18 Spent morning sleeping. Had bath just before lunch. Went up to 'A' Co in afternoon. Only got as far as Co H.Q. as I could not go round lines apparently in day time. Went in at night to see RBs saw them. Sending out a 2 patrols during day located Bosch positions normal. Also gave orders for two patrols at night. Owing to gas projector & ..... not sure they could be managed. Finally failed to get out.

3-10-18 Had a slack morning. Went up to 'C' Co in afternoon meaning to go round trenches but they told me conditions foul owing to mud. G.O.C. Grogan went up to 'A' Co. Got orders at night when I intended going round lines that we would have to do an attack & all reconnaissance had to be done possible. Also G.O.C. conference at 9.0 next morning

4-10-18 G.O.C. conference lasted till midday. Orders to take Fresnes Rouvroy line on Sunday morning. Various small details & main scheme were issued. Got back & had O.C. Company's conference & told them

---

[166] Due to a rebellion by troops at Radomir, Bulgaria was forced to seek and accept an armistice on 30 September 1918.

main scheme. Spent all night writing orders. Late at night it came in show postponed 24 hours. Gunners could not do their work.

5-10-18   G.O.C. conference at 10.0. when I got to Bgde H.Q. Lt Col D Grant Dalton D.S.O. had reported to take over Batt. Seemed quite a nice fellow. Had been Commanding a Pioneer Batt for 2 years or so previously. I had to carry on still with the show. Rode back with him. O.C. Company's Conference & then spent all evening writing our orders

6-10-18   Had another G.O.C.s conference in the morning. G.O.C. came to our H.Q. & talked to the officers. Huge ovation After that we had company commanders' conference & bit of other conference & then moved up at night to 'A' Co H.Q. on top of the Greenland Hill. Got in quite safely.

7-10-18   Zero at 5 a.m. Huge attack & huge barrage & a huge success. All went swimmingly ..... about 45 prisoners for about 35 casualties 5 killed. Got all our objectives & exploited move right up to Victory Marches & Gloster Wood. C.O. went up at night or rather afternoon. I felt very rotten at night awful headache owing to eating chocolates. Went to bed & slept the night through.

8-10-18   All quiet. Went up & round companys with C.O. in morning. Afternoon stayed in & were relieved at night by the Devons. Went back to old B.H.Q. at night. North on leave.

9-10-18   Went out after lunch. Went & saw Reynolds East Lancs & Lawson R Berks before lunch. Stayed till last man out from Batt H.Q. & then returned to Stirling Camp in Railway Embankment just East of Arras. Rogerson to dinner & Bridge.

10-10-18 Spent morning going through papers with C.O. Afternoon inspecting Transport & Q.M. stores with C.O. Heard moving up again tomorrow to fight. Mathews to dinner. No bridge owing to move.

11-10-18 Moved at 7 a.m.to Greenland Hill to support Devons & Middlesex who were taking the Quéant-Drocourt line. Got up there about 10 a.m. & stayed there all day. At dinner time C.O. & myself went to Brigade to arrange about going through the ..... battalions & exploiting success as far as the Scarpe Deviation or Harte Du..... Canal.

12-10-18   I went up early about 4 a.m.to see the Devons & Middlesex. Got up there & then Batt came up & I went up & saw the start of the show. Got them away to time & then returned dog tired to B.H.Q. Owing to them shelling it we changed it to close to the mine. 'C' & 'B' Companys had the show but 'D' got engaged also & only 'A' remained in support. They did very well & got to the Rhine but Huns held the far bank too strongly & we could not get across. We had about 67 casualties. C.O. met B.G.G.S. of Corps Aspinall & had a talk with him. Something went wrong & the C.O. was sent back to the Details at once. Grogan came in & said I was to command the Regiment. C.O. stayed over night.

13-10-18   C.O. went down to Details & I had to carry on. Horrible wet night. Nothing happened. We got orders that we were to be relieved by the Devons at night so I did not go out. Devons came in & we handed over. Got away about 11 p.m. & all companies went back to the Quéant-Drocourt line. R.H.Q. is some old Pill boxes.

14-10-18   Stayed in bed till about 10.30. Orderly Room at 12 but there was nothing for it. Spent the morning wandering round saw 'B' & 'C' Co. Afternoon I went down to the Transport & saw them. Grogan came round to see us. All very comfortable.

15-10-18   Wandered round in morning & saw the Brigade. Had a drink with Grogan. Bourne up there talking about the push for Douai so I asked to have it done by us but he would not promise it. Late for Orderly room. After lunch played bridge all afternoon & evening. Quin & Pearce to tea. Just after Rogerson turned up & we played all night. Bed about 2 a.m. Rogerson on fairly good form.

16-10-18   Spent morning wandering round 'A' Co & 'D' Co. Spent afternoon in. Col. Price came to see us & after tea General Grogan came & told me I should be commanding the Battalion some time so I had better pick a C.O.2. No post & we were relieving the Middlesex tommorow night. Stuart & Winterton went up to see rough dispositions & got badly bumped.

17-10-18   Went up in morning with Brigadier & Harris to take over from Middlesex. Groggy would not believe that Bosch was still there so we went up & they had 2 shots at us. Got back to lunch. Called in at Middlesex H.Q. on the way & heard Bosch were back N & S of us & we had to go over at night. During afternoon Middlesex established bridge heads & sent a patrol to Douai. We followed up & went right through to the other side. Middlesex got a patrol into Douai first. I went up in front to see how the bridges were getting on & then went back & established B.H.Q. at Corbehem. Later moved up to Courchelettes. I went up & saw the Companys at night. Got back about 2 a.m. Beautiful moonlight night.

18-10-18   I went up early morning & saw all Companys. B.H.Q. moved up to Douai. Bridges etc over the canals were blown up in every direction. Also all bridges on railway. Every house was systematically looted & ransacked. We found a billet marked No 3 Destruction Company. All transport etc came up at night as they had bridged the canals.

19-10-18   Rode round the companys with Rogerson in morning. Got orders just before that they wanted small working parties on the main road north from Douai. So saw the places. Got back for lunch. Wrote letters in afternoon & wandered round the cathedral with Stuart & saw the organ etc. Got back for tea & then went out to see working party. Harris the B.M. came to dinner & we sat up till about 2 a.m. talking.

20-10-18   Orders at 6.30 a.m. to move to Catelet at 10.30 a.m. Huge ..... to get going. Got going alright but held up at Râches through bridge not being ready. Halted in ..... area & had dinner & we had a very good lunch. Got in about 3.0 a.m. & started filling in shell holes straight away. Very comfortable all round. Civilians in the place very pleased to see us. Orders at night to work next day on roads.

21-10-18   All Battalion working on roads. Went round work & billets in morning. Saw G.O.C. & many red hats. Afternoon went over to Q.M. Stores & Transport.

22-10-18   All on roads again. 'C' Co sent out early. Found road done so I had a row with Brigade & Div over it also saw Col Fielding about it. Job was done finally. Rode round with Green round Hem, Bouvignies & Marchiennes & back. Raining pretty bad. Richards went to England so Green took over 'D' Co. Slade & Pascoe came in to dinner & we had quite a hilarious time & bridge.

23-10-18   Company's drilling went round them. Devons with Grant-Dalton turned up. Also found Le Gros[167] had been posted to East Lancs as C.O. & met him in the street. Groggy was in very great form in the

---

[167] Major Philip W. Le Gros, C.O. 2nd Bn. East Lancs.

morning. Also saw old Padre Hamilton. Thompson of Bedfords was ill so we took him some books etc round for which he was very thankful. He was just off to join Brigade. After dinner lost 20 francs to Stuart at bridge.

24-10-18   Stuart on leave. Had 1 hour Batt drill in morning - very good show considering the ground was so rough. Saw Grant-Dalton in afternoon. Had 2 or 3 company commanders conferences. Heard we were going into the line again shortly. Padre Hamilton came in to dinner at night & talked for an hour or so.

25-10-18   Had companys practising new attacking formations in morning. I saw Grant-Dalton on his way to Manchesters. Afternoon a bit showery. General Grogan came & talked to all officers & men on the new formations & tactics & then stayed to tea. Camp ..... the guard. Told me we were moving the next day. Kiddy arrived early in morning. I had a wire on 29th about it.

26-10-18   Cancellation of move early in the morning. So we did a mornings work & had ½ hr Batt drill. They were pretty good at it. At 2.45 p.m. we got orders to move to St Amand over Millonfosse. 15 miles march. We got going at 4.30 p.m. Route given by Brig. to us was hopeless in all places 3 sides of a rectangle with the 4 & shorter side quite good so had to about turn the Batt & come back. Then we luckily met a gunner in Brillon who told us a bridge would not take transport so we side tracked the Transport & the Batt. came on. Got in about 7.30 p.m. with only 4 men falling out. Got to bed about 1.30 a.m. Orders just arrived before turning in to move next day into St Amand.

27-10-18   Started for St Armand at 11.30 & got into Billets at 1 a.m. Met & had a chat to Brig Aspinall B.G.G.S. of VIII Corps. Saw Mortimer DADM 8th & various other celebrities including Col Nicholson. Spent afternoon going round Billets also Transport & Q.M. Stores. Mortimer in to lunch & bridge. Took 20 francs off him. Good fellow. Also saw Fielding who was very sick. Farrar to Hospital & North back from leave.

28-10-18   Morning going round Companys. Had a special call to go & see the G.O.C. I thought it meant Hennecker but it only meant Groggy. When I got there he had nothing at all to say to me but that we are probably taking over from the Devons. I had to round up all officers to reconnoitre the line with a view to crossing the canal at the first opportunity. Got back & found shortly after order for us to move our Billets in St Armand. Only about 70 minutes walk from here.

29-10-18 Went up to see Brigade about changing but I had to move the mess but ..... not near Q.M. Stores. Got back & went up all O.C. Companys. Went up after lunch & saw Prior. He & Grogan had had to get into a ditch to stop some Bosch firing at them. Got back for tea. Orders to take over from Devons came in at night. I had arranged to take over from them in afternoon. Late at night a wire came to see G.O.C. next morning at 9.15 a.m. Had Carr & Winterton in to dinner. Rather a ..... & quite a .....

30-10-18 Rode over to Brigade in the morning to hear about the Show. We were to take the second canal in front of Conde. Henecker turned up & ignored me! Said Show had to take place on night of 1st/2nd. Rode back to lunch. Mortimer & Stow to lunch. Started off after lunch & got orders that Devons were going to take canals. Had to change everything & got in to Odomez as best we could leaving the Devons in. We did not take over Forrester House as B.H.Q. but went forward into Odomez into a forward House. Very good billet. Settled in OK for the night. Devons got over the first canal during the night.

31-10-18 Went down & saw Prior. We had orders to go on the second canal at night. Then as Devons had such a pasting & nearly all came back, we were ordered to make good the ground in between the canals. Finally that was cancelled & we were ordered to take over outpost line instead. Great relief on everyones part. Devons had about 50 casualties. Parky went to Hospital ill. Pearce very bad.

1-11-18 Changed dispositions, went round in morning with gunner officer & saw Matheson & then went to 'C' Co new billets at Bruille & then to 'B' Co & back in afternoon I went along to see Billets in S.E. of Odomez & back by 'A' Co's. Shelled the village very heavily at night & quite a bit round orderly room. Farrar[168] reported died of Influenza.

2-11-18 Orders in for taking over Batt frontage of the Canadians on our right the 3rd C.M.R.s & to hand over our left half to the 52nd Div. I went along to the 7th Scottish Rifles with North & saw their Brigadier. Got back about midday. Got shelled on the way back. Went straight in with Doc & Armitage to see Canadians. Grogan there. Got back for

---

[168] 2/Lt (Act. Capt.) John F. Farrar.

lunch. Moved on in afternoon & took over finally in evening. My front was then over 6000. From Chateau sur Forêt to South of Condé. Newton made a thoroughly bad show of things so I decided to have Carr up & send him back to transport. Relief complete about 10.30. I went out to 'B' & 'A' Co with North.

3-11-18   Slack day all day. Had nothing but visitors 14 in the morning mostly gunners. Graham marched in midday. Carr took over from Newton to transport. Farnsworth & Ibbetson back. Crick ordered to go to RAF. North ordered to report to Brig for a day or two. Then changed & Farnworth ordered to join the Brigade as Intelligence Officer on the 5th. Had orders late in evening that 52nd Div was taking over from us & the Div was being relieved by them & then going out. Relief next day. Farnworth & Ibbetson rejoined.

4-11-18   C.O. of 7th H.L.I. Col Foster came over in morning to see me & arrange the relief. A muddle was caused by Rogerson telling the cook transport was turning up when it wasn't. 'C' Co relieved on daylight all others by night. Relief completed by 8.15 p.m. Very quick considering. Carr seemed very good & energetic. Rode back to Bousiquiers & got in there by 10.30 & to bed. Relief complete then by 2.15. Took over from 2nd East Lancs. Had authority for 9 M.M.s & 2 bars. 16 Div parchment certificates out of 28 given to the Div. Also during the day I recommended Graham for the MC. Heard various rumours. One the Div was going out for a rest & 2 that we were going straight into a front.

5-11-18   Pouring wet day. Wandered round billets in morning & to transport lines. Missed Hinchcliffe. Afternoon spent handing out certificates to men from Corps Commander. Gen Sir Aylmer Hunter-Weston KCMG D.S.O. M.P. Parrots making huge row. Crick to leave Brigade but did not go in the end. Bridge at night. Poured incessantly.

6-11-18   poured incessantly all night & day. Went along to Brigade in morning. Afternoon spent inspecting Billets. Very wet.my room almost flooded out. Holmes went home to England. Sharpe returned & Fawcett came into division. Sharpe & I lost 10 frs at bridge. Bosch delegates for peace left for France.

7-11-18   Heard G.O.C. was going to inspect us tomorrow, great excitement. Room very hot at night half the ceiling fell in. my appointment to Lt Col came in & Rogerson to Major. Afternoon spent inspecting Companies. Grogan walking round & met him. Seemed quite bucked.

Farnworth returned to me from Brigade earmarked for Brigade Intelligence Officer. Had Mathews in to dinner in evening & played bridge, took 15 francs with North of him & Rogerson.

8-11-18   Wet day again in the morning did nothing all morning. Afternoon we played M.G.C. at Rugger. Harris & Slade played & we lost 17-0. Went to tea with Gardner O.C. 'A' Co M.G.C. Poured with rain. Peace in the air very much with rumours of the Division going to India after peace. Played Bridge with Rogerson v Doc & Armitage. Got orders to move to Fresnes near Condé next morning early. Orders came in very late not much sleep. Armistice delegates came to G.H.Q. (Albert).

9-11-18   Started off beautiful frosty day at 6.30 a.m. Marched via Brillon, St Armand, Escautpont to Fresnes. Passed the Middlesex en route as they had mistaken orders. Got to Levres & found we had to move on by Bruay via Valenciennes to a place called Pommereuil half way from Condeé to Mons. Set off at 4 p.m. but buses which should have started at 5.0 but did not till about 8 & then went frightfully slowly at first. Bus nearly fell over a bridge so everyone had to get out there & over & in again. Ended up at The..... about 2 a.m. & then had to find our own billets. Dreadfully cold all night. Everyone nearly frozen. I slept at the Priests place. dear old chap who did me very well. Got to bed about 4 a.m. Walked into Vieux Condé the 2 houses we ..... at Fresnes. Result of armistice terms to be published by 11 a.m.11.11.18.

10-11-18   General in to see me about 9 a.m. Had breakfast about 10.30 a.m. Felt a bit rocky but quite OK after dinner. Orders to move at 3.0 to a place called Tutu. Middlesex again late so we led off. Passed our starting point to the ..... a bit early at the Brigade. Grogan came with me to the front half quite chatty. Seemed to think the Armistice imminent. We were in support to the Div. Middlesex taking the front line. Nothing doing as Bosch had gone a long way back. People awfully glad to see us. First troops properly in their village. B.H.Q. quite a good spot.

11-11-18   Carr came in early to say wire from Corps that Hostilities ceased at 11 a.m.11-11-18. So I had a Batt parade & read the telegram out to them. Got orders to move in the afternoon to Donorain up about 2 miles at the most. Set off at 4 p.m. & got in about 4.40 p.m. Very good spot with splendid billets. Middlesex attached in the morning but apparently nothing to attack. My appointment to C.O. came through from the First Army. Had Matthews to dinner but orders came in to move at 7 a.m. next morning to Maisières so it broke up the dinner party.

The German People Offers Peace.

The new German democratic government has this programme:

"The will of the people is the highest law."

The German people wants quickly to end the slaughter.

The new German popular government therefore has offered an

Armistice

and has declared itself ready for

Peace

on the basis of justice and reconciliation of nations.

It is the will of the German people that it should live in peace with all peoples, honestly and loyally.

What has the new German popular government done so far to put into practice the will of the people and to prove its good and upright intentions?

a) The new German government has appealed to President Wilson to bring about peace.

It has recognized and accepted all the principles which President Wilson proclaimed as a basis for a general lasting peace of justice among the nations.

b) The new German government has solemnly declared its readiness to evacuate Belgium and to restore it.

c) The new German government is ready to come to an honest understanding with France about.

Alsace-Lorraine.

d) The new German government has restricted the U-boat War.

No passengers steamers not carrying troops or war material will be attacked in future.

e) The new German government has declared that it will withdraw all German troops back over the German frontier.

f) — The new German government has asked the Allied Governments to name commissioners to agree upon the practical measures of the evacuation of Belgium and France.

These are the deeds of the new German popular government. Can these be called mere words, or bluff, or propaganda?

Who is to blame, if an armistice is not called now?

Who is to blame if daily thousands of brave soldiers needlessly have to shed their blood and die?

Who is to blame, if the hitherto undestroyed towns and villages of France and Belgium sink in ashes?

Who is to blame, if hundreds of thousands of unhappy women and children are driven from their homes to hunger and freeze?

The German people offers its hand for peace.

12-11-18   Orders went all wrong. T.O. & Q.M. never got their orders so transport was ½ hour late in morning. Batt got on all right & got in about 9.15 Had a big straffe on with Carr as he seemed totally mad over affair of who was to blame for orders going wrong. Had an exceptional good billet. Bosch had only left 2 or 3 days before. Quite near Mons. In afternoon Doc & I walked into Mons. When we got there we saw the Prince of Wales go into the Town Hall so we went in after him & drank champagne & I asked him to come & see the Regiment as it was the P.W.O. He said he was very full up & would come if he could. Got back for tea. Church turned up as C.O. Seemed quite a nice fellow but rather a loner. He is a New Zealander or Australian or something belonging to the Suffolks att Royal Berks. Hinchcliffe & Sharpe in to dinner. Took about 15 francs off Hinchcliffe.

13-11-18   Church & I rode over to Brigade. G.O.C. had not very much to tell us - all C.O.s were there. Baker as usual very officious. Saw Slack. Afternoon spent going round the defence scheme plan with Church - a very nice ride. Fox turned up. Had Hamilton out to dinner - he drank rather heavily & left infernally late. Fox got going very quickly. Rogerson to transport Newton assistant transport officer. Beautiful day rather a hard frost in the morning. Heard we were moving on 16th to the 3rd Corps. From the VIII

14-11-18   Took O.C. companys round defence scheme in morning. Chased a hare but it went to earth. Got a wire to say General Houn was making a beautiful entry into Mons & we had to turn out next day as a ceremonial parade & received him in Mons. Rode over hell for leather to Brigade office & had a talk about it & got back & inspected the Batt on parade. B..... work good. Equipment very bad. Went round at night to see the Middlesex show - arrived 1 hour late owing to them changing the time - bad show.

15-11-18   Had Battalion parade at 8.0 a.m. Turnout much better but parade start members all wrong. Marched off at 9.0 a.m. & found when we got to Mons we had to line a bit of the streets. Did that OK & then fell in behind the procession & marched through the town & past the general. Marched past just after 12.0. Then had to go back to Glyn & take part in a presentation of the French Cordon to the Devon Reg. Got on the way there & had just had our ..... rations at about 2:30 p.m. & Davis came up & said it was a washout & too late. So we turned round & got back for lunch about 3 p.m. Transport & all our things had gone on ahead for a two days trek.

INFORMATION CONCERNING RECENT STATE OF AFFAIRS BEHIND GERMAN
LINES.

I. INFORMATION FROM CIVILIANS.

1. Nature of German Withdrawal. Reports indicate that the German troops were on the whole avoiding BRUSSELS in their retirement. Some were passing through the town though, and there caused disturbances on Sunday, Monday and Tuesday.

Their march in and round BRUSSELS was, on the whole orderly; they wore red cockades and carried red flags, their officers were with them and bands were playing. Though the general tone was orderly, some cases of looting, rioting and disorder occurred.

Various reports showed that officers had been insulted, their shoulderstraps torn off them, and that some were shot. The troops were stated on Monday to be firing Machine guns on the Metropole Hotel, the Grand Hotel and the Palace Hotel, where German officers and Nursing Sisters had taken refuge. The Nurses were seen firing revolvers on the attacking troops, whilst the officers took cover and merely loaded the revolvers. The troops were desperate and quite willing to set fire to these hotels.

Most of the rioting took place between LA GARE DU NORD and the EXCHANGE, those concerned in it were mostly drunken looters and bad characters, possibly incited by Bolshevik agents.

On Sunday last Bolsheviks, to the number of about a thousand, clad in marines' uniforms, arrived by special train. They tried to start rioting against KING ALBERT, but failed except in a few insignificant cases. The Stations of VERVIERS, LIEGE and LOUVAIN are stated to be under their control. In some quarters of LOUVAIN and BRUSSELS, they forced the population to take down the Belgian and Allied Flags and put up Red ones instead. They have also taken down the German Flag on the BRUSSELS COMMANDATUR and put up a red one over the building.

Some German troops are selling all their equipment. Rifles can be bought for a mark apiece, complete uniforms for 10 marks, horse and cart for 40 or 100 marks, motor cars for 1,000 marks, a train of foodstuffs was sold to the inhabitants of ENGHIEN at very cheap rates e.g. an 80 kilo sack of cornflower for 30 francs. The same sales were taking place at HARCK.

There were at the beginning of the week some 4,000 released P.O.W. of ours in BRUSSELS. They were under the command of a Major, and were waiting the departure of the Germans to arm themselves and organise a Police service in the City.

Between NINOVE-HAL on Tuesday the enemy were blowing up ammunition, and firing off machine guns to celebrate the armistice. (This may account for the firing heard in that direction on Tuesday).

II. INFORMATION RECEIVED FROM OTHER SOURCES.

(a) Riots. Rioting in BRUSSELS, mainly drunken brawls between soldiers, and soldiers and civilians.

(b) Extent of Revolutionary Feeling. Majority of the troops in favour of the Revolution, and showing their sentiments by carrying red flags and wearing red cockades.

Stripping shoulderstraps off officers was fairly general on the first few days of the Revolution. An order was then issued by the Councils of Soldiers and Workmen forbidding this, and stating it was only conducive to disorder.

(c) Moves of Headquarters and Divisions. The Headquarters of the VI Army was at LOUVAIN on the 15th November and likely to move further back to destination unknown on the 16th inst.

/Prince

Prince RUPPRECHT'S of BAVARIA H.Q. moved from LILLE to TOURNAI
and thence to BRUSSELS. A few days ago, the rumour went round
VI Army H.Q. that RUPPRECHT of BAVARIA was at INNSBRUCK.

The IV Corps moved from GRANDMETZ to BRUSSELS on the 6th November
and on the 7th November the 2nd Gd.Res.Div. left FRASNES. On the
7th November all area troops left FRASNES for RUNSBROEK via
GAMMERAGES.

About 4th November 4th Ersatz Division entrained for ALSACE
where it was to relieve Austrians.

119th Division in RENAIX area from 2nd to 6th Nov., and 187th Div.
recently in PERUWELZ area.

(d) Boundaries. Boundary between 6th and 17th German Armies ran
through PERUWELZ and WIERS.

Boundary between IV and LV Corps ran through FRASNES to a point
just South of BRUSSELS.

(e) Counter-revolutionary Feeling. On 14th inst a Division
marching from BRUSSELS to LOUVAIN was stopping and turning back any
cars met flying red flags or bearing red cockades. The men were
furious against the revolutionaries and slight disturbances took
place.

(f) Situation in GERMANY. Very little news of late has been
coming through from GERMANY. There is great fear of starvation.
Great chaos reigns at the Frontier where trainload after trainload
of men come pouring in.

The whole Army is discussing: where is the food going to come
from ? If the food does not materialize Bolshevism will set in for
certain.

Great fears of Bolshevism getting hold of the people were
expressed by officers. Up to now the revolution had been peaceful.
"Soviets" had been established at all Headquarters, who counter-signed
all orders.

III. INFORMATION FROM OUR OWN ESCAPED AND RELEASED PRISONERS OF WAR.

Treatment. There has been considerable variation in the treatment
in various camps but any disinclination to work(even owing to
weakness) was always greeted with a kick or a blow with the butt end
of a rifle.

Prisoners had always to walk to their work, often 20 kilos. a
day. If any transport accompanied them, the prisoners had as a rule
to push the wagons as there was a shortage of horses

Since July no parcels seem to have been received by any prisoners
owing no doubt to difficulties of transport, and to disorganisation
in the enemy's L.of C.

Enemy Moral. Moral has been exceedingly low of late. Common
talk has it that from 30-40 officers have been shot in the last few
days in BRUSSELS - both German soldiery and civilians taking part in
these fracas.

Much confusion exists on the roads in rear and little order
prevails among the men. Cases are commonly occurring of motor cars
being held up and commandeered by rebellious soldiers.

Up till July moral in military matters was still good though
the shortage of food at home was then making itself felt very much.

There was much envy among even officers when parcels arrived
from ENGLAND, and prisoners who got parcels were told they were
feeding better than the German officers.

For the last few months many hundreds of defaulters have been
seen marched down the line, having refused to go into the trenches.

/Pay

Pay. Three francs every 10 days, lately this has been reduced in several instances to 1.90 frs.

General. In several cases the officers in charge of P.O.W. Companies were given such posts as a punishment. One was so employed on account of a self-inflicted wound. He treated the prisoners well, but could not of course increase the ration as food was very scarce.

All the prisoners testify to the kindness of the Belgian civilians without whose surreptitious help many more would have died. The Belgian Relief Commission did much to alleviate distress. Very few examples have been discovered of parcels being detained until the recent disorganisation.

The daily ration since July has been meagre in the extreme – ½ loaf rye bread per man per day, acorn coffee, and watery soup at midday. No set meal times were allowed; in most cases the ration was eaten whilst walking along the road to their work. Transport was never provided and often 12 to 18 kms. had to be covered without any extra rations being issued.

Whilst in TOURNAI recently the civilians offered to look after the feeding of the British prisoners of war, but the Germans forbade the carrying out of that intention.

Some of the prisoners were used to carry aeroplane bombs to the planes that bombed ENGLAND and opportunity often occurred for the prisoners to tamper with the 'planes by removing a nut or cutting a wire and so either prevent the plane starting or make its return doubtful. Casualties particularly on return from bombing raids were very heavy. On a raid in the spring 7 machines started from the aerodrome where prisoners were working and only one returned safe.

III Corps "I".
16th November, 1918.

16-11-18   Cold fine day again. Were supposed to leave at 10 a.m. Buses never came till about 11:35 a.m. Got going at about 12. Picked up Devons at Glyn & Brig H.Q. Came in by a circuitous route through Tournai to within 1 Kilo of Taintignies. Got to Tournai at about 4:30 p.m. just as it was getting dark. Lost our way in Tournai & got in about 6 p.m. Settled in about 7 p.m. Toye C.O.2 Middlesex V.C. came in fact all the way with me

17-11-18   Beastly cold day. Found my window broken in my billet. Spent the morning running round. Afternoon Church & I walked to Tournai. Saw Boys S..... in a shop & also one of the old R.F.A. liaison officers. Got a lift back in a car. Saw Grogan & Harris. Grogan going to Paris for French leave. Heard Pearce[169] had died of flu. Church parades only.

18-11-18   Another cold day. Started to rain & sleet in morning. Winterton returned from leave. Went round in morning & had various conferences. Afternoon spent doing nothing. Pasloe & Howe came in for dinner. Had bridge. Lost 20 Francs. Stayed up fairly late.

19-11-18   Had a very hard day. Spent morning inspecting 'A' & 'B' Companys. Caught them out in various things. Then Batt Drill & afternoon spent looking at football & then we went round Church & I to Esplechin & saw the 2nd R. Berks. Most of them in. ..... & Richardson there. Doc & others promised to come & see us. Got back about 6.30 p.m. Bridge after dinner. Rogerson out to Brigade. Grogan went on Paris leave & Prior took over the Brigade.

20-11-18   Inspected Billets. 'A' Co very good others bad. Afternoon spent messing round. Isaac & Doctors did not turn up in spite of a very good lunch for them. Afternoon very foggy. Went round to watch football. No good.

21-11-18   Nothing doing all day. Companys had the day to themselves. Isaac & ..... got the D.S.O.. Lawson & Riley got the M.C. & Paton a bar. Went in to tea to Brigade. Gray came. Had mess meeting & lecture by Hinchcliffe on the Regiment at night. Winterton in to dinner & bridge afterwards. Lost 3 francs to him & Newton.

22-11-18   Got up early to inspect 'C' & 'D' Companies & they had taken the wrong days training so I did nothing all morning but look at musketry

---

[169] 2/Lt. James Pearce D.C.M. M.M.

& then Batt. Drill. Beautiful day. Afternoon watched football & then Myers & Reynolds came in to tea rather struck at our mess. Prior C.O. 2nd Devons who was acting as Brigadier as Grogan was on French leave & Harris came into dinner & was in good form. Parrots were in exceptional form.

23-11-18 Had inspection of 'C' & 'D' companys - very much better, Batt. Drill then Corps commander turned up, Butler C.B. C.M.G & said very little. Watched football in afternoon. Capt. Lee of train came into dinner & stayed a long time Peacroft in good form.

24-11-18 Late breakfast spent most of the day in orderly room. Some officers turned up Rushworth, Merman, Greensmith & Barker. 'D' Co beat H.Q. in the final company match. Rogerson's brother came over for tea. Went to see Harris about Woodward shooting his servant by accident but he was out. Hinchcliffe came in to dinner. Weather changed to warm & like rain.

25-11-18 Usual parades in morning. Battalion parade. We tried Brigade stunts seemed to work alright. Afternoon 'D' Co beat H.Q. of Devon's for brigade football. Had 2 Devon officers in to lunch & Prior & another Devon officer & the referee in to tea. Xmas cards came. 1 rubber of bridge with Rogerson v Fox & Newton. Draft of 125 arrived also Frost & Calderick

26-11-18 Inspected new draft & then went round companys. Batt parade on 'A' Co's ground. Officers frightfully shoddy drill. Afternoon cross country run. Went round with them. Bridge at night. Sharpe to dinner.

27-11-18 Brigade parade in morning - Drill was not good but the turn out of officers & men was better than the other regiments. In afternoon Stuart returned & also we were beaten at football 'D' Co beaten by Brig. H.Q. Winterton in to play bridge. Won 5 francs.

28-11-18 Beastly wet day. Battalion Bathing at Froidmont so went over to see the Baths with Fox. Church went to baths. Saw Myers, Ronald & Lyons there & also Carrfort. Spent afternoon in my room fed up with nothing to do. Bridge at night.

29-11-18 Div General round to see us in the morning. Hugely ..... with life & couldn't find anything wrong. Never known him so pleasant. Complimented us on our soft caps etc. In afternoon went & saw

Brigade & they said I could go on leave on the 3rd that meant crossing on the 3rd leaving here the 1st. Rode in with Church to Tournai. Saw Prior & the cathedral. Had a mess meeting & passed the buying of decent crockery etc. at 6 p.m.

30-11-18   Expected Corps Commander in morning but he did not come. Rode over in afternoon with Church to RAF Froidmont to cadge a motor for tomorrow but they had left.

1-12-18   Sunday. Set off with Church for Lille. Rode on to Tournai-Lille road. Left at 10 a.m. & got into Lille about 12 & had lunch & we left about 3 p.m. Walked out to Loos after tea & heard I could catch the train at station Porte des Postes earlier with shorter walk. Saw Spider Quott & also Symons J.I. Major in ..... Slept at the club.

2-12-18   Caught the train at Porte des Poste at 9.30. Big walk & heavy bag to carry. Got to Bethune at about 12. Then had to change. Train supposed to go at 2.59 did not leave till about 8.35 p.m. Got into Calais next morning. Not half as cold as I expected but very squashed & dirty.

3-12-18   Got in just in time to walk down to pier & catch boat going at 9 a.m. Train got in about 7.50. Had no breakfast & heard I was O.C. Ship so had a cabin. Very rough indeed so had the expected result & I felt rotten all the way. Managed a shave. Had late breakfast when I got in the Pulman. Got to Town about 2.55 p.m. Went & saw Pat at Princes & then to Wenos but she was out. Caught the 4.45 to Lancaster & got in about 10.45. Good journey.

4-12-18   Stayed in all day getting things straight just. Down town in morning. Concert at night. Elaine ....., Ada Ashby & 2 others in Aston Hall. V.G. Lights went out & they finished by candle light.

5-12-18   Caught morning train to Silverdale.. Mother met me & I brought Karl's motor back. Got back for tea. Billiards at night.

6-12-18   Town in morning. Afternoon fetched Mr Malcom & had lunch at club. Played a single & he won giving him a half. Took him back to work..

7-12-18   Fetched Mr Malcolm & had lunch at club. He & I beat Storey & Clark giving them 3 holes. Also won .....by.

8-12-18   Went & saw Crosslands & Greta Hel...... v. nice homes. Afternoon want a walk with Mr Malcolm & in evening caught a train to Carlisle. Stayed at Carlisle for night.

9-12-18   Caught 7.10 to Glasgow arrived 9.40 left Buchanan St Station 11.0 Troon 12.4. Mr & Mrs Townsend met me. Rained hard in afternoon so we got no golf but cleared a bit & we watched Willie Fernie[170] & Anderson play.

10-12-18   Fine morning so we got a game in & 4 holes. I easily beat Mr Townsend who was very off. Caught 2.2 to Glasgow arrived 3.20. Hope & Mrs Townsend met me & I left 3.50 & got in to Lancaster at 9.45 instead of 9.1. Kaye had brought Karl's car but it gave up the ghost half way down.

11-12-18   Took Kaye & Babba to lunch at Silverdale & stayed night. Lunch Fred & Mabel there. Played Billiards all afternoon & puzzle at night. Kaye & .....

12-12-18   Brought Uncle over to lunch at golf club. Storey & Duncan & Mr Malcolm to lunch. Uncle & I played Storey & Mr Malcolm & beat them 2 up. Uncle to tea at ..... & I took him to catch 6.45 train.

13-12-18   Left by the 02.50 Train to Wolverhampton, saw Brooke on station. Changed at Preston & Crewe. Had tea at Crewe. Met Walford at Wolverhampton going to Election meeting at Tipton. Took his train & got up to Ash Hill for dinner. Davis up but not very fit.

14-12-18   Breakfast early as Walford had to go off to town. In morning went along to Efandem & saw Peter Smith & a few of the old hands. Talked things over & arranged to meet at Gibbons on Monday. Visited Kemp & Wilson. Spent the afternoon doing nothing.

15-12-18   Got taxi to come at 10.30 & took Kaye to Oriel Lodge[171]. Went over it very thoroughly, a ripping house with great possibilities. Afternoon spent wandering round garden with Dai. Clarence Smith in to tea. Same as ever .

16-12-18   Went up at 9.0 a.m. with Peter Smith who called for us in his Humber to see Gibbons. Got back about 10.30 a.m. Gibbons seems

---

[170] Troon club professional from 1887 until 1924.
[171] A. T. Champion's post-war house in Wolverhampton.

a very funny but straight fellow. Kaye & I caught 11.50 G.W.R to London. Got in about 2.50 to Paddington. Went straight to Redbourne. Had dinner at Savoy with Thomas & Elsie Sturridge & two friends of hers - Waters I think, a smashed up fellow - gammy leg & Donald or Dunbar a Yank Naval Officer - very quiet. Waters was very good fun. Went on to the Hippodrome & saw Harry Tate[172] - not a particularly brilliant show for him.

17-12-18   Saw Weno in early morning. She looked very tired & run down. George in bed with flu. Their Christmas visit to Lancaster seemed doubtful. Stopped all morning & found out about Staff train. Lunched at Princes. Pat not there. Went to Kings Cross & met Edith from New Barnet. Tea at Britains after vainly trying to see the Red Cross Pearls[173]. Dinner at Savoy with Thomas - then went to see The Naughty Wife at The Playhouse. Haughtry, Gladys Cooper & Ellis Jeffreys in it. The latter was especially good. Got a very nice Darracq[174] car for the morning.

18-12-18   Caught Staff train at 11.5 a.m. from Charring Cross. Boat left Folkestone about 2 p.m. Very rough crossing many people ill but I did not perform. Got to Boulogne at 4.0 p.m. Spent the night at the Service Officers Club. Talking to a few Middlesex Officers.

19-12-18   Caught 4.45 a.m. train to Calais. Had to cross Calais to Fontainette. Man carried the bag. Caught 8.30 a.m. to Lille. Devons colours travelled by same train. Got to Lille Gare St Andre at about 2.30. Had to cross Lille to Gare Port d'Arras to get to Tournai. Train supposed to go at 1.30 p.m. so I stayed at Officers Club. Actually I heard it went at 1.0 a.m. 20.12.18. Saw Fenn & Giles & had tea with them & then went to see The Cranks, a thoroughly bad show. So we left & they went back to Douai. At Dinner I saw Squire 2nd R.B.s, Humphry an R.G.A. Major he introduced me to & Leslie Henson. Squire had been having French leave.

---

[172] A successful comedian who performed in music halls and in films, well known for his impressions of Dan Leno and George Roby. When the Royal Aircraft Factory R.E.8 biplane was introduced its "R.E.8" designation spoken aloud sounded similar to Tate's name so fliers nicknamed the aeroplane the "Harry Tate".

[173] During the war the Red Cross appealed to the public for pearls to be used to make a necklace which would be sold with the proceeds going to the sick and wounded. A total of 3,597 pearls were donated and made into 41 neckalces which were sold by Christie's after three days viewing. The auction raised £84,383.

[174] A a French motor vehicle manufacturing company founded in 1896 by Alexandre Darracq.

20-12-18   Humphrey & I went up to Pont St André & fetched his luggage. Took it & mine to Port d'Arras & then returned to lunch at the Club. Got lunch about 2 p.m. Train supposed to go at 1.35 p.m. Actually went at 4.30 p.m. Met a Padré from near Seascale at a Church Army Hut. Arrived at Tournai about 7.30. Found Ward's train was there so he had dinner with him. He was Lt Col. DSO Croix de Guerre. Gave us a good dinner sent us on at 9.30 instead of 10.30 by a supply train. Frightfully slow & got us in at 2.30 a.m. to Ath.

21-12-18   Stuart met me & conducted back to mess. Got to bed about 3.30 a.m. Breakfast at 9.30 a.m. Humphrey off to Hal. to join 3rd Corps H.A. Henecker round in morning not favourably impressed. Went out in afternoon on Big Jim. He was fearfully excited & nearly landed us into the canal. Lo..... in to dinner. Bridge after. I won 12 francs.

22-12-18   Sunday so got up late. Grogan & Slade round to see us over the accommodation. Spent whole of the day messing around. Ours & the men's Christmas dinner seemed in jeopardy as nothing had turned up. Hinchcliffe & Bucher in to dinner. Hinchcliffe just off on leave also Carr. Took 15 francs off me.

23-12-18   Got up with a beastly cold. Went round the billets in the morning - pretty tidy but a lot required still to do to them. Afternoon I did nothing owing to rain. After tea went & saw 1/7th. Quite a good show. North came in to dinner after. Lost 10 francs at bridge.

24-12-18   Rode Ginger in morning. Very fresh. Did not stay on him long. Walked round with Church after lunch. Grogan in to see me after tea. Bridge at night. Went round to 'D' Co after dinner & then on to 'A' Co & had a hilarious evening after that. The T.M.B.s & Clayton came in to H.Q. mess & drank & sang. After that a very inebriated band of ours turned up & had more drinks. Finally got to bed at about 2.30 a.m. Saw Major Hammond Liv Scottish. He is O.C. 8th Div. Rec Camp.

25-12-18   Started the day by visiting Brig. & had drinks - then Middlesex & then Devons. Then went round all the company dinners. Snatched a lunch & went down to Transport. Then went & played silly football. 15 a-side. Officers v W.O.s & Srgts & had soccer & rugger got very muddy & after a bath tea. Then the Srgts dinner & then our own. A very good dinner. Much cheering at all the company & Srgts dinners but not any at the Officers. Also no speeches. Church & I went round to the Officer's Café after. Bad place. Got to bed about 11.30 p.m.

26-12-18   Had another holiday & eat the remains of the Xmas dinner up. Gave all H.Q. men servants a day off. So after lunch went round & spent the afternoon with Maxwell. Had tea then found Mumford then came back & wrote some letters & then changed & went back & had a most excellent dinner with him. Went a jolly ride for 2 hours on Big Jim in the morning. Then Australians ran amok at night.

27-12-18   Parades had to be cancelled owing to rain. Spent the morning wandering round the Barracks etc. Afternoon in the mess. Raining. Maxwell & Mumford came to dinner. There was a fire at the station after dinner & a lot of shells blew up. Quite an excitement. Several people damaged. Batt. turned out but did not have to proceed to the station.

28-12-18   Spent the whole of the morning & afternoon writing up the confidential reports on officers. Mortimer & a Belgian officer called Grisard came to lunch. He was at Clifton with Karl. Afternoon spent on working & evening writing letters. Played bridge at night & lost. Also attended a lecture in Y.M.C.A. on Kipling. Poor attendance but General was there.

29-12-18   Walked all morning & went to Church. Afternoon rode over to Maffle & watched a football match v. 55 Bgde RFA. We were 2-0 at half time but had the advantage of wind & slope. Big explosion as I passed the station. Got back to tea. The band turned up. 39 men & boys including Band Master & about 23 instruments. Dinner at Brigade. Church, Ho..... C.O.2 Devons also there. Good dinner & we had quite a good time.

30-12-18   Inspected the band. A Frightfully amusing set of tiny kids! Had a battalion parade which Matthews took & in afternoon went on ride with Maxwell along the canal. Dinner at night Brigadier, Harris, Albermarles R.F.A. Bill Adams & Sharpe came. A most hilarious dinner as the general had much fizz etc & really thoroughly enjoyed himself. Great success.

31-12-18   Rained as usual in the morning. Messed around. Watched football match v Sherwoods. They drew with us but got their last goal about 7 minutes after time. Our goalkeeper was v.g. or they could have beaten us badly. Their C.O. came in to tea also their Yanky D.O.C.

Went out to 'D' Co for dinner. Matthews & Yates to dine at H.Q. mess. Also Thompson & Linley. They were my guests & I had forgotten that I had asked them. Came round to H.Q. mess after & sank the new year in with much gusto. Stuart brought the Midlesex piper in to play & there was liquid flowing round. Harris, Parsloe, Town Major & a few others blew in & we had dancing etc to the piper. A few things smashed but not many. Everyone in great form. They went off to the Devons after & I to bed.

1919

1-1-19 Spent the morning with General on Transport inspection. Went round to Boxing & tried to find the Baths which the Battn were at but failed. Found the M.G. mess & saw Gardner in there. Afternoon went a ride with Maxwell. I on a chestnut very fresh but all was well. Got back for tea. Band played in the afternoon. Went out to M.G.C. to dinner a very poor dinner indeed. Room cold & food likewise. Had bridge & got back about midnight.

2-1-19 Usual stuff in the morning. Wilson brought me Ginger for Batt Parade & I had to give it up & be on foot. Went out on ride with Maxwell after on Big Jim he on Ginger. Had a shower & got in about 3.30. Took him over the Transport lines. Parsloe & Winterton to dinner. Matthews in after.

3-1-19 Matthews & Rogerson on leave. Inspected 'C' & 'D' Companys, very bad. Afternoon spent watching Rugger football. Evening no one to dinner. Clench, Sharpe Stuart & I went to a M.G.C. dance in the theatre. Bad show so got back early. Draft of leave came & I wrote a copious letter to Dai. Bridge with Newton v Fox & Stuart afterwards. General went on leave at the same time as Matthews & Rogerson. He took them in his car.

4-1-19 Most energetic morning. Inspected 'A' & 'B' Cos kits & ran round all the billet including Transport. Afternoon Harris & I were ..... committee for the Div Officers Rugger Team. Harris & Thirlby in to dinner & bridge. A good evening. Had tea at Maxwells.

5-1-19 Church in morning the same padre Andrews M.C. came & preached a fearfully broad winded sermon in plain Khaki & then came to lunch. He knew Sharpe & Stuart. Good fellow. Went a walk with Church in afternoon & watched them put an engine on the line which had come off. Took gramophone to bits after tea. Angel & Garten to dinner & bridge. Hamilton came in .... as he was off home on demobilization.

6-1-19 Had breakfast in old mess & then moved round to new mess. Battalion mess. H.Q. had lunch there & all the officers tea & dinner. Quite successful but the heating was not on & also not enough chairs. Band played & then we had bridge. Stuart & I took 15 francs out of Church & Winterton.

7-1-19 Went down to Transport & Bequiry in morning. Afternoon played football for H.Q. v 'D' Co beat them hollow. Spent evening writing. Saw Maxwell just before he went off on leave. Went to bed very early.

8-1-19 Fine day. Spent morning on Ceremonial parade. Had the colours en cased. Hunter came down to see us & was apparently very pleased. Afternoon went a short walk but had some work to do. Bridge at night. Great night but no band as they had not practised anything new.

9-1-19 Pouring wet day. Church to Brussels. Wandered round Barracks & went down to the Boxing 'A' Co performing. Went a walk with Winterton in the afternoon. His dog had two puppies. Bridge at night. Ambler & I won 20 francs Sharpe & Winterton.

10-1-19 Wandered round all morning. Afternoon went about 14 mile ride. Thompson & a gunner in to tea. M.O. & Padre of the Middlesex came in to dinner. Band played. Did nothing but talk after & early to bed. MGC had a dance but no one from this regiment went.

11-1-19 Had kit inspection in morning. Went round to Brigade but Harris not up from his debauches the night before. Afternoon watched the 2nd R Berks beat us 4-2. Two officers Smith & Capt came to lunch & tea. No one to dinner. Bridge after with Winterton & Fox & Sharpe. Went to transport twice about Ward on classing horses. Board due to arrive at 11.30 came at 4 p.m.

12-1-19 Did not go to church not a full parade. Spent most of the morning at Transport. Played Rugger v a side of Gunners from the Devons all officers & beat them 5-3. A very good game indeed. Had them in to tea after. Bridge after dinner. Church came back from Brussels.

13-1-19 Went wandering all round with Church in morning & inspected 'C' Co. Better than before but not a patch on what they were. Afternoon spent watching Rugger match 8th Div v 7th they had not been beaten & we won 6-3. Some very good play. Fox played very well. Also Squ..... St....., Slack. Bird & Birchall. Ch..... R.E. Major & 2 others to tea. Mess at 7.30 owing to Brigade dance. Went round there for a few minutes & came back with Yates.

14-1-19 Wandered round all morning round barracks & transport & went down & saw Boxing. Summers down there. Prior also. Afternoon nothing doing. Went a stroll with Clench round the place. Bridge at night.

15-1-19   Went up with Stuart & the soccer football team we were going to lorry ..... it into Hal & see the Corps Rugger trial match. ..... playing in it but it was pouring with rain & the lorry was late. We had lunch at the Royal Berks & did not get out till 2.20. So we watched our football match & then went round to East Lancs. After to tea at 25th Brig. Col Green had taken over the East Lancs. Saw him & Isaac. Got back about 6.30. Slade & Horn to dinner. Bridge after with Slade. Horn & the others to a dance by the Field Ambulance.

16-1-19   Wandered round in morning. Watched boxing all afternoon. We won 2 finals. Su..... gave an exhibition. Jolly good show. At night went with Church to the Lilly Whites[175] the East Lancs show. A jolly good show considering they had only been going about 2 months.

17-1-19   Went round in the morning to transport etc. After lunch Winterton had his company photoed. Wandered about all afternoon. At night went with Doc who returned for tea then to Lilywhites also Stuart. Got out just in time to change for mess. Prior, Harris & the East Lancs Oi/c Lilywhites came to mess & also Thirlby. Good show. Band played & Bridge after.

18-1-19   Had rather busy morning rushing round also to baths & transport. Afternoon spent talking to Andrews the S.C. 8th Div. Went to show again at night with Sharpe & Bucher. Band had their photo taken at midday. Quiet mess & bridge after.

19-1-19   Missed church by going to Y.M.C.A. instead of theatre - it was changed & they did not tell Church & I. Went a walk instead. Flag turned up. Andrews to lunch. Just after tea Heggs & Lyons 2nd East Lancashires turned up to see their show so we had them to dinner & bridge after with Frost. Frost & I took 10 francs off them. Between tea & dinner I saw those going off demobilized. R.Q.M.S. Gu.....y, Sergt Newman then Sergt. ..... & about 28 others leaving the next morning early. C.Q.M.S. Purd.....es 'A' Co took on R.Q.M.S. Drivers were amalgamated with Band. Asked G.O.C. to mess on Wednesday. Ellis left demobilized.

---

[175] A white Fluer-de-Lys was the demi-official emblem of 2nd East Lancs, the old 59th, who were accordingly known as 'the Lilywhites'.

20-1-19   Wandered round all morning. G.O.C. went through in his car. Afternoon watched 13 Platoon v Transport final football. 13 Platoon won 3-1. Wrote all evening & bridge after dinner with Matheson who returned with Rogerson from leave against Fox & Winterton. We won. A gunner Colonel from 74th (?) Brig R.F.A. army Brigade came in on his way from Lille to ..... for his horses so I sent him back on Old Jim.

21-1-19   Set off in motor bus with Stuart, Sharpe & Doc & 21 O.R. to see Waterloo. Bus kept on breaking down & we did not get there till 1.45 leaving Ath at 9.15. under 50 kilometers. Had lunch at Browns Hotel. Each had a Veal & Pork chop, beer except M.O. & coffee. Cost 65 francs. Then wandered round & saw nearly all there was to see & got the bus back at 4 p.m. Landed in about 8 p.m. coming right round by Hal. Got out there & got in a lot of fruit for tomorrow's dinner. Wrote after dinner.

22-1-19   Spent the morning being photographed. Battalion with colours, colours by themselves, also the officers. Later the transport & my little chestnut. Afternoon we played M.G.C. & were beaten 8-0. At night we go to a pucka dance. General Henecker & Grogan, Col Prior, Harris & A.D.C. Hon Plunkett to dinner. After Baker & Toye, another Dixon, 2 M.G.C. & 4 came in unofficially rather tight who had to be ejected, 2 from 15th Ambulance & 2 from Australian Ambulance. Very good show indeed. I proposed General Hunter's health & Rogerson General Grogan. Both answered in very good speech. Band played & everyone seemed to thoroughly enjoy themselves. All over at 2 a.m. General Grogan went early - General Henecker went about 12.

23-1-19   Wandered round & did rather a lot of orderly room stuff. Afternoon watched our match v 33rd Brigade R.F.A. beaten 4-1. Afternoon went to a lecture to officers at Devons mess by A.C.G. 5th Army Col. Talbot by name very good indeed lasted 1½ hours. Andrews there. Bridge after dinner with Fox against Stuart & Farnworth won.

24-1-19   Messed about all morning saw Grogan. Afternoon spent signing papers & went a walk with Sharpe. Fox's slip as a Pri.....al or demobilization man came in after tea. Went down to A & D Coys before dinner. Not very popular but warming up. Clayton to dinner. After went to the Australian dance but did not stop a minute. Played Petunia after.

25-1-19   Church went to Court Martial at Enghien & then to Brussels. I got up early & saw draft off. spent morning wandering round with Grogan & signing papers for demobilization. Afternoon watched Basket ball. After tea & dinner played bridge.

26-1-19   Went by car at 9.0 to Brussels horrid snow all the way. Put Grogan & Baker in same car. Got there about 10.45 & went to the Palace to see the show. Had no ticket but pushed my way in. Saw the march past. King Albert - Prince of Wales & Prince Albert there. Saw most of the Division including Henecker. After had lunch at Palace Hotel with others then Church wandered in. Prior & I went off after with Church. Saw first part of performance at the Scala Revue. Then wandered round & saw the sights & went to the Palace for tea - awfully funny show & fearfully crowded. Saw Col Green, Gen Bellsmythe,. Heggs & Lyons there. Also Slade. Left about 6.20 & got back at 7.30 in time to change for dinner. Bridge after dinner.

27-1-19   Church stayed on at Brussels. Spent morning wandering round & down at the Boxing. Afternoon spent in writing & also during evening. Bridge after dinner with Winterton v Church & Sharpe. Had to propose Padrés & ..... health as they were going off next day. Church returned from Brussels.

28-1-19   Morning spent wandering round, boxing hall transport etc. Church closed up the Battalion & the Band boys went into Barracks. Harris in bed with quinzy[176]. Saw funeral in morning. Started to ..... guards on the trains. Went down & saw them in afternoon. Spent evening writing. Church went to Enghien to gunners dance with Blaber. Doc returned. Wrote all the evening.

29-1-19   Inspected Billets in morning. Were to have officers photo taken but snow intervened so had a snowball fight. Afternoon spent playing Shiny or Shinty 7 a side jolly good game. Wrote between tea & dinner. Bridge up till 11.45 with Stuart against Winterton and Frost.

30-1-19   Had haircut in morning. Wandered about most of time. Played shinty again in afternoon. Not such a good game owing to more a side & the ground being much bigger. Went & saw Harris in morning & saw General. Slade back. After mess I went round with Br..... to a dance at the Devons. Did not stay long. Came back with the General. He was in very good form. Just before dinner poor old Douai Coctoo died.

---

[176] Quinsy, a rare and potentially serious complication of tonsillitis.

31-1-19   Felt pretty rotten all day with a cold. Had nothing to do all morning but an officer photograph taken. Afternoon spent in the mess reading. After tea played bridge. After Dinner when Fox was going we toasted him (with speech) had bridge & early to bed as I was feeling so rotten.

1-2-19   Got up early to see Fox off at 8.30 for demobilization. Did nothing all morning. Afternoon went a walk with Clench. Wrote after tea & bridge after dinner. Very cold still.

2-2-19   Got up late. Stayed in all the morning. Went a walk in afternoon with Clench & Hinchcliffe. Wrote letters after tea. Bridge after dinner.

3-2-19   Saw draft off in the morning. Morning spent wandering round. Afternoon played shinty against the sergeants & beat them 8-5. After tea spent at Brigade conference. Talked about demobilization to the Cadre which was expected very shortly. All men for P..... Bal.....s Army were expected to go soon & then which division was moving to Ath. We had to close up & the Northants were coming into the Barracks on Tuesday (6th). Played bridge after mess.

4-2-19   Company Commanders conference in morning about billeting etc. At 11 o'clock Col Prior came to inspect demobilization books. Andrews S..... C..... & Bourdilliers D.A.D.M.S. came to lunch also a corps gunner. After lunch Officers played H.Q. Company & lost 9-6. Officers seemed rather tired. Maxwell & Andrews came in for a drink before lunch. Asked Maxwell & Thirlby to dinner on Wednesday. Went round & had dinner with Maxwell ..... & then went on after playing picquet with him to the Middlesex dance. Saw General & others there & came away with the General about 10.30. Called in at Maxwells on the way back. Asked Blaber to mess on Wednesday night. Heard Hinchcliffe was leaving us.

5-2-19   Saw Slade & General in the morning. Fixed up a cot in the orderly room. Afternoon snowed but we played the Devons Officers at shinty. We had only a bad team out & lost 19-4. Two or three officers of ours were absolute passengers. Wrote after tea. Maxwell & Blaber in to dinner. Also Thirlby who was going next morning. Good dinner & they were great fun. Fairly early to bed as they did not play bridge.

6-2-19   Morning spent wandering about. Afternoon Doc & I went to the Devons & played Badminton. Had a lot of very good games. Afternoon I wrote & then went round to Devons for dinner.

Henecker, Scarlett, Grogan, Plunkett & Slade were all there. They gave an exceptionally good dinner which lasted till 11.15 owing to speeches by Prior, Henecker, Horne & Grogan who gave a wonderful one as usual. Came back with General & Slade about 12 midnight.

7-2-19   Wandered about in morning. Afternoon they played shinty but I gave it a rest. Slade, an Australian Captain & Bucker in to Dinner & bridge with Slade after.

8-2-19   Nothing doing in morning, saw General about Hinchcliffe's ..... book. Afternoon spent playing Badminton with Doc at Australian C.C.S. After tea lecture by McNally on Bolshevism. V. good. He is an Englisised Pole. Layfield Rye left in morning. Clayton to mess with us. After dinner went round to Sergeants dance for half an hour. Beastly cold so did not stay longer. Early to bed.

9-2-19   Got up late & spent morning rearranging the Cadre of the Battalion. After lunch played Shinty against the Devons & they beat us again 8-4. An awfully good game & they were certainly the better side but we gave them a jolly good game. Matthews could not turn out as he was going ..... Clayton played & had not played before but played quite well. We were bad forward. Wrote after tea. Rogerson showed very bad spirit in not playing. Am very disappointed in him. He seems to have gone quite to pieces & is a Bolshevist in the Regiment!! Parsloe back from leave. Middleton sent 300 men to the Army of Occupation.

10-2-19   Spent morning inspecting Devons Demobilization books & watching Belgian funeral. Afternoon I inspected M.G.C.'s books & the Doc & I saw over the old citadel of the village. Parsloe in to tea. Matthews & Hart left the Batt. Wrote after tea. After dinner played bridge with Doc, Farnworth & Newton won 22 francs. Hinchcliffe's last night.

11-2-19   Hinchcliffe left by 9 a.m. train for 2 months leave. Sharpe left on ordinary basis. I went round billets etc, saw 26th Field Amb for demobilization papers. Went round to 2nd Co R.E. but no one in. Blaber & P..... came in before lunch. A Colonel Rudd came into lunch. He was an 1st Army R.A.V.C. & had been directed here on a job that did not exist, had to go on to Tournai. Spent afternoon playing Badminton at the Devons & had tea there. A.D.M.S. came in & told Doc the only way of getting out was to go in the 24th F.A. Cadre so he decided to do that. After tea wrote. After dinner Bridge with Newton v. Farnsworth & Woodward. Won 25 francs.

12-2-19   Spent morning rushing round inspecting the demobilization books of 1st/7th DLIs & 2nd F.Co R.E. Afternoon went a walk with Maxwell & had tea with him. Wrote after tea. Asked Town Major & Blaber in to mess. Was going to play M.G.C. at Shinty but they cried off. wrote after tea. Talked with Blaber & Town Major till 11.45 p.m. Then bed.

13-2-19   Saw draft off including Rogerson & Sergt Cain. Aldwich went as conducting officer & for leave afterwards. Morning spent rushing round & seeing Middlesex demobilization scheme. Spent afternoon with Stuart walking. We saw the Citadel & then went for a walk to the quarry at Maffles & saw Angel, Prior, Garton & the two docs skating. Wrote after tea. After dinner played bridge with Woodward against Doc & Farnworth lost 10 frcs.

14-2-19   Spent morning arranging about ammunition being handed in, with Yates, Stuart & Slade. Afternoon watched soccer match v Worcesters lost to them 5-3. Not too good a game owing to the snow. Wrote after tea. Padré of the Devons came in to dinner & we had bridge after. I & he won 15 francs.

15-2-19   Messed around all morning. Batt at Baths. Met B..... Hill by old ..... now in Worcesters he said he was going to be demobilized shortly. Afternoon spent walking with Maxwell, Padré Hamilton came in & had lunch with us. Saw Blaber after tea. Wrote most of the time. Was going to play Worcesters at Shinty but owing to the thaw I put it off. Wrote after tea & then went round & had dinner with Maxwell. Also went a walk with him in the afternoon. Didn't do anything after dinner but talk. Was a German fellow there too.

16-2-19   Got up at 8.0 to see draft off although it was Sunday but they went off absolutely to time & I was 3 minutes late so I missed them. Got a wire to say a car would call for me to take me to see the Cross Country Corps running at Hal. Called at 11 p.m. Prior, Angel & Garden in it. Took us to D.H.Q. Enghien & then Garden disappeared to lorry ..... it to Hal. We had lunch at A mess with Bourne. Lord Denbigh there. After lunch we went with Bourne to watch the run. Very well organised show but frightfully difficult course. Saw Pat Fraser, ... Miller & Lewis (XI S Lancs) there. First two in 15th Div & Lewis with 74th. 8th Div did rather badly we were about last. From there we all went in to Brussels. Had tea at the Palace. No one there we knew much except one or two Middlesex officers. After tea Garden came in. He & Angel stayed to dinner then Prior & I went to Menniers or some such name near the Opera. Very good & a splendid dinner. He saw two old friends there out of 49th Div. Then we returned to Palace. Met Andrews, Squire & B.....ford an M.G.C. Major. They had been to a soccer match 8th Div v Belgians who beat us 6-0. From there we went to the Gaiety, saw Tautz & Richardson & Micky O'Sullivan there. From there we went back to the Palace & after a few more left about 7.30 a.m. Car went wrong all the way down, punctures etc & we only got in at 5 a.m. after a most strenuous day.

17-2-19   Rushed round all morning. Sent 12 Lorries (Y) away at midday. Afternoon played the Devons at Shinty a most mucky strenuous game. We lost about 8-3. Wrote all after tea. Played bridge after dinner. Doc & I won 6 francs off Farnworth & Daddy.

18-2-19   Messed around all morning. Afternoon the Northants beat us at soccer 6-0. Wrote after tea. Wrote between tea & dinner. Went out to dinner at Brigade. Angel & Stacey there too. Played bridge with Parsloe against Angel & Ho..... & won 3 francs out of them. A very merry evening and a jolly good dinner.

19-2-19   Messed around all morning. Blaber came in & offered to take me to Antwerp. Spent the afternoon getting leave from General & going a walk with Maxwell who came to tea. Saw Prior & Baker got D.S.O. Mathews the bar to his MC. Harris Sta..... & another also got MC. Wrote after tea. Bridge after dinner.

20-2-19   Started off at 9.30 with Aldeston, Maxwell , Blaber & ..... Q.M. Martin to Antwerp. Got to Enghien & messed about there for a bit then went in to Hal & messed about there & then went on to Brussels. Decided to go through straight to Antwerp so we had a sandwich lunch just the other side of Brussels & Riddel past on his way to Hal. Went on & got there by 3.0 p.m. Went strolling round till 7.0 & then had dinner. Jolly good one. Had the best Oyster I have ever tasted. Then went on to the French Opera & heard Lakmé. Jolly good show but not very interesting. We stayed the night at the Y.M.C.A. Quite a good clean but sheets hideous. That & breakfast 5 francs. Town seemed very interesting. Had dinner at Restaurant a Lepage quite near Y.M.C.A. which used to be the Hotel Webus.

21-2-19   Had a very poor breakfast at 9.30 a.m. & then went out in the car & saw the sights, including Cathedral, Hotel de Ville, Church of St Marie. We had a guide for them then we went in & saw the old inquisition House called the Steel[177]. Went back & had lunch at Y.M.C.A. Set off home about 2.30. Got to Brussels for tea & stayed there till 6.0. Saw Pat Fraser, Bill Buily & J. Pristinan O.R. A.E.D. Got back about 8.15 to find Church back. Rang up the General to ask for leave for the ..... & played bridge with Newton v Farnworth & Frost.

22-2-19 Started off at 8.15 to go to see C.C. with Stuart in a Field Ambulance from 25 F.A. Major Mottram. Got to 8 Kilos from Mons & we had had to stop for engine trouble, one puncture & the step..... had broken off & he had no pump. So borrowed a pump after the step..... had broken off again & when the tyre went down again we ..... back. Returned on flat tyre. Got in time for lunch. Wrote all afternoon. After tea went with Church to a show by 12th Div Sig Coy. Very good. Played bridge after dinner.

23-2-19 Messed about all morning. Asked Blaber in to dinner as I heard he was going on Tuesday. Got up late. Wrote all afternoon. After tea went with Church & Blaber to see the Buzzers again. Blaber very struck with the beautiful girl in the show. Everyone said the prettiest in Ath. Of course a boy made up. He was v. good. Show started at 6 p.m. We left at 8.20 p.m. Heard after it stopped at 9.20 p.m. Blaber came to dinner & we opened the last bottle of fizz. Did toasts etc after & he left about 11.30.

24-2-19 Messed around all morning. Doc going on Tuesday with Blaber Afternoon he & I went round & beat the M.G.C. people at Badminton. After that we had tea at their mess & then came in & went to their Amiens show, a very poor effort. Alderson & Blaber had a very good ..... & went to their Sergts Dance after a very good show indeed. Back about 11.30.

25-2-19 Doc & Blaber went off at 9.30. Birchall O.C. D.L.L came to inspect our Demob books in morning. In afternoon went a walk with Maxwell & after tea wrote, after dinner played petunias.

26-2-19 Went round all morning. Borrowed a pierot costume for dance from MGC. Afternoon was going a walk with Maxwell but started to rain so returned. Gorman in to lunch. Maxwell in to tea. Wrote after tea & went to dance at 25th E.A. after dinner. Northants fellow in to

---

[177] Actually Steen Castle, now a visitor centre.

dinner. Stayed at dance about 2 hrs. Good show but very small in numbers. Got back about 10.30 p.m.

27-2-19   Wandered round all morning, saw General, Prior, Harris, etc. After lunch went to a lecture by Alderson on Venereal & then went round to M.G.C. & played pingpong. Wrote after tea. Went round & had dinner with Maxwell & talked all night after.

28-2-19   Wandered round all morning. Church & Stuart to Enghien. Afternoon went a walk with Church all round the railways. Wrote after tea. Had Davies to mess & two Gunners Bains & Randal. Went round to Dance at C.C.S. given by Un Groupe de Dances. Did not stay long. Came back with Stuart & played bridge with Stuart v Newton & Farnworth. Slade came in & rather upset things. Stayed till midnight.

1-3-19   Had haircut & then Church & I beat Angel & Platt at Badminton 4 games to 1. Afternoon we played the Northants at Shinty & beat them 8-5. We were beaten at 6 a side soccer by the D.L.I.s 5-1. Wrote after tea. Bridge after dinner.

2-3-19   Went to Church in morning, Neville Talbot son of Bishop of Winchester A.C.G. 5th Army took sermon. Went round to Maxwell's after. After lunch watched Final Div Cup. D.A.C. beat Northants 2-0. Henecker presented cup & medals after. Sta..... left for Train Guard duty at Dunkirk. Sharpe & Campbell returned from leave. Wrote after tea. Bridge after dinner.

3-3-19   Had a conference at 9.30 to decide what the Batt wanted doing with canteen profits. Five men, three Sergts & 2 officers. All decided to divide it & put it to charity in the Regiment. G.O.C. had a conference of C.O.s at 10.30 to talk about the same thing. They had had a committee who decided to hand it over to C.O.s for their use but G.O.C. disagreed so he ruled we must put it to our old comrades society. Also talked about an 8th Div yearly dinner. That lasted till about 12.0. In afternoon I went up with Church to Enghien & saw Isaac & the R Berks. They were just sending their Army of Occupation draft so I saw them off & then went to their mess. After that went round & had tea with B....., Church & Mitchel. Henecker turned up later. Returned about 5.30. Fidler & Ch..... Woods to tea & dinner. They were going with the draft. Bridge after dinner. Went round & talked to Maxwell after tea. He could not come to dinner on Tuesday.

4-3-19   Wandered round all morning. Rained hard most of the day. Afternoon spent going over to Maffles to watch 6 a side football v R.Es. We won 5-1 but Church & I turned up late for the show. Wrote after tea. Alderson & Parsloe to dinner, good dinner with champagne etc. They stayed & played bridge till about 1 o'clock. They thoroughly enjoyed it.

5-3-19   Wandered round all morning. Got various documents from Ministry of Labour including 215a. Afternoon watched a match v the Middlesex. They turned out an officer team. We won easily. Wrote after tea. After dinner went round to Devons Dance. Stayed about 20 minutes & then came away & went & talked to Maxwell. Bed early.

6-3-19   Spent morning wandering round. Afternoon went & watched 24 Brig officers beat 23rd Brig at soccer & then went a walk with Church. Wrote after tea. Angel rang up to say he was very unfit & could not come to dinner. Garten came in his place. Grogan, Prior, Harris & Garten came. Prior & I played Grogan & Church & took 10 francs off them. Garten played in another four. They went at about 11.15 p.m. Talked to Garten for a bit after & got to bed about 1 a.m.

7-3-19   Wandered round all morning. General said farewell to 25 men going to R.O.D. Ardricq from Army of Occupation. I then went up by ambulance to Enghien to see Officers Rugger match v Aust Heavy Brig Art. Had lunch at R Berks with Isaac & Richardson & went onto Hal after. No match as Australians failed to turn up. Had tea & returned for dinner. Cross was playing also Slade & Padré. Bridge after dinner. Two men escaped from our Guard room.

8-3-19   Wandered round & went in to see Maxwell in morning. Church in Court Martial. The C.M. officer & Reynolds in to lunch. Also a fellow Davies A.D.I. to General Daly G.O.C. 25th Div. Watched soccer 6 a side after. 25th F.A. beat us 2-0. Spent afternoon writing & bridge after dinner.

9-3-19   Did not go to church. Went round & saw Maxwell. After lunch walk with Church. Spent from tea to dinner playing bridge with Ambler against Farnworth & Newton. Harris & Slade came to dinner. Harris ..... his demobilization on Tuesday, with a hilarious evening. I did not get any writing done or to bed till about 1 a.m.

10-3-19   Padré gave us a lift in a car to see the football match. Sharpe came too. We got to Brussels about 1.0 & then had a not good lunch. Saw

Green & Reynolds there at Mourain's. went up & saw the match. Saw old Kentish there. M.G.C. v 165 Brig R.F.A. they drew after playing 10 min extra each way. We then came straight back bringing Green with us, dropped him at Enghien & picked up some canteen stores & an A.S.C. waller. Got in about 7.0. I dined at 'B' mess with Prior & the others. Took 24 francs out of Padré & Prior with D.A.D.M. Simeon rather an ass. Got away about 12.

11-3-19   Went up in morning with the players to Rugby match. Had lunch with Small at 'A' mess & then on to Hal. 8th Div playing 30th. Green..... & an interpreter were playing. I knew no one else. 8th won 6-0. Squa..... & Wallace were both crocked but Slade, Brown & P..... played very well. Had tea with the team & returned by ambulance about 4.30. Sharpe & I went to M.G.C.s to dinner, they played ..... but I did not compete. Plenty of drink but not a very good dinner seemed cold. Padré Andrews, Prior, Franklin, his C.O.2 & Parmiter to dinner. Got back about 12.0.

12-3-19   Messed around all morning as Padré was going to take me to see match M.G.C. v Gunners again but he could not get a car so we did not go. Went a match in afternoon with Church & Sharpe. Wrote after tea. Changed my billet from old mess to new mess. Maxwell & Cross to dinner. They went fairly early. Gunners beat M.G.C. 3-1.

13-3-19   Henecker came to say goodbye to all officers of Area as he was off to command the Southern division of the Rhine. Wandered round all morning. Afternoon I was going out to watch match v Middlesex when I met Hamilton, P..... & McLoughlin also Alderman who said he was off to see an old Chateau with some sisters would I care to go. So I went there & came to an old chateau happened to be the second in Belgium owned by Prince de Ligue at Briociel. Gardens were supposed to be a copy of Versaille. Chateau very grand & lovely tapestries & pictures & very gaudy but not much of a place really. On returning had tea at C.C.S. with Martin Sandbach & 5 sisters. Got back to find Padré could not come owing to being ill to dinner so asked Horn. He & Davies came & we played bridge with Church losing 15 francs.

14-3-19   General Grogan said farewell to a few men at 11 o'clock & then Church & I went to 24th F.A. & had a scrap lunch & then went up in 2 ambulances to Ghent. Party consisted of Alderson, two Padrés, the nurses, McLoughlin & another doc. Ryan got there about 2.30 p.m. & looked round. Saw the Belfry, Cathedral and an old Castle. Had tea at

La Porte cost us 96 francs & got back about 9.0. A very good day & very interesting. Funny old town but we did not have half time to see at all. A good run only the roads were bad.

15-3-19   General saw some more men off. Played hockey in afternoon. 23rd Brig v 24th. The 23rd team was made up of Devons & Newton & self. Prior & Tricket were playing. We won very easily 18-1. Wrote after tea & bridge after dinner. Stuart & I lost to Sharpe & Newton.

16-3-19   Sunday got up as usual to see men off on demobilization. Wandered round & worked in morning. Afternoon went a walk with Church. Had tea at the C.C.S. with Martin Sandbach & the Sisters. Stuart came too. Wrote after tea. 2Lt Strange from Berks came in as 25th Brig were coming in tomorrow to billet. He & his men attached themselves to us. He had mess with us & then we played bridge. He & I lost to Church & Sharpe.

17-3-19   25th Brig came in in the morning. I wandered round all morning & then Green & Reynolds came to lunch. Had a short walk before tea. Wrote after tea. Maxwell heard he could be demobilized tomorrow so I went & had dinner with him. Alderson was there. We stayed & talked till about 11.0 & then went back together.

18-3-19   Nothing doing all morning. Owing to other Battalions coming in a huge squash all over the place. Played shinty in the afternoon Middlesex 2 Northants 2 & ..... 3 played Devons they won 6-1. Jolly good game. Wrote after tea. Had a dance after dinner. A very good show nearly everyone turned up but lots of men were late. I held a party in my room & Slade & I played picquet. Ended about 2.30 a.m.

19-3-19   Up at 8.30 to see draft of demobilized. Sergt Thompson the duty room sergt went. Wandered round all morning, afternoon went a walk with Church. Wrote in evening. Nothing doing all day. Had dinner at Alderson's. Franklin there. Jolly dinner then went round to M.G.C.'s dance. Rag time show was on there - rather a bad show. Announcement of an engagement between an M.G.C. officer & a Belgique. Came away with Alderson about 2.30 a.m. Heard from Gray we are sending 160 men away to P. of W. camps.

20-3-19   Spent morning working out draft for P of W camps Dieppe & Cherbourg. Beastly wet day. Church & I had a very short stroll round rubber necking. Spent after tea writing. Colonel Green, Reynolds, a Northants officer & the Padré at 26th F.A. came to dinner. We had a mess night. Green & I played Reynolds & Church & won ? Got to bed about 12.0.

21-3-19   Messed around all morning. Church went off for two days tour. Watched ..... of Ath officers beat 24th Brig at soccer. Padré in to tea as he was off on Sunday to Northern Div Rhine old 3rd Division. Deveril. Heard Bourne was also off to G.S.O. II 3rd Corps. Angel to Henecker's div the Southern Div. M.G.C.s draft off 22nd. Remainder home on 26th. R..... Berks & RBs off on 25th. Bridge after dinner for a short time. Went round after tea & saw Isaac & Richardson. They told me the Belgians were going to have a revolution as soon as we left the country & guaranteed a republique by Nov 11th.

22-3-19   Wandered around in the morning & also went to the Hospital & saw Alderson & the docs & nurses. Afternoon a walk with Sharpe. Wrote after tea. Tautz & Parsloe came to dinner. Davis & Goodman were coming but put it off & I asked Tautz instead. We played bridge. Tuckett came too so we cut in & Tuckett & I played Ambler & Farnworth & took 20 francs out of them. Parsloe got rather merry & ended by singing lustily all sorts of songs & Yeodling. Got to bed about 12.30 a.m. All leave etc stopped owing to strike of Railways in England.

23-3-19   Messed round all morning. Ssaw Angel, Garden, Green & Prior. Asked Rollo for a car for Tuesday for Green & I to go off a few days jaunt. He would not provide. In afternoon played shinty. mixed side v Devons lost badly. T. M. Ward supposed to leave. Wrote after tea. Quiet mess. Church returned & we had a game of bridge. Early to bed. Padre Andrews came in early & said goodbye finally as he was off at 7 a.m. tomorrow.

24-3-19   Messed round in the morning, General said goodbye to some men at 11 o'clock & then came & said goodbye to the officers of the Regiment at 12.45. After lunch was going a walk with Church but went in & saw Alderson & he played pingpong & then went over the chain factory of Mr Canbin. Church went & wrote some letters. Had tea then & they gave us an awful non price 1½ with ..... tax! Got back about 6 p.m. Played bridge after dinner. Bed about 11 p.m.

25-3-19   Got up at 6.45 to see General Grogan off. He left by car & I went back to bed again. Messed around all morning & got wire to say draft for Cherbourg left next morning. Afternoon shinty pick up game. Many sticks got broken so many last game. Went round & played bridge with Alderson, Church & Sharpe after tea. Isaac, Prior & Richardson in to mess. Richardson & I took 11 francs out of the other two.

26-3-19   Newton, Farnworth & Campbell left with draft of 80 for Cherbourg at 7 a.m. Went to see them off. Band turned out. Spent morning wandering round, also afternoon. M.G.C. cadre & Rhine personnel went off during the day. Went & had tea at the mess. Most of them out. Alderson came too & returned & played bridge. He & I won 1 franc from Frost & Ambler. Went out to dine at Worcesters. General Livsey, Prior, Eastwood & Gray there. They had Franklin Pelly Adj. Parker & Padré. Exceptionally good dinner & wine. Bridge after. Eastwood & I v Franklin & Prior - no score. Back about 2 a.m.

27-3-19   Messed round in morning. Spent most of it at Berks. Afternoon I spent at C.C.S. Had tea with General L.....ont, Major Maxwell R.F.A. Alderson & Doc M.....y. Wrote after tea. Church & I took 10 francs out of M.....y & Alderson. Went to R Berks for dinner. Very good dinner. Eastwood was there & he & I lost 5 francs to Richardson & Isaac. Left there about 12 and went round to Devons as it was probably Prior's last night. Church, Sharpe & Slade to dinner there. They had all gone but I stayed till about 2.30 a.m.

28-3-19   Messed around all morning. Saw Green & he suggested we tour to Ghent etc for Monday. Afternoon went with Alderson to Frelinghem for shell cases. Church to Lille. Saw Livsey in the morning. Wrote after tea. Saw Colonel Green about Ghent etc. Had no one in to dinner though there were two subalterns Worcesters & Northants in. Bridge & early to bed.

29-3-19   Snowing hard when I got up. Col Green in to see me about Bruges etc. Went on st..... with Church in afternoon. Nothing doing all day. Wrote after tea. Bridge after dinner.

30-3-19   Did nothing all day. Wandered round in morning with Church. Stayed in room & read all afternoon. Westre at night & played bridge after. Went & saw Green but nothing heard of the car.

31-3-19   Saw Green in morning & we chased round and finally found Rollo. Got a car from him at 10.30 to go as far as Ghent. Green, Hinde & myself. Got there for lunch at 1 o'clock. Spent afternoon seeing Cathedral & other places of interest. Spent night there at De La Porte Hotel. Quite a good one.

1-4-19   Left Ghent by the 10.20 train & got in to Bruges about 11.15. Had lunch & put up at the Flanders Hotel. Not a good hotel turned out after a very bad one. No change in menu & dirty & noisy. Went in afternoon to Zeebrugge by tram, & steam train to Heyst. A good walk along the front. The canal was quite blocked & the work was very badly blown up but there were no signs of fighting in the way of bullet holes or splashes. Bosch had made a terrific lot concrete places. Just caught a steam train back & got in for dinner. Bosch not done much damage except to Railway station & round that on the line.

2-4-19   Wandered about all morning. Very little to see but the Belfry about 370 ft high & a very interesting huge mechanical music box to work the 50 bells. Afternoon went to Ostend. Front slightly damaged but not much. Old Vindicator there but pulled to one side other two boats were miles out of it. Not much shell fire damage & nothing blown up much though they had sunk a few boats in the harbour. Got back for dinner.

3-4-19   Caught the 12.40 to Brussels. Wandered round in morning. Got in about 4.15. Stayed at the Metropole not very comfortable. Dinner at Monnais. Good dinner. No bathroom at our disposal.

4-4-19   Wandered about in morning & caught 12.20 back to Ath. Got in at 2.10. Spent afternoon at Hospital playing bridge with Alderson. Tea with nurses. Wrote all evening. Got news of Louisa's chill. Bridge after dinner with Slade, Sharpe & Stuart. Found Ambler & Fawcett had gone in my absence.

5-4-19   Messed around all morning in Barracks etc. Gray went. Afternoon had a walk with Isaac & tea then. wrote after tea. Temporary Lt Col came through. Bridge at night. Won a few francs off Sharpe & Stuart playing with Frost.

6-4-19   Stayed in all morning and played with mess accounts. Green came round & fixed Tuesday for Antwerp. Afternoon I went with Slade to Leopold Club Brussels & watched England v Belgium at soccer. We won 4-2 a very good match indeed. Got back about 6.45. Wrote & then went to bed soon after dinner & read. Church returned & the piece of plate for Madame from the officers arrived very nice indeed.

7-4-19   Nothing doing all day. Went a walk with Church morning & afternoon. Band played at C.C.S. so Sharpe & I went to tea there & played rings after. Then went round & saw Livsey & asked to go to

Antwerp. All OK. Bridge after dinner. Clayton left for demobilization.

8-4-19   Caught 8.30 train to Brussels. Lunch at Lamonage. Caught 1.0 train to Antwerp. Quite a comfortable train with loose seats. Got there about 2.30. Went to Y.M.C.A. Gave us an awful room, two beds, no other furniture in the annexe. Tried Hotel de Londres but no good. Then went & saw the Steen, walked back to tea at a place in Place de Lys. Afternoon walk to canteen - it had moved so we had rather a long walk. Dinner at Laplage. Walk after through the Park. Many couples there. Party consisted of Col Green & myself & our two servants.

9-4-19   Breakfast at Y.M.C.A. Saw in morning the Cathedral, Town Hall & Church of St Paul. Then walked along the docks & back by the Palais de Justice. Lunch at Laplage. Afternoon we saw Musee & ..... Plantin only a bit of the latter. Tea at same place & then a walk & saw the Zoo. Changed rooms at Y.M.C.A. & got good ones. Dinner at Laplage. Too tired for a walk after so to bed after playing billiards for a bit in Y.M.C.A.

10-4-19   Breakfast at Y.M.C.A. Saw rest of the Musee Plantin, bought an old brass or an imitation of same. Lunch at Laplage & just caught 2.0 to Brussels. YMCA would not give Green's servant his coat as he had not paid his bill for both. Got to Brussels about 3.15. Tea at Palace. Caught 5.25 from Gare de Midi to Ath. Saw General La..... there. Got in for dinner & bridge after.

11-4-19   Spent morning wandering round & writing. Saw Isaac & arranged to go a walk in afternoon. 8th West Yorkshire Cadre turned up. Major Brooke, Captains & Arrived about 6 a.m. Q.M. & C.O. coming on next day. Went a walk in afternoon with Isaac round Bosch Bombing School. Had tea with him. Got news after tea we were leaving here on the 15th.
on the 14th 2 F. Co. R.E.
on the 15th Ourselves Devons & Middlesex
on the 16th Northants & Worcesters
Also we were going to York. Stevenson Adjutant for Worcesters came to dinner & played bridge after.

12-4-19   Raining hard in morning. Spent the whole day messing round writing & packing. Church went off in the morning to England. Our move cancelled but only temporarily. Played bridge after dinner.

13-4-19   Messed around in the morning packing. Afternoon went on & saw Alderson. Watched him play pingpong he & padre both awfully good. Then went to tea at Hospital. Nearly everyone there. Stayed with him and talked to the matron till 7.30. Franklin, Walker & Stevenson to dinner. Bridge after till 1.15 a.m. Good evening. Orders changed to all 5 cadres of ..... & 2 R.E. cadres on one train midday 16th.

    8th W York took over from us.
    1st Leicester "   "   " Northants
    4th Worcesters " "   " 1st Worcesters
    1st Herefords "   "   " Devons
    1st London Scottish   " Middlesex

14-4-19   Messed round in morning. Inspected the Cadre & Band. Afternoon played bingo & bridge at Hospital, first with Alderson, McLean & Harris before lunch. Started to rain so we gave it up. After lunch bridge with two sisters. Tea there & back to write after tea. Green came in & said a goodbye. Had dinner at Worcesters. Frost there - had a final turn. Very funny everyone had laughing fit. Got back about 1 a.m.

15-4-19   Went round to Bules in morning & messed around. Afternoon at Alderson's. Played 3 handed bridge & won. Tea then after tea went to C.C.S. & then picked up a lot of things. Dinner at own mess & then went round & played Pingpong up J..... etc at C.C.S. Returned about 12.30 a.m. Col Greene on leave.

SECOND BATTALION WEST YORKSHIRE REGIMENT.

INSTRUCTIONS FOR CADRE.

REDUCTION TO CADRE:- (C.R.O. 6582) to be notified to Command Paymaster
BASE.

SUSPENDED SENTENCES. (A.R.R. part 1. para 959. II)
If the unexpired portion of the sentence exceeds
28 DAYS the offender is to be posted to another unit, of the
same record office.
If under 28 DAYS to proceed home with cadre and sentence will
be remitted on day of dispersal in part II orders and Soldiers'
papers. I - "........days remitted under R.R. para 959."

DESCRIPTIVE ROLLS. (para 1105 I, c and d.)
To be rendered in triplicate. One copy to
Secretary XX War Office, M.R.
one copy to H.Q Command direct
and one copy to O.C. Records.

CLEARANCE CERTIFICATE FOR COMMANDING OFFICER (A.F. Z.42)
(para 1105 III- 606 -c. - 1730 - 1734)
To be signed by the officer to whom he hands over or
by his immediate superior officer.

A.F.B.213 - (para 1113)
To be rendered while with the R.E.

NOMINAL ROLLS- A.F.Z.9. (para 1114)
On receipt of movement orders, to be prepared in
triplicate. Two copies to Embarkation Staff and one
retained.
NOMINAL ROLLS TO D.E.A.C.(O.R.O. 6543)
At least 6 days before embarkation.

CLEARANCE CERTIFICATES - A.F. Z.42. (para 1175)
All officers must have these completed before
embarkation.

ALLOWANCE CLAIMS. (para 1176 II)
Made up to and for date of embarkation. To Command
paymaster, Base.
(Also see para 1704)

ALLOWANCE CERTIFICATE - A.F. Z.41 (para 1176 II)
All officers to be in possession of these.

CERTIFICATE OF HANDING OVER. (para 1604 V)
Certificate to H.Q. via Bde etc. that he has correctly
handed over all surplus stores either to another Unit or
to A.O.D.

IMPREST ACCOUNT. (para XXX 1714)
Take to Base or Field cashier with
i.   The original vouchers (if any) connected with the
     account.
ii. The last statement received from the Clearing House.
iii. Duplicate Remittance rolls for 6 months.
iv. Cash balance (if any).
v.   A.F. W.3100 for 3 months.
vi. Clearance certificate for signature.
ANIMAL
CLOSING OF ANIMAL ACCOUNT. (A.R.I. Chapter XIX para 82 to 84)
Close current account and forward it to Financial Adviser
as soon before embarkation as possible.
CENSOR STAMPS (C.R.O. 6582)
To officer i/c publication Dept, A.P. & S.S. BOULOGNE.
before embarkation.

Orderly Room keep care off of Infbattln H.Q. date & name of Embarkation Camp for O.R.S
to join Cadre. - - - - - - - - - - -

16-4-19 Had a lot of work arranging for move all morning. Afternoon the same. Had tea at 1.15 & 2.0. Left there 4.30. Parade 4.45. Band to play us down. Train left at 6.0 only cattle trucks provided. Officers in them we had to share ours with Worcesters. At first they arranged 3 cadres officers in one truck. Had that altered. Train left at 6.0. Everyone down to see us off bar Livsey. Matron & Alderson turned up at last minute. Special train to take 7 cadres.

2 Devons		Captain
2 W Yorks	\ 23 Brig	Self
2 Middlesex	/	Baker
1 Worcesters	\ 24 Brig	Franklin
2 Northants	/	Haynes
2 F. Co R.E.		

Haynes in charge. Bands of RB Berks East Lancs & Northants to play us off.

17-4-19 Arrived Dunkirk about 12.30. No one heard of our arrival. Heard all were to have bath & clean clothes (deloused) Then to No 2 camp. Franklin & I walked over & saw about it. No accommodation for officers so went to Brigade (78) found Taylor (late of Worcesters & 24th Brig) was Brig Major so got all fixed up. Officers less C.O.s in No 3 Camp. Got in late & had tea & dinner there. Bed about 12.

18-4-19 Lounged about all day. Read in bed in afternoon. Evening at 6.0 Taylor Brig Major took Franklin & self down & car & met Sharpe, Yates & Stevenson. Later ..... had dinner at Arcardian Hotel. Back by 9.30 by car. Early to bed.

19-4-19 Taylor took Franklin & self down to docks in car. Cadres paraded 9.45. Boat left at 12.0 the Autumn. Had quite ..... of a crossing & got to Dover at 2.30. Goat of Worcesters got free at Dover & then they refused to let it go further. Train for Town at 5.50. Cadres split up then. We were to go to Chipenham not York stay over Sunday in Town. Got to Town at 8.0. Awful trouble about luggage. I billeted at Savoy, men in Great Peter St., Officers at Eaton Square. I got in about 10.0. Supper & bed. Had a suite in Savoy Court. Had to take luggage to Marylebone. Frost, Yates & Aldwich saw it in. Sharpe could not come as ..... account not O.K. Left him at Dunkirk. They got luggage across by 12.0 p.m. Yates went off to his people at Watford.

20-4-19   Frost & Aldwich came round at 10.30 for orders. Aldwich then went off to his people. So Frost & I wandered round trying to get money. He got £5 at ..... I failed no one in town. Got on to Blaber at Princes where we had lunch. He said he would dine & after gave in & said urgent call to Taplow! Wandered round all afternoon. Tea at Cu..... dinner at Picadilly Grill.

21-4-19   Left by train to Marylebone & caught 8.45 north. Frost, Yates Aldwich & every one of the men including the men we left sick at Dunkirk & also Sgt Batty from Ban. Got to Cl..... at 12.45. Met by Hinchcliffe & the Brigadier. Changed at Nottingham only. Room in camp & we all went off that afternoon on leave till Monday. Yates & I caught train to Manchester changing at Worksop. Got in there about 6.45. Had dinner at an awful place & I caught 9.5 to Lancaster got in about 11.0. Phoned from County then walked up found they had all gone to bed. Left my luggage & Cocko to be sent up next day.

22-4-19   Went down to Town. Mr Sharpe gave me a lift out to golf. Played with him after lunch at club v. Downes & Jerry Sharpe. Beat them easily & gave them nothing. After I played .....ball of Warlick & Mr Malcolm gave them 1 up in 9 holes & won. Then 6 holes & won again.

23-4-19   Caught 11.55 to Silverdale. Stayed the night. Mabel there.

24-4-19   Saw A..... Caught 1.55 to Lancaster. Kaye met me. Tea at Holmes.

25-4-19   Messed about in morning. Took car to lunch & golf. Picked Frank Storey up at his office & went out to golf. Lunch at Club. Jerry & I played Sam & Mr Storey & gave them 3 holes & we won 1 up. Then had 9 holes & they were bye & we bye bye. Dinner 6.45. Then all went off to Victory Ball. Holmes all there & Eric White. Came away about 1 a.m.

26-4-19   Went down town for show full up so came back. Got up at 10.30. No water. Shaved & rushed off & picked Mr Malcolm up. Lunch at Club. Palmer & I played Turner & Mr Malcom after tea. Before Edward Storey & I played Mr Malcolm & Storey gave them 4 up & had them 2 up. Billiards.

27-4-19   Nothing in morning. Went over in car with Kaye & Louisa & saw Egerton & Gladys. Afternoon played golf. Oglethorpe & I v Malcolm

& Hall. Beat them giving them 4 up. Lost the next nime. Played 11th in snow storm.

28-4-19   Caught 7.45 from Midland to Nottingham. Met Edwards there & had lunch. Got to Cl..... about 4.0.

29-4-19   Half the men, Frost & Aldwich, Demobbed. Sharpe returned in afternoon.

30-4-19   Await board in morning. All square. Left by 12.2. train. Met Edwards at Nottingham. Gave him lunch. Caught train on to Birmingham had to change at Derby. Got 4.5 to Wolverhampton. Clond..... met me.

1-5-19   Hilda went off to London in morning. I spent time going over Oriel Lodge. Afternoon played a round with Dai. Gave him a half - played badly, he well & won 1 up.

2-5-19   Went over to Tipton in morning. Saw Miss Cole, chose door furniture & a grate for dining room. Lunch then caught 1.40 back. Peter Smith met me - went to Efandem & had a talk, he ran me up to Ash Hill. Wrote in afternoon.

3-5-19   Dai & I went to Golf - gave him a half played shockingly & halved. Lunch at Ash Hill. Hilda returned & we went up to station picked up Miss Cole & went on to Oriel Lodge. Met a gardener there & fixed it all up. Got back, calling by Trinity to see lecture given by Sam Bayliss.

4-5-19   Went to Kirk. Quarter of an hours extra sermon consecrating lectern. Wrote afternoon & then we three went over to Oriel by car. Tea at Johnson's - saw grandniece & Min & Charley Wright.

5-5-19   Over to Oriel Lodge in morning. Caught 11.30 to Lancaster for tea.

6-5-29   Messed round all day.

7-5-19   Caught 11 train to Glasgow. Changed Carlisle. Lunch & got to Glasgow about 4.30. Caught 5.0 to Troon. Got in about 6.9. Mrs T met me.

8-5-19   Golf with Turner v Hood & Mr T. Lost. Rained afternoon so only had a few holes. Bridge after with Findley. Mrs T from Glasgow.

9-5-19   Findley & self lost to Hood & Mr T. morning. Afternoon Townsend & self beat Hood & Mr T. Bridge after.

10-5-19   Stuart & self lost to Mr T & George Law. Single v Mr T afternoon.

11-5-19   Stayed in all morning. Tea with Mr & Mrs Allan Mrs & Miss Dumpy ....

12-5-19   Ron & self beat Mr T & George Law 3&2. I did about 79. Motored to Kilmarnock caught 5.15 to Carlisle. Carnforth 9.40. Kaye met me in motor. Lancaster about 10.30.

13-5-19   Did nothing all day.

14-5-19   Went to Golf after lunch. Played Sam 15 holes long course beat him 1 up giving him 2 lives. Played 9 holes 3 ball v Wolstenholme & Oglethorpe & lost. Mr Malcolm joined in next 9 & we beat them. Kaye & Thomas & us two went to Opera The Bohemian Girl. Fairly good.

15-5-19   Mrs M returned in evening. Did nothing but go down town.

16-5-19   Kaye & I started at 10.12 to motor to Wolv. Lunched at Aunty Edie's at 1.0. Set out at 1.45 & arrived at 5.15 at Oriel having a puncture just before Warrington. Looked round for an hour & then on to Ash Hill for dinner.

17-5-19   Caught 8.40 to Birmingham. Miss Cole met us at Tipton & we went to Chamberlain & King & Jones[178] & bought £520 of furniture. Got back after lunching at L.N.W.R. Birmingham by 2.45. Tennis all afternoon & evening with Dai & Hilda, Mr & Mrs Richards, Mr & Mrs Thomas & Mr Allen & Jack. Very good tennis.

18-5-19   Went to Oriel Lodge in morning. Set off at 1.45 to Lancaster tea at Warrington at Uncle OE's at 5.0. Left at 5.30 & got in at 7.45. No puncture but petrol tap turned off by mistake.

19-5-19   Nothing all day but go down town & tear up letters.

---

[178] A large and prestigious company established in 1851; cabinet makers, carpet factors, upholsterers and decorators.

20-5-19   Game with Sam. 13 holes gave him 2 ..... & beat him 3 & 2. Mrs Malcolm & F Storey came down. Wrote afternoon.

21-5-19   My birthday. Caught 10.37 train to Wolverhampton with Kaye. Johnsons first van of luggage arrived at Oriel Lodge.

22-5-19   Went over to Oriel Lodge.

23-5-19   Carpets arrived at Oriel Lodge.

24-5-19   Moffat arrived by 2.50 train at Oriel. Got them in & back to tennis at Ash Hill.

25-5-19   Caught 1.36 train to Lancaster. Got in 6.7. Changed at Stafford & Warrington. Went up to see Mrs R Holmes.

26-5-19   Rushed round Lancaster.

27-5-19   Set off en famille to Wolverhampton. Rosalind & I in Belsize. Got to Warrington 12.30. Left 10.15 others got in at 1.0. Lunch at Lion Hotel. Left at 2.0 & got to Wolv. 4.45. others at 5.30. Hilda met us. Second car had Kaye 2 infants Kevin & Sarah. Beds & furniture for bedroom just arrived.

28-5-19   More furniture from Chamberlain King & Jones. Also another van from Johnsons. Also Hilda's stuff.

29-5-19   Worked all day.

30-5-19   More from Chamberlain King & Jones All but 2 chest of drawers & 2 chairs. Saw Will Lyle at Ash Hill.

31-5-19   Men finished inside. Hilda Dai & Jack Lyle to Church Stretton.

1-6-19   Stayed in & worked all day.

2-6-19   Started at Efandem. After 5.0 went over & had some tennis & dinner at Ash Hill.

3-6-19   At work & working in Wolverhampton.

4-6-19   At work & hard at it after 5. Putting up curtain rods.

5-6-19   At work, curtain rods till 7.0. Hilda & Dai to dinner.

6-6-19   At work. Hard at it after returning.

7-6-19   At work. All went over at 3.0 to Ash Hill for tennis. Couldn't play at all afternoon, no excuse as everything OK. Mr & Mrs Howell & McAllum to tennis. We three stayed to dinner.

8-6-19   Kaye & Rosalind went to Kirk. I stayed in & did a lot of work.

9-6-19   Went over to Dai in morning his Birthday. Worked all rest of day wheeling rubbish away.

10-6-19   Work all day in Works.

11-6-19   Work at Efandem in morning. Half a day off owing to hands wanting it. Went in afternoon to see Peter. Hilda & her servants to tea. Saw Charley Wright.

12-6-19   Kaye & Rosalind to Birmingham all day. I saw Taulius in morning. He promised personal attention. Met them at 5.19. C. K. & J. delivered lots of goods.

13-6-19   Work all day. Works in evening. Saw Gibbons.

14-6-19   Work in morning. Sir Archibald Gould, Mr Brown of Brown B..... & Mincham & S..... came down. Showed Sir Archibald round works. Very good fellow. After lunch ..... a bit. Ash Hill at 3.0. Had very good tennis indeed stayed supper. Jack, Charlie & Mrs Wright two Allen brothers & Miss Swift there. Back at 10.30 p.m. Demobbed.

15-6-19   Did not go to church. Worked all day.

16-6-19   Worked all day. Went to concert at 7.30. Hilda & Jack there. At Grand Theatre by Wolv. Orchestra & Choral Societies. Quite good. Norman Allin sang, sea solos - very good.

17-6-19   Worked all day. Lunch late. Had a row with Rosalind & Kaye. Kaye upset over it.

18-6-19   Worked all day. Not recovered from Row - every one very d.....y.

19-6-19   We had all day & evening. Harold arrived to take Belsize ..... Karl landed at Southampton.

20-6-19   Sarah, Rosalind & Harold all went. Sarah in morning by train other two by Belize in afternoon.

21-6-19   Hilda & Dai went in their motor. Run to S Wales & Devon. We went in afternoon to Charles Wright & played Tennis hard till 7.50. Allen, Theo & a Mr Graham there. Jolly good tennis. Got notification from W O I could be demobbed.

22-6-19   Jack came in morning & stayed the day. Got papers from demobbing centre (Sloane Square). Fetched Miss Cole from station 3 3. & took her back at 7.10. Just caught train owing to petrol giving out. Went after Jack left.

23-6-19   Received papers saying I was demobbed on 14 Jun 1919.

"Every noble life leaves the film of it interwoven for ever in the work of the world"

Addendum

GD2051 60,000 3/19 HWV(P) H3163

Any further communication on this
subject should be addressed to—

The Secretary,
    War Office,
        Whitehall, S.W.1,
and the following number quoted.

Telephone: Victoria 9400.

WAR OFFICE,

WHITEHALL, S.W.1,

14ᵗʰ *October,* 1920.

Nº 31161/8. (M.S. 4. K. 3).

SIR,

    I am commanded by the Army Council to inform you that in consequence of the demobilization of the Army, a notification will be published in the *London Gazette* at an early date, to the effect that you relinquish your commission on completion of service.

    You will ~~retain~~ be granted the rank of *Lieut-Colonel* but such grant does not confer the right to wear uniform, except on ~~~~ *appropriate* occasions of a military nature. ~~~~

    I am to take this opportunity of conveying the thanks of the Army Council for your services during the late war, and for having done all in your power to assist in bringing it to a successful conclusion.

Lieut Colonel A. T. Champion,
South Lancs Regt.
Oriel Lodge,
Ford House,
Wolverhampton.

I am,

SIR,

Your obedient Servant,

B. B. CUBITT.

Lt.-Col. Champion Dies Suddenly At S. Staffs Golf Club

A week after he had been elected to serve for a second year as captain of the South Staffs Golf Club, Lieutenant - Colonel A. T. Champion collapsed at the club this morning and died shortly afterwards. His home was at Oriel Lodge, Fordhouses.

Until he retired for health reasons last September; Lieutenant-Colonel Champion commanded the 26th (Wednesfield and Willenhall) Battalion Staffordshire Home Guard.

In the last war he joined the South Lancashire Regiment in 1914, and served in France from 1915 to 1919. At the end of the war he was commanding the 2nd Battalion West Yorkshire Regiment.

KEEN GOLFER

He started "B" Company of the Wolverhampton Battalion L.D.V. in May, 1940.

Being on the reserve of officers, he was called up a month later, but as there was no vacancy, he returned to command "A" Company, 24th Battalion.

When "A" and "E" Companies were combined he took command of the new 26th Battalion.

A keen golfer, he had been a member of South Staffs Golf Club for many years and was a member of Wolverhampton Sportsmen's Association, Ltd.

Lieutenant - Colonel Champion leaves a widow, three sons in the R.A.F. and three daughters, one of whom is in the W.R.N.S. and one in the Land Army.

Lieut.-Colonel A. T. Champion, of Oriel Lodge, Fordhouses, who, as reported in the "Express and Star," died suddenly on Saturday. Until September, 1943, he commanded the 26th (Wednesfield and Willenhall) Battalion Staffordshire Home Guard, and he was captain of the South Staffs Golf Club.

Lt.-Col. A. T. Champion

HOME GUARD PAYS A LAST TRIBUTE

A large representative body of the 26th (Wednesfield and Willenhall) Battalion Staffordshire Home Guard, of which he was a former commanding officer, were present with an escort at the funeral, at Bushbury parish church this afternoon, of Lieutenant-Colonel A. T. Champion, Oriel Lodge, Fordhouses, who collapsed and died at the South Staffs Golf Club on Saturday.

It is only just over a week ago that Lieutenant-Colonel Champion was elected to serve for a second year as captain of the club.

He was a member of the Wolverhampton Sportsmen's Association, Ltd.

Officers of the battalion lined the path on either side from the lichgates to the church, while the coffin was carried by six members of the battalion, with pall-bearers on each side, followed by mourners.

"LAST POST" AND "REVEILLE"

Draped drums beat slowly as the escort moved in slow march. The coffin was draped with the Union Jack, and on it were Lieutenant-Colonel Champion's sword and hat.

The service was choral and the Rev. J. T. Crathorne (vicar) officiated. Major Griffiths read the lesson.

As the coffin was lowered into the grave, officers came to the salute, and then buglers sounded the "Last Post" and "Reveille."

PALL BEARERS

Pall-bearers were Major A. V. Whitehouse, Major H. Legg, Major R. J. Griffiths, Captain J. Adey, Captain J. Round, Captain H. Wrigglesworth, Captain H. G. V. Norton and Captain H. F. J. Weaver.

Family mourners were Mrs. A. T. Champion (widow), Lieutenant-Colonel C. C. Champion, D.S.O. (brother), Flying-Officer and Mrs. Eric C. Champion (son and daughter-in-law), Pilot-Officer Ronald T. Champion (son), Flight-sergeant Ian D Champion (son), Mrs. Mark Avent (daughter), Miss Elma H. Champion, W.R.E.N. (daughter) and Miss Brenda R. Champion, W.L.A. (daughter), Lieutenant-Colonel H. A. James, Captain J. Swales (adjutant), and Captain H. A. Stirzaker (quartermaster).

Among the sector and battalion commanders were Colonel W. J. Beddows (commander, G Sector), Colonel G. Elwell (commander, J Sector), Lieutenant-Colonel the Right Hon. the Earl of Dartmouth (who represented the Garrison Commander), Lieutenant-Colonel E. W. Page (20th battalion), Lieutenant-Colonel C. L. Riley (21st battalion), Lieutenant-Colonel W. T. D. Morgan (22nd battalion), Lieutenant-Colonel A. Gameson Lane (23rd battalion), Lieutenant-Colonel A. J. Parkes (24th battalion), Lieutenant-Colonel C. Hatton (25th battalion), and Lieutenant-Colonel J. Pitkeathley (34th battalion).